TAKING SIDES

Clashing Views in

Public Administration and Policy

TAKING SIDES

Clashing Views in
Public Administration and Policy

Selected, Edited, and with Introductions by

William J. Miller
Southeast Missouri State University

and

Jeremy Walling
Southeast Missouri State University

TAKING SIDES: CLASHING VIEWS IN PUBLIC ADMINISTRATION AND POLICY

Published by McGraw-Hill, a business unit of The McGraw-Hill Companies, Inc., 1221 Avenue of the Americas, New York, NY 10020. Copyright © 2013 by The McGraw-Hill Companies, Inc. All rights reserved. Printed in the United States of America. No part of this publication may be reproduced or distributed in any form or by any means, or stored in a database or retrieval system, without the prior written consent of The McGraw-Hill Companies, Inc., including, but not limited to, in any network or other electronic storage or transmission, or broadcast for distance learning.

Some ancillaries, including electronic and print components, may not be available to customers outside the United States.

Taking Sides® is a registered trademark of the McGraw-Hill Companies, Inc.
Taking Sides is published by the **Contemporary Learning Series** group within the McGraw-Hill Higher Education division.

1 2 3 4 5 6 7 8 9 0 DOC/DOC 1 0 9 8 7 6 5 4 3 2

MHID: 0-07-805040-5
ISBN: 978-0-07-805040-4
ISSN: 2164-1552 (Print)
ISSN: 2164-165X (Online)

Managing Editor: *Larry Loeppke*
Senior Developmental Editor: *Jill Meloy*
Permissions Supervisor: *Lenny J. Behnke*
Senior Marketing Communications Specialist: *Mary Klein*
Lead Project Manager: *Jane Mohr*
Design Coordinator: *Brenda A. Rolwes*
Cover Graphics: *Rick D. Noel*
Buyer: *Nicole Baumgartner*
Media Project Manager: *Sridevi Palani*

Compositor: MPS Limited, a Macmillan Company
Cover Image: © Image Ideas Inc. / Index Stock RF

Editors/Academic Advisory Board

Members of the Academic Advisory Board are instrumental in the final selection of articles for each edition of TAKING SIDES. Their review of articles for content, level, and appropriateness provides critical direction to the editors and staff. We think that you will find their careful consideration well reflected in this volume.

TAKING SIDES: Clashing Views in PUBLIC ADMINISTRATION AND POLICY

First Edition

EDITORS

William J. Miller
Southeast Missouri State University

and

Jeremy Walling
Southeast Missouri State University

ACADEMIC ADVISORY BOARD MEMBERS

Editors/Academic Advisory Board continued

Preface

If nothing else, politics involves differences. Our Founding Fathers dreamed of the day when Americans would be able to openly discuss their differences in an open, deliberative forum. They viewed dissent as healthy for governance. Yet, we highly doubt they would have looked happily on the America they see today. Civility is at an all-time low (see Joe Wilson or Samuel Alito's behavior during presidential addresses); polarized partisans celebrate an American city not winning the rights to hold an Olympics, booing the awarding of a Nobel Peace Prize to our president, and explaining that the opposing party's view on health care is for Americans to die quickly. In our nation today, polarization risks taking what used to be simple differences and turning them into canyons that separate Americans from each other.

Given how policy decisions can lead to debate and disagreement, it is essential that we work to understand how we differ in matters related to public administration and policy. Our high school civics courses—and even many introductory college courses—walk us through how bills become laws, yet fail to present the full picture. Once a bill becomes a law, it becomes the responsibility of public employees to implement the law to the best of their ability. In this process, myriad of variables enter play that can lead to even greater debates and disagreement. For students, what an analysis of these disagreements and alternative points of view will hopefully lead to is the acknowledgement that public administration and policy do not have to be the inactive, allegedly boring elements of government that many claim them to be.

Indeed, no matter where we find ourselves in a debate, we must realize that there are two sides. When it comes to matters of public administration and policy, there will always be opposition regardless of how right we know we are or how badly we want to believe in unanimity. Today, an American could turn on the television and easily find individuals proposing government takeovers of any number of private industries. A quick flip of the dial could lead to an interview with Representative Ron Paul, arguing against the mere existence of many bureaucratic agencies that have long been considered vital to preserving American government. In this environment, it is even more important that the average American be well-versed in both sides to an argument given that a vast majority of Americans—despite living in a polarized nation—find themselves located between the poles.

Despite how many Americans are set in their ways regarding their attitudes toward government and bureaucracy, we firmly believe that there is far more to still be learned and understood from examining both sides of the major issues facing public administration and policy today. No matter how set one may be in their own view, they can still learn by studying the opposition. For public administration and policy, our efforts strive to reach both practitioners and academics. Although public administration has long been considered a practitioner-based discipline, the past century has helped us real-ize how truly academic much of the research can be. To be successful, we rec-ognize the importance to remain relevant to both sides of this coin by asking pertinent questions and providing useful readings. We simply ask students, instructors, and the average citizen to allow us the opportunity to demonstrate the lively nature of public administration and policy. Only by doing so can we fully claim to be aware of how American government actually functions. For under the surface of partisan bickering and alleged media biases lies a bureaucrat—paid for by public tax money—attempting to make sense of some policy aimed to serve the average citizen.

Acknowledgments   This book sprang from the realization that *Taking Sides* had yet to venture into the realm of public administration and policy. When we realized that this book was yet to exist, we set off to bring it to fruition. We are grateful to Larry Loeppke, Leonard Behnke, Jill Meloy, and David Welsh for guiding us throughout this process. Larry and Lenny helped us with the initial framework and in shaping questions that would appeal to a broad audience. Jill made sure we remained on task and was always available to respond to our frequent questions. And Dave stepped in and assisted us as we moved toward production. Without these four, this book would never have been.

   We also appreciate the assistance of our wives—Jill and Breanna—for their patience and willingness to remind us when we were falling behind. Rick Althaus—our great colleague—helped us regularly by suggesting articles or looking at our progress. And our Academic Advisory Board Members shaped the book by responding to our survey of possible topics and letting us know what they considered to be truly useful in the project. It goes without saying but any errors that remain fall squarely on our shoulders.

William J. Miller
Southeast Missouri State University

Jeremy Walling
Southeast Missouri State University

Contents In Brief

Contents

UNIT 1   THE STUDY OF PUBLIC ADMINISTRATION AND BUREAUCRACY   1

Issue 1.   Is Contemporary Public Administration Theory More Influential Than Its Classical Counterpart?   2

YES: Jocelyne Bourgon, from "Responsive, Responsible, and Respected Government: Towards a New Public Administration Theory," *International Review of Administrative Sciences* (March 2007)   *6*

NO: Herbert Kaufman, from "Emerging Conflicts in the Doctrine of Public Administration," *American Political Science Review* (December 1956)   *16*

Jocelyne Bourgon argues that public administration is in need of new, unifying philosophies that will allow the discipline to keep up with the advancements occurring throughout the public sector. By providing a new public administration theory, we can make the discipline relevant to what occurs in government every day. Herbert Kaufman, writing in the 1950s, argues that traditional public administration—founded through experimentation with government structures—would be capable of remaining relevant regardless of future changes in public service. The key values expounded by Kaufman remain relevant today and even form the backbone of what we expect from public administration.

Issue 2.   Can Public Administration Be International in Scope?   29

YES: Woodrow Wilson, from "The Study of Administration," *Political Science Quarterly* (June 1887)   *32*

NO: B. Guy Peters, from "The Necessity and Difficulty of Comparison in Public Administration," *Asian Journal of Public Administration* (June 1990)   *37*

Woodrow Wilson argues that administration, as a discipline, finds its roots throughout Europe. Given the generic central tenants of administration theory, Wilson asserts that our young nation was only unable to improve administrative mechanisms and procedures by looking to the experiences of other nations. B. Guy Peters argues that while the discipline needs more meaningful comparative studies, there are several impediments that make it difficult to conduct such studies. As long as minute and subtle differences make great deals of differences, it will be difficult to have meaningful comparative studies—making public administration best studies as a country-specific phenomenon.

Charles T. Goodsell argues that American bureaucrats are among the best in the world and that they are not mere agents of waste and red tape. Using empirical evidence and cases, he helps paint a picture of public servants working as best as possible to carry out the functions of government for the citizens they serve. Ralph P. Hummel argues that although public servants may be well-intentioned, bureaucracy is inherently dark and causes managers, workers, and clients to all behave in manners inconsistent with the goals of government service. Despite a public servant's good intentions, the corrupting influence of bureaucracy will eventually lead to inefficiencies emerging.

UNIT 2   DILEMMAS OF PUBLIC POLICY   69

Kristen Norman-Major argues that even though equity was identified as the fourth pillar of public administration by the National Academy of Public Administration, we can—and should—go further to ensure policies are both efficient and equitable. Only through concentrated efforts can we make equity as important as economy, efficiency, and effectiveness. Julian Le Grand argues that the trade-off between efficiency and equity is not as easily solved. Rather than attempting to solve the tradeoff, he believes we can best help impact policies by challenging the tradeoff framework.

The U.S. House of Representatives argues that the Federal Emergency Management Agency was unprepared to respond successfully to the effects of Hurricane Katrina. While acknowledging the difficulties posed by the magnitude of the storm, it becomes clear that the House places more blame on the bureaucrats than the legislators who were largely responsible for funding and monitoring the agency. Douglas J. Amy argues that the failures of Katrina are more directly related to a lack of financial support from the president and Congress to assure that bureaucrats are in a position to successfully carry out their assigned tasks. The stereotypes of modern bureaucracy, in his eyes, are undeserved given the effort put forth by today's public servants.

Jenna Bednar argues that federalism can be an effective government format to help ensure that policies are ultimately efficient. Through successful coordination of federal, state, and local governments, it is possible to make implementation less costly and more effective for citizens. Thomas Birkland and Sarah Waterman argue that a lack of coordination contributed significantly to the outcomes of Hurricane Katrina. Without being coordinated from the beginning, policy had no chance of being carried out smoothly in a time of crisis. The more we attempt to coordinate, the less efficient policy outcomes are likely to be.

David Lewis argues that federal programs administered by politically appointed bureau chiefs perform less effectively than those run by bureau chiefs drawn from the civil service. Career managers have more direct bureau experience and longer tenures in office. Both factors are believed to lead to better performance. William West argues that nonpartisan objectivity within the career bureaucracy does not necessarily serve the interests of presidents and other members of government. If bureaucrats must be neutral, many scholars believe they are unable to be fully responsive, thus potentially limiting their ultimate effectiveness.

performance management does not necessarily improve the performance of public agencies. In his view, performance management has not led to improved performance as much as scholars have simply succeeded in finding some successful agencies where these programs are in place.

Issue 11.   Is Employment Equity Necessary?   241

President John F. Kennedy argued that government contractors needed to take action to ensure applicants are considered without regard to any characteristic such as race, color, or nationality. In 1964, his arguments led to the creation of the Equal Employment Opportunity Commission through the Civil Rights Act. Justice Anthony Kennedy argues that tests that are vetted properly can be used for merit promotion even if there are apparent racial divides within the results. In this light, affirmative action should be devoted to ensuring that minorities are equally prepared for tests, not in assuring actual equity.

Issue 12.   Is It Possible to Motivate Workers in a Manner That Increases Job Satisfaction in the Public Sector?   265

James L. Perry and Lyman W. Porter examine comparative motivational contexts in public organizations to determine what can be done to increase motivation. They ultimately find out monetary incentives, goal setting, job design, and participation all have different impacts on motivation. Seong Soo Oh and Gregory B. Lewis argue that some employee motivation tools, such as performance appraisal systems, can decrease employee productivity. The authors find that this is especially true for intrinsically motivated workers.

Issue 13.   Should Incrementalism Be the Guiding Budgeting Philosophy of Public Agencies?   287

Aaron Wildavsky and Naomi Caiden argue that incremental budgeting accurately reflects the nature of the political process in the United States. Conflict is minimized by accepting this reality and focusing on only a handful of discretionary items. Aidan Kelly argues that incremental budgeting has not been shown to occur throughout many social service departments in England. Most troubling, however, is that much of the success in the departments occurred within nonincremental budgeting frameworks.

Victor A. Thompson argues that since public employees are human, they inevitably pursue individual preferences and goals, sometimes at the expense of organizational goals. Thus, he advocates external controls over public employees. H. George Frederickson argues that administrative discretion is essential to effective public service. The author acknowledges that while external controls such as codes of ethics and ethics legislation will likely increase democratic accountability, such external controls often amount to "gotcha" mechanisms that punish offenders rather than inculcate ethical mores and encourage proper conduct.

Amanda Huffman argues that the Wisconsin showdown from spring 2011 demonstrates a clear need for public employees to have collective bargaining rights. The challenge, in her eyes, is to discover how to maintain a balance and integrity in public sector employment relationships that provides appropriate checks on both employer and union power. Daniel DiSalvo argues that public union members will need to willingly make concessions in the future or risk seeing dramatic changes due to the faltering economy. Highlighting the efforts of New Jersey Governor Chris Christie, DiSalvo believes citizens will eventually begin questioning the demands of public employees if they do not begin coming to their senses.

UNIT 6   GOVERNMENT IN THE TWENTY-FIRST CENTURY: NEW AVENUES OF STUDY   385

Sang M. Lee, Xin Tan, and Silvana Trimi examine the impact e-government has had on countries that have been early and leading adopters. Such transitions toward e-governance have created a self-sustaining change in a broad range of closely connected technological, organizational, cultural, and social effects. Victor Bekkers and Vincent Homburg argue that many of the myths associated with e-government—such as technological inevitability, a new and better government, rational information planning, and empowerment of the intelligent citizen—are not supported by

Correlation Guide

The *Taking Sides* series presents current issues in a debate-style format designed to stimulate student interest and develop critical thinking skills. Each issue is thoughtfully framed with an issue summary, an issue introduction, learning outcomes, and critical thinking and reflection questions. The pro and con essays—selected for their liveliness and substance—represent the arguments of leading scholars and commentators in their fields.

Taking Sides: Clashing Views in Public Administration and Policy is an easy-to-use reader that presents issues on important topics such as *equity in public policy, budgeting and spending,* and *administrative ethics.* For more information on *Taking Sides* and other *McGraw-Hill Contemporary Learning Series* titles, visit http://www.mhhe.com/cls.

This convenient guide matches the issues in **Taking Sides: Public Administration and Policy** with the corresponding chapters in two of our best-selling McGraw-Hill Public Policy textbooks by Berkley and Rosenbloom.

Taking Sides: Public Administration and Policy	The Craft of Public Administration, 10/e by Berkley	Public Administration: Understanding Management, Politics, and Law in the Public Sector, 7/e by Rosenbloom
Issue 1: Is Contemporary Public Administration Theory More Influential Than Its Classical Counterpart?	**Chapter 1:** The Administrative Craft **Chapter 2:** The Ecology of the Administrative Craft **Chapter 3:** The Anatomy of Public Organizations	**Chapter 1:** The Practice and Discipline of Public Administration: Competing Concerns **Chapter 4:** Organization: Structure and Process
Issue 2: Can Public Administration Be International in Scope?	**Chapter 1:** The Administrative Craft **Chapter 2:** The Ecology of the Administrative Craft **Chapter 10:** Administrative Law and Government Regulations	**Chapter 2:** The American Administrative State: Development and Political Environment **Chapter 3:** Federalism and Intergovernmental Relations: The Structure of the American Administrative State
Issue 3: Is Bureaucracy the Best Option for Organizing Government?	**Chapter 4:** The Physiology of Public Organizations **Chapter 7:** Communication and Leadership **Chapter 10:** Administrative Law and Government Regulations	**Chapter 2:** The American Administrative State: Development and Political Environment **Chapter 3:** Federalism and Intergovernmental Relations: The Structure of the American Administrative State **Chapter 4:** Organization: Structure and Process

(Continued)

Taking Sides: Public Administration and Policy	The Craft of Public Administration, 10/e by Berkley	Public Administration: Understanding Management, Politics, and Law in the Public Sector, 7/e by Rosenbloom
Issue 4: Is It Possible to Balance Efficiency and Equity in Public Policy?	**Chapter 5:** People and Personnel **Chapter 9:** The Productivity Challenge: Working Smarter While Doing More with Less	**Chapter 5:** Public Personnel Administration and Collective Bargaining **Chapter 7:** Decision Making **Chapter 12:** Accountability and Ethics
Issue 5: Do Bureaucrats Have More Influence on Public Policy Than Other Branches of Government Do?	**Chapter 4:** The Physiology of Public Organizations **Chapter 6:** Public Sector Labor-Management Relations **Chapter 10:** Administrative Law and Government Regulations	**Chapter 2:** The American Administrative State: Development and Political Environment **Chapter 9:** Regulatory Administration: An Illustration of Management, Politics and Law in the Public Sector **Chapter 10:** Public Administration and the Public **Chapter 11:** Public Administration and the Democratic Constitutionalism
Issue 6: Is It Possible to Coordinate Federal, State, and Local Governments in a Way That Allows Policy Making to Be More Efficient?	**Chapter 8:** Taxing, Budgeting, and Spending **Chapter 9:** The Productivity Challenge: Working Smarter While Doing More with Less **Chapter 10:** Administrative Law and Government Regulations	**Chapter 2:** The American Administrative State: Development and Political Environment **Chapter 7:** Decision Making **Chapter 9:** Regulatory Administration: An Illustration of Management, Politics and Law in the Public Sector **Chapter 10:** Public Administration and the Public
Issue 7: Do Bureaucrats Need to Be Politically Neutral to Be Effective?	**Chapter 5:** People and Personnel **Chapter 7:** Communication and Leadership **Chapter 10:** Administrative Law and Government Regulations	**Chapter 2:** The American Administrative State: Development and Political Environment **Chapter 9:** Regulatory Administration: An Illustration of Management, Politics and Law in the Public Sector **Chapter 11:** Public Administration and the Democratic Constitutionalism
Issue 8: Should Government Be Run Like a Business?	**Chapter 4:** The Physiology of Public Organizations **Chapter 10:** Administrative Law and Government Regulations	**Chapter 2:** The American Administrative State: Development and Political Environment **Chapter 8:** Policy Analysis and Implementation Evaluation **Chapter 9:** Regulatory Administration: An Illustration of Management, Politics and Law in the Public Sector **Chapter 10:** Public Administration and the Public

Taking Sides: Public Administration and Policy	The Craft of Public Administration, 10/e by Berkley	Public Administration: Understanding Management, Politics, and Law in the Public Sector, 7/e by Rosenbloom
Issue 9: Should Governments Use the Private Sector to Deliver Public Services?	**Chapter 6:** Public Sector Labor-Management Relations **Chapter 10:** Administrative Law and Government Regulations	**Chapter 1:** The Practice and Discipline of Public Administration: Competing Concerns **Chapter 2:** The American Administrative State: Development and Political Environment **Chapter 9:** Regulatory Administration: An Illustration of Management, Politics and Law in the Public Sector **Chapter 12:** Accountability and Ethics
Issue 10: Does Performance Management Lead to Better Policy Outcomes?	**Chapter 5:** People and Personnel **Chapter 6:** Public Sector Labor-Management Relations **Chapter 7:** Communication and Leadership	**Chapter 5:** Public Personnel Administration and Collective Bargaining **Chapter 12:** Accountability and Ethics
Issue 11: Is Employment Equity Necessary?	**Chapter 5:** People and Personnel **Chapter 6:** Public Sector Labor-Management Relations **Chapter 10:** Administrative Law and Government Regulations	**Chapter 5:** Public Personnel Administration and Collective Bargaining **Chapter 12:** Accountability and Ethics **Chapter 13:** The Future
Issue 12: Is It Possible to Motivate Workers in a Manner That Increases Job Satisfaction in the Public Sector?	**Chapter 5:** People and Personnel **Chapter 6:** Public Sector Labor-Management Relations **Chapter 7:** Communication and Leadership	**Chapter 5:** Public Personnel Administration and Collective Bargaining **Chapter 8:** Policy Analysis and Implementation Evaluation **Chapter 9:** Regulatory Administration: An Illustration of Management, Politics and Law in the Public Sector
Issue 13: Should Incrementalism Be the Guiding Budgeting Philosophy of Public Agencies?	**Chapter 6:** Public Sector Labor-Management Relations **Chapter 8:** Taxing, Budgeting, and Spending **Chapter 9:** The Productivity Challenge: Working Smarter While Doing More with Less Regulations	**Chapter 6:** Budgeting and the Public Finances **Chapter 7:** Decision Making
Issue 14: Do We Need More Budget Flexibility for Discretionary Spending Compared to Entitlements?	**Chapter 8:** Taxing, Budgeting, and Spending **Chapter 9:** The Productivity Challenge: Working Smarter While Doing More with Less	**Chapter 6:** Budgeting and the Public Finances

(Continued)

Taking Sides: Public Administration and Policy	The Craft of Public Administration, 10/e by Berkley	Public Administration: Understanding Management, Politics, and Law in the Public Sector, 7/e by Rosenbloom
Issue 15: Should Whistleblowing Be Encouraged in the Public Service?	**Chapter 5:** People and Personnel **Chapter 6:** Public Sector Labor-Management Relations **Chapter 7:** Communication and Leadership **Chapter 10:** Administrative Law and Government Regulations	**Chapter 9:** Regulatory Administration: An Illustration of Management, Politics and Law in the Public Sector
Issue 16: Are External Controls Effective Tools for Ensuring Principled Conduct?	**Chapter 5:** People and Personnel **Chapter 6:** Public Sector Labor-Management Relations **Chapter 7:** Communication and Leadership	**Chapter 1:** The Practice and Discipline of Public Administration: Competing Concerns **Chapter 5:** Public Personnel Administration and Collective Bargaining **Chapter 9:** Regulatory Administration: An Illustration of Management, Politics and Law in the Public Sector
Issue 17: Should Public Employees Have Collective Bargaining Rights?	**Chapter 5:** People and Personnel **Chapter 6:** Public Sector Labor-Management Relations **Chapter 8:** Taxing, Budgeting, and Spending	**Chapter 5:** Public Personnel Administration and Collective Bargaining
Issue 18: Has e-Governance had a Dramatic Influence on Public Administration?	**Chapter 9:** The Productivity Challenge: Working Smarter While Doing More with Less **Chapter 10:** Administrative Law and Government Regulations	**Chapter 2:** The American Administrative State: Development and Political Environment **Chapter 4:** Organization: Structure and Process
Issue 19: Should Public Agencies Use Social Media to Reach the Citizenry?	**Chapter 5:** People and Personnel **Chapter 9:** The Productivity Challenge: Working Smarter While Doing More with Less	**Chapter 4:** Organization: Structure and Process **Chapter 7:** Decision Making **Chapter 13:** The Future

Topic Guide

This topic guide suggests how the selections in this book relate to the subjects covered in your course. You may want to use the topics listed on these pages to search the Web more easily. On the following pages, a number of Web sites have been gathered specifically for this book. They are arranged to reflect the units of this Taking Sides reader. You can link to these sites by going to http://www.mhhe.com/cls.

All issues, and their articles that relate to each topic, are listed below the bold-faced term.

Affirmative Action

11. Is Employment Equity Necessary?

Budgeting

13. Should Incrementalism Be the Guiding Budgeting Philosophy of Public Agencies?
14. Do We Need More Budget Flexibility for Discretionary Spending Compared to Entitlements?

Bureaucracy

3. Is Bureaucracy the Best Option for Organizing Government?
5. Do Bureaucrats Have More Influence on Public Policy Than Other Branches of Government Do?
7. Do Bureaucrats Need to Be Politically Neutral to Be Effective?

Business

8. Should Government Be Run Like a Business?
9. Should Governments Use the Private Sector to Deliver Public Services?

Classical Theory

1. Is Contemporary Public Administration Theory More Influential Than Its Classical Counterpart?

Codes of Ethics

16. Are External Controls Effective Tools for Ensuring Principled Conduct?

Collective Bargaining

17. Should Public Employees Have Collective Bargaining Rights?

Comparative Public Administration

2. Can Public Administration Be International in Scope?

Contemporary Theory

1. Is Contemporary Public Administration Theory More Influential Than Its Classical Counterpart?
18. Has e-Governance Had a Dramatic Influence on Public Administration?

Discretionary Spending

14. Do We Need More Budget Flexibility for Discretionary Spending Compared to Entitlements?

e-Governance

18. Has e-Governance Had a Dramatic Influence on Public Administration?

Efficiency

4. Is It Possible to Balance Efficiency and Equity in Public Policy?
8. Should Government Be Run Like a Business?
9. Should Governments Use the Private Sector to Deliver Public Services?

(Continued)

Introduction

At this moment, Americans across the country are demonstrating (most of them unknowingly) why public administration and policy are concepts that deserve attention and discussion. This book asks us to read about classic and contemporary issues related to these disciplines by painting a picture of how truly relevant they are in America.

The United States Post Office

The mailman: an American hero of sorts who cannot be deterred by rain, wind, sleet, or snow. He fights off our dogs, willingly walks through the rain, and takes extra care to ensure citizens are satisfied. Yet, we tend to not recognize the diligent work the postal carrier performs. Instead, we seemingly take for granted the consistency of mail delivery and only seem to recognize it on the one day out of the year where it takes an extra four hours. A larger debate is growing within our country at present, however. As the United States Postal Service continues to seemingly hemorrhage money despite rapidly increasing stamp prices and efforts to remain competitive with private competitors, such as FedEx and United Parcel Service, citizens and politicians, alike, are calling for changes.

The most regular suggestion—which seems to be gaining even more traction—is to cut back the number of postal processing centers located throughout the country. With the volume of first-class mail dropping by 25 percent in the past five years, there are simply not as many opportunities to make money. As a result, the Postal Service is considering closing 252 processing locations to save approximately $3 billion per year. Further, they will be cutting the transportation network—leading to a one-day delay on most first-class mail. Now, citizens who have long oft ignored the presence of their local post office processing center are up in arms about its possible closure. To ensure that an independent agency of the federal government does not continue to lose money, citizens will face slower mail service. It is possible—though not guaranteed—that pieces of mail will travel further to get to a processing center than they would have for typical delivery.

The Tea Party and Future of Government

Libertarian ideals are making a popular comeback throughout segments of the United States under the guise of the Tea Party movement. During the 2010 midterm elections, the American public appeared fascinated by the Tea Party movement; much time and effort was devoted to attempting to determine exactly what the movement stood for. David Brooks defined the movement as "a large, fractious confederation of Americans who are defined by what they are against. They are against the concentrated power of the educated class.

They believe big government, big business, big media, and the affluent professionals are merging to form a self-serving oligarchy—with bloated government, unsustainable deficits, high taxes, and intrusive regulation."

In an animated rant, given in the wake of the passage of the American Recovery and Reinvestment Act of 2009, Rick Santelli roared on CNBC's *Squawk Box*: "We're thinking of having a Chicago Tea Party in July . . . all you capitalists that want to show up to Lake Michigan, I'm going to start organizing it." With that, Santelli reflected to a national audience a sentiment that been developing on a regional basis. A few weeks earlier, on January 24, a few dozen citizens of Binghamton, New York, poured soda into the Susquehanna River. The familiar symbolism of the Native American headdress was utilized to protest a slate of taxes endorsed by Governor David Paterson, particularly a tax on soft drinks.

Although the antitax attitude can certainly be understood, Tea Party favorite Ron Paul ultimately goes one step further by advocating for a shutdown of most government agencies supported by taxpayer money. His list includes the Internal Revenue Service, Federal Bureau of Investigation, the Federal Reserve, and the Department of Education. He also opposes current military interventions, the PATRIOT ACT, and the North American Free Trade Agreement. Paul's argument is not that some aspects of government are bad. Instead, as a self-acclaimed libertarian purist, Paul largely opposes the existence of government.

Tennessee Fire Case

In September, 2010, Gene Cranick's home in Obion County, Tennessee, caught fire. In Obin County, homeowners must pay $75 each year for fire protection from a nearby city. If they fail to pay the fee and their home catches fire, the city will not assist, even if firefighters are already in the area. In the case of Cranick, the firefighters appeared after a neighbor called to report the flames moving toward his property. At that point, the perimeter was controlled while Cranick's home continued to burn. In the aftermath of the event, pundits from all sides took to the airwaves and Internet to discuss why they believed the fire department was correct (or incorrect, depending on their personal viewpoint). Supporters of the fire department labeled the nonpaying citizens of Obion County "jerks, freeloaders, and ingrates" who had no more right to the fire services than protection from the New York City Police Department. Those in opposition, however, raised questions since they had already responded, were capable of stopping it, and are typically expected to put out fires.

Just this one occurrence that resulted in the destruction of a mobile home in rural Tennessee leads to questions about public worker ethics, free riders, collective goods, and public policy intentions. Consider, for example, that if a firefighter had entered the home despite Cranick not paying the $75, then he would potentially have not been covered under his life or health insurance given the nature of the incident. Although on face value, the fire presents moral questions regarding human life, when we consider it from the perspective of public administration and policy, however, even more questions arise. In this situation, bureaucrats made a policy decision that negatively impacted the lives of citizens.

National Aeronautics and Space Administration

When the National Aeronautics and Space Administration (NASA) was created as an executive branch agency of the federal government in 1958, it was a goal and vision-driven entity. To begin, NASA was expected to conduct space exploration. As the Cold War boomed, NASA aimed to stay one step ahead of the Soviets. In its aftermath, they aimed to go further into space and to continue crafting technology that the world had yet to see or imagine. But among crunching budgets and shuttle delays and disasters, NASA began to fall out of the public's favor. Many asked why we are concerned with the mineral content of Mars when children are hungry. Others questioned the need for a continued space program given the relative lack of competition today.

Despite public criticisms and the eventual shutdown of the shuttle program, NASA has not simply closed up shop. Organizations—particularly public and nonprofit ones—have an almost protean nature. There is a resistance to simply closing up shop and disappearing. Think of the March of Dimes. Originally formed to battle polio, the organization continues to function today with a different mission given that polio has been eradicated. Once the goal of the organization was met, they simply found another, larger goal to attempt to achieve. In the case of the March of Dimes, this cause was all childhood diseases. With public agencies, there are times where we may need to walk away more permanently. Bureaucratic inertia logically makes sense since individuals tend not to advocate that their jobs are no longer necessary. But the continued funding of programs that serve nonessential functions in times of budget difficulty needs to be thoroughly questioned.

Public Labor Unions

Few current events have received as much attention as the protests in Wisconsin related to the rights of public employees to collectively bargain. Governor Scott Walker has been vilified or turned into a hero by individuals based on their opinion of his effort to prevent collective bargaining among public employees. In the wake of legislation being proposed (and subsequently passed and signed into law), we have seen members of a state legislature running across state lines to prevent a vote, recall elections, and the spread of the idea passing to other Midwestern states (especially Ohio). The debate over public labor unions highlights the importance of the administration aspect of public administration. There is a large number of government employees throughout the United States at a multitude of levels, and each day they work to serve citizens. Whether they see their job as a calling or merely a career, these workers have the same needs and wants as their private counterparts. The public attention paid to the protests in Wisconsin show that Americans can be convinced to care about the work of government.

Synthesis

The five aforementioned stories may seem to be disjointed and unrelated. Yet, at their core, they introduce us to the importance and relevance of public administration and policy. Often considered to be a practitioner-focused, technical field within the study of government and politics, one could argue that public administration and policy are the most relevant components of the American political system to the average citizen. After all, have you ever met the president? What has he done in the past two days to directly affect you? How about a member of Congress? The Supreme Court? We are even unlikely to have had a recent experience with a city council member. Yet, each day, knowingly or unknowingly, bureaucracy has a direct impact on our lives. Your mail is delivered, garbage leaves your curb, and potholes get filled. The police officer lets you off when you are going six miles per hour over the speed limit rather than pulling you over. Or perhaps someone ensures that your student loan refund is issued in a timely manner. Whether we realize it or not, public administrators surround us in everything we do and they are normally working off of some public policy.

When we think about the United States Post Office and NASA, we have two agencies that are struggling to determine how they fit into the twenty-first century. Both have been challenged by technology and competition (after all, no one in the 1950s would have guessed that private companies would be offering flights into orbit so soon), and both face heavy pressure to trim costs and improve efficiency. Where they differ, however, is that most Americans still see the value in mail delivery while some question the need for NASA to exist as it does today. The firefighter case presents us with a series of ethical questions. As bureaucrats try to properly implement policy, they are often faced with difficult questions that carry potentially severe consequences. Do firefighters have an ethical obligation to attend to all fires they are in the vicinity of? Should citizens have to pay for basic services such as fire protection? But most importantly, who gets to make these decisions?

What all of the examples taken together demonstrate is that public administration and public policy are very real phenomena. Although in text, the concepts and cases battled by government workers everyday can seem monotonous and boring, when discussed in the context of the real world, we see how truly exciting they can be. The Wisconsin protests, Tennessee fire case, battles over NASA and the Postal Service, and the antigovernment attitudes in America show that large groups of citizens can come together and exert influence on behalf of or against public administrators. As long as Americans can be riled up by perceived government misdeeds or alleged poor policy decisions, there will always be the potential for genuine discussion about public administration. However, as history has demonstrated, this not merely a contemporary realization.

American Statelessness

Visiting the United States to ostensibly study the American penitentiary system, Alexis de Tocqueville discussed the particular state of American administration. He observed in *Democracy in America* that "public administration is, so to speak, oral and traditional . . . little is committed to writing, and that little is wafted away forever, like the leaves of the Sibyl, by the smallest breeze." His experience with the advanced, formal administrative system of France no doubt affected Tocqueville's assessment of the American administrative state in the 1830s. Tocqueville remarked the following:

> The instability of administration has penetrated into the habits of the people; it even appears to suit the general taste, and no one cares for what occurred before his time: no methodical system is pursued, no archives are formed, and no documents are brought together when it would be very easy to do so.

Tocqueville argued that the lack of an American administrative state was congruent with American culture. However, his specification of the direction of the relationship is unclear. He seems to imply that the unstable character of the administrative apparatus infected the political culture. It seems more likely that Americans' lack of reverence for historical developments and formalized documentation are a reflection of the political culture at that time. One should also note that Tocqueville visited the United States in its nascent stages, at a time when the scope of the national government was minimal and the balance of power in the federal system shifted heavily toward the states.

Public Administration Theory

Richard J. Stillman described the American administrative state (in *Preface to Public Administration*) as "half-formed." He states, "Our administrative system grew piecemeal, attempting to cope with the shocks of change in an ad hoc manner without any grand design." Certainly, Stillman's argument reflects Tocqueville's observations. American bureaucracy, to the extent that it existed at all, functioned more as an adhocracy, merely reacting to drastic change with no vision, plan, or forethought. Years before his presidency, Woodrow Wilson wrote a seminal essay (an excerpt of which appears in this volume) in 1887 that would eventually form the cornerstone of American public administration orthodoxy. Wilson recognized a division between the policymaking component of government and the administrative machinery, arguing for a clear distinction between the two. The distinction between politics and administration was further codified by Frank Goodnow's (1900) definitions of politics as the expression of state will and administration as the execution of state will. Today, the politics–administration dichotomy is often the first anchor dropped in any introductory public administration course. Wilson's normative claim is endlessly debated, despite repeated examples of administrative organizations, such as the Environmental Protection Agency, issuing regulatory policy with the weight of law and street-level bureaucrats, such as police and social workers, tailoring policy to particular circumstances.

American public administration theory developed along with the expansion and elaboration of the administrative state. Although Cabinet-level executive offices existed from the first presidency, the first independent agency of the national government was the Interstate Commerce Commission, established in 1887 to regulate the railroads, eventually serving to oversee interstate trucking and busing. Three years earlier, Congress passed the Pendleton Act in response to the assassination of President Garfield. The legislation attempted to wrest control of the civil service from the hands of political officers and institute merit-based hiring and employee policies, although the act initially affected a small fraction of the national government workforce. With increased industrialization and urbanization came the recognition of a need for increased public administration to nurture, support, and regulate emerging commercial enterprises and the citizenry at large.

With Wilson and Goodnow leading the movement, public administration theory developed significantly with the turn of the Twentieth Century. Frederick Taylor testified before the U.S. House of Representatives in 1912, advocating the analysis of jobs using scientific measurement principles to determine the "one best way" of completing a task. Taylor's scientific management placed the burden of the analysis on the employer, with the ultimate task of finding employees who fit the job and replacing those who do not. Overall understanding of bureaucratic organizations was enhanced by the English translation of Max Weber's description of the "ideal-type" form of bureaucracy. The 1937 Brownlow "Report of the President's Committee on Administrative Management" reflected on changes to the administrative state, observing the following: "Since the Civil War, as the tasks and responsibilities of government have grown with the growth of the nation in sweep and power, some notable attempts have been made to keep our administrative system abreast of the new times." The report boldly stated that government efficiency is a function of "the consent of the governed and good management," specifically recommending enhanced executive control over the management and reorganization of agencies within the executive branch. Luther Gulick (1937), a member of the Brownlow Committee, contributed to public administration theory by recommending management principles such as division of labor, span of control, and the awkward acronym POSDCORB (planning, organizing, staffing, directing, coordinating, reporting, and budgeting).

Taken collectively, the writings of Wilson, Goodnow, Taylor, Weber, Gulick, and the Brownlow Committee serve to form the basis of public administration theory in the United States. Soon, much of this orthodoxy of public administration theory was challenged by the next wave of scholars. Herbert Simon (1946), in a work that was originally his doctoral dissertation, demonstrated that the principles of administration recommended by Gulick could be demonstrated to be conditional and contradictory, more like proverbs than principles. Chester Barnard (1938) and Mary Parker Follet (1926) observed the behavior of organizations, noting that employees' humanity and the conditional nature of environmental conditions can challenge Taylor's "one best way" approach to management. Robert Merton (1940) noted that in its effort to generate efficiency and standardization, bureaucratic organizations can also be dysfunctional, producing workers who are unable to adapt to changing circumstances. These scholars and others effectively shattered the orthodoxy paradigm of a clear separation of politics and administration, organizations based on established bureaucratic norms, general principles of management, and the notion of "one best way." Nevertheless, even a casual observation of contemporary organizations will reveal that many of the component parts of early public administration theory continue to be utilized.

The Plan of the Book

Understanding that public administration and policy have historical roots and contemporary relevance, we have attempted to bring together a series of issues that demonstrate the past, present, and future struggles of the discipline. In Unit 1, we focus on the larger questions surrounding the discipline by looking at the difficulty in determining when to apply classical and contemporary theory, the potential for internationalizing the study of the discipline, and perhaps the most pressing question of all—whether bureaucracy is a suitable organizational mechanism for contemporary governance. In Unit 2, we turn the focus toward public policy through an examination of the practical application of the four "E"s of public administration—efficiency, equity, effectiveness, and economy. The questions in the unit look at efforts to balance efficiency and equity, the ways bureaucrats can influence the policy process, and the difficulty in coordinating multilevel government responses to policy issues. Unit 3 looks more closely at Goodnow's politics–administration dichotomy through debates on bureaucratic neutrality, government efforts to run more like a business, and privatization. Unit 4 leaves the abstract and more closely concentrates on the actual workings of government. The five issues in this unit examine performance management, employment equity, public service worker motivation, budgeting strategy, and budget flexibility. Continuing with a focus on the actual work of bureaucrats, Unit 5 turns toward administrative ethics through examinations of whistleblowing, the debate between internal and external controls, and collective bargaining rights for public sector unions. The final unit (Unit 6) turns toward the implications of modern technology for governance in the United States by discussing the effects and impacts of e-governance along with the usage of social media.

The aim of including these particular issues is to present material that will remain relevant beyond the present day. Given that many of the questions posed are ones debated routinely by both academics and practitioners, we believe we have successfully done so. Ultimately, we hope readers leave the book with a greater appreciation for the importance and relevancy of public administration and policy as key parts of the American political system.

Internet References . . .

American Society for Public Administration

The American Society for Public Administration is a membership organization for practitioners and academics that provides information to individuals interested in public administration and policy.

http://www.aspanet.org

American Political Science Association

The American Political Science Association possesses a vast array of information on issues and matters related to public administration and policy specific to academics along with useful knowledge for practicing administrators.

http://www.apsanet.org

United Nations Public Administration Network

The United Nations Public Administration Network is a global network that connects relevant international, regional, subregional, and national institutions worldwide for the promotion of better public administration.

http://www.unpan.org/

International Public Management Association for Human Resources

IPMA-HR is an organization that represents the interests of human resource professionals at the federal, state, and local levels of government.

http://www.ipma-hr.org/

International City/County Management Association

ICMA provides member support; publications; data and information; peer and results-oriented assistance; and training and professional development to nearly 9000 city, town, and county experts and other individuals and organizations throughout the world.

http://www.icma.org

Masters in Public Administration

A web site devoted to prospective MPA students. It presents data on career possibilities, salaries, and most importantly, links to many of the MPA programs currently available in the United States today.

http://mastersinpublicadministration.com

UNIT 1

The Study of Public Administration and Bureaucracy

*O*n its face, public administration studies the actions of government. It examines the way administrative agencies are structured and how they fit into the complex puzzle of governance. But more importantly, public administration allows scholars and practitioners to examine the nuances of the American political system and how the way the system is structured impacts governance and policy. As a discipline, public administration has already undergone a series of paradigm shifts with different dominant theories finding prominence at different times. In this unit, we examine three issues that deal with some of the overarching questions in public administration today.

- Is Contemporary Public Administration Theory More Influential Than Its Classical Counterpart?
- Can Public Administration Be International in Scope?
- Is Bureaucracy the Best Option for Organizing Government?

1

ISSUE 1

Is Contemporary Public Administration Theory More Influential Than Its Classical Counterpart?

YES: Jocelyne Bourgon, from "Responsive, Responsible, and Respected Government: Towards a New Public Administration Theory," *International Review of Administrative Sciences* (March 2007)

NO: Herbert Kaufman, from "Emerging Conflicts in the Doctrine of Public Administration," *American Political Science Review* (December 1956)

Learning Outcomes

After reading this issue, you should be able to:

- Gain an understanding of contemporary public administration theory.
- Gain an understanding of classical public administration theory.
- Discuss the differences between contemporary and classical public administration theory.
- Understand the applicability of each paradigm to modern governance.
- Discuss the relationship between emerging societal trends and long-term theory building.
- Understand the relationship between theory and practice as it relates to public administration and policy.

ISSUE SUMMARY

YES: Jocelyne Bourgon argues that public administration is in need of new, unifying philosophies that will allow the discipline to keep up with the advancements occurring throughout the public sector.

By providing a new public administration theory, we can make the discipline relevant to what occurs in government every day.

NO: Herbert Kaufman, writing in the 1950s, argues that traditional public administration—founded through experimentation with government structures—would be capable of remaining relevant regardless of future changes in public service. The key values expounded by Kaufman remain relevant today and even form the backbone of what we expect from public administration.

Like any discipline, public administration has undergone fundamental changes in thinking through sweeping paradigm shifts throughout its existence. From its classical roots—where it seemingly had to advocate for its right to exist—through today, public administration has been a discipline where issues ebb and flow as academics and practitioners strive to determine the necessary areas of study for the modern state of the discipline. Given that public administration is a practitioner-focused field of study, it faces the hurdle—like business, medicine, and law—of needing to be responsive to the times. As the world changes, public administration, to at least some degree, will be expected to as well. However, in recent years, a debate has begun regarding which of the two major paradigms—classical or contemporary—are best suited to describe the current happenings of American public administration.

At its classical core, public administration falls back on Max Weber's six principles of bureaucracy. Although written from a theoretical standpoint to describe the ideal type of bureaucracy, Weber's characteristics (espoused in the early 1920s) have stood the test of time and remain the litmus test of sorts for measuring these organizations. According to Weber, bureaucracies exist in formal hierarchical structures where each level controls the level below while being controlled by the level above. Such a structure allows for centralized decision making and more mainstreamed planning operations. Second, bureaucracies have management by rules. The use of rules permits for high-level decisions to be implemented consistently throughout the organization with minimalized questions or concerns. Third, bureaucratic agencies are organized by functional specialty. Workers are organized based on skill sets and organizations aim to have specialized workers in place to maximize efficiency and effectiveness. Fourth, bureaucracies have an up-focused or in-focused mission. They aim to serve either the agency that empowered them or the organization itself. Fifth, bureaucracies are purposely impersonal. In this vein, bureaucracies treat all employees and customers equally without concern for status, race, gender, or any other distinguishing characteristic. Lastly, in Weber's ideal type, employment is based on technical qualifications. Individual workers are protected from arbitrary punishments, and promotion decisions will be based on merit rather than patronage.

Although Weber wrote in a different era, in a different country, from the approach of a different field of study (sociology), his descriptions of ideal types ring true today. Yet, despite the prominence of his description of bureaucracy, public administration—in practice—dates back to antiquity where Pharaohs would require tax collectors and pages to carry out the business of government. In the American sense, Woodrow Wilson introduced the concept of public administration in his seminal essay "The Study of Administration." Published in 1887, he wrote that "it is the object of administrative study to discover, first, what government can properly and successfully do, and, second, how it can do these proper things with the utmost possible efficiency and at the least possible cost either of money or of energy." Further, he made four larger claims that have to some degree shaped what we know today. First, he stated the necessity of separating politics and administration. Second, he pushed for a comparative analysis of the public and private sectors. Third, he sought ways to implement successful business practices into the sphere of government. And last, he aimed to develop ways by which we could improve the overall effectiveness of the public sector. All these points are still continually raised and debated today.

Luther Gulick was a second-generation scholar of public administration who worked to determine a generic idea of the duties of administration in wake of the behavioral and organizational research conducted by individuals like Henri Fayold, Frederick Taylor, and William Willoughby. Developed in the 1940s, Gulick's POSDCORB (standing for planning, organizing, staffing, directing, coordinating, reporting, and budgeting) suggested roles for public administrators through his administrative theories. Between Weber, Wilson, and Gulick, we have a fairly clear picture of American public administration today. Yet, their writings were composed in a different time under different contexts.

More modern theories have emerged through the contemporary paradigm, however, which take alternative angles on how best to study public administration. In the late 1980s, a new class of scholars emerged and began operating around New Public Management. Originally proposed by David Osborne and Ted Gaebler, New Public Management advocated public use of private sector-style models and values. By doing so, they believed government would become more efficient. Likewise, we witnessed the advent of the representative bureaucracy movement wherein it was assumed that citizens preferred when bureaucracies have workers with the same pattern of gender, race, and other demographic characteristics as society as a whole. Largely, scholars assumed that a Hispanic male would be more at ease if talking to a Hispanic male about his issue or concern. Since the promotion of this ideal, it has remained hotly debated and contested.

By the end of the 1990s, New Public Management was already being ushered out of the mainstream academic debate due to the emergence of digital era governance through which scholars and practitioners realized the technological wave that was quickly approaching them. Further, New Public Governance entered the debate as an approach that looks to centralize power, increase partisan bureaucrats, and aim to allow government to work more on behalf of the current government than as a neutral party. Neither of these theories have yet to fully work themselves into the public or scholarly debate, but each maintains levels of support and curiosity.

In the YES selection, Jocelyne Bourgon argues that the new, unifying philosophies of public administration are more influential than their classical counterparts given their relevance and applicability to modern governance. On the other side, in the NO selection, Herbert Kaufman, writing in the 1950s, argues that traditional public administration theory was crafted in such a manner as to be relevant regardless of future changes. Ultimately, the debate comes down to whether one believes that contemporary approaches build off of something besides traditional theory. As both authors discuss, the key is ensuring that public administration theory serves a useful purpose for practitioners, academics, and students alike.

YES

Jocelyne Bourgon

Responsive, Responsible, and Respected Government: Towards a New Public Administration Theory

Public administrations are a vehicle for expressing the values and preferences of citizens, communities, and society as a whole. Some of these values and preferences are constant; others change as societies evolve. Periodically, one set of values comes to the fore, and its energy transforms the role of government and the practice of public administration.

Recent decades have been marked by tremendous change, both nationally and globally. Not surprisingly, public administrations are in a period of transition. Current practice of public administration draws key strengths from past models: the Classic model, with its emphasis on control and organizational design; the Neo-bureaucratic model, built upon rational decision-making processes; the Institutional model of the 1950s and 1960s, which was deeply rooted in behavioural sciences; and the Public Choice model, with its reliance on political economy.

In many ways, public administrations are pushing ahead. With one foot in the past, they are also eager to keep stride with—and indeed anticipate—the rapidly advancing sectors that will shape the future. Thus, the practice of public administration is no longer totally consistent with the Classic theory; nor is it yet supported by a 'new' and unifying philosophy.

This text aims to explore the rich tapestry of contemporary public administration, from a practitioner's perspective. Following the threads of academic theory and practical experience, it offers some of my 'best guesses' in relation to emerging trends and characteristics that will define innovative patterns and textures in this dynamic field. . . .

The question of whether we need a 'new synthesis,' a new 'integrating framework' or a new 'theory' of public administration is one of degree. As I was preparing these notes, I was struck by the considerable gap between modern concepts of government and those that held sway in the past. As a result, I became more concerned about the growing gap between the reality of those serving in the public service and the theory that, in principle, is there to guide them.

'There is nothing so practical as a good theory'. I would add that there is nothing so dangerous as a theory that lags behind the times and yet remains the yardstick for making decisions and passing judgments.

Our concepts or understanding of situations shape the way we think and act. Concepts of citizenship, democracy or public interest have evolved over time and they are continuing to evolve. Consequently, the role of government and the role of the public service are being transformed in ways that push beyond the constraints of the Classic model.

A journey towards a New Public Administration theory must start at the most basic level. It begins with the concept of citizenship.

Citizenship

Citizen involvement was not a trademark of the public service of the late nineteenth and early twentieth centuries. Originally, 'citizenship' was used strictly in a legal sense—i.e. to define citizens as equal under the law. Over time, the term has taken on a broader meaning. First, it took on an economic aspect (i.e. property rights or the right to dispose of assets), which helped to ensure a well-performing market economy. The concept later expanded to include a social dimension, i.e. it came to incorporate social rights such as health and education.

Today, we would readily agree that citizenship encompasses all of these dimensions and that citizens are more than constituents, voters, clients or customers. I would argue that citizenship is the starting point of a New Public Administration theory.

Citizenship is considered an 'integrating' concept in that it helps individuals to reconcile their multiple roles in society. It recognizes that my interests as a parent, an employee or a member of my local community sometimes conflict. However, my role as a citizen extends beyond my conflicting self-interests and prompts me to consider the welfare of the community as a whole. Today's citizens examine and reconcile various kinds of individual and collective interests.

Citizenship also helps to integrate individuals and communities. Individuals belong to many communities simultaneously. 'Families, work groups, churches, civic associations, social groups ... help establish connections between individuals and the larger society. Collectively, these groups constitute a civil society in which people work out their personal interests in the context of community concerns'.

In recent years, we have learned a great deal about the importance of civil society. In addition, we now have a better understanding of the importance of government's role in encouraging community building and civil society. Governments can contribute to social capital by encouraging citizen involvement in government activities that enrich both government and the community.

Many factors work in favour of greater citizen involvement. Greater involvement can lead to better policy decisions. It helps to ensure that government initiatives meet the needs of the greatest number of citizens—and increases the likelihood of successful implementation. Equally important, greater involvement enhances the legitimacy of government.

Figure 1

Towards a 'New' Public Administration Theory: Citizenship

Factors	From	Towards
Citizens	Legal being ⟶	Political being
Citizenship	Equal bearer of rights ⟶	Member of a social and political community including rights and responsibilities
Role of government	Representing citizen's ⟶ interests	Promoting citizenship, public discussion and public integration

Figure 1 attempts to illustrate how the concept of citizenship has changed over time and will continue to evolve over the coming years (although it does not propose a pre-determined end point). Despite all the risks inherent in oversimplification, I believe that this figure is a useful reminder of the trends that are transforming the role of government in modern society.

As mentioned in the introductory paragraphs, much has been written about declining trust in government. One possible interpretation is the growing frustration of citizens who feel excluded by a political system that is becoming the reserve of professional politicians, powerful lobbyists and campaign managers. Declining trust may also be a signal of declining support for 'power politics' that have been practiced in the past—and a growing demand for citizen engagement in policy debate, citizen involvement in government services and citizen participation in policy decisions. The 'politics of citizenship' is the 'politics of participation' . . . of ordinary citizens engaged in dialogue about the directions of society.

In the past twenty years, we witnessed a sustained push towards a market model. It has not been entirely satisfactory. Over the next twenty years, developed democracies will need a concept of citizenship that reconciles the 'economic man', the need for effective public institutions, and for proper checks and balances. We will need to integrate our concept of citizenship with the fact that we are becoming world citizens and that the threats to our well-being are no longer found solely within the borders of the nation-state. In this context, national citizenship and national governments assume even greater importance: they become the main instrument for exerting influence in the international community of nations.

Public Interest

The second concept I'd like to examine is that of 'public interest'—which has been alternately dismissed, applauded and, most recently, revived. Clarke Cochran gave us a schema of four different schools of thought on the subject, defined as normative, abolitionist, political process and consensualist.

For the normative group, public interest is an ethical standard for decision-making. The abolitionist school argues that public interest cannot be measured and, therefore, does not exist (see Figure 2).

Figure 2

Towards a New Public Administration Theory: The Public Interest

Factors	From	Towards
Public interest	The aggregation of individual interests	$\longrightarrow$ The common (or shared) interests of citizens
	The interplay of special interests	
Role of government	To express the public will	$\longrightarrow$ To articulate and realize the public interest

The political process school refers to the mechanism through which policy is made. It is less concerned with 'what' decisions are made and more interested in 'who' decides and 'how'.

In the Classic model of public administration theory, the public interest is determined by elected officials: Their decisions amount to carrying out the 'public will'. Public administrators had no role in it, or to quote Woodrow Wilson: 'it [the public service] will have no taint of officialism. . .'. Citizens themselves had no direct role, other than by electing their representatives.

At one time, the prevailing view was that interest groups and political parties best represented the interests of citizens in the public policy process, and that the mediation between these views would approximate the public interest. Miller later argued that this school of thought turns liberal democracy 'on its head' because it replaces the public interest with the will of the winning coalition.

The consensualist school of thought views the public interest as a policy debate to achieve a public value consensus. The concept was developed further by the work of Paul Appleby and Deborah Stone, and can be best described through direct quotation:

> The public interest is never merely the sum of all private interests. . . .
> It is not wholly separate from citizens with many private interests; but it is something distinctive that arises within, among, apart from, and above private interests focusing on government some of the most elevated aspiration and deepest devotion of which human beings are capable.
>
> It [public interest] 'is about communities trying to achieve something as communities. . . . The concept of public interest is to the polis (the political community) what self-interest is to the market'.

The way we perceive the public interest has profound ramifications for the role of government and the way public servants are expected to act. If we see the public interest as distinct from special interest, then the role of government is to help articulate and satisfy the public interest. It is to ensure that the public interest dominates in the solutions and in the processes by which public policy solutions are achieved.

The decline in trust referred to earlier may be due in part to a growing perception that elected officials and administrators are seeking to maximize their self-interest rather than to help articulate a shared vision for society. Coupled with a modernized concept of citizenship, a richer definition of the role of government in serving the public interest would provide the foundation for a New Public Administration theory.

Service to Citizens

In the early days of public administration, service delivery (i.e. the implementation of public policies) was not considered a distinct function of government. It was the whole of public administration. The purpose of public agencies was to implement politically determined policies and programmes.

The process of policy implementation was top-down, hierarchical and unidirectional. Public agencies were expected to translate policy directives with as little variation and as little discretion as possible. It was not a matter of using discretion responsibly but of avoiding it altogether by adhering to laws, procedures and directives. In this context, responsiveness was unnecessary.

The influence of scientific management led to an expectation that it would be possible to define the 'correct' procedures and to control clearly defined and predictable tasks.

It was not until the early 1970s that the service delivery function of government started to receive some attention. (The work of Pressman and Wildavsky is worthy of note.) We came to realize that the implementation process is a determinant of policy outcome, and that the institutional capacity to deliver is central to the design of policy options. In short, we learned that policy formulation and policy implementation are an integrated and interactive process of discussion involving both policy makers and administrators.

In the 1990s, the attention focused on new and different types of government services. This was largely the result of new modern information and communication technologies and the changing expectations of citizens. The 'new' services share a number of common characteristics:

- First, they are **knowledge based**, which means that the service provided depends on the accumulated knowledge of the organization and on the human capital of the people working for the organization.
- Second, they use a **holistic approach** to service delivery, which implies a 'whole-of-government' method involving multiple service agencies within a government or among levels of government. They also favour a holistic approach to citizens' needs, which implies addressing multiple demands, depending on the circumstances of service recipients.
- Third, they encourage **citizens' participation** in service design and delivery.

All of these changes can be seen, to varying degrees, in public administrations around the world. They have profound ramifications for the role of government and raise issues that merit inclusion in a New Public

Figure 3

Towards a New Public Administration Theory: Implementation of Public Policy

Factors	From		Towards
Policy and implementation	Separation	$\longrightarrow$	Integration
Guiding principles	Compliance	$\longrightarrow$	Results within the law
Exercise of discretion	Rule based	$\longrightarrow$	Constrained by accountability
Criteria of success	Output	$\longrightarrow$	Outcome
Citizens	Non-interference	$\longrightarrow$	Participation/co-production

Administration theory. This gives rise to issues of accountability. It also entails a transformation of the interface between the political and administrative realms and of the relationships between the public service and citizens. Figure 3 summarizes this change and provides an initial impression of the magnitude of the change that has taken place in the implementation of public policies over the past thirty years.

In academia and in government, I have witnessed three types of reactions to the transformation of the role of government in service delivery. The first is to dismiss it as a fad or to think that 'this too shall pass'. The second is to oppose these changes on the grounds that they are not in keeping with the traditional principle of accountability. The third is to carefully, but vigorously, explore ways of making government more responsive to citizens' needs in the twenty-first century while ensuring fairness and adherence to the rule of law. I believe there is a tremendous opportunity to strengthen the role of government. I also believe that there is no turning back.

Public Policy

Today, no government can claim to have all the tools or all the powers necessary to effect a complex policy outcome. Certainly, government is an important player, but one that must work with others to move society in a certain direction. Increasingly, government's role is to set the agenda, bring the appropriate players to the table, and facilitate and broker sustainable solutions to public problems.

The contemporary policy process is characterized by a dispersion of power and responsibility. There are many reasons for this: global markets have given rise to new issues of public concern that require global solutions; governments must increasingly work with other governments and many international organizations; and technology enables greater public access to the public policy process.

The dispersion of power combined with the capacity of modern information and communication technologies are at the root of the policy networks that have emerged as privileged arenas for public policy debates. In this context, it makes more and more sense to speak of governance:

> Governance can be defined as the traditions, institutions and processes that determine the exercise of power in society, including how decisions are made on issues of public concerns and how citizens are given voice in public decisions-making. Governance speaks to how society actually makes choices, allocates resources and creates shared values.

The OECD has studied various forms of citizens' involvement in policy development and defines the primary characteristics of three common approaches:

- **Information:** A one-way relationship in which governments provide information to citizens;
- **Consultation:** A two-way relationship in which citizens provide feedback to governments.
- **Active participation:** An ongoing exchange in which governments and citizens are involved in the content of policy making.

As the process of policy development changes, so do the roles of government, of elected officials and of public servants. Governments will continue to play the key role in setting the legal and political rules of governance, balancing interests, and ensuring that the principles of democracy and social justice are respected. In contrast, public servants are called upon to play new roles of facilitation, negotiation, and conflict resolution. These changes add complexity to the policy–administration relationship. (see Figure 4). . . .

As mentioned earlier, nothing is really 'new'. Each aspect mentioned in this presentation has previously been discussed elsewhere. A rich and abundant body of literature is available on any one of these issues. However, the field of public administration lacks a *unifying* set of values, themes and principles to express today's reality, as well as to inspire and assist public servants.

Allow me to pick out some specific 'threads' so I can begin 'weaving' them together.

A 'new' theory should start with the ideal of democratic citizenship. The public service derives its true meaning from its mandate to serve citizens to advance the public good. This is the raison d'être of the institution, the source of motivation and pride of all those who choose to make it their life, whether for a season or for an entire career.

Public administration seen from this perspective refocuses our attention on the ideals of democracy, the public interest, citizenship and human dignity, civic values, and commitment to service. These ideals are the starting point that defines the role of government, of elected officials and of professional public servants.

To be pragmatic public servants need a dear point of reference. In most countries (though not all), the constitutional law is the source of all powers and the authoritative basis for citizens' rights and responsibilities. It is above

Figure 4

Towards a New Public Administration Theory: Public Policy

Factors	From	Towards
Policy/Administration interface	Separation $\longrightarrow$	Interaction
Public policy	The result of political decision process $\longrightarrow$	The result of multiple interactions
Citizens' role	Compliance $\longrightarrow$	Engagement
Role of government	Legislation $\longrightarrow$	Deliberation

majority voting, above the laws creating public agencies and granting authorities to elected officials. Thus, it is a solid and reliable basis for action by public servants.

Starting from the concept of *democratic citizenship* opens up new perspectives. In this context, the role of public administrators cannot be reduced to simply responding to users' demand or carrying out orders. It involves:

- Building collaborative relationships with citizens and groups of citizens.
- Encouraging shared responsibilities.
- Disseminating information to elevate public discourse and foster a shared understanding of public issues.
- Seeking opportunities to involve citizens in government activities.

Democratic citizenship is not a concept wherein 'benevolent bureaucrats' substitute their superior wisdom for that of elected officials. This concept recognizes that elected officials hold the ultimate responsibility for setting the agenda and making public choices. It also values the constitutional authority of the courts as the ultimate interpreter of the law. Democratic citizenship implies an interactive process in which public servants deal with citizens as citizens within the broader systems of political governance. It affirms public service values and clearly differentiates public administration from the market model.

Let me weave in a second thread. A New Public Administration theory would propose a *unifying vision of policy, politics and policy implementation* as one circular, integrated, and interactive process that brings together all relevant actors. This principle of active and democratic interactions would replace the doctrine of strict separation—a doctrine that has long been discredited but is still considered as a point of reference, particularly when things go wrong. The new theory would recognize the fact that both policy makers and administrators are *actively involved* in all aspects of policy research, policy development and policy implementation. It would help elected officials and professional civil servants act responsibly, ethically and in accordance with democratic principles. It would also recognize that, in the twenty-first century, discretion is necessary in policy implementation and, thus, would help to explore how the exercise of discretion could be informed by citizens' choices and participation. Finally, the new theory would help to address the issue of professional responsibility and accountability.

In seeking to address all of these individual issues, the new theory would effectively take on the difficult task of proposing a *unified doctrine of accountability* that encompasses the full range of professional, legal, political and democratic responsibilities.

In recent years, both elected officials and public administrators have been reaching out to citizens and exploring various forms of engagement, including use of the Internet. The underlying message to citizens is that 'having a say' does not mean 'having a vote'. The new theory would therefore seek to better reconcile the governments commitment to citizens' participation with its own role in establishing the legal and political rules of engagement, setting the agenda, and making the final decisions. In essence, the new theory would help to reconcile the role of responsible public administrators and the democratic responsibility of elected officials.

Public administrators are neither masters nor mercenaries. They are professional individuals who serve the functions of analysts, managers, facilitators, moral leaders, and stewards of public values and are called upon to be responsible actors in a complex system of governance. It is a demanding, challenging and sometimes heroic endeavour involving accountability, adherence to the law, judgement and responsibility. A strong theory reduces the need for heroism by showing the way and guiding one's steps. Public administration theory should help public servants fully exercise their multi-faceted role.

In closing, and in further pursuing the analogy of the weaver, I would remind readers that even the most complex tapestry is created by combining warp (vertical) and woof (horizontal) threads. In the context of the public service, I would propose that *trust* is the warp thread—the thread that gives the fabric its shape and sturdiness.

At the most basic level, citizens expect their government to be legitimate, honest and responsible: in a word, to be trustworthy. They expect government to respect democratic principles, abide by the rule of law and serve the collective interest. As taxpayers, they expect value for money, efficiency and responsiveness. They expect public servants to abide by high ethical standards and to carry out their duties with competence and integrity.

Trust in government, in public institutions and in the fairness of government decisions is the ultimate test of good government. It is the frame on which the multitude of threads representing various aspects of government and society can be interwoven to create a pattern that reflects reality. Trust is both a pre-condition for, and the result of, government actions. Maintaining public trust between governments and citizens is an essential element of democracy and a prerequisite for good government. It is also a constant 'work in progress'.

Signs of declining trust should never be taken lightly: no country is rich enough to afford the cost of distrust. Declining trust in existing public institutions leads to a lower rate of compliance, corruption, black markets, more tax avoidance strategies and increasing litigation costs. Disaffected citizens may stop participating in public affairs. Eventually, it leads to the erosion of the social fabric. Declining trust of elected officials in the professional civil service may be less visible but is also corrosive. It leads to increasing external controls, the higher costs of which divert money from service delivery to internal processes. It may also deprive elected officials of the best advice on policy decisions. Ultimately, it leads to growing dissatisfaction among citizens and public servants. Declining trust in an incumbent government reduces the scope for new public initiatives, particularly when benefits are not equally shared or will only materialize in the mid to long term.

The most common outcome of declining trust is a democratic change of government.

However, if the declining trust applies to both government and to institutions, rather than a single political party or an individual, it may lead to social conflict and ultimately to an overthrow of government and a return to military rule, dictatorship or civil war.

We have seen the growing signs of disenchantment. Decades of reforms to make governments more efficient and transparent have clearly fallen short of enhancing public trust. Decades of pressure to reduce the role of the State have not generated more trust, a greater sense of security or greater citizen satisfaction.

The current discontent signals the need to reconcile, yet again, freedom in the private sphere with collective deliberation over common values in the collective sphere. I would argue that we are in a better position than ever before to tackle this challenge. Everything that has taken place to date has been part of a learning process. Everything that lies ahead of us will be part of a journey of discovery for there is no end to our quest for better governance. I believe that the time is ripe for a New Public Administration theory that is adapted to the dilemmas and challenges of governance in the twenty-first century.

Herbert Kaufman

Emerging Conflicts in the Doctrine of Public Administration*

. . .

Three Core Values

The central thesis of this paper is that an examination of the administrative institutions of this country suggests that they have been organized and operated in pursuit successively of three values, here designated representativeness, neutral competence, and executive leadership. Each of these values has been dominant (but not to the point of total suppression of the others) in different periods of our history; the shift from one to another generally appears to have occurred as a consequence of the difficulties encountered in the period preceding the change.[1] Much of the early literature commonly identified as within the province of public administration was written during the transition from the first to the second of these values, and the great flood of materials produced after World War I often reflected both the second and third values when these for a time (and for reasons to be explained) pointed in the same direction for governmental improvement. Lately, however, the courses of action indicated by the second and third values have been not only different, but contradictory; the cleavage is becoming increasingly apparent in the doctrines of public administration. What the effects will be on the fraternity of practitioners and on their aspirations to professional status is difficult to say, but it seems clear that commitments to values that have become incompatible can produce only gulfs in the realm of ideas and confusion in proposals for governmental reform.

The Quest for Representativeness

The earliest[2] stress was placed on representativeness in government, the quest for which clearly had its roots in the colonial period, when colonial assemblies were struggling with royal governors for control of political life in the New

* This is a revision of a paper prepared for the Panel on "The Study of Public Administration Since Woodrow Wilson" at the 52nd Annual Meeting of the American Political Science Association on September 7, 1956, at Washington, D.C.

World and "No taxation without representation" was a slogan that expressed one of the principal interests and anxieties of the colonists. The legislatures thus became the champions of the indigenous population, or at least of the ruling elements in the colonies, against what was regarded in many quarters as executive oppression. When the Revolution drove the British out, the legislatures in the new states were, with but a couple of exceptions,[3] enthroned in positions of leadership of the new governments, and, although the franchise continued to be limited to a relatively small proportion of the people, it was through the legislatures that governmental policy was formulated and legitimated. Even in the states that continued to operate under their colonial charters in the post-Revolutionary years, the governors were reduced to figureheads with little influence in the making of governmental decisions. In ten of the states, the governors were elected by the legislatures, most of them for only one-year terms; in just one state did the governor have a veto, and even that was limited by present-day standards. Governors had few powers of appointment and removal, or of administrative supervision and control. They did not function as legislative leaders. Lacking in status and in constitutional and administrative strength, governors had no source of political strength, and they therefore remained subordinate to the legislatures in every respect; they had no leverage with which to exert influence even if they had been so inclined. Hence, the office was regarded as primarily ceremonial and a symbol of honor rather than as a seat of power, and it therefore rarely attracted men of distinction in the early days of the Republic. Consequently, as late as the opening years of the Twentieth Century, the governorship was a dead-end road. As one authority has remarked, they served their short terms and returned to private life with few accomplishments behind them and nothing before them but the pleasure of being called "Governor" for the rest of their days.[4] The legislatures ruled virtually unchallenged.

In local government, too, collegiate bodies were in charge. Whether they were truly "representative," and whether one ought to refer to the governing organ of a community that is not "sovereign" as a legislature, are questions we need not consider here. Suffice it to say that local executives labored under the same or perhaps greater handicaps than their state counterparts and therefore presented no more of a challenge to the local institutions corresponding to legislatures than did the governors to the state bodies.

The constitutional specifications for the Presidency constituted a countertrend to the apparent value system of governmental designers in early America. For the President was invested with greater authority than almost any other chief executive of the time. Yet even at the federal level, there were clearly widespread expectations that the Congress would provide the primary motive power for the government, a view shared, according to Binkley, even by many incumbents of the White House whose "Whig conception" of the Presidency as subservient to the legislature may be contrasted with the "stewardship theory" of independent Presidential authority to be enunciated much later in history. While Washington and Jefferson fought to protect and extend executive power from the very first, it is probably not stretching the facts to argue that Presidents for a long time had an uphill struggle in this effort, and that many chose to yield to the sentiment of the day and the strength of the giants in Congress. Whether or not the legislatures were actually the most representative institutions need not be explored here; there is ample evidence that they were thought to be so.

The enthronement of the legislature was one of the two major tangible indications of the value placed on representativeness; the other was the rather uncritical faith in the electoral principle. It began with the extension of the franchise and a thrust toward universal adult suffrage. But the faith in elections also took the form of an increasing number of official positions filled by balloting. The first half of the Nineteenth Century saw the number of elective offices sharply increased, especially after the Jacksonian Revolution burst upon the country. The ballot grew in length until almost every public official from President down to dogcatcher came to power via the electoral route. Moreover, with the rise of the party organizations to new influence as a result, even those positions which were not made elective were filled by party faithful; the spoils system came into its own. By the time of the Civil War, voters found themselves confronted by hundreds of names on their ballots, and each change of party brought with it a change in virtually all government employees.

The Quest for Neutral Competence

As early as the middle of the Nineteenth Century, it had become clear to some people that legislative supremacy, the long ballot, and the spoils system did not in fact increase representativeness; as a matter of fact, they often seemed to have just the opposite effect. For one thing, they tended to confuse both voters and interest groups and thereby opened the way to power to political bosses who, while providing a measure of integration in the bewildering pullulation of government, often utilized their positions to advance their personal interests and the interests of the organizations they headed without regard for the interests of many of the governed. For another thing, legislators and administrators at every level of government proved themselves peculiarly vulnerable to the forces let loose by the burgeoning industrial system; corruption beset legislatures from county boards and city councils right up to Congress itself, and the venality and incompetence of many public officers and employers were common knowledge.

Disillusionment with existing governmental machinery was a result. State and local constitutions and charters grew longer and more detailed as reformers tried to reduce the discretion of legislative bodies. Limitations on the length and frequency of state legislative sessions were imposed to limit the amount of harm they could do. And at every level, reformers began to cast around for new governmental machinery that would provide a high level of responsible government service while avoiding the high costs of unalloyed representative mechanisms.

Thus began the quest for neutral competence in government officials, a quest which has continued to the present day. The core value of this search was ability to do the work of government expertly, and to do it according to explicit, objective standards rather than to personal or party or other obligations and loyalties.[5] The slogan of the neutral competence school became, "Take administration out of politics."

This school produced its own rationale and mechanisms for this purpose. The rationale was the now-familiar politics-administration dichotomy, according to which politics and administration are distinct and separable processes that should therefore be assigned to separate and distinct organs. The mechanisms were independent boards and commissions and the merit system, which were designed to insulate many public officials and public policies from political pressures.

The movement gathered momentum after the Civil War, although the first agitation for some of its objectives goes back even further. In local and state governments, library boards and park boards and police boards and boards of health and finance boards and utilities commissions and boards of education and boards of assessment and equalization and boards and commissions for a dozen other purposes mushroomed up all over the governmental landscape. At the federal level, the Interstate Commerce Commission came into being, to be followed in the Twentieth Century by a host of like bodies. These agencies, at every level, differed from each other in details, but had the same underlying structure: their members were appointed for overlapping terms supposedly on the basis of their reputations for general ability and character and specialized knowledge. They were granted wide discretion and secure tenure for substantial periods, and were expected to formulate policy on nonpolitical premises. Objectivity was reinforced in some instances by mandatory bipartisan membership on the boards. The exigencies of the times made it necessary for legislatures to delegate power to administrative agencies; the advocates of neutral competence deflected delegation from the chief executives and the departments under their control to what was later to be branded "the headless fourth branch of government."

The merit system, peculiarly, made its greatest advances where boards and commissions were slowest to gain a foothold—the federal government. Pressure for the merit system began before the Civil War; its first fruit was the federal Civil Service Act of 1883. Initially, the objectives of the program were confined principally to controlling the selection of government workers by taking the power to hire staff from the hands of executive heads (who were politicians) and lodging it with experts who, if they did not actually appoint personnel, at least could screen out all but those who could pass tests of one sort or another. This aspect of the program spread rapidly in the federal government; despite the subsequent growth of the federal service, about nine out of ten government employees today are under some form of merit appointment. But the process did not stop with the removal of the appointing power from politics; over the years, the Civil Service Commission extended its surveillance to dismissal, promotion, and position classification; eventually, with the aid of new legislation, the political activities of civil servants were reduced to little more than voting. A wall was erected between the government bureaucracy and the politicians, a wall policed by the Civil Service Commission.[6]

The quest for neutral competence, though it began about a century ago, has never waned. The training of civil servants became steadily more formal and systematic as time passed; courses, departments, and even schools of administration appeared in universities. Organization and methods analysis became a profession in itself. Boards and commissions are still common modes of handling administrative problems—witness, for example, the Atomic Energy Commission. Supporters of the merit system continue unabated their efforts to extend it "upward, outward, and downward." The desire to make government employment an attractive career service was given new voice by the Commission of Inquiry on Public Service Personnel a generation ago, and by the Task Force on Personnel and Civil Service of the Second Hoover Commission more recently. The city manager plan—and even the town, county, and state manager plans—have continued to score successes. Neutral competence is still a living value among students of government, career civil servants, and, perhaps more significantly, among much of the general populace.

The Quest for Executive Leadership

Just as the excessive emphasis on representativeness brought with it bitterly disappointing difficulties unforeseen by its advocates, so too the great stress on neutral competence proved to be a mixed blessing. And just as the failures of the machinery established with an eye primarily to representativeness helped produce the reaction toward neutral competence, so too the weaknesses of the governmental arrangements devised by the latter school—or, more accurately, the weaknesses of government resulting from the work of *both* schools—gave impetus to the supporters of a third value: executive leadership.

For both earlier philosophies, and the mechanisms to which they gave rise, created a thrust toward fragmentation of government, toward the formation of highly independent islands of decision-making occupied by officials who went about their business without much reference to each other or to other organs of government. Neither elected administrative officials nor independent boards and commissions welcomed direction from the chief executives; the former were supported by constituencies in much the same way as governors and mayors, and their tenure was linked largely to their vote-getting prowess, while the latter generally remained in office longer than the chief executives and depended very little on them for support. Besides, as these officials and agencies became more accomplished in their respective areas of specialization, they tended to resent efforts of "laymen" and "amateurs" to intervene; this tendency revealed itself even in some civil servants nominally under the chief executives, who, though formally subject to dismissal, turned out in practice to have quite secure tenure, and who, by adept maneuvers in negotiating bureaucratic armistices ("memoranda of agreement") and in forming alliances with legislative committees and clientele groups, succeeded in carving out for themselves broad areas of discretion free of real supervision by their political chiefs.

The drive toward fragmentation could not be effectively countered by legislative bodies, despite their vast statute-making, financial, and investigative powers. Even Congress can exercise only a general and intermittent oversight over administrative agencies, and has had to confine itself to providing general standards guiding the exercise of administrative discretion and to occasional intervention to correct abuses or to force specific changes in policy. And state legislatures and city councils and county boards operate under still greater limitations; many of these bodies are in session for only brief periods out of each year (or biennium), and administrative officials conduct the business of government with great latitude in the long intervals between meetings. Moreover, even if legislatures met often enough and had enough technical assistance of their own to exert control over administration, their composition and procedures would render them incapable of providing integration; working through tens of committees, reaching decisions through processes of compromise and concession among representatives of small territorials units, functioning increasingly as reviewing bodies for proposals placed before them by executive and administrative agencies and by interest groups, they are generally too slow and too fragmented to perform this function effectively.

Neither have the courts been able to integrate the component elements of American government. They were not designed for this responsibility, and they are completely unable to discharge it. Limited to refereeing disputes between contending parties, formal in procedure and deliberate in method, they could not play this role even had they been willing. In fact, they have increasingly moved toward acceptance of findings of fact by administrative organizations and toward restriction of their own activities to review of questions of jurisdiction and procedure.

The centrifugal drives of the representativeness and neutral competence institutions thus found no important counter-force in the legislatures or in the courts. So the efforts to maximize these values brought with them the dispersion of governmental policy-making processes.

There were widespread criticisms of this fragmentation.[7] It bred chaos; agencies pursued contradictory policies in related fields. It fomented conflict; agencies engaged in bitter bureaucratic warfare to establish their spheres of jurisdiction. It opened gaps in the provision of service or of regulation; clienteles were sometimes denied benefits or escaped supervision because they fell between agencies. It was costly; many agencies maintained overhead organizations that could have been replaced more cheaply and effectively by a common organization, and citizens had to make their own way through bureaucratic labyrinths. And, most important of all, it led to irresponsibility; no one quite knew how the pattern of organization and program came into existence or what could be done to alter it, each segment of the fragmented governments became a self-directing unit, the impact of elections on the conduct of government was minimized, and special interest groups often succeeded in virtually capturing control of individual agencies. No one seemed to be steering the governmental machinery, though everyone had a hand in it. At best, it seemed to be drifting (and just when the growth of the economic system appeared to make greater direction necessary), while at worst it showed signs of flying apart or grinding to a stop. These were among the forces that persuaded many students of government that chief executives had to be built up to take charge of the machinery.

The office of the chief executive became their hope because it furnished the only available means of achieving the end sought.[8] Movement toward strengthening chief executives began long before there was an explicit body of doctrine to explain and justify it. In the federal government, it took the form of struggles between Presidents and Congress for control of policy. Since the Presidency was set up with strong constitutional powers at the very start, the battle raged over the breadth of the powers conferred rather than over formal constitutional changes. Those powers were firmly defended, liberally interpreted, and gradually expanded under the strong Presidents from Washington on. The governors, on the other hand, having been granted few powers at the start, gained strength slowly, largely through constitutional amendment, in the course of the Nineteenth Century. In the same period, many city executives developed from mere chairmen of councils to weak mayors and then to strong mayors, and there was even an occasional step in this direction among the rural units of government. These things were taking place even while the emphasis on representativeness was predominant; they continued after the pursuit of neutral competence became the order of the day; but the Twentieth Century was well on its way before executive leadership became a systematic quest supported by articulate theories, and before it really began to gather speed.

One of the first signs of the new emphasis was the rapid spread of the executive budget in government. For a long time, agency requests for funds were considered individually, and there was no central point at which total expenditures were reviewed and the competing claims balanced against each other in the light of the resources available; indeed, very often, the only way governments could figure out how much they were spending was to add up the appropriation bills after they had been passed. The reformers turned to the chief executives to rationalize the spending process, and out of it came the now familiar phenomena of executive review and adjustment of agency requests, and the submittal of a comprehensive budget supposed to make it possible to see the overall spending pattern. The practice was often far short of ideal, but, for the first time, chief executives were given a powerful instrument with which to control administrative behavior; it was a major advance in striving to equip them to integrate American government. A few large cities and states adopted budgetary legislation during the first two decades of the Twentieth Century, and the Taft Commission on Efficiency and Economy in 1912 urged such a measure upon the federal government. By the middle of the third decade, many of the largest cities, virtually all of the states, and the federal government had budget laws on the books. Since then, in general, the tendency has been toward continued increase in the budgetary powers of chief executives, and toward adoption of the process by those jurisdictions in which it did not previously obtain. A large body of literature now backs up this practice, and, though the lack of a *theory* of budgeting (as contrasted with beliefs about the appropriate *machinery* for budgeting) has been pointed out, the executive-budget doctrine is widely accepted and rarely challenged.

Another indication of the concern with executive leadership is the administrative reorganization movement. It is frequently described as having begun in 1917, when Illinois adopted a sweeping change in its administrative structure, although such measures had been unsuccessfully urged in other states several years earlier. Under this plan, the number of agencies was reduced, and they were grouped into comparatively few departments headed by officials appointed by the governor; an administrative pyramid, with the governor standing at the apex, was the goal, and if it was rarely achieved completely, the extent to which it was approximated is indeed remarkable considering the degree of fragmentation prior to the changes. The number of elected administrative officials was sharply diminished, and ballots became correspondingly shorter. The appointing and removal power of the governor was also increased. In a single vast upheaval, the reorganizers sought to elevate him from an almost impotent exhorter to a powerful leader; if their efforts did not—as they could not—*immediately* produce the consequences sought, it was not very long before they began to bear fruit. Administratively and politically, the Illinois governor ascended to new eminence and influence. And more than half the states, some cities, and a few counties and towns, followed Illinois' lead. All during the 'twenties and 'thirties, surveys of government machinery were commonplace, and they became even more so after World War II as the first federal Hoover Commission touched off a wave of "little Hoover Commissions" in the states and many cities. "Concentration of authority and responsibility," "functional integration," "direct lines of responsibility," "grouping of related services," "elimination of overlapping and duplication," and "need for coordination" echoed through state capitols, city and town halls, and even through some county courthouses as chief executives became the new center of governmental design.

At the federal level, there were occasional adjustments and readjustments in the machinery of government in the early part of the century, and the President was even invested with broad powers of reorganization during the emergencies of World War I and the depression. But it was not until the mushrooming agencies of the New Deal strained that machinery to its limits that the practices and supporting dogmas of the reorganizers made their appearance in strength in Washington. Few clearer statements of the executive leadership value than the *Report of the President's Committee on Administrative Management* have ever been published;[9] with its recommendations on pulling the administrative functions of the independent regulatory commissions back under the President,[10] on drawing the government corporations back into the hierarchy,[11] on bringing personnel management under close direction by the President, on strengthening the White House staff, on getting the General Accounting Office out of the pre-auditing field and returning this operation to the executive branch, and in the tightly reasoned explanations of these recommendations (which were tied to the peg of the separation of powers), the Committee offered the classic presentation of the reorganization aspects of the executive leadership school.[12]

The Reorganization Act of 1939, which reversed one formal relationship of the President to Congress by conferring initiatory responsibility for reorganization plans on the former and authorizing the latter in effect to veto such proposals, reflected in practice the theory of the Report; even the frequent use of the legislative veto does not reduce the significance of this expansion of executive power, and the fierceness of the periodic battles over renewal of the Act suggests both Congressmen and Presidents are conscious of this significance. In the course of the years since the Report, without much fanfare, other recommendations of the Committee have been put into practice, too; the influence of the Committee continued to make itself felt for a long time.

The first Hoover Commission was considerably less emphatic about strengthening the chief executive than its predecessor, and the second Hoover Commission has displayed, if anything, some coldness (if not outright hostility) to the concept. It is conceivable, therefore, that the reorganization movement has for the time being run its course in the federal government. But it would probably be an error to write off entirely this phase of the quest for executive leadership.

A third index of this quest, an index related to, but distinguishable from, the developments in budgeting and administrative reorganization, is the increase in the size of executive staffs. The archetype is the Executive Office of the President with its hundreds of specialists providing the President with advice on every aspect of policy, reviewing legislative proposals to work out the Presidential attitude, studying administrative management from the President's point of view, planning, researching, furnishing legal counsel, serving as a source of information alternative and supplementary to the formal hierarchy, and studded with "the President's men," responsible and loyal to him and him alone. This is a far cry from the days when a President's secretariat consisted of a few aides who helped him with his official correspondence; it has helped to give the chief executive the means with which to direct the administration he heads and to formulate programs and press them into statute and then into operation; it has helped make him a real center of political and administrative power. In like fashion, the executive offices of many of the governors have been transformed into instruments of leadership, and some local executives have been similarly equipped; at these levels, the evolution as been somewhat less dramatic, but not much less effective. The tendencies may be uneven in their fulfillment, but they are pronounced.

Doctrinally, the sharp conceptual cleavage between politics and administration, which gained currency during the years when neutral competence was ascendent, and which served as such a useful philosophical prop for the machinery favored in those years, became an impediment to the justification of executive leadership. For one thing, chief executives, in whom administrative responsibility and power were to be lodged, were also partisan politicians. Moreover, one of the main reasons advanced for seeking integration was elimination of the fragmentation resulting from acceptance of the idea of the separability of politics and administration. Gradually, therefore, the politics-administration dichotomy fell out of favor in public administration, and the doctrine of the continuity of the policy-formulating process, better suited to the aims of executive leadership, began to replace it. Before long, the traditional orthodoxy became old-fashioned and found few defenders. . . .

Notes

1. To be sure, the three values, which will be examined in turn, are not the only ones to be fulfilled by the governmental system, but the design and functioning of the government have been such that these appear to have received prime stress in the ordering of our political life.

2. It is impossible to date any of the periods with precision, except arbitrarily, and it is probably unnecessary to do so for most purposes, but their origins can be identified. and so, roughly, can their zeniths.

3. New York and Massachusetts. These states provided important models for the federal executive, which ultimately was set up as an even stronger— and perhaps better—office than its prototypes.

4. There were notable exceptions of course. Cleveland became President after serving as Governor of New York, Hayes and McKinley had both been Governors of Ohio before moving to the White House, and other governors became influential in national politics. As a general rule, however, the governorship was not a springboard to power or prominence.

5. Proponents of this value generally did not demean representative institutions; on the contrary, they claimed their programs would strengthen those institutions by rationalizing governmental operations and improving their quality to such an extent that elected officers would be in a position to exert greater control over policy than they ever could hope to do in the prevailing political jungle. The case for neutral competence has normally been made not as an alternative to representativeness, but as a fulfillment of it.

   The disillusionment of some was so thorough, however, that they lost faith completely in representativeness, in the capacity of a people to rule themselves, and returned to advocacy of rule by an aristocracy of talent. Civil service reform was, in fact, a movement which found its leaders among the grandsons and great-grandsons of the "Patricians" of early days, among the "Old Whigs" and their sons, among those who had been enamored of, or grew up under, British or German or French institutions (for example, the Adamses, Godkin, Schurz, Villard, Rosengarten), and among the urban mercantile and older businesses or professions rather than among the new industrialists. Distrust of the populace may still be observed in some modern writers and even in some current supporters of the neutral competence idea, but, for the most part, the concept of representation was so deeply ingrained in American thinking—and, indeed, in American emotions, for the word has become a revered one—that few dare to attack it openly whatever their beliefs may be.

6. The states and localities were slow to follow suit. By the turn of the century, only two states had enacted civil service legislation and only a few of the largest cities. Even today, the formal merit system still has a long way to go at these levels: states and localities remain the prime targets of the civil service reformers. But they have made some impressive gains during the last quarter-century, and the idea is still spreading.

7. Criticisms, that is to say, of the fragmentation "in general." When it came to the particular fragments over which they exerted their greatest influence, legislators, bureaucrats, party organizers, and interest groups were often defensive of their special positions and hostile to integrating remedies which might disturb their control.

8. Party bosses occasionally did serve this function, but only occasionally, for it must be remembered that our political parties are really congeries of smaller organizations in most places and therefore hardly equipped to provide governmental integration. Besides, they were phenomena from

which governmental designers were seeking to deliver the governmental process.

9. And no clearer or more scholarly justifications of this value than E. Pendleton Herring, *Public Administration and the Public Interest* (New York, 1936).

10. This point of view received additional support at the state level, although in restrained tones, from James W. Fesler in his *The Independence of State Regulatory Commissions* (Chicago, 1942).

11. See also, for example, V. O. Key, Jr., "Government Corporations," in Fritz M. Marx, ed., *Elements of Public Administration* (New York, 1946).

12. To be sure, the Committee also advocated expansion of the merit system, and restated the argument that stronger executive leadership would mean greater popular control of government (i.e., representativeness), thus indicating how deep-seated these parallel values were. But this cannot obscure the basic premises of the Committee's Report, nor negate its general impact: it is overwhelmingly for executive leadership in sentiment.

EXPLORING THE ISSUE

Is Contemporary Public Administration Theory More Influential Than Its Classical Counterpart?

Critical Thinking and Reflection

1. What are the central tenets of contemporary and classic public administration theory?
2. In what ways are these theories complementary? In opposition?
3. How much influence should emerging societal trends have on shaping long-term theories?
4. How do theory and practice relate when it comes to looking at public administration and policy?
5. Which paradigm do you believe is best suited to examine bureaucracy in America today? Why?

Is There Common Ground?

Classical and contemporary public administration theories will have no choice but to continue coexisting and attempting to influence the decisions of practitioners and academics alike. The classical theories of individuals like Max Weber, Luther Gulick, Woodrow Wilson, Frank Goodnow, and Dwight Waldo came together to give birth to the discipline in the first place, and their influence is felt in even the most modern and contemporary of theories. Whether discussing New Public Management, representative bureaucracy, or e-governance, there are elements of the classical theorists underlying new ideas.

Although these classic theories are unquestionably still relevant, one can see that their impact has become muted as government has changed since the time of their writing. In the current American society, existing under modern American government, classical theories are not always directly relatable to the issues of today. Weber, for example, could not have imagined the questions that would face public administrators of the twenty-first century. As a result, perhaps rather than arguing the merits of classical theories compared to more contemporary ones, our time would be better spent determining ways to build new theories that integrate more fully classical ideas into a contemporary context—thus ensuring public administration maintains its roots while properly asserting its continued relevance.

Additional Resources

Dolan, J. and D.H. Rosenbloom, *Representative Bureaucracy: Classic Readings and Continued Controversies* (New York: M.E. Sharpe, 2003)

Dolan and Rosenbloom provide an edited volume examining one of the more modern theories of public administration—representative bureaucracy. By focusing on classic arguments and modern applicability, the book strives to show how classic and contemporary theories can work together in improving the discipline for practitioners and academics alike.

Osborne, S., *The New Public Governance? Emerging Perspectives on the Theory and Practice of Public Governance* (New York: Routledge, 2010)

Osborne uses this edited volume to examine new trends in public governance. While slightly different from traditional public administration, this book demonstrates how classical and modern public administration theory can be merged together to examine questions that the founders of the discipline would not have necessarily considered.

Shafritz, J.M., and A.C. Hyde, *Classics of Public Administration*, 7th ed. (New York: Wadsworth, 2011)

An anthology of the classic works of public administration from the discipline's founding through the modern era. Shafritz and Hyde present the vital readings for students of public administration.

Shafritz, J.M., J.S. Ott, and Y.S. Jang, *Classics of Organization Theory*, 7th ed. (New York: Wadsworth, 2010)

An anthology of the classic works of organization theory from the field's founding through the modern era. Shafritz, Ott, and Yang present the vital readings for students of public administration.

Stillman III, R.J., *Public Administration: Concepts and Cases*, 9th ed (New York: Wadsworth, 2009)

Stillman presents a series of telling case studies to demonstrate both classic and contemporary elements of public administration. The cases help to show the continued relevance of classic theory while also explaining the issues that earlier scholars would have been unable to anticipate.

ISSUE 2

Can Public Administration Be International in Scope?

YES: Woodrow Wilson, from "The Study of Administration," *Political Science Quarterly* (June 1887)

NO: B. Guy Peters, from "The Necessity and Difficulty of Comparison in Public Administration," *Asian Journal of Public Administration* (June 1990)

Learning Outcomes

After reading this issue, you should be able to:

- Understand the uniqueness of American public administration.
- Describe the difficulties in attempting to compare different bureaucratic structures across countries.
- Identify patterns and regularities in administrative action and behavior.
- Discuss the difficulty in examining similarities and differences between advanced industrial democratic countries and developing countries.
- Describe the historical attempts to internationalize the study of public administration.
- Understand the historical rationale as to why public administration can be studied comparatively.

ISSUE SUMMARY

YES: Woodrow Wilson argues that administration, as a discipline, finds its roots throughout Europe. Given the generic central tenants of administration theory, Wilson asserts that our young nation was only unable to improve administrative mechanisms and procedures by looking to the experiences of other nations.

NO: B. Guy Peters argues that while the discipline needs more meaningful comparative studies, there are several impediments that make it difficult to conduct such studies. As long as minute and subtle differences make great deals of differences, it will be difficult to have meaningful comparative studies—making public administration best studied as a country-specific phenomenon.

When we think of public administration, most Americans immediately look to domestic institutions for examples and relevancy. We do this not because we do not care about other nations or structures of government but because it is simply what we are more familiar with and aware of. The fact is that understanding the way public administration is set up and operates within a country is difficult enough on its own. As the previous issue explained, much of what we know was originally framed decades ago and has remained applicable to the present day. Yet, context matters. In fact, a variety of contexts matter.

To begin, the domestic political setting directly impacts public administration within a country. At the highest possible level, whether a government is democratic or autocratic impacts all of the structures described next. Yet, even if we see two countries with similar structures, it does not mean they are performing the same tasks in the same ways for similar reasons. Civil service means different things in different parts of the world. So does bureaucracy. Beyond domestic political structures, the political environment impacts the meaning and function of public administration in different areas around the world. For example, countries that have long histories of political corruption may have citizens with different ideas of what qualifies as a "good" public servant. In all, the idea of comparative (or international) public administration leaves us with many issues to consider.

From a perspective of comparison, the first question we must think through is whether comparative public administration is most suitable from a most different or a most alike framework. After all, despite the contextual difficulties quickly highlighted earlier, bureaucrats perform roughly the same tasks regardless of where they are located and what kind of system they operate in. Yet, the country-specific factors still have great impact. As a result, we must wonder about the academic–practitioner divide as it relates to the potential internationalization of public administration. Although academics can gain a more fertile research agenda by moving toward comparative studies, how applicable will this knowledge be for public administration? At the systemic level, governments could perhaps encounter new (or different) ways of structuring public agencies, but does that knowledge impact the lower level government worker? With these questions remaining relevant, one must ask, from a practitioner's perspective, if there is enough to be gleaned from the findings to justify the cost of analysis.

In terms of its place in the discipline, in the mid- to late 1990s, comparative public administration was a growing subfield and seemed to be poised to be a career worthy of research for students who chose to specialize in it. There were endless possibilities. Research looked at the differences in public administration in democratic and autocratic regimes, between developing and advanced industrial nations, between parliamentary and presidential systems, between nations with constitutions and unwritten constitutions, and between nations from different geographic regions. Although many findings were reported and new theories hatched, the impact on actual practitioners appeared to be minimal. Consequently, those in the field who aim to undertake practical research backed away from the subfield and left it for the more theoretical side to continue dissecting. As time has passed, it has become less and less of a fad topic and has been replaced by areas such as disaster management, information technology, and nonprofit management as hotbeds in the discipline. In higher education in the United States, public administration programs typically aim to prepare students to work in some area within the American system. With that as an end goal, it seems clear why the idea of internationalizing the curriculum has little traction. Beyond merely showing how and why our system is unique, there is little knowledge gained that will impact day-to-day performance in bureaucratic settings.

Perhaps the larger problem for internationalizing public administration is the difficulty in developing theoretical models that we can then scientifically test. Without these types of models present, all of our comparative work ends up being little more than snapshots in time of a few countries existing under different contexts with some shared similarity or difference. Although insights will be gleaned from such studies, the results will most likely not be able to be generalized back into larger theories that permit for testing in other countries or areas. Without the ability to do this, we cannot determine the actual contextual factors that shape the structures and functions of public administration across the globe.

Ultimately, what public administration must decide is whether it is a discipline best served by country-specific examinations of relevant factors that impact one nation's structures and functions or if there is a useful, meaningful way that we can make comparisons between systems operating in different contexts. In the selections for this unit, we encounter two divergent viewpoints related to whether it is possible to have public administration that is international in its scope. In the YES selection, Woodrow Wilson discusses how administration—as a discipline—comes to us from European traditions and as a result can only fully grow by looking to other countries' structures for guidance. Since we were an even younger nation at the time of Wilson's writing, it makes sense to top view public administration as a concept that can be borrowed from other countries and improved upon. After all, we were not the first nation to attempt to create a bureaucracy, so clearly we borrowed at least some aspects from others. In the NO selection, B. Guy Peters, on the other hand, believes that while such comparative efforts are useful, there are too many impediments to this line of research to find meaningful results. Most importantly, Peters notes that as long as small, difficult-to-notice differences continue to matter, it will be nearly impossible to have any truly meaningful comparisons.

YES

Woodrow Wilson

The Study of Administration

. . . **A**dministration is everywhere putting its hands to new undertakings. The utility, cheapness, and success of the government's postal service, for instance, point towards the early establishment of governmental control of the telegraph system. Or, even if our government is not to follow the lead of the governments of Europe in buying or building both telegraph and railroad lines, no one can doubt that in some way it must make itself master of masterful corporations. The creation of national commissioners of railroads, in addition to the older state commissions, involves a very important and delicate extension of administrative functions. Whatever hold of authority state or federal governments are to take upon corporations, there must follow cares and responsibilities which will require not a little wisdom, knowledge, and experience. Such things must be studied in order to be well done. And these, as I have said, are only a few of the doors which are being opened to offices of government. The idea of the state and the consequent ideal of its duty are undergoing noteworthy change; and "the idea of the state is the conscience of administration." Seeing every day new things which the state ought to do, the next thing is to see clearly how it ought to do them.

This is why there should be a science of administration which shall seek to straighten the paths of government, to make its business less unbusinesslike, to strengthen and purify its organization, and to crown its duties with dutifulness. This is one reason why there is such a science.

But where has this science grown up? Surely not on this side the sea. Not much impartial scientific method is to be discerned in our administrative practices. The poisonous atmosphere of city government, the crooked secrets of state administration, the confusion, sinecurism, and corruption ever and again discovered in the bureaus at Washington forbid us to believe that any clear conceptions of what constitutes good administration are as yet very widely current in the United States. No; American writers have hitherto taken no very important part in the advancement of this science. It has found its doctors in Europe. It is not of our making; it is a foreign science, speaking very little of the language of English or American principle. It employs only foreign tongues; it utters none but what are to our minds alien ideas. Its aims, its examples, its conditions, are almost exclusively grounded in the histories of foreign races, in the precedents of foreign systems, in the lessons of foreign revolutions. It has been developed by French and German professors, and is consequently in all parts adapted to the needs of a compact state, and made to fit highly

From *Political Science Quarterly*, June 1887.

centralized forms of government; whereas, to answer our purposes, it must be adapted, not to a simple and compact, but to a complex and multiform state, and made to fit highly decentralized forms of government. If we would employ it, we must Americanize it, and that not formally, in language merely, but radically, in thought, principle, and aim as well. It must learn our constitutions by heart; must get the bureaucratic fever out of its veins; must inhale much free American air.

If an explanation be sought why a science manifestly so susceptible of being made useful to all governments alike should have received attention first in Europe, where government has long been a monopoly, rather than in England or the United States, where government has long been a common franchise, the reason will doubtless be found to be twofold: first, that in Europe, just because government was independent of popular assent, there was more governing to be done; and, second, that the desire to keep government a monopoly made the monopolists interested in discovering the least irritating means of governing. They were, besides, few enough to adopt means promptly.

It will be instructive to look into this matter a little more closely. In speaking of European governments I do not, of course, include England. She has not refused to change with the times. She has simply tempered the severity of the transition from a polity of aristocratic privilege to a system of democratic power by slow measures of constitutional reform which, without preventing revolution, has confined it to paths of peace. But the countries of the continent for a long time desperately struggled against all change, and would have diverted revolution by softening the asperities of absolute government. They sought so to perfect their machinery as to destroy all wearing friction, so to sweeten their methods with consideration for the interests of the governed as to placate all hindering hatred, and so assiduously and opportunely to offer their aid to all classes of undertakings as to render themselves indispensable to the industrious. They did at last give the people constitutions and the franchise; but even after that they obtained leave to continue despotic by becoming paternal. They made themselves too efficient to be dispensed with, too smoothly operative to be noticed, too enlightened to be inconsiderately questioned, too benevolent to be suspected, too powerful to be coped with. All this has required study; and they have closely studied it.

On this side the sea we, the while, had known no great difficulties of government. With a new country, in which there was room and remunerative employment for everybody, with liberal principles of government and unlimited skill in practical politics, we were long exempted from the need of being anxiously careful about plans and methods of administration. We have naturally been slow to see the use or significance of those many volumes of learned research and painstaking examination into the ways and means of conducting government which the presses of Europe have been sending to our libraries. Like a lusty child, government with us has expanded in nature and grown great in stature, but has also become awkward in movement. The vigor and increase of its life has been altogether out of proportion to its skill in living. It has gained strength, but it has not acquired deportment. Great, therefore, as has been our advantage over the countries of Europe in point of ease and health of constitutional development, now that the time for more careful administrative adjustments and larger administrative knowledge has come to us, we are at a signal disadvantage as compared with the transatlantic nations. . . .

Government is so near us, so much a thing of our daily familiar handling, that we can with difficulty see the need of any philosophical study of it, or the exact point of such study, should it be undertaken. We have been on our feet too long to study now the art of walking. We are a practical people, made so apt, so adept in self-government by centuries of experimental drill that we are scarcely any longer capable of perceiving the awkwardness of the particular system we may be using, just because it is so easy for us to use any system. We do not study the art of governing: we govern. But mere unschooled genius for affairs will not save us from sad blunders in administration. Though democrats by long inheritance and repeated choice, we are still rather crude democrats. Old as democracy is, its organization on a basis of modern ideas and conditions is still an unaccomplished work. The democratic state has yet to be equipped for carrying those enormous burdens of administration which the needs of this industrial and trading age are so fast accumulating. Without comparative studies in government we cannot rid ourselves of the misconception that administration stands upon an essentially different basis in a democratic state from that on which it stands in a non-democratic state.

After such study we could grant democracy the sufficient honor of ultimately determining by debate all essential questions affecting the public weal, of basing all structures of policy upon the major will; but we would have found but one rule of good administration for all governments alike. So far as administrative functions are concerned, all governments have a strong structural likeness; more than that, if they are to be uniformly useful and efficient, they *must* have a strong structural likeness. A free man has the same bodily organs, the same executive parts, as the slave, however different may be his motives, his services, his energies. Monarchies and democracies, radically different as they are in other respects, have in reality much the same business to look to.

It is abundantly safe nowadays to insist upon this actual likeness of all governments, because these are days when abuses of power are easily exposed and arrested, in countries like our own, by a bold, alert, inquisitive, detective public thought and a sturdy popular self-dependence such as never existed before. We are slow to appreciate this; but it is easy to appreciate it. Try to imagine personal government in the United States. It is like trying to imagine a national worship of Zeus. Our imaginations are too modern for the feat.

But, besides being safe, it is necessary to see that for all governments alike the legitimate ends of administration are the same, in order not to be frightened at the idea of looking into foreign systems of administration for instruction and suggestion; in order to get rid of the apprehension that we might perchance blindly borrow something incompatible with our principles. That man is blindly astray who denounces attempts to transplant foreign systems into this country. It is impossible: they simply would not grow here. But why should we not use such parts of foreign contrivances as we want, if they be in any way serviceable? We are in no danger of using them in a foreign way. We borrowed rice, but we do not eat it with chopsticks. We borrowed our whole political language from England, but we leave the words "king" and "lords" out of it. What did we ever originate, except the action of the federal government upon individuals and some of the functions of the federal supreme court?

We can borrow the science of administration with safety and profit if only we read all fundamental differences of condition into its essential tenets. We have only to filter it through our constitutions, only to put it over a slow fire of criticism and distil away its foreign gases.

I know that there is a sneaking fear in some conscientiously patriotic minds that studies of European systems might signalize some foreign methods as better than some American methods; and the fear is easily to be understood. But it would scarcely be avowed in just any company.

It is the more necessary to insist upon thus putting away all prejudices against looking anywhere in the world but at home for suggestions in this study, because nowhere else in the whole field of politics, it would seem, can we make use of the historical, comparative method more safely than in this province of administration. Perhaps the more novel the forms we study the better. We shall the sooner learn the peculiarities of our own methods. We can never learn either our own weaknesses or our own virtues by comparing ourselves with ourselves. We are too used to the appearance and procedure of our own system to see its true significance. Perhaps even the English system is too much like our own to be used to the most profit in illustration. It is best on the whole to get entirely away from our own atmosphere and to be most careful in examining such systems as those of France and Germany. Seeing our own institutions through such *media,* we see ourselves as foreigners might see us were they to look at us without preconceptions. Of ourselves, so long as we know only ourselves, we know nothing.

Let it be noted that it is the distinction, already drawn, between administration and politics which makes the comparative method so safe in the field of administration. When we study the administrative systems of France and Germany, knowing that we are not in search of *political* principles, we need not care a peppercorn for the constitutional or political reasons which Frenchmen or Germans give for their practices when explaining them to us. If I see a murderous fellow sharpening a knife cleverly, I can borrow his way of sharpening the knife without borrowing his probable intention to commit murder with it; and so, if I see a monarchist dyed in the wool managing a public bureau well, I can learn his business methods without changing one of my republican spots. He may serve his king; I will continue to serve the people; but I should like to serve my sovereign as well as he serves his. By keeping this distinction in view,—that is, by studying administration as a means of putting our own politics into convenient practice, as a means of making what is democratically politic towards all administratively possible towards each,—we are on perfectly safe ground, and can learn without error what foreign systems have to teach us. We thus devise an adjusting weight for our comparative method of study. We can thus scrutinize the anatomy of foreign governments without fear of getting any of their diseases into our veins; dissect alien systems without apprehension of blood-poisoning.

Our own politics must be the touchstone for all theories. The principles on which to base a science of administration for America must be principles which have democratic policy very much at heart. And, to suit American habit, all general theories must, as theories, keep modestly in the background, not in open argument only, but even in our own minds,—lest opinions satisfactory only to the standards of the library should be dogmatically used, as if they must be quite as satisfactory to the standards of practical politics as well. Doctrinaire devices must be postponed to tested practices. Arrangements not only sanctioned by conclusive experience elsewhere but also congenial to American habit must be preferred without hesitation to theoretical perfection. In a word, steady, practical statesmanship must come first, closet doctrine second. The cosmopolitan what-to-do must always be commanded by the American how-to-do-it.

Our duty is, to supply the best possible life to a *federal* organization, to systems within systems; to make town, city, county, state, and federal governments live with a like strength and an equally assured healthfulness, keeping each unquestionably its own master and yet making all interdependent and co-operative, combining independence with mutual helpfulness. The task is great and important enough to attract the best minds.

This interlacing of local self-government with federal self-government is quite a modern conception. It is not like the arrangements of imperial federation in Germany. There local government is not yet, fully, local *self*-government. The bureaucrat is everywhere busy. His efficiency springs out of *esprit de corps,* out of care to make ingratiating obeisance to the authority of a superior, or, at best, out of the soil of a sensitive conscience. He serves, not the public, but an irresponsible minister. The question for us is, how shall our series of governments within governments be so administered that it shall always be to the interest of the public officer to serve, not his superior alone but the community also, with the best efforts of his talents and the soberest service of his conscience? How shall such service be made to his commonest interest by contributing abundantly to his sustenance, to his dearest interest by furthering his ambition, and to his highest interest by advancing his honor and establishing his character? And how shall this be done alike for the local part and for the national whole?

If we solve this problem we shall again pilot the world. There is a tendency—is there not?—a tendency as yet dim, but already steadily impulsive and clearly destined to prevail, towards, first the confederation of parts of empires like the British, and finally of great states themselves. Instead of centralization of power, there is to be wide union with tolerated divisions of prerogative. This is a tendency towards the American type—of governments joined with governments for the pursuit of common purposes, in honorary equality and honorable subordination. Like principles of civil liberty are everywhere fostering like methods of government; and if comparative studies of the ways and means of government should enable us to offer suggestions which will practicably combine openness and vigor in the administration of such governments with ready docility to all serious, well-sustained public criticism, they will have approved themselves worthy to be ranked among the highest and most fruitful of the great departments of political study. That they will issue in such suggestions I confidently hope.

B. Guy Peters  **NO**

The Necessity and Difficulty of Comparison in Public Administration

All scholars have a tendency to conceptualize politics, economics or other social phenomena in terms of our own national or even personal experiences. This may be especially true of the social sciences in the United States where so much of the development of contemporary social science theory has taken place. However, it is crucial for the development of meaningful theoretical perspectives in those social sciences to examine each national experience in light of that of other nations. This allows us to understand the effects which differences in structures, cultures, and values have on each other, and on the performance of the particular aspect of the social system that is being investigated. In that regard, the tendency of academic disciplines to isolate comparative studies from other subfields represents a barrier to theoretical development and enrichment within those disciplines.

The tendency to extrapolate and develop theory on the basis of a single national experience is perhaps especially true of the administrative experience and public bureaucracy of the United States. Much of our discussion of public administration (not only in the United States) has been very much bound to a particular time and place. This has had rather unfortunate effects for theory development concerning public administration within the social sciences. There can hardly be said to be anything approaching a "paradigm" for the study of public administration, especially if we are so difficult as to demand a paradigm that would be applicable outside Washington, DC, the United States, or most especially the industrialized world. While a single paradigm may not be necessary, or even desirable, the absence of any successful and broadly-shared attempts at the development of such comprehensive approaches represents a major weakness in the theoretical development in this field of inquiry. Some attempts have been made, but appear driven as much by normative concerns as by the need to understand public administration in a broader theoretical perspective.

The Necessity of Comparison

In some ways the need to justify and defend the practice of comparative public administration represents the incomplete conquest of political science, and especially public administration, by scholars concerned with the construction

From *Asian Journal of Public Administration,* June 1990, pp. 3–6, 8–12, 21–23. Copyright © 1990 by University of Hong Kong. Reprinted by permission.

of meaningful social theory. It is almost trite to argue that theory in the social sciences proceeds largely through comparison, or through the development of abstract concepts (such as Weber's ideal types) against which to compare observations in the real world. Therefore, to think about comparative public administration as somehow distinct from public administration, or indeed to think of comparative politics as distinct from the study of politics more generally, is to be trapped in the "stamps, flags and coins" school of comparative politics and comparative administration. That is, comparative public administration has all too often been considered excursions into the exotica of world political systems with the intention to describe different administrative systems and, with any luck, to develop a repertoire of amusing anecdotes based on field work. As such, it was distinct and isolated from the mainstream of conceptual and theoretical developments.

Such a stereotypical conception of comparative administration could, however, be justified by much of the literature in the field. That literature has been largely descriptive and based in a single country rather than seeking to provide broader analytic and theoretical perspectives. In this subfield, as in some others, "comparative" really has meant "somewhere else" rather than comparative. As Riggs wrote once, ". . . inevitably a new framework for 'comparative' administration will evolve—not as a 'subfield' but as the master field within which 'American public administration' will be a subfield."

While Riggs is perhaps excessively optimistic, that direction would certainly be the one with the opportunity for the greatest theoretical development. Significant work in the philosophy of social science and the methodology of empirical research demonstrates that a strategy of triangulation—using two or more approaches and two or more contexts—is practically the only way to separate theoretical bias from actual observations in the field. Observers impose any number of biases in their observation, and any complex social phenomenon such as public administration is especially prone to such biases. Therefore, it is crucial for theoretical development to foster more and better comparative studies. How, then, should we proceed with the task of comparison? To aid in that theory construction, it will be important to make the comparisons along at least three dimensions.

Cross-National

As indicated by the statements above, we are thinking of comparative administration as something substantially more than simply the accumulation of descriptive material about a number of different countries. In particular, we would not consider the presentation of such material on a country-by-country basis as the most useful form of discussion. Some description of that nature is useful as a means of beginning a more theoretical inquiry. It is certainly pedagogically important for students who initially may not know a *Beamte* from an *ENArque*. However, using countries as nominal categories for describing systems of public may not be the most efficient means of understanding why those systems function as they do. For example, the extremely fragmented form of policy-making by the public bureaucracy in the United States has little or nothing to do with national character *per se* (other than the fear of strong government at the time of the founding of the Republic) and has a great deal more to do with the nature of the governing institutions—both bureaucratic and political—which have been developed within the Constitutional framework. Of course, at times there may be patterns which are more explicable by cultural variables, for example, possibly the legalism of administration in West Germany. However, until we begin to move away from the country-bound approach to comparative administration it will be difficult to ascertain which patterns of behaviour are peculiarly national.

It may be especially important to attempt to understand public administration—and indeed government more broadly—in the United States in a broader comparative context. So much of the conceptual thinking about public administration which by now has become pervasive worldwide—Gulick and Urwick, Simon, March, Lindblom, Waldo, Wildavsky, Mosher, Levine, *et.al.*— is American in origin. There is a danger, therefore, that to some extent the professional study of public administration is extremely culture-bound even when conducted outside the United States. These approaches to administration are not ethnocentric simply because of their origins (the genetic fallacy), but because the constructs, hypotheses and theories are not necessarily representative of reality (and therefore not meaningful or valid) in other contexts. Therefore, there is a pressing need to think of the United States as but one of many industrialized, capitalist democracies and to point out the uniqueness of the system. At the same time, however, the many points of similarity to other political systems must also be understood. To do that, however, requires the development of a set of research questions and a set of categories which can be used for comparison. It is hoped that this discussion can be a first step towards the development of a broader comparative perspective on public bureaucracy in the United States, as well as something of a statement about the conduct of the enterprise of comparative public administration. At a very minimum, we will present something of a list of dependent variables which will be useful in the process of comparison across nations. . . .

The Low Level of Development of Comparative Administration

The importance of comparison for the development of our thinking about public administration having been recognized, we now come to the awful truth that the comparative study of public administration is perhaps the least well-developed aspect of the study of comparative politics and government. This is true despite the long and honourable history of this field. Comparative administration was a central component in the traditional approaches to comparative government. Many of the classic textbooks in the field of comparative government contained extensive sections on administration and the execution of law through the public bureaucracy. The comparative study of public bureaucracy also had a central place in development studies in the 1950s, 1960s and 1970s as scholars attempted to understand the role of the bureaucracy in implementing development programmes, as well as differences in administrative behaviour related to levels of development.

Despite these strong and promising foundations, the comparative study of public administration has waned. It is perhaps especially instructive that although the comparative study of public policy began as an explicit "sub-field" within academic political science much later than comparative administration, most people would argue, I believe, that it has made greater progress than has comparative administration, especially if progress is to be measured by the canons of normal social science. Any number of models and theories to explain differences in policy have been developed, and at least some of these models have been subjected to empirical testing. This *certainly cannot be said to be true of the comparative study of public* administration, where few if any rigorous models have been developed and fewer tested empirically. It is indeed rather amusing now to reconsider the rosy predictions about the developments in this field published in the 1960s and 1970s, including those that argued that comparative public policy studies were a virgin field for exploration. It is unfortunate, but also fair, to say that there has been something of an intellectual malaise surrounding comparative administration.

Why should there be such a malaise in this important area of study? There is certainly rich material for comparative study. As noted above, the public bureaucracy is in some ways the easiest of the major political institutions to study comparatively because of the relative identifiability of the structures and the relative uniformity of the activities carried out. Of course, there are some interesting and important variations in this presumed identifiability and uniformity, perhaps the most important being the increasing use of "third party government" to exercise many nominally governmental functions. However, when one knocks on the doors of bureaucratic offices one is likely to find more similarities than when knocking on the doors of legislators or even chief executives.

Weberian Assumptions: Little to Compare

One answer as to why there has been this malaise in the study of comparative administration is that one important approach to this field might argue that there is little or nothing to compare and that the uniformity would be overwhelming. If one accepts the logic of Weberian and/or Wilsonian approaches to public administration one might be tempted first to say that all public organizations will, over time, tend towards the bureaucratic form. However, even if public bureaucracies were differently structured and organized, they would be uninteresting because the public bureaucrat is not involved in politics but in the "mere execution of the laws."

While the above statement may appear perilously close to the old politics/administration dichotomy which presumably has been debunked, it is important to remember the durability and longevity of that dichotomy. This is especially true for those who participate in government. The dichotomy may be equally durable for some scholars who work on other political institutions such as the presidency and assume that members of the bureaucracy are indeed supposed to accept the legitimate orders of the President. This concern for the proper execution of the law has to some degree come into the study of public administration through the backdoor in the guise of implementation studies. Frequently, failures to achieve policy goals are blamed on the recalcitrance of the public bureaucracy rather than on any inherent weaknesses in the legislation which was enacted. In general, the assumption in implementation studies appears to be that if the civil service would behave as they should then government might be able to function properly as well.

In addition to the problems with the politics/administration dichotomy, there are significant problems in assuming that public organizations will tend towards bureaucratic principles. For example, if we examine the structure and functioning of organizations in the governments of many industrialized democracies, we can find some organizations, for example, in the Executive Office of the President or a ministerial *cabinet,* which might closely resemble patrimonial organizations in which the members are personally loyal to the leader. Also, an increasing number of organizations, for example, in areas such as health or legal services, might be organized around professional rather than hierarchical values. We would expect a declining number of organizations to be characterized by the more rigid organizational structure expected in a bureaucratic organization. What we are less certain about, however, is how differences in structures translate directly into differences in the behaviour of the members of the organization, or in the outputs of the organization. There is a good deal of evidence relating structure to performance in private sector organizations but substantially less for public sector organizations.

Education and Training

Another factor, closely related to the first, in why comparative public administration does not appear to have made the strides of some other aspects of comparative politics is the training which many people received during the "behavioural revolution" in the study of politics. To a great extent comparative administration, and to some degree the study of all political institutions, was denigrated while greater emphasis was placed on the study of "inputs" into the political process such as voting, attitudes, and socialization. The institutions of government were largely condemned to live out their existence in a "black box" which was deemed to be an uninteresting place to explore.

The above paragraph may be a bit hyperbolic, but certainly there was some over-reaction to the traditional dominance of formal institutional studies in the comparative politics prior to this "revolution." In fairness some of this over-reaction is now being corrected with some of the resurgence of institutional analysis in the discipline. In addition, the burgeoning interest in the concept of the state may, as it develops, require greater attention be paid to political institutions, such as the public bureaucracy, which are manifestations of the state. However, there is a still a great deal to be done to develop approaches to comparative public administration which will be respectable to other colleagues in the social sciences. Further, this development must be done while capturing the nuanced interpretations so necessary for an understanding of the operations of the modern bureaucracies and their roles in making public policy.

The Emergence of Policy Studies

Another factor affecting the development of the study of comparative public administration was the emergence of policy studies and the swelling concern with issues of public policy. This concern was for the output side what the behavioural revolution was for the input side of the black box of government. That is, by directing attention towards outputs and outcomes of government, much of what went on in making that policy got lost. In part that loss took place in the rush to quantify when studying public policy. Politics became the readily quantifiable indicator of partisanship, with perhaps a few institutional factors thrown in. It is therefore not terribly surprising that many of the early analyses found that "politics doesn't matter." Fortified by those empirical findings, then, it appeared reasonable to drop or downplay the role of politics—especially the very subtle and difficult-to-quantify politics that may go on within political institutions—when attempting to understand public policy.

The comparative study of public policy was able to drive out or at least threaten the comparative study of public administration in part because of the presumed greater ease of measurement and hence the appearance of greater "scientific" rigour. In public expenditures there was a ready-made ratio level measure which (at least presumably) could be used in any and all political systems. Other also seemingly ready-made indicators were available for measuring not only government expenditures for a particular purpose but some of the actual impacts of government programmes on social and economic conditions. The availability of these indicators gave the study of policy a decided advantage in the race to appear scientific over the study of administration which had fewer indicators, and fewer still agreed-upon indicators (see below). The public policy component of the discipline of political science could publish in the "mainstream" journals while those interested in public administration, and especially comparative administration, had a much more difficult time doing so. . . .

Except for counting the number of personnel and perhaps determining their social backgrounds, the research problems for comparative administration outlined above may be difficult to undertake. Even if we can agree on the set of dependent variables discussed here there is a great deal of work to be done before they can be used within the methodologies and approaches of the conventional social sciences. As noted above, while comparative policy studies appear to have been making significant progress, the comparative study of public administration has appeared mired with little or no progress being made. There are at least three reasons for the greater difficulties experienced in generating and analyzing data.

The first is the absence of a theoretical language which is useful for the comparison of public administration. This is not to say that there have not been attempts. For example, Riggs and other members of the Comparative Administration Group of the American Society for Public Administration developed a huge number of neologisms attempting to capture differences in political systems and administrative systems. While to some extent useful as classificatory systems, looking back over them today they appear curiously locked in time. That language clearly represents the developmental concerns of the 1950s and 1960s and does not appear sufficiently nuanced to capture differences among, say, the administrative systems of France, Spain and Italy, all of which are at least on the surface similar but which have deep and important differences when examined more extensively. Our own earlier work on the comparison of administrative systems developed its own share of neologisms, especially for the relationships between interest groups and the bureaucracy but these in many ways appear to have fallen on deaf ears. The language of more general organization theory also provides a series of classificatory schemes for organizations and their structural attributes but appear more concerned with the nature of private sector organizations than public sector ones so that many variables appear inapplicable. In many ways the language of the old and much-maligned traditional public administration (Gulick and Urwick, Fesler, Waldo, and so on) still has a great deal to offer in way of a language to discuss the *structure* of public administration. That language has many of the defects which Simon and others have so thoroughly discussed, most importantly its absence of very clear connections to the behaviour of individuals occupying positions in those structures, but is still a very useful way of beginning to understand government structure.

Associated with the absence of clear theoretical language for discussing many of the issues associated with comparative public administration is the absence of indicators. This is an even more daunting deficiency in some ways than the absence of a language. The comparison with comparative public policy is again useful. That latter field of inquiry has been able to get a great deal of mileage from utilizing public expenditure data as their dependent variable although arguably the real theoretical meaning of those data has not been crystal clear. Data analysis has been able to preceed theoretical developments, or at least an adequate conceptual development, and justification of the major dependent variable of many or most empirical studies. Were there such a ready-made indicator then a number of studies might be undertaken that could inductively develop a better idea of how governments are structured.

This is by no means a plea on behalf of mindless "number-crunching," but rather is an observation that to some extent comparative policy studies have been able to make more apparent advances because it went ahead and crunched some apparently meaningful numbers. Further, some progress in organization theory has been made by analyzing large bodies of data on organizations from a number of cultural settings and generating "grounded" concepts. Exploratory analysis using data need not be mindless so long as the scholars involved remain aware of the tentative nature of the findings, and perhaps even of the data themselves.

Finally, in comparative administration minute and subtle differences appear to make a great deal of difference. This is to some degree Pollitt's argument on behalf of social action theory as a means of approaching organizational change in the British central government. The meaning attached to organizational change was subtle and had to be understood within the context within which it was made. Imposing a pre-assigned theoretical framework, therefore, would in this argument have been folly. While this argument extended to its logical conclusion would appear to deny the possibility of comparative analysis, it points to the extreme importance of contextual and highly nuanced knowledge when attempting to interpret the characteristics of institutions such as the public bureaucracy. Comparison then becomes that much more difficult as indicators may become less reliable and fewer people will have the type of detailed understanding required to make the comparisons appropriately, or indeed even to know how to ask the appropriate questions. . . .

EXPLORING THE ISSUE

Can Public Administration Be International in Scope?

Critical Thinking and Reflection

1. What aspects of public administration in the United States make it unique?
2. What historical attempts have been undertaken in an effort to internationalize the study of public administration?
3. What makes it difficult to comparatively study public administration across countries?
4. In what ways is public administration similar and different between advanced industrial democracies and developing nations?
5. What are the different historical rationales as to why public administration can in fact be studied comparatively?

Is There Common Ground?

Despite much of our classic public administration theory being developed by scholars from outside the United States, the discipline has largely been considered American-centric. To a degree, this is understandable since American public administration is composed of a complex series of institutions that have taken time to understand. Without a complete knowledge of our own bureaucratic system and structures, it is difficult to determine how we compare to the rest of the world. At the same time, however, we cannot necessarily appreciate our own system without understanding our unique structures and values.

As an advanced industrial democracy, our government structures will always be examined by other nations that are attempting to move toward democracy. The environment we have created for public administration will not be exempted from these comparisons. Although the classical facets of public administration are written in a way to attempt to be universal in applicability, the country-specific contexts of each nation make applying them difficult. As a result, even the most internationally applicable aspects of public administration will require that politicians and bureaucrats have a comprehensive knowledge of their own domestic bureaucratic structures in order to implement them properly.

Additional Resources

Jreisat, J.E., *Comparative Public Administration and Policy* (Boulder, CO: Westview, 2002)

Jreisat provides readers with an analytical, evaluative text that examines public administration in a global context.

Jreisat, J.E., *Globalism and Comparative Public Administration* (New York: CRC Press, 2011)

Jreisat describes comparative public administration since the 1960s while paying special attention to the role of globalization and technological developments. By doing so, he hopes to help readers understand the need for a global field of learning in public administration and policy.

Kim, P.S. and M.S. De Vries, *Value and Virtue in Public Administration: A Comparative Perspective* (New York: Palgrave Macmillan, 2011)

Kim and De Vries offer a comparative examination of how values differ in public administration depending on the context of where decisions are being made in this edited volume. In doing so, they attempt to show the potential for international changes in a post–New Public Management world.

Peters, G.B., *The Politics of Bureaucracy: An Introduction to Comparative Public Administration,* 6th ed. (New York: Routledge, 2009)

Peters discusses the role of bureaucracy in countries across the world with specific case studies in North America, Western and Eastern Europe, and Africa.

Schiavo-Campo, S. and H.M. McFerson, *Public Management in Global Perspective* (New York: M.E. Sharpe, 2008).

The authors focus specifically on public management in this volume that attempts to show the different understandings of the concept across the globe.

ISSUE 3

Is Bureaucracy the Best Option for Organizing Government?

YES: Charles T. Goodsell, from *The Case for Bureaucracy: A Public Administration Polemic*, 4th ed. (2003)

NO: Ralph P. Hummel, from *The Bureaucratic Experience: The Post-Modern Challenge*, 5th ed. (2007)

Learning Outcomes

After reading this issue, you should be able to:

- Describe the differences between bureaucracy and bureaucrats.
- Understand the positive and negative facets of both bureaucracy and bureaucrats.
- Gain an understanding of the potential corrupting nature of bureaucracy.
- Describe the intentions of bureaucrats.
- Discuss when bureaucracy can offer assistance to citizens and when it is more likely to cause problems.
- Understand the impact bureaucratic structures have on government functioning.

ISSUE SUMMARY

YES: Charles T. Goodsell argues that American bureaucrats are among the best in the world and that they are not mere agents of waste and red tape. Using empirical evidence and cases, he helps paint a picture of public servants working as best as possible to carry out the functions of government for the citizens they serve.

NO: Ralph P. Hummel argues that although public servants may be well-intentioned, bureaucracy is inherently dark and causes managers, workers, and clients to all behave in manners inconsistent with the goals of government service. Despite a public servant's good intentions, the corrupting influence of bureaucracy will eventually lead to inefficiencies emerging.

If we think back on historical examples of regimes that aimed to strictly follow Weber's understanding of bureaucracy, we would be hard pressed to find a more poignant example than the National Socialist German Worker's Party in their efforts to ethnically cleanse Europe in the 1940s. Although their actions were reprehensible, the Nazis were effective bureaucrats. Meticulous record keeping, absolute hierarchy, and impersonal relationships were hallmarks of concentration camps. Their efforts were efficient and effective. Yet, due to the fact that what occurred throughout Germany and Poland in the era was so morally unfathomable, we rarely discuss—even in the context of public administration—the way bureaucracy made the holocaust possible. From this framework, we can examine the ways that bureaucracy, and bureaucrats, can be both good and bad for government.

This enduring debate arises from the fact that both Ralph Hummel and Charles Goodsell have their claims supported by common sense and experience. As Americans, we can clearly relate to both good and bad bureaucratic images put forth. The reasons for this popular negative attitude toward bureaucracy cut across numerous elements of American life—perhaps none so poignantly as the shared bureaucratic nightmare of the Department of Motor Vehicles. The popularly perceived shortcomings of the American bureaucrat are regularly exacerbated by the inability of the bureaucrat to achieve cultural acceptance.

Politicians run entire campaigns against the bureaucracy, turning the government workers into their opposition in a quest for office. Intellectual scholars tend to portray bureaucrats as out of control and responsible to no one. The media makes bureaucrats and other governmental workers the antagonists of plot lines. Presidents speak negatively of the difficulty they have in their dealings with the bureaucracy. Perceptions in political culture, such as editorial cartoons and political jokes, show the bureaucracy as a mass of hypocritical and foolish individuals. Newspapers and television states love to run bureaucratic horror stories.

When all of these elements come together, it is easy to imagine why the popular perception is that the bureaucracy acts against the interests of everyday Americans. Americans presume that government exists to bend to their will and address peoples' needs and wants. On the positive end, however, some bureaucrats are exceptionally friendly. The mail typically comes at the same time every day, allowing Americans to build a routine of sorts around their scheduled delivery. Some of us even have regularly positive experiences at the Department of Motor Vehicles (DMV). Street-level bureaucrats can be as helpful as they are disabling—the police officer that tickets you today may be the one who saves your life tomorrow. As Goodsell points to, the "public encounter" can be a powerful influence on how citizens ultimately judge bureaucrats.

To examine these questions, let us consider a modern example. Sergeant Kimberly Munley is a classic bureaucrat. With years of military training, she retired from the armed forces and entered life as a street-level bureaucrat—a civilian police officer at Ft. Hood, Texas. In November 2010, she became a household name after mortally wounding Nidal Malik Hasan after he shot and killed 13 individuals, wounding 38 others, despite being shot twice in both legs with cop killer rounds. Texas Governor Rick Perry, after the ordeal, deemed her "the classic public servant . . . not interested in anything other than getting on with her life." After undergoing hours of surgery, her doctor reported that her initial words upon awaking in recovery were "Did anybody die?" Munley is clearly a steward of the public interest. She was willing to sacrifice herself to ensure the safety of others.

The actions of Kimberly Munley add credence to the claims of both Goodsell and Hummel. In the light of Goodsell, Munley illustrates everything that is good about American bureaucracy. Although many complain about the behavior of bureaucrats and their supposed rigidness, Munley—a street-level bureaucrat—was willing to sacrifice her own life to fulfill her duties. In this light, America sees the good in the individual bureaucrat even if it does not recognize the bureaucracy. Goodsell would find that her actions refer not to compliance with technical police rules, but the police credo that in a gun battle your aim is to kill the shooters but allow the innocents to go home safe." Hummel, however, would likely take exception to Munley's question immediately upon awakening. Although one cannot question the intent, Hummel would be prone to view the pressures of bureaucracy as having stripped Munley of the ability to even be concerned about herself before wondering about the success of her actions.

What Goodsell would see as altruistic concerns of a dedicated public servant, Hummel would claim as the dehumanizing influence of a form of an organization, stripping an individual of his or her ability to think outside of the bureaucratic realm. In this difference, we can begin to see where the truth lies in the now almost three decade-long debate between Goodsell and Hummel. Looking back to the Nazi example presented earlier, we can clearly see the applicability of this debate. Eichmann's response that he was following orders in executing thousands of innocent individuals speaks volumes to the idea presented by Hummel of how bureaucracy can be corrupting. For Goodsell, the debate shows how bureaucrats can be effective in fulfilling goals (even though there is a clear value conflict present in this example).

Some scholars argue that the debate poses a false duality. Whereas Goodsell specifically sets his focus to studying the public's perceptions and understandings of American bureaucracy and how they typically fail to value the well-working system that we have, Hummel centers his examination on the ideal-type concept of bureaucracy and the effects that the more generalized conditions ultimately have on human and bureaucratic nature. In the YES and NO readings, we will see why Goodsell believes bureaucrats are honest, hardworking individuals that aim to assist citizens while Hummel believes the structures they work under simply give them no opportunities except to become jaded. By looking at this dichotomy, we can better understand if bureaucracy is the optimal way to organize government.

YES

Charles T. Goodsell

The Case for Bureaucracy: A Public Administration Polemic

Bureaucracy Despised, Disparaged, and Defended

To make the case for bureaucracy. What a ridiculous idea! The author must be a Lucifer incarnate or just plain mad. Only the devil himself would make a case for evil. Only a lunatic would come to the defense of the indefensible.

I hope, dear reader, that you will eventually lay aside any such initial suspicions about your author's character or sanity. Several pages may have to be turned before you do so.

Clearly, I have a large task ahead to convince you to accept my case for bureaucracy. We have all heard about police raids that are brutal, welfare departments that are heartless, defense contracts that waste billions, and public schools that graduate illiterates. Also, we have all personally encountered individual government employees who are arrogant, rude, lazy, condescending, apathetic, and incapable of writing in clear English. How, then, can any self-respecting person write a book on *behalf* of bureaucracy?

Before launching into the rational and logical side of my argument, let me begin by indicating exactly where I am "coming from" emotionally. As the reader, you deserve to know. I do this by relating a few personal experiences with bureaucracy. Perhaps you have had similar things happen to you. As you will see, they are quite ordinary and simple events.

Being a good citizen who likes to stay clear of the law, I take care to pay my income taxes on time. In Virginia the state income tax is paid to the Commissioner of the Revenue of your county. One tax season, after sending in my return, I got a call from a woman at the commissioner's office who said I had misinterpreted the tax form instructions and had paid too much. Even though the tax deadline had by this time passed, she told me to drive over to the county seat that afternoon and come to her office. Upon arriving at the courthouse, I found her behind a well-worn wooden counter. On the spot, she rewrote the form in front of me, had me re-sign it, tore up the old check, and waited until I wrote a new one—at a considerably lower figure.

Once I was driving across my university campus, trying to get somewhere quickly. At a congested area across from the gym, I encountered several cars double-parked, blocking my lane. Despite a double yellow line in the center of the street, I carefully passed all of them . Just as I pulled clear of the last car, I noticed that it was marked "police." Instantly its motor sprang to life and roof lights flashed. I gulped, pulled over at the next driveway, and resignedly got out my driver's license. When the officer came up to the window, he said with a big grin, "Now *that* was a dumb thing to do, wasn't it?" Embarrassed, I readily agreed. He then went back to his cruiser, checked me out on the computer, and returned to give me my license back with the comment, "Now you won't do that again, will you?" Again, I agreed.

In preparing this fourth edition of *The Case for Bureaucracy*, I needed some updated census data for one of the tables. I called my university library to see if the document in question was available. The librarian said no, but provided a Web page address at the Census Bureau. Upon reaching the page, I located the report but saw that it was too long to download. Noticing an 800 contact number on the page, I dialed the number. After two rings, a friendly voice answered, asking what document was needed and requesting my address, so that a copy could be put in the mail right away. I asked how much it would cost. The voice replied, "Let's not look that up, because if I charge you it will take much longer to get the report in the mail." It arrived three days later.

On another occasion, my wife and I landed at Dulles Airport after a trip to Great Britain. The United Kingdom had been badly hit that year by foot-and-mouth disease, and as we prepared to go through Customs we were warned that we must state whether we had visited a farm while overseas. Since we had in fact spent three nights at a farm bed-and-breakfast in Dorset and had tramped all over the barnyard, I debated whether to admit the truth. Others had told us that if we did so we could experience long delays and perhaps be forced to clean our outer clothing. I decided to risk telling the truth to the Customs official, who sent us to a Department of Agriculture inspector nearby. The inspector asked in a friendly way whether the shoes we were currently wearing had trod about the farm. We said yes, whereupon he told us to turn around and lift up our feet one at a time. After looking carefully at the underside of each, he merely said, "They look all right," and sent us on.

For me, these simple experiences say something important. Despite the negative images of bureaucrats to which we are subject from every quarter, when we interact with them in our daily lives, their actual conduct often is much different from what we have been led to expect. Whether tax officials, police officers, Customs employees, or agricultural inspectors, it is possible to encounter bureaucrats who work hard, show concern for our interests, do not flaunt their authority, exhibit courtesy and good humor, and go the extra mile to help out. Yet these very same people are not well paid in their jobs. Their daily work is often tedious, difficult, or even dangerous. In our private-enterprise culture, they are subject to kidding if not taunts for "doing government work." In my mind and heart, these bureaucrats and their bureaucracies are worth a closer look than we usually give them.

These thoughts are not learned propositions. They are personal feelings. It is from them that this case for bureaucracy springs. If that be madness, you have been forewarned.

A Brief for Bureaucracy

Lawyers prepare *briefs* to conduct their cases. My brief for bureaucracy, most simply put, is that governmental administration in America may be regarded as generally competent and effective if we look at it in a balanced way and in relation to what is possible. Whereas public bureaucracy in the United States, at all levels of government, inevitably involves individual instances of waste, incompetence, abuse of power, and breakdown, it does, *on the whole and in comparison to most countries and even the business sector in this country, perform surprisingly well.*

I say "surprisingly" because we Americans are taught throughout our lives, from hearth and home on through school and career, that our government is a sea of waste, a swamp of incompetence, a mountain of unchecked power, an endless plain of mediocrity. Our media and politicians tell us that public bureaucracy is bloated in size, inefficient compared to business, a stifling place to work, indifferent to ordinary citizens, the problem rather than the solution. *Bureaucrats*—with the word uttered in contempt—are alleged in all quarters to be lazy, incompetent, devious, and even dangerous.

We encounter this attitude everywhere we look. T-shirts mock bureaucrats. Bumper stickers ridicule them. Movies stereotype them. Parlor games parody them. A nationally televised presidential campaign ad subliminally flashes the word *BUREAUCRATS*, highlighting the last four letters. A full-page newspaper ad placed by a tobacco company features the heavily jowled face of a smugly grinning man. The caption below asks, "Who should be responsible for your children, a bureaucrat or you?"

Government as a whole and bureaucracy by implication are condemned even inside government. The web site of a prominent congressman displayed a "Waste-O-Meter" that tallied the ongoing flow of uncovered waste that supposedly exists in government. The Commonwealth of Virginia issued a "GOVT SUX" vanity license plate. The county executive of Montgomery County, Maryland, bans the word *government* from official letterheads because of its negative connotations. A right-wing religious broadcaster suggested that the Department of State be blown up by a nuclear device.

Bureaucrat-bashing is not confined to political broadsides or to the popular media. Many books and tracts have been devoted to the cause. Just a few examples: *The Federal Rathole, Fat City, Burning Money, Alice in Blunderland, The Government Racket, B.S.: The Bureaucratic Syndrome, America by the Throat,* and *Why Government Fails or What's Really Wrong with the Bureaucracy.*

Also, academic instruction in our colleges and universities is not immune to a grossly negative portrayal of America's administrative institutions. Examining the image of public administration presented in eighteen introductory college texts in American government, Beverly Cigler and Heidi Neiswender found that the books overwhelmingly stressed bureaucracy's size and permanence, its unintelligible language and political power, and its uncontrollability by the president. Not one of the texts made any reference at all to the profession of public administration or the call to public service.

While perpetuating this deeply embedded mistrust of public administration may be a good way to fuel our spirit of individualism, love of liberty, and readiness to revolt against injustice, it leads to a drastically misleading picture of our public employees and government agencies. Even worse, instead of addressing the many problems that *do* exist in bureaucracy, this attitude can exacerbate them by encouraging the kinds of political rhetoric and public policy that demoralize agencies, adversely affecting their performance and encouraging the best staff members to leave. Furthermore, it promotes a set of negative assumptions about government employment that keeps the brightest of our young people from considering a public service career.

The thesis of this book, then, is that a wide gap exists between bureaucracy's reputation and its record. Despite endless rantings to the contrary, American bureaucracy *does* work—in fact, it works quite well. It is something like your ten-year-old car, an immensely complex mechanism made up of tens of thousands of parts, which is by no means perfect or totally reliable. But it starts more often than it stalls, and it completes the vast majority of trips you take. In fact, the old thing is usually working so well that you do not even think of the possibility that you may get stuck somewhere. The first time you are stuck, however, you take notice, and if this happens more than once, you, too, start to rant.

It is the same with government agencies, especially big ones. They are imperfect, vastly complex, and usually reliable, and they come to our attention only when they break down. One of the most visible, and certainly one of the largest and most complex, is the U.S. Postal Service, which collects and delivers 650 million items to 130 million addresses six times a week, with 93 percent of them arriving on time. Rarely is *any* piece lost. Still, we take this service for granted—and without knowing a thing about the immense administrative, processing, and transportation systems needed to make it work. We complain when one letter is a few days late, allowing that one late letter, not the thousands of on-time deliveries we have received, to shape our image of the whole.

One way to keep the quality of American bureaucracy in perspective is to realize that it is far better than that found in many other parts of the world. We may not sense this if we have not traveled or lived abroad. To the billions of people who reside in the poor nations of the world, the routine hallmarks of government bureaucracy are inordinate delays, long lines, undependable service, officious indifference, immense waste, and, not infrequently, corruption. The principal aim of bureaucrats in many countries is not to help the public at all but to get through the day with minimal work. The aim of the bureaucracy as a whole is not to increase the quality of national life but to support the current regime and give employment to friends and relatives. Most people on this planet would be thrilled to receive even a small part of their mail safely and on time, let alone most of it.

But wait a minute, you might say. We are talking about *American* bureaucracy here, and we need an *American* standard of comparison. How does government bureaucracy in the United States measure up to what is really efficient in America, private business? It clearly does not, will be your instant reply. Business *must* be efficient, because it has to outperform competitors, control costs, adopt new technologies, and satisfy customers—so that it can make profits and survive. Government agencies, by contrast, are legal monopolies, supported by annual appropriations from revenues collected by compulsory taxes and staffed by bureaucrats who cannot be fired. How could they *possibly* be efficient, adopt change, or please citizens?

Yet, as we see later in this book, this seeming irrefutable argument is undermined by facts that do not confirm its assumptions. Many comparative studies have been made to assess private and public organizations doing comparable work, and their overall conclusion is essentially that in terms of operational efficiency, performance, productivity, and service, the differences between the two realms are greatly exaggerated or even minimal. The mantra that business works and government fails—no matter how frequently repeated in legislative chambers, luncheon club speeches, economics textbooks, and the local bar—must be reexamined.

We observed earlier that the Cigler-Neiswender study concluded that American government textbooks stress bureaucracy's size, power, and uncontrollability. Our brief must address these matters, for they raise the possibility that bureaucracy is an enemy of democracy. We deal with this question at length later, but let us make two preliminary points here. First, the singular term *bureaucracy* refers not to one aggregate mega-institution but to thousands of separate organizations. These departments, bureaus, agencies, commissions, and countless other kinds of bodies do not act in concert or in conspiracy. In fact, they often have little to do with one another and in some ways are rivals. Moreover, as we later see, huge size is not necessarily characteristic of bureaucracy—in fact, small size is more common.

Second, our bureaucracies, just like our citizens, operate within the context of regular elections, representative government, and a system of constitutional law that provides for divided and limited governmental power and guaranteed rights. They are continuously monitored and investigated by auditors, judges, budget examiners, performance evaluators, legislative committees, public watchdog groups, clientele associations, citizen bodies, and media organizations eager for a good scandal. While public agencies clearly can and must possess political clout in varying degrees in order to do their jobs, they are channeled and checked in more ways than one might think. In fact, sometimes the checks are nearly disabling.

We conclude this brief by explicitly defining the word *bureaucracy*. Some uncertainty arose on this point in response to earlier editions of this book, so let me be clear about how I define the term. When using the word *bureaucracy* I am referring, quite simply, to the institutions of public administration in America. By this I mean the organizations and their unit offices whose employees are paid from public funds, at all levels of government in the United States. This includes the ubiquitous county welfare office, the departments of transportation (DOTs) in every state, the Environmental Protection Agency headquartered in Washington, D.C., the Centers for Disease Control and Prevention in Atlanta, the thousands of police departments and public schools scattered across the nation, and—don't forget—the several branches of the U.S. armed forces.

The descriptive category, then, is vast. It embraces thousands of institutions and millions of people. It incorporates an incredible variety of activities, from investigating child abuse to filling potholes to combating AIDS to negotiating international treaties and conducting wars. The very enormity of the category speaks eloquently of the critical importance of our subject. The vast range of organizations included cries out for thoughtful assessment of individual bureaucracies rather than characterization by stereotype.

Many readers will be aware of the sociological model of bureaucracy posited by Max Weber early in the past century. To Weber, a bureaucracy was an organization with specified functional attributes: large size; a graded hierarchy; formal rules; specialized tasks; written files; and employees who are salaried, technically trained, career-appointed, and assigned stated duties requiring expert knowledge. Weber regarded his model as an ideal type, useful for description and analysis.

Many academic theorists and researchers contend that by possessing these characteristics, an organization tends automatically to exhibit certain patterns of behavior. These include rigidity, proceduralism, resistance to change, oppressive control of employees, dehumanized treatment of clients, indifference to citizen input, use of incomprehensible jargon, and tendencies toward empire building and concentration of power. These ascribed traits are, obviously, all pejorative. They also happen to spring, for the most part, from predisposed beliefs about large organizations rather than from empirical study. When academic writers on bureaucracy reflect negatively on the consequences of the "Weberian model," they are often being not neutral social scientists at all but ideological critics of hierarchical organization—a position shared by many intellectuals. As if by a kind of original sin embedded in its organizational form, bureaucracy is seen as automatically and perpetually condemned to incompetence and antidemocratic excess.

Returning to my own use of the word, I do not deny that much if not most of American public administration is made up of organizations that answer to many if not all of Weber's basic structural characteristics. Yes, steps are often taken to flatten chains of command, create flexible roles and teams, empower employees and citizens, and stress service to citizens. Still, most public-sector organizations and jurisdictions continue to feature differentiated levels of office, bounded areas of authority, internal rules, electronic or paper files, career or at least long-term employees, and professional experts of one kind or another. So, to that extent, most administrative components of U.S. government are still essentially "bureaucracies" in the Weberian sense—whatever that may mean in terms of resultant behavior. (They are not, however, necessarily very big, as we discover later.)

Let me make myself abundantly clear. I do not deny that selected attempts to deemphasize these structural characteristics in our public administration institutions would be helpful in many instances. I do not, however, accept the deterministic thought implicit in theories of bureaucracy that automatically equate *any* substantial presence of Weber's characteristics with incompetence or rigidity, dehumanized or oppressive conduct, or imperialistic behavior. Hence I am not, obviously, using the term *bureaucracy* in the typical pejorative sense. To put the matter another way, my debating opponents and I disagree not over whether American public administration is essentially bureaucratic, but over whether that means it is inevitably pathological. . .

Several themes can be identified in pro-bureaucracy writings. One is what the Beards were probably worried about, the damage done to the public service and government agencies by incessant attacks on them. In the early 1980s Werner Dannhauser urged us to realize that "nothing will be gained and a great deal can be lost by magnifying the bureaucracy problem out of all proportion." Herbert Kaufman characterized the fear of bureaucracy as a "raging pandemic," and Zahid Shariff lamented that "public administration is clearly the whipping boy." At the very time I was writing my first edition, two friends, Brinton Milward and Hal Rainey, were penning, without our realizing the coincidence, a stimulating essay entitled "Don't Blame the Bureaucracy!" . . .

A second theme in the pro-bureaucracy literature echoes Harlan Cleveland's "outrageously tolerate thoughts" about government departments. A number of books say that bureaucracy's critics exaggerate the problems and do not acknowledge that government is capable of working quite well. George Downs and Patrick Larkey note that comparisons between the efficiency of business and government are often invidious, and they conclude that government often performs better than the public thinks, and business worse. Mark Holzer and Kathe Callahan assert, "By no means is the public sector 'dead in the water.'" Kenneth Meier and John Bohte, having analyzed student failures in the Texas public schools (i.e., absentees, hold-backs, and drop-outs), found that the frequency of such failures had no statistical relation to proportion of bureaucrats per 100 students. Steven Kelman, in what he calls "a hopeful view of American government," says that the policy process of this country performs better than its reputation and thereby deserves the people's participation. Christopher Leman, analyzing the direct performance of tasks by government bureaucracies as opposed to indirect means such as grants and loans, points out that distrust of government may lead to reliance on third parties when in-house action by public agencies could get the job done better. Lewis Mainzer goes so far as to state that the quality of the American public service "is no mean achievement."

> Compared with governmental bureaucracies elsewhere or in other times, it achieves an impressive record combining competence, dignity, and responsibility. The variety in quality and style of American public administration is incredible, the worst is admittedly bad, but a fair amount is quite decent and the best is impressively good. In a world so bungled, whatever worth has been achieved merits a restrained word of praise.
>
> . . .

In addition to urging us to stop attacking bureaucracy and start realizing that it may not be as bad as we thought, a third theme in the supportive literature is more aggressive. It asserts outright that government and its administration make crucial, indispensable contributions to the society. "There is much to celebrate in terms of the public's achievements through the use of democratic governance," states Max Neiman, ". . . operating through its government institutions." "Bureaucracy is the cod liver oil of social institutions," Barry Bozeman writes. "It smells bad and leaves a nasty aftertaste, but sometimes it is just what you need."

To Gary Wills, government is "a necessary evil" that protects liberties as well as endangering them. H.T. Wilson observes that bureaucracy mediates contending interests in the political system; without it powerful forces favoring capital would always win out. Gyorgy Gajduschek asserts that one of bureaucracy's important contributions to society is uncertainty reduction, a feature identified by Weber but ignored by his interpreters. Larry Preston argues that bureaucracies—both public and private—support individual freedom by giving us the ability to make choices, learn, create, and achieve higher purposes. In a striking reappraisal of Weber's model, Paul du Gay contends that the notion of ethos of office permits the democratic state to act forcefully, morally, and accountably, contrary to managerial or entrepreneurial concepts of administration. My former professor Carl J. Friedrich, to whom bureaucracy is "the core of modern government," used to say that the success of democracy itself depends on a successful bureaucracy, for without it no elected government can succeed. . . .

. . . A fourth and final theme on the "pro" side of the debate supports bureaucracy not at the institutional level but at the individual level. Several books and articles have been written on the work of individual public administrators. Probably the first was Theodore Taylor's 1984 *Federal Public Policy,* which presents the personal stories of ten federal senior civil servants, which, Taylor holds, it is impossible to read "without being emotionally moved and mentally exhilarated." Shortly thereafter two additional works in this vein appeared. One was Howard Rosen's *Servants of the People,* which noted that most of the Nobel prizes in medicine and physiology over the previous twenty-five years had been awarded to scientists employed by or supported by the federal government. The other was Jameson Doig and Erwin Hargrove's *Leadership and Innovation,* which explores how administrators such as Gifford Pinchot, David Lilienthal, Hyman Rickover, Austin Tobin, and James Webb possessed remarkable skills both to manipulate symbols and build coalitions in behalf of public innovation.

 **NO**

The Bureaucratic Experience: The Post-Modern Challenge

Understanding Bureaucracy

One city planner, shown a plan of a road cutting through a medieval city's houses: Won't people object?
Second city planner: One must force them to be free!

—From a documentary on the medieval
city of Rothenburg on the river Tauber

It was a series of random events that killed thousands and saved hundreds. Not many people did anything right that day, but not many people did anything wrong either.

—A firefighter who escaped the North Tower

What are we calling postmodernity? I'm not up to date.

—Michel Foucault

This is a practical guide to bureaucracy. Or, it will be if you can make it so. Not an easy job, when you consider: "As soon as you step into bureaucracy, the handcuffs go on your mind as well as your hand."

If you can't at some point in reading this say, "Yeah, that's how it is on my job, in my life;" you have not made the practical connection. This is not a message from me to you; if you understand, you understand only because in some way you already knew *what* I was going to say.

Doing something practical means letting go of some illusions and delusions. One illusion is that bureaucracy is compatible with democracy. A delusion is that, whatever the faults of modern organizations, these are just anomalies that can be fixed. We all subscribe to this delusion. Without it there is no hope. Yet behind this delusion stands a grim reality. It is captured in defense computers run amuck, international aid that starves populations, but most directly in the desperate phone call of a friend who announces, without introduction or saying who is calling:

"Ralph, it's worse than you say it is."

Imagine having adopted a baby. A year later, you get a phone call: "Return the baby!" "What!?" you say. "The father didn't sign the papers," they say.

Bureaucratic Experiences

In some way, we have all had our experiences with bureaucracy. Everyone has trouble with bureaucracy. Citizens and politicians have trouble control-ling the runaway bureaucratic machine. Managers have trouble running it. Employees dislike working in it. Clients can't get the goods from it. Teachers have trouble getting a grip on it. Students are mystified by the complexity of it.

Let's take a closer look at what is so troubling.

Firefighters

New York firefighters are civil servants. Are they bureaucrats, too? Kicked off the fully manned rigs, some of those off-duty took the bus to the World Trade Center. Some came without clear direction. Some came without working radios. Some came against orders. All came because they heard behind the sirens and the alarms a silent call. Sixty of the total of 343 firefighters who died on 9/11 were off-duty. Would better support from the administration of the fire department have helped?

Consultants called for stricter training, routine obedience to orders, tauter command and control, better coordination with the police. These can enhance the ability to take care of our fellow human beings. Can they create or command sacrifice? (Contrast this with the Fire Department of the City of New York, 2002.)

And this is the practical case against bureaucracy. It is at the same time the moral case. Bureaucracy beats what we do freely into order, and it does so blindly. It multiplies the potential of organizations to get things done, but it does not do the doing. Bureaucracies set up the invasion of Normandy; human beings won the battle. Bureaucracy, whether too much of it or not enough, set up the organization of firefighters—it did not create the will to self-sacrifice. No matter how tough the rules, how rational the plans, how tight the tol-erances and controls, some human being somewhere has to judge whether, when, and how there is an opening for applying those rules.

This is not only a judgment of technical fit. It is to judge whether what you do next upholds or damages the potential of human beings to whom you do it. We not only judge whether rational plans are objectively reasonable, but whether they fit the human being. Freedom, not order, opens the room for sacrifice. Know-how and freedom are inescapably partners.

One thing we know about you who choose public service, whether you become immersed in bureaucratic demands or not. You, in contrast to those choosing business, are not in it for the money. You do not blanch or pull a wry smile at the word "service." Service, not profit, is your aim. But service is freely given. No one has warned you that you would be entering not a world of service but a world of control. When you first enter a bureaucracy—and most organizations today are—you are entering an entire new world.

Welfare Managers

In this brave new world, a baby entrusted to a welfare agency may die of neglect while sleeping on the floor of the welfare office while welfare workers for days step gingerly around it—and yet the welfare administrator will be able to say sincerely that "everyone concerned did his or her job conscientiously."

Corporate Executives

In this new world, parallels are enacted (but more easily defended) in the business bureaucracy. When the accounting firm of Arthur Andersen missed a $3.5-billion discrepancy because the communications firm of WorldCom had disguised operating expenses as profits, the *New York Times* reporters thought "it was conceivable that Andersen's auditors at WorldCom could have done their job properly and nonetheless failed to detect the problems with the company's financial reports."

FBI Agents

In this new world, nearly 3,000 people are killed in an attack on the United States and a tip by lower-ranking officials does not get to the top because, in the words of one whistle-blower, "We have a culture in the F.B.I. that there's a certain pecking order, and it's pretty strong. And it's very rare that someone picks up the phone and calls a rank or two above themselves."

The IMF—International Bureaucrats

In this world of global reach, nations are asked to change their cultures to meet the demands of the macro-bureaucracies—the International Monetary Fund or the World Bank—in other words, that they modernize or be killed in economic competition. In the words of a former global bureaucrat: "To heap paradox upon paradox, because I worked with investment bankers I was surrounded by free-market fundamentalists who roamed the globe preaching a triumphant gospel of deregulation from which all freedoms would flow, yet returned to a bureaucratic roost perfectly Soviet in its rigidity."

Computerized Citizens

In this world's most intimate touch, we ourselves become prisoners of a micro-bureaucracy of the mind. We willingly carry it with us even as it distorts our reasoning. Each use of the laptop, palm pilot, pager, and so on trains us daily in a kind of thinking that is so logical that we forget we have to make it sensible. Inner logic becomes the standard rather than the question: Does this serve the ultimate human capacity to set our own purposes? Instruments that technically connect us practically keep us apart. No need for a central power to force us to obey a central law. We happily subscribe to the electronic network. This provides not orders but only a matrix for all thinking, sensing, and acting. Within it we are free to think we are free.

Nitwits begin to say that when air controllers and a computer disagree, the solution is "removing the human from the loop." In a flurry of sneers at science fiction horribles, conveniently forgotten are examples from the Cold

War. Then humans repeatedly saved computers from launching a war based on reading a flock of geese or a rising moon as a missile attack.

There is a danger in this wired world. It is not only that the baby died, that the economy was endangered, that peace collapsed, or even that we are hardwired to be part of the techno-bureaucracy. The danger lies not in technology or bureaucracy themselves, but in the ease with which we fall into lockstep with their programs and reproduce their excuses: Everybody did their jobs, but the baby died. Somebody didn't do their job: same result: Return the baby!

Bureaucratic Patterns

There is a pattern in all this, a consistent pattern of misunderstandings covering up the understanding of what bureaucracy is and does.

Consider its word origins. Bureaucracy: from the Greek for power (*kratos*) and from the French for office (*bureau*). In conceiving the thought that an office could rule, the designers had made a discovery: people could orient their actions toward an idea instead of a human leader. This idea could become law for them. And this law would be legitimate, a product of their own making, by becoming embedded and available to all in published rules. To assure compliance, there would be regulation and enforcement by the impersonal office. In this office, the present tenant is held accountable. But he or she will claim to be not personally responsible as long as he or she follows the rules, the law, the impersonal idea.

All these—idea, law, legitimacy, even force—could be made thoroughly intelligible to human reason, technical and moral. Promised was a power of social control never before seen on this earth. The price simply was that the particular human being would be subjected to the general rules.

Now consider the implications: The office rules, not the man or woman in it. It rules by policies, programs, and standards. These are the most inhuman of standards that can be imagined: the general laws of pure reason untainted by the particular individual or situation determine the fate of each of us. Without fear or favor does this office uniformly apply its assigned tasks; but also without compassion or sensibility. A mis-fit is unavoidable.

Reason rationalizes. It modernizes. It creates the modem world. Modernity replaces tradition: the sentiments and sensibilities of the family, the clan and tribe, the kingdoms of faith or fear.

The cradle of modernity lay in Europe. There bureaucracy was expected to carry into human affairs reason's light—the light that would enlighten the world. Europeans called it the Enlightenment, and named bureaucracy to be its administrator. Just so do we still rely on schools, armies, prisons and world bureaucracies to modernize the globe.

What happened?

For centuries we have lived that failed promise. The system developed its own inner logic. Its logic runs contrary to what humans who have desires, feelings, and emotions might consider reasonable. Bureaucracy—as distinct from civil service in general—structures that service under dehumanizing

Exhibit 3.1

Misunderstandings and Understandings of Bureaucracy

Misunderstandings	Understandings
Socially Bureaucrats deal with people.	Bureaucrats deal with cases.
Culturally Bureaucrats care about the same things we do: justice, freedom, violence, oppression, illness, death, victory, defeat, love, hate, salvation, and damnation.	Bureaucrats aim at control and efficiency.
Psychologically Bureaucrats are people like us.	Bureaucrats are a new personality type, headless and soulless.*
Linguistically Communication with bureaucrats is possible: We all speak the same language, we think the same way.	Bureaucrats shape and inform rather than communicate.
Cognitively Bureaucrats think the way we do: logically *and* sensibly.	Bureaucrats use logic only: They are trained to think the way computers think.
Politically Bureaucracies are service institutions accountable to society and ruled by politics and government.	Bureaucracies are control institutions increasingly ruling society, politics, and government.

*The terms "headless" and "soulless" here evoked strong protests from some employees of modern organizations. It may be worthwhile to point out that these terms reflect a tendency that bureaucratic life forces on bureaucrats, rather than the actual characteristics of specific individuals.

conditions. These favor top-down control but guarantee insensibility to outsiders and a pathological lack of care for the health of its inmates. The claim that it is the most perfect control instrument for its masters in business or government has long been disproved; yet its myth persists.

Consider our conventional expectations (I call them misunderstandings) in contrast to cues from reality (I call them understandings) (see Exhibit 3.1).

Today these misunderstandings and understandings work themselves out in three distinct arenas of human struggle for the human spirit.

Conventional bureaucracy. Exhibit 3.1 covers this familiar arena of bureaucratic struggles that we are used to. The institutions are in local, state, and national arenas of power. But today there are two more: computer bureaucracy, the bureaucracy without bureaucrats; and global bureaucracy, the bureaucracies of globalization.

Computer bureaucracy. With the coming of the computer, bureaucracy has become a state of mind. With every stroke of the laptop keyboard, we key in to the demands of the perfectly rational machine, the machine totally without human sensibility.

Global bureaucracy. Here the Enlightenment project continues unabated. It claims to bring the light to "dark" continents. It spreads the economics of modernity along with the gospel of democracy.

Bureaucracy is spreading, rather than contracting. It spreads across the globe. It invades our minds. Where is the light?

Modern Self-Critique

In the Enlightenment project something seems to have gone wrong. Who will tell us what it is?

The project had expected free men (and eventually women) to use their own imaginative reason to construct their own political order. In the transition, an administrative mechanism would keep a delicate balance of order.

By 1900, this temporary order had, in the words of the sociologist Max Weber, become "a cage of steel." Bureaucracy places order before freedom, Its inmates distrust imagination. Reason, the source of light, becomes half-reason. Without imagination of how things might be otherwise, it becomes the mere logic of turning other traditions into carbon copies of the modern Western original.

By 2000+, in personal life, in computer use, in globalization, we still face the same familiar bureaucratic problem: How can human imagination be free to construct an order fit for human beings when the tools are in the hands of a force heading in another direction?

Modern social science critical of this contrary development asks typically modern questions. As the father of modern bureaucracy study, Max Weber, put it in regard to the increasing bureaucratization of life:

1. How can we save *any* remnants of "individualist" freedom in any sense?
2. How will democracy even in a limited sense be *at all possible*?
3. How will politics remain possible?

These are profound questions. But they seek to protect the essential concepts of modernity from itself. Post-modernism questions today's validity of the use of concepts like freedom, democracy, even politics. Such terms are considered out of date. They no longer cover experiences and entities in reality (a concept also threatened). On top of that, post-modernists ask about the choices presented. The individual, freedom, democracy are defined by the Enlightenment itself. How can its laughing heir, modern social science, protect their integrity when its tools are tainted?

Yet Max Weber's questions have profound consequences. They orient us to the vast indifferent expanses of the modern world. Most recently similar questions were extended to apply to other aspects of modern life. In the study of public administration, private management, policy, and planning, a whole critical school appeared.

This critical school, believers in full reason and hopeful of modernity, now stands confronted by a school we may call post-modern, unbelievers or at least challengers of reason.

If bureaucracy is a state of mind, this school asks, how did we get into that state of mind? And how do we get out of that state without losing our mind? Perhaps traditional institutions—individualism, freedom, politics itself—are not the issue. Perhaps the problem is precisely in thinking of human beings as individuals, of freedom as license, of politics as power, of reason as just logic. In which case, modern self-critique is not enough.

Modern self-critique of modern institutions begins with Max Weber. Still the first and foremost student of bureaucracy, Weber even today presents us with his definitive outline of what it takes to construct this control instrument without compare.

Post-modern critics do not fundamentally disagree with the tally of the costs:

- *Socially,* bureaucracy cancels *who* you are and tells you *what* you are— your assigned role in the program or the job.
- *Culturally,* the substance of what is worthwhile to you is translated into a formal shadow of your values: for example, justice into law.
- *Psychologically,* you are asked to surrender your full personality to fit into program or job identity.
- *In speaking,* you learn a strange new language that enables you to speak without meaning what you say.
- *In thinking,* you learn to be strictly logical—even if the result makes no sense.
- *Politically,* you accept being managed and are taught to despise politics because it falls far short of rational administration.

But post-modernists go beyond this list. They ask: Is there any other way of thinking about how this became so? And: What are the furthermost implications of where we are headed? A version of Exhibit 3.1 was first published in 1977 as a modern anti-bureaucratic manifesto. Today even we moderns realize that, as the adoptive father of the baby said, it's really worse than that.

. . .

EXPLORING THE ISSUE

Is Bureaucracy the Best Option for Organizing Government?

Critical Thinking and Reflection

1. How are bureaucracy and bureaucrats different? Similar?
2. In what ways can bureaucracy corrupt the individuals working for it?
3. How can bureaucratic structures effect the functioning of government? Is there a way to better design bureaucracy to allow bureaucrats to fulfill their goals of helping citizens?
4. What are the positive facets of bureaucracy? Bureaucrats? How about the negatives of each?
5. When is bureaucracy most likely to offer assistance to citizens? When can it instead cause problems?

Is There Common Ground?

As Goodsell and Hummel make clear, there is a distinction between bureaucracy as a structure and the bureaucrats that work to accomplish the goals of government every day. Goodsell makes a strong argument that the individuals who work for bureaucratic agencies are generally well-intentioned and aim to ensure citizens receive positive outcomes within the regulations set forth by statue and legislation. In doing so, they provide a necessary service and are able to interact with and assist citizens in a way that other branches of government are not. They are allegedly mistreated by academics, citizens, and the media alike.

Hummel, on the other hand, argues that bureaucracy is a corrupting influence that turns well-intentioned workers into drones of the state—speaking their own language and incapable of making their own decisions. Bureaucracy, as a result, leaves neither citizens nor workers satisfied. Although Hummel does not present a different organizational structure better-suited for American government, he does strongly suggest the need to make changes. Perhaps, the proper course of action is to work on the assumption that bureaucracy will continue to be the way we choose to organize our government and determine ways to make it better. By determining ways to ensure that citizens receive proper outcomes without corrupting the individual bureaucrats, we can move toward a better system of government organization rather than a different one.

Additional Resources

Kettl, D.F., *The Transformation of Governance: Public Administration for Twenty-First Century America* (Baltimore: The Johns Hopkins University Press, 2002)

Kettl examines the contemporary challenges in the field of public administration and undertakes a critical examination of how governance has changed in recent decades.

Osborne, D. and T. Gaebler, *Reinventing Government: How the Entrepreneurial Spirit Is Transforming the Public Sector* (New York: Plume, 1993)

Osborne and Gaebler present ways to increase efficiency and effectiveness in American public administration by reviving government. This book served as an impetus for the decisions of President Bill Clinton when attempting to remove red tape from the federal bureaucracy.

Stillman III, R.J., *Public Administration: Concepts and Cases*, 9th ed (New York: Wadsworth, 2009)

Stillman presents a series of telling case studies to demonstrate both classic and contemporary elements of public administration. Most importantly, Stillman's case studies highlight the positive and negative aspects of using bureaucracy to organize government.

Weber, M., *Economy and Society* (Berkeley, CA: University of California Press, 1978)

In this two-volume set, Weber lays out his beliefs on bureaucracy and its potential impact on bother government and society. A must read for students of public administration.

Wilson, J.Q., *Bureaucracy: What Government Agencies Do and Why They Do It* (New York: Basic, 1991)

Wilson highlights how policy is largely created by those with no understanding of how it will be implemented. As a result, neither liberal nor conservative views on how to improve bureaucratic behavior can fully be successful on their own.

Internet References . . .

Center for American Politics and Public Policy

CAPP focuses on research that relates to public policy processes, including issues of agenda setting, decision-making, implementation, regulation, the development of quantitative measures of policy change, and the role of ideas and dialogue in policy change.

http://www.cappp.org/

American Enterprise Institute for Public Policy Research

The American Enterprise Institute (AEI) is a community of scholars and supporters committed to expanding liberty, increasing individual opportunity, and strengthening free enterprise. AEI pursues these unchanging ideals through independent thinking, open debate, reasoned argument, facts, and the highest standards of research and exposition.

http://www.aei.org/

Brookings Institution

The Brookings Institution is a nonprofit public policy organization based in Washington, DC. Their mission is to conduct high-quality, independent research and, based on that research, to provide innovative, practical recommendations that strengthen American democracy; foster the economic and social welfare, security, and opportunity of all Americans; and secure a more open, safe, prosperous, and cooperative international system.

http://www.brookings.edu/

Stateline: State Politics and Policy

Stateline is a nonpartisan, nonprofit news service of the Pew Center on the States. Since 1999, it has reported and analyzed trends in state policy.

http://www.stateline.org/live/issues/Politics

Public Agenda

Public Agenda's mission is to improve democratic problem solving. We pursue this nonpartisan mission through research, engagement and communications that bridge the divisions and disconnects among leaders and publics so that sustainable solutions to tough challenges can be achieved. By doing so, we seek to contribute to a democracy in which problem solving triumphs over gridlock and inertia, and where public policy reflects the deliberations and values of the citizenry.

http://www.publicagenda.org

Dilemmas of Public Policy

*T*he policymaking process in the United States is methodical—designed to allow different groups to have input in shaping the laws that emerge. The fact that we are a federal system adds extra layers of complexity to the already difficult process, however. Not only do we need to determine what values citizens are expecting to be instilled in policy, but we also must labor through the process of determining which level of government is best suited to execute the policy and how the different levels will work together when needed. Only by examining these issues can we begin to fully understand the dilemmas of public policy.

- Is It Possible to Balance Efficiency and Equity in Public Policy?

- Do Bureaucrats Have More Influence on Public Policy Than Other Branches of Government Do?

- Is It Possible to Coordinate Federal, State, and Local Governments in a Way That Allows Policy Making to Be More Efficient?

ISSUE 4

Is It Possible to Balance Efficiency and Equity in Public Policy?

YES: Kristen Norman-Major, from "Balancing the Four *Es*; or Can We Achieve Equity for Social Equity in Public Administration?" *Journal of Public Affairs Education* (Spring 2011)

NO: Julian Le Grand, from "Equity Versus Efficiency: The Elusive Trade-Off," *Ethics* (April 1990)

Learning Outcomes

After reading this issue, you should be able to:

- Define what makes a public policy efficient.
- Define what makes a public policy equitable.
- Discuss the merits of having policies that are both efficient and equitable.
- Describe the difficulties of attempting to solve the trade-off between efficiency and equity.
- Understand the importance of values to public policy.
- Gain an understanding of the complexity of modern public policymaking.

ISSUE SUMMARY

YES: Kristen Norman-Major argues that even though equity was identified as the fourth pillar of public administration by the National Academy of Public Administration, we can—and should—go further to ensure policies are both efficient and equitable. Only through concentrated efforts can we make equity as important as economy, efficiency, and effectiveness.

NO: Julian Le Grand argues that the trade-off between efficiency and equity is not as easily solved. Rather than attempting to solve the tradeoff, he believes we can best help impact policies by challenging the tradeoff framework.

In America today, everyone seems to expect something different from public policies. Rather than being concerned with larger policy goals and outcomes, we take a fairly self-serving view in many cases and as a result lose the forest for the trees. Historically, policy followers have lumped outcome goals into four broad categories: efficiency, equity, effectiveness, and economy. Where policymaking becomes so difficult is when we realize that in the ideal world policies would fit neatly into each. By efficiency, we mean that policies should do the maximum possible for the minimum cost necessary. Equity, on the other hand, implies that policies should be fair and impartial. In terms of effectiveness, we want policies that do what they are intended to. We do not necessarily concern ourselves with cost when thinking about effectiveness because we simply want the right outcome. With economy, we focus on the cost of programs and assuring the lowest cost option is utilized (with or without regard to other possible value).

What these definitions present us with is a baseline understanding of what the four leading values of public policy are. Yet, by digging deeper, it becomes clear how these values can oftentimes come into conflict with one another or can be duplicative. Economy, for example, offers little to our understanding of policies and programs that we cannot see within the scope of efficiency and effectiveness. As a result, our analyses—when they look at all four values—are already being inefficient! Most importantly for the students of policy and public administration is the fact that these values oftentimes conflict. Consider the relationship between equity and equality. If equity is expected, then the policy will always be provided in a suboptimal manner. We will try to have the most efficient and equitable policy, but that will be a different outcome from simply the most efficient one. Simply put, values clash more often than they coordinate.

When we try to evaluate public programs and policies, we tend to focus on three key questions (which just so happen to align with the values of interest to public administration). First, we ask if the policy/program is achieving its intended results. Next, we examine if it is possible to achieve the results at a lower cost. Lastly, we explore whether people are being treated fairly under the policy/program. Although all three questions are worthy of consideration, the debate centers on which question gets asked first for which policies. This may seem like a fairly simple decision, yet within each policy framework, different groups of individuals will have different priorities and consequently ask different questions. Typically, most American policy analysts have been most concerned with equity and efficiency given the political nature of policy debates within our country's political framework. Let us examine this debate through some more concrete examples.

Public health debates are one of the areas where efficiency and equity come into conflict. When there are concerns about potential epidemics entering a region—whether it be a form of influenza or something more severe like SARS—health workers work to determine the most vulnerable populations and ensure they are provided with available preventative measures. However, as with most things, the amount of preventative measure is oftentimes scarce. As such, in some instances only the most at-risk groups will receive vaccines. This signifies the efficiency–equity tradeoff. An equitable solution would involve all members of the possibly affected region receiving the vaccine and being spared the possible impact of the epidemic. Yet, this is simply an inefficient process. If the epidemic is not predicted to be life threatening, only the vulnerable populations (perhaps children, elderly, and those with already weakened immune systems) may need the vaccine. In the debate over public health, we can easily see where questions of efficiency and equity regularly come up in the interests of American citizens.

To some degree, questions of efficiency and equity emerged when the American government attempted to determine how best to assist the banking industry in response to the mortgage crisis. The federal government took an efficient approach by bailing out banks through a basic one shot, top–down policy. However, a more equitable process would likely have been to pass a law that forced us to reexamine each mortgage individually and then refinancing bad mortgages in a way that allowed individuals to remain fiscally solvent as opposed to the banks. So why did our country's politicians choose to accept the efficient policy rather than the equitable one? This question is still being debated—and needs to be addressed in a different volume than this—but the point rings true. It is not easy to determine which values to emphasize more in policy decisions.

What these examples were intended to do was to demonstrate in concrete terms how almost any policy decision reached in the United States can be looked at through both lenses: efficiency and equity. Through the YES and NO selections, we will look more closely at the alleged value clash between efficiency and equity as it applies to American public policy. In the YES article, Kristen Norman-Major discusses how even because it was the fourth value proposed by the National Academy of Public Administration, we need to make more efforts as practitioners to ensure that equity is viewed as being as important as efficiency, economy, and effectiveness. On the opposite side of the argument, in the NO article, Julian Le Grand argues that practitioners and academics alike spend far too much time and energy attempting to solve the tradeoff debate when they could instead be trying to figure out ways to create policies that better encompass all of the values. Although such a suggestion alters the frame of the debate, it does provide a different way of considering the long-standing question of how best to bring together divergent values in American policy.

YES

Kristen Norman-Major

Balancing the Four *Es*; or Can We Achieve Equity for Social Equity in Public Administration?

In 1968, a group of young public administration scholars gathered in Minnowbrook, New York, to discuss a new direction for the study and practice of public administration. Rejecting the traditional ideas of a politics-administration dichotomy and public administration practiced by neutral competents, these young scholars argued that public administration by its nature cannot be neutral; it must consider the values of American society, including responsiveness, public participation in decision making, social equity, citizen choice, and administrative responsibility.

One of the strongest advocates of the need to practice a "new public administration" was H. George Frederickson. Frederickson argued at the time, and still does, for the inclusion of values in the practice of a new public administration, especially the inclusion of social equity as a key component. His passion for this issue is illustrated in his 2005 reflection on the state of social equity in American public administration:

> But in public administration I insist that we engage with the problem of inequality, that we dirty our hands with inequality, that we be outraged, passionate, and determined. In short, I insist that we actually apply social equity in public administration.

Over 40 years after the first Minnowbrook conference and the call for adding values to the practice of public administration, social equity—while named the fourth pillar of public administration by the National Academy of Public Administration in 2005—still struggles to find equal footing with its partners, economy, efficiency and effectiveness. As Wooldridge and Gooden have argued, it is the rare public administrator who has the courage to make social equity the primary goal of policy. The question for this work is, "Can we achieve *equity* for social equity among the pillars of public administration?" The argument to be made here is that how we define and measure the pillars matters and that a lack of a clear definition and measures of social equity are largely responsible for its struggle. To change this, we must clearly define *social equity*; develop clearer measures for it; and, most important, educate public

From *Journal of Public Affairs Education*, Spring 2011, pp. 233–237, 241–242, 250–251.

73

administrators to include equity at the same level of consideration as economy, efficiency, and effectiveness when developing and implementing public policies.

Defining, Measuring, and Practicing the Four Pillars

Economy

Of the four pillars of public administration, economy is arguably the one most scrutinized by the public. When it comes to spending public dollars, especially in times of tight budgets, the expectation is that public services will be provided in the most economical manner possible. In general, economy is thought of as the careful or sparing use of resources. Frederickson defines *economy in public administration* as the "management of scarce resources and particularly with expending the fewest resources for an agreed upon level of public services." In practice, economy in public administration often involves such things as getting the lowest bid on contracts for agreed-upon services or materials, outsourcing or privatization of public services, using network governance to partner across sectors in providing services, and generally figuring out how to do more (or sometimes less) with fewer resources.

It should not be difficult to convince students and practitioners of public administration of the need for economy in providing public services. Economy is an objective concept, and good stewardship of the public dollar is a long-held principle. Economy can also be easily measured through evaluation of expenditures, calculating cost savings, and monitoring the inputs to a program compared to the stated goals or agreed-upon level of service.

Economy is most often considered in the short term, that is, by looking at immediate cost savings in providing services. However, given sufficient short-term resources, public administrators are sometimes willing to sacrifice economy in the short term to gain efficiency, effectiveness, and economy in the longer term. For example, governments will invest larger sums to develop technology, data systems, or computer applications that are expensive to build in the short term but expected to create money-saving efficiencies in the longer term. This willingness to sacrifice short-term economy for longer-term gains in efficiency or effectiveness is not usually shared when it comes to increased short-term investments that are expected to provide long-term gains in equity.

Efficiency

To many, efficiency in public administration might seem an oxymoron. After all, the stereotype of a public servant is not of one who is productive, well organized, and works to get the best outcome with the least amount of wasted effort or expense. However, in practice efficiency is a key pillar in public administration. Frederickson defines *efficiency* as "achieving the most, the best, or the most preferable public services for available resources." Weimer and Vining define *efficiency* as "maximizing the total value to the members of society obtained from the use of scarce resources." In practice, efficiency in public administration is often thought of in terms of process efficiencies reflected in measures such as timely plowing of streets, short turnaround times on applications, and short lines at government offices. It can also be reflected through reduced waiting times for trials, faster responses from emergency services, and "one-stop shopping" options for social services. Tied to this, however, are economic considerations. All of these services must be provided at minimum cost and using a balanced distribution of resources.

As with economy, it is relatively easy to get agreement on efficiency as a key value of public administration. Despite stereotypes to the contrary, most governments strive to provide services in the most efficient manner possible. Ironically, efficiency is often reflected in the lack of attention paid to government. When things work well, people don't complain or think much about government's role in providing services that affect their daily lives. It is only when things go wrong—streets aren't plowed, days are spent in line at the Department of Motor Vehicles, or Public Works employees are caught taking too many breaks—that attention is paid to how government is working. While inefficiencies are put in the spotlight, efficient operations are rarely recognized or publicly praised.

Increasingly, public administrators are using practices such as Balanced Scorecards, LEAN processes, customer satisfaction surveys, and process and output evaluation to measure how efficiently services are being provided. These measures are concrete and provide objective information on the efficiency of services. As defined here, efficiency, like economy, is also considered mostly in the short term; but administrators are often willing to invest resources to develop systems that are assumed to improve process efficiencies in the longer term.

Effectiveness

Simply put, effectiveness is being successful in producing a desired result or accomplishing set goals. As a pillar of public administration, effectiveness became more prominent with increasing calls for accountability that began with the National Performance Review in the Clinton administration and continued through the George W. Bush administration. While government may operate in an economical and efficient manner, it is also important that it is doing what it set out to do in the first place. In the practice of public administration, effectiveness is reflected in such things as reduced welfare roles, increased employment rates, improved test scores, lower crime rates, better roads, improved water quality, reduced pollution, and the like. Effectiveness is usually considered in the short term, especially when renewing budgets. Policy makers' patience for long-term outcomes is often limited by election cycles. Results that need to be proven within a 2- to 4-year time frame make it harder to propose investment in longer-term programs and services that may not show clear results for several years.

While there is not always agreement on which outcomes should be used to define effectiveness, it is not difficult to find objective ways to measure outcomes for many public services. Common tools include tracking of outputs, program evaluations, pre- and post-tests, client follow-up, economic indicators, report cards, and benchmarking. Some outcomes are less tangible and thus harder to measure than others, and often costs of data collection can be prohibitive. In times of budget shortfalls or decreasing revenues, program evaluation is often one of the first items cut; many times, it never makes it to the table when programs are initially established. However, when desired public agencies have a wealth of tools available to help them measure program effectiveness.

Like its partners economy and efficiency, effectiveness is not a hard sell as a value of public administration. It is a concrete concept with proven tools for measurement. Few, if any, would argue that public services shouldn't be effective. The main arguments arise when defining what the final goals should be and then what variables serve as clear measures for the given outcomes. A key example of this is the debate in the past several years over standardized testing as the best way to measure educational effectiveness under No Child Left Behind.

Social Equity

In calling for the inclusion of social equity as a pillar of public administration, the scholars at Minnowbrook argued that it is not sufficient to have economical and efficient government services if we don't also consider who is being served at the same time. As Frederickson wrote in an essay almost 10 years after the first Minnowbrook conference, "the most productive governments, the most efficient governments, and the most economizing governments can still be perpetuating poverty, inequality of opportunity and injustice." However, part of the challenge in raising equity to a level playing field with economy, efficiency, and effectiveness is that it is a normative concept that lends itself to debate over what it looks like and what the proper role of government is in establishing it once defined. While economy, efficiency, and effectiveness deal with how government operates, equity delves into questions of for whom government operates. In Frederickson's words, this is the debate over "for whom is the organization well managed? For whom is the organization efficient? For whom is the organization economical? For whom are public services more or less fairly delivered?"

In 2000 when the National Academy of Public Administration (NAPA) established the Standing Panel on Social Equity, it put forth the following definition for social equity in public administration:

> The *fair, just and equitable* [emphasis added] management of all institutions serving the public directly or by contract; and the fair and equitable distribution of public services, and implementation of public policy; and the commitment to promote *fairness, justice and equity* [emphasis added] in the formation of public policy.

This definition clearly dismisses the idea of public administration as the neutral implementation of public policy by calling for fairness, justice, and equity in the provision of public policy, However, unlike the relatively objective nature of economy, efficiency, and effectiveness, the terms *fair, just, equitable,* and *equity* are highly normative and make it more difficult to reach agreement on what they mean and how they are incorporated in practice. The combination of highly normative concepts along with the lack of a clear and applied definition of social equity exacerbates the struggle in raising the status of equity as a pillar of public administration. As Svara and Brunet noted in their 2004 article examining coverage of social equity in introductory public administration texts, it is a "skeletal pillar" that needs to be filled with more solid definitions and measures.

This confusion over just what social equity is and what the appropriate role of government is in implementing it makes it harder for public administrators to advocate for social equity as an equal to economy, efficiency, and effectiveness, much less for them to have the courage to argue that trade-offs with short-term economy or efficiency can lead to long-term gains in equity. The remainder of this article looks at ways to better define and measure equity, its relationship with the other pillars, and ways to educate public administrators so they can be courageous advocates for social equity. . . .

Cost-Benefit Analysis and Social Return on Investment

While the measures just discussed are helpful, only some may be available in the immediate term. There is still the issue of longer-term results from investments in social equity. Along with the recognition that the payoffs for social equity are often long term, there is also a growing recognition that the effects of investments in equity can fall outside of the issue area where the immediate investment is made. One of the most prominent examples of this is the increasing amount of research done that shows the long-term return on investment for programs that provide high-quality early education to children considered to be at risk for failure in school.

For years, advocates for early childhood education argued that investing in high-quality preschool experiences for children was not only the morally right thing to do but also that it would save money in the long run through such things as a decreased need for special education, reduction in juvenile crime and welfare roles, and increased graduation and employment rates. However, the evidence for these claims was merely anecdotal and often dismissed by policy makers. Over the past decade, however, an increasing amount of work has been done by economists and policy analysts that shows concrete evidence of long-term social returns on investment of between 9 and 16 percent for every dollar invested in early childhood education for children considered to be at risk of school failure. Through cost-benefit analysis, these studies have shown that the savings or social return on investment (SROI) to the public for these programs comes in the form of long-term reductions in educational remediation, juvenile crime, and welfare roles as well as increases in graduation rates, higher education attainment, and productivity in the marketplace, among other things. Thus the payoffs for these programs spill over into several issue areas other than Pre-K–12 education and immediate school readiness. The challenge for advocates of such investments is that many of these broader payoffs often come 5 to 20 years or more after the initial investments, well outside the range for policy makers needing proof of effectiveness and efficiency. The question then is, in what time frame do we demand to see results of investments that reduce inequity?

A Second Look at the Efficiency-Equity Trade-Off

As noted earlier, Vining and Weimer define *efficiency* as "maximizing the total value to the members of society obtained from the use of scarce resources." The key question, however, is *when* the return to society is measured, particularly when looking to counter the assumption of an equity-efficiency trade-off.

In the field of economics, efficiency is often described using the concept of Pareto optimality. Under such conditions, the distribution of resources in a society is considered efficient when at the balancing point where you can't make one person better off without making someone else worse off. It is realized that in reality, however, few redistributions of resources in society can occur in a Pareto optimal way; that is, at least one person is made worse off in the transaction. It is even more challenging to argue for redistributions of resources if it is not clear that those intended to be made better off actually are, at least in the short run.

As a way of looking at the distribution of resources a bit differently, Nicholas Kaldor and John Hicks, two economists, postulated that an exchange could still be considered efficient if those made better off could eventually compensate those made worse off. Kaldor-Hicks efficiency, as it is referred to, opens the door to justifications for investments in social equity by allowing for those benefiting from the exchange to pay back society in other ways in the future. . . .

Social equity among the values of public administration has gained ground in acceptance since the first Minnowbrook conference. But over 40 years later, it still struggles to gain traction as an equal among its partners economy, efficiency, and effectiveness. Despite continued scholarship, including this and other symposia in the *Journal of Public Affairs Education,* the work of the Standing Panel on Social Equity in NAPA and its annual Social Equity Leadership Conference, and the establishment of a Democracy and Social Justice Section in the American Society for Public Administration, the field of public administration has not fully accepted the role of social equity in public administration. In part, this is due to the lack of clear definitions and measures for social equity. It is argued here that social equity can be simplified to maintaining or creating equality of opportunity in the provision of public services and that it can take three different forms in public administration:

1. Simple fairness and equal treatment
2. Distribution of resources to reduce inequalities in universal programs and services
3. Redistribution of resources to level the playing field or increase equality of opportunity through targeted programs

It is also possible to measure outcomes for social equity in the short term given proper data collection, the setting of benchmarks, use of program evaluation, and similar tools. The difficulty is not in how to measure, but in clearly defining what to measure. A simpler and more applied definition of social equity should help.

Also important to creating equity for social equity is adjusting the definition of efficiency to look at longer-term, broad payoffs to society of investments in reducing inequity. Use of cost-benefit analysis to calculate social return on investment is a growing field and one where partnerships between economics and public administration need to be strengthened. Finally, public administration educators must be more forthright in discussions of social equity across the curriculum and not reserve such conversations for specialized electives taken only by a limited number of students. From the simple (procedural fairness and equal access) to the complex (targeted programs to increase equality of opportunity), social equity is essential to the practice of public administration. Educators and practitioners alike must do a better job of recognizing the role of government in providing social equity. We must also call for more measurement, particularly of long-term outcomes. Courageous educators who discuss equity on equal terms with other public administration values will lead to courageous public administrators willing to do the same.

Julian Le Grand*  **NO**

Equity Versus Efficiency: The Elusive Trade-off

The objectives of equity and efficiency appear high on most lists of the aims of welfare policy. That a welfare program should be assessed at least in part by its ability to promote equity, fairness, or justice seems almost axiomatic.[1] That a program should not at the same time create inefficiency or, indeed, that it should actually reduce it, is also a widely accepted criterion for assessment. There will, of course, be other criteria for evaluation—the impact of the program on individual liberties, for example—but none perhaps with the salience of these two.[2]

It is also commonly asserted that there is, or that in most situations there is likely to be, a trade-off between these objectives. That is, the implementation of a program designed to "increase" one may result in a "decrease" in the other. For example, a social security system that reduced poverty, thus promoting greater equity under most interpretations of that term, may also reduce individuals' incentives to work or to save, thus creating inefficiency—at least under some interpretations of that term. Another example concerns comprehensive education, widely thought to improve equality of educational opportunity and thus equity, but accused by some of simultaneously damaging educational "excellence," thus damaging efficiency. Yet another case might be a health-care program on the dangers of smoking that increased the average life expectancy of all groups in the population, thus promoting efficiency, but produced a greater increase in life expectancy for the better off (who, for various reasons, were more responsive to the message) than for the poor, thus increasing the gap between them and arguably increasing inequity.[3]

Now, there are a number of questions that can be asked about this trade-off. Some of them are empirical: Does the social security system really discourage people from working? Does comprehensive education actually produce worse exam results on average than selective systems? Do antismoking campaigns have a greater impact on the better off than the poor? and so on. These

* This article forms part of the Objectives of Welfare project of the Welfare State Programme at the Suntory Toyota International Centre for Economics and Related Disciplines (ST/ICERD), London School of Economics, whose support is gratefully acknowledged. I am also grateful for comments from A. B. Atkinson, Brian Barry, Robert Goodin, David Miller, and other participants at the ST/ICERD Tenth Anniversary Conference on Political Philosophy and the Welfare State, June 1988.

are important and controversial questions, but they are not my concern here. Rather, I want to concentrate on the more philosophical issues concerning the intrinsic nature of the equity-efficiency trade-off. In particular, I want to examine the question whether the general notion of a trade-off between the two actually makes sense. A necessary condition for it to do so is that efficiency is a social and economic objective in the same sense that equity is an objective. But does efficiency have the same status as equity or, indeed, as other possible objectives of economic and social organization, such as liberty? If it does not, and it will be one of my contentions that at least in one important sense it does not, then what do people mean when they talk of the equity- efficiency trade-off? It is to these questions that this article is addressed.

The article begins with a distinction between two kinds of trade-off, either of which could form the basis for *the* equity-efficiency trade-off. It then discusses various possible interpretations of the term *efficiency,* and their implications for the existence or otherwise of the trade-off. There is a brief concluding section. Some of the arguments are a little technical.

Types of Trade-off

The first point to be made is that there are two different kinds of phenomenon to which the phrase "equity-efficiency trade-off" could refer. The first concerns values; the second, what might be termed production.

The ideas underlying the value trade-off were, I believe, first laid out systematically by Brian Barry. He argued that when evaluating social outcomes, it was not necessary for rationality in that evaluation to assume that attaining one objective should always dominate attaining another. Rather, the "extent" to which one objective was attained could be traded off, or substituted for, the extent to which another was attained. In the equity-efficiency context (the example actually discussed by Barry) it would be perfectly consistent with most notions of rationality for someone to consider an allocation of resources that was highly efficient but grossly inequitable as equally good (or equally bad) as one which was extremely equitable but highly inefficient. "The fundamental idea . . . is that although two principles need not be reducible to a single one, they may normally be expected to be to some extent substitutable for one another. The problem of someone making an evaluation can thus be regarded as the problem of deciding what mixture of principles more or less implemented out of all the mixtures which are available would be, in his own opinion, best."[4]

The idea that in making social evaluations people might be indifferent between various combinations of objectives or principles, just as in making their consumption decisions they might be indifferent between various combinations of goods, seems eminently sensible. Moreover, it is a way of resolving dilemmas concerning apparent inconsistencies in people's moral decisions that have puzzled some thinkers.[5] However, I do not think that, when people refer to the equity-efficiency trade-off, it is generally value-substitutability that they have in mind. It is more likely that they are concerned with what might be termed "production-substitutability"; that is, with the ability of a welfare program or of other aspects of the economic and social system to deliver different combinations of objectives. The sort of questions involved here are not value ones but are more empirical in nature; they concern the possibility or feasibility of alternatives. Is it possible or feasible to allocate resources within the economy in a way that is both "fully" equitable and "fully" efficient? If not, then what are the various combinations of degrees of equity and efficiency that are feasible? How much equity has to be sacrificed to obtain a given level of efficiency or vice versa? These kinds of questions relate to the productive capacities of different kinds of social and economic organization rather than to the values of the person making an assessment of them. . . .

The definition is this: *An allocation of resources is efficient if it is impossible to move toward the attainment of one social objective without moving away from the attainment of another objective.* . . . This implies that all points on the objective possibility frontier are efficient, whereas all points inside the frontier are inefficient.[6] . . .

If this interpretation of efficiency is indeed a plausible one, what is the implication for the equity-efficiency trade-off? Simply that the notion of a trade-off is meaningless. For acceptance of this interpretation implies that efficiency can be defined only in relation to the ability of forms of social and economic organization to attain their primary objectives and that therefore efficiency cannot itself be one of those primary objectives. In this sense, if equity is one of the objectives it is meaningless to talk of a trade-off (either in value or production) between equity and efficiency. Efficiency is not an objective in the sense that equity is an objective; rather, it is a secondary objective that only acquires meaning with reference to primary objectives such as equity.[7]

Other Interpretations of Efficiency

What, then, do people generally mean when they are talking about the trade-off between equity and efficiency? For the reasons explained, they cannot be referring to a trade-off between equity and efficiency in the sense of the latter outlined above, yet they clearly have some phenomenon in mind. The explanation has to be that they are using the term *efficiency* in some different way. One common interpretation is to identify efficiency with growth in aggregate economic production; another is to identify it with Pareto-optimality. Both create problems for the notion of the equity-efficiency trade-off, as I now hope to show.

Efficiency as Economic Growth

The identification of efficiency with economic growth is widespread in both popular and academic discourse on the economy. It is also often asserted that the attainment of efficiency in the sense of economic growth is incompatible with the attainment of equity and, hence, there is a trade-off between the two. Examples of this abound; an influential one is Arthur Okun's famous volume *Equality and Efficiency: The Big Trade-off.*[8]

A similar interpretation underlies many of the debates concerning the trade-off between efficiency and equity in the context of social security. A system of unemployment benefits that provides the unemployed with a basic income and/or that imposes high marginal tax rates on earned income may discourage people from seeking employment and, hence, from increasing their work effort; and if hours of work are reduced, so will be economic growth. A system of state pensions may reduce the incentive of individuals to save to provide for their old age; unless this is offset by an increased propensity of the state to save, then this will result in smaller aggregate savings, smaller investment, and, hence, a lower rate of economic growth.

This identification of efficiency with economic growth has an obvious appeal; and undoubtedly any production trade-off between equity and economic growth that may exist would have serious policy implications. However, a single-minded concentration on growth does have its curious aspects. Increasing economic production does not seem a sensible objective on its own. Presumably, the only point of doing so is if the increase can be put to use in some way, that is, if it can provide want satisfaction—generate utility—for one or more individuals. The relevant objective then becomes one of increasing individuals' utilities, presumably aggregated in some way.

Again, it is of obvious importance to establish, so far as possible, the existence of any trade-off between equity and aggregate want satisfaction. But there are complications. The exact method of aggregation has to be established. Is it to be a form of utilitarianism, with individual utilities being simply added together, or are they to be weighted in some way? Can utilities be "added" in any reasonable fashion? These are standard problems, but their very familiarity does not mean they can be ignored.

Moreover, there are other, less well-known, difficulties. For example, if the reason for identifying efficiency with economic production and thereby elevating it to the status of a primary objective is because increases in production lead to increases in individuals' utilities, then the utility costs of increased production should also be taken into account. Yet these are frequently neglected. The argument concerning the impact of social security on work effort, for example, often seems to ignore the possibility that work itself can have costs—that it may create disutility. This may have perverse consequences. In the Appendix an example is given of the impact on an individual of a change in social security that reduces benefits to the unemployed but also lowers marginal tax rates on earned income. The result is an increase in the individual's work effort, an increase in his or her money income, but a reduction in his or her utility.[9]

In short, the identification of efficiency with economic growth and, hence, its elevation to the status of a primary objective, will indeed raise important issues concerning possible trade-offs with equity. But economic growth itself is far from unproblematic as an objective. Moreover, its identification with efficiency robs the latter of the more general interpretation discussed in the previous section, an interpretation that concerns the ability of society to achieve any or all of its objectives. In many ways, it would seem preferable to divorce the idea of efficiency from that of economic growth and to discuss the issue of any trade-offs between growth and equity explicitly rather than obscuring the issue by reference to efficiency.

Efficiency as Pareto-Optimality

Another common interpretation of efficiency, at least among economists, is that of Pareto. Under this definition an allocation of resources is efficient if it is impossible to make one individual better off without making another worse off. An allocation of resources with this property is described as Pareto-optimal or as Pareto-efficient. On this interpretation, an equity-efficiency trade-off will exist if there is no feasible allocation that is simultaneously equitable (according to a chosen definition of equity) and Pareto-optimal.

To establish the existence or otherwise of such allocations has been a preoccupation of many economists. As an illustration of the at times rather bizarre directions which this activity can take, it is worth digressing briefly to consider the literature concerning the relationship between Pareto-optimality and one particular definition of equity that has recently attracted attention. This relates the existence of equity or inequity to the existence or otherwise of envy. More precisely, it defines an allocation of resources as equitable if no individual envies any other's position.

This conception of equity was first put forward explicitly by D. Foley, although its origins lie in the much older conception of the "I cut; you choose" method of equitably dividing a cake. It was developed by S. C. Kolm and by H. Varian in the mid-1970s. Since then the literature has expanded enormously, culminating in a book by William Baumol which also provides a brief history of the development of the idea."[10]

It might be thought that in promoting a new idea of equity the first concern would be to establish its acceptability by, for instance, direct reference to intuition or by using impartiality mechanisms such as a Rawlsian social contract or the "undistorted rational discourse" of Habermas or Ackerman.[11] But no. Varian, perhaps the most influential of the writers concerned, provides little by way of moral arguments in support of the conception; in the recent book by Baumol, the most sustained treatment of the concept, less than two pages (out of 266) is given to a discussion of the idea's philosophical underpinnings. Instead, the principal concern of most of these writers is with the equity-efficiency trade-off or, more precisely, with the trade-off between this conception of equity and efficiency defined as Pareto-optimality. Batteries of intellectual artillery are deployed to establish the conditions under which allocations exist that are simultaneously equitable (under this definition) and Pareto-optimal—allocations that, it should be noted, are termed by Varian "fair," thus confusing fairness with Pareto-optimality and displaying a disregard for the English language that may be symptomatic of a lack of a philosophical base for the ideas.

A related feature of this literature is that if no "fair" allocations are found to exist under certain realistic conditions, then the definition of envy-freeness—indeed, of envy itself—is altered so as to ensure that some do exist. For example, one of the early results established in the literature was that in economies with production it may be impossible to find allocations that were simultaneously envy-free and Pareto-optimal. Accordingly, Varian proposed an alternative definition of envy, for which such allocations do exist, namely, that envy does not exist (and, hence, an allocation is equitable) if an individual, i, prefers his or her own consumption and work effort to the consumption of any other individual, j, and the work effort that i would have to make in order to produce as much as j. In effect, this is saying that no one envies another's superior abilities, a statement that seems factually incorrect as well as having little apparent connection with intuitive or other interpretations of equity. In fact, no moral argument is put forward to support it; the only justification presented is that defining both envy and equity in these ways means that "fair" (according to Varian's definition of the term) allocations exist.[12]

Nor is Varian alone in devising interesting but apparently ad hoc notions of equity that will permit the existence of allocations that are equitable and Pareto-optimal. Another example is the suggestion that an allocation be defined as equitable if its distribution of utilities could have been achieved by an equal division of any set of commodities.[13] Again the principal argument put forward to justify this definition is that it permits "fair" (equitable and Pareto-optimal) allocations to exist. Again, no moral justification is offered; indeed, it is hard to see what it would have been.

The rationale for this emphasis on the importance of finding a definition of equity such that feasible allocations exist which are simultaneously equitable and efficient is not immediately apparent. In a pluralistic world, it seems quite plausible to suppose that there may be objectives whose simultaneous achievement is impossible. Economists, in particular, should be sympathetic to the possibility of trade-offs between objectives—in other contexts, after all, the trade-off is the hallmark of the profession. There seems to be nothing intrinsic in the concept of equity (or, indeed, of any other moral value) which requires that, for a particular conception to be acceptable, feasible allocations must exist that are simultaneously equitable and Pareto-optimal; discovery of concepts with this property, although doubtless a worthy endeavor in some respects, does seem an essentially secondary task.

Moreover, there is another problem with this trade-off. This concerns the nature of Pareto-optimality. Frequently offered as a definition of efficiency, it is more correctly interpreted as a form of value or social welfare function, one that, in certain forms, actually incorporates a notion of equity—rather a curious one, as we shall see. This perhaps can be best illustrated by reference to the literature concerning potential Pareto-optimality or the Hicks-Kaldor compensation principle. There it is asserted that there is an increase in welfare from a particular economic change if the gainers from the change can compensate the losers and still remain gainers. In the words of Sir John Hicks himself: "If A is made so much better off by the change that he could compensate B for his loss, and still have something left over, then the reorganisation is an unequivocal improvement," a test that he goes on to describe as "perfectly objective."[14]

What this implies is that a potential Pareto-improvement always constitutes an increase in welfare. One of the assumptions underlying this is a welfarist one: that social welfare depends only on individuals' utilities. . . .

Suppose there is a change of some kind that benefits a rich person by an amount estimated as ten dollars but also imposes a cost on a poor person of nine dollars. Clearly, the rich person could fully compensate the poor person and remain a gainer. So, according to the compensation principle, whether or not the compensation actually takes place there has been an increase in social welfare. But now consider the utility changes involved. On the not unreasonable assumption of diminishing marginal utility of income, if there is no compensation it is likely that the reduction in utility for the poor person due to the change is greater than the increase in utility for the rich person. Therefore, the only way that there could be a net increase in social welfare (in the absence of any actual compensation) is if the (smaller) change in utility for the rich person is weighted in such a way that it increases welfare more than the (larger) utility change for the poor person reduces welfare. And this could only occur if the social welfare function weights rich people more (values them more) than poor people.

All this is an illustration of the general point that Pareto-optimality is perhaps better viewed as a specialized form of social welfare or value function rather than as an objective or universal definition of efficiency. In that case, investigations of the trade-offs between various interpretations of equity and Pareto-optimality are not really concerned with the trade-off between equity and efficiency at all. Instead they are investigating what is, at least in part, actually a trade-off between two different kinds of equity: that whose properties are being explored and that embodied in the Pareto social welfare function.

Concluding Comments

This article has argued that the idea of an equity-efficiency trade-off is an elusive one. There are three main points. First, there are two types of trade-off to which the concept could refer: a value and a production trade-off. In practice it is usually the latter that is of concern, but the two must be kept distinct.

Second, at least according to one general definition of efficiency—one that refers to society's ability to attain its primary objectives—the notion of a trade-off between equity and efficiency literally does not make sense, for trade-offs can only occur between these primary objectives, of which efficiency is not one. Third, even if efficiency is interpreted in such a way as to make it a primary objective, in terms of economic growth or of Pareto-optimality, for instance, there are serious problems in teasing out precisely what is being traded off against what (in either value or production terms). Moreover, although establishing the existence or otherwise of trade-offs between equity and these objectives is undoubtedly important, the relevant discussions are often confused by their identification with the broader notion of efficiency.

A final point. It is conventional in economics to treat efficiency, in contrast to equity, as a concept that is relatively unproblematic. If I have done nothing else in this article, I hope I have demonstrated that this relative complacency is misplaced. The interpretation of efficiency is as much a complex and value-laden business as the interpretation of equity, a fact that complicates even more the interpretation of the trade-off between them.

Notes

1. I shall use the terms *equity, fairness,* and *justice* synonymously throughout this article.

2. On the aims of welfare policy, see J. Le Grand and R. Robinson, *The Economics of Social Problems* (London: Macmillan, 1984); and N. Barr, *The Economics of the Welfare State* (London: Weidenfeld & Nicolson, 1987), chaps. 3, 4.

3. The equity status of inequalities in life expectancy is discussed in J. Le Grand, "Three Essays on Equity," Discussion Paper WSP/23 (ST/ICERD Welfare State Programme, London School of Economics, 1987).

4. B. Barry, *Political Argument* (London: Routledge & Kegan Paul, 1965), p. 6. As Barry notes, any reference to the extent to which an objective can be attained clearly contains within it the assumption that movement toward the objective can be measured or quantified in some way. In making this assumption it is not intended necessarily to imply that meaningful numbers can be constructed that represent, e.g., the level of efficiency or equity that characterizes an economy (although even that is not as hopeless a task as it might seem; indicators of both have been constructed). All that is necessary for this discussion is that it is meaningful to say that one outcome is more equitable or more efficient than another, a not unreasonable requirement.

5. Milton Friedman, e.g., gives two examples of the trade-off between equity and liberty that he thinks provokes inconsistent reactions (*Capitalism and Freedom* [Chicago: University of Chicago Press, 1962], p. 165). One is where three individuals are starving and a fourth has food but refuses to give it to them; the other is where four people are walking down the street and one finds a ten-dollar bill in the gutter and refuses to share it with the others. Friedman thinks that a common judgment would be that the three poorer individuals in the first case would be justified in overriding the liberty of the fourth and forcing a more equitable distribution, but that they would not be justified in doing so in the second case, a reaction that he would consider inconsistent. But all the examples show is that people are prepared to trade off more liberty to promote equity if the initial situation is already grossly unfair than if it is already broadly equitable, an outcome that seems to be perfectly reasonable.

6. This definition presumes that there is more than one social objective to be considered. If there is only one (as is arguable in the case, e.g., of utilitarianism) then the definition of an efficient allocation of resources becomes simply that which moves as close as possible to the attainment of the objective.

7. The argument that efficiency can only be defined in terms of wider objectives has an apparent similarity to that made in R. Goodin and P. Wilenski, "Beyond Efficiency: The Logical Underpinnings of Administrative

Principles," *Public Administration Review,* November/December (1984). How-ever, their point is rather different. They argue that efficiency as narrowly conceived by administrators (presumably, something like least resource cost) cannot be justified except by reference to what they term a metaprin-ciple, such as want satisfaction or respecting persons, and that at times pur-suit of the metaprinciple may require overriding the administrator's narrow conception of efficiency. For the latter is simply one among many ways of satisfying the metaprinciple; others include equity, democracy, due proc-ess, etc. But this is saying that equity and (one particular interpretation of) efficiency are objectives of similar status, which may have to be traded off against one another; this is quite different from the argument here, which provides an interpretation of efficiency in terms of the ability to attain any objective or set of objectives.

8. A. Okun, *Equality and Efficiency: The Big Trade-off* (Washington, D.C.: Brookings Institution, 1975).

9. In fact, one suspects that much of the expressed concern over work incen-tives stems not so much from worries over aggregate production but from a perception by politicians and other policymakers of a general reluctance among taxpayers to subsidize laziness—to give money apparently for nothing. In other words, a social security system that apparently encour-ages people not to work is thought to reduce the utility of those paying for it by more than if the payments did not apparently discourage work effort. In that case the supposed trade-off between equity and efficiency becomes a trade-off between increasing the utility of recipients and not reducing the utilities of taxpayers, a trade-off that has meaning, indeed, but one that seems a little way from the rather grander notions of equity versus efficiency.

10. D. Foley, "Resource Allocation and the Public Sector," *Yale Economic Essays* 7 (1975): 45–98; S.-C. Kolm, *Justice et Equité* (Paris: Editions du Centre National de la Recherche Scientifique, 1972); H. Varian, "Equity, Envy and Efficiency," *Journal of Economic Theory* 9 (1974): 63–91; W. Baumol, *Super-fairness: Applications and Theory* (Cambridge, Mass.: MIT Press, 1986).

11. J. Rawls, *A Theory of Justice* (Cambridge, Mass.: Harvard University Press, 1971); J. Habermas, *Legitimation Crisis* (London: Heinemann, 1976); B. Ackerman, *Social Justice in the Liberal State* (New Haven, Conn.: Yale University Press, 1980).

12. To be fair (in a more usual interpretation of the term), some other con-tributors to the literature have expressed moral reservations about this conception of equity: e.g., E. Pazner, "Pitfalls in the Theory of Fairness," *Journal of Economic Theory* 14 (1977): 458–66.

13. E. Pazner and D. Schmeidler, "Egalitarian-Equivalent Allocations: A New Concept of Economic Equity," *Quarterly Journal of Economics* 92 (1978): 1–45.

14. J. R. Hicks, "The Rehabilitation of Consumer Surplus," *Review of Economic Studies* 8 (1940–41): 108–16.

EXPLORING THE ISSUE

Is It Possible to Balance Efficiency and Equity in Public Policy?

Critical Thinking and Reflection

1. What makes a policy efficient? Equitable?
2. Why would we ultimately want policies that are both efficient and equitable? What makes it difficult to achieve this outcome?
3. Why do we worry about values such as efficiency and equity when we are designing public policy? What could happen if we did not?
4. Is public policymaking too complex? What steps could we take to make the process simpler?
5. If policymakers opt to favor one value over another, what are possible long-term effects?

Is There Common Ground?

Determining ways to create policies that are both efficient and equitable has been a difficult task for academics and practitioners for many decades. There are a series of values that Americans seemingly expect public policies to consider and include in their design. Although these values assist in ensuring different outcomes, difficulties arise when the values come into conflict with one another. When we consider efficiency and equality, we find such conflict. If we want efficient policies, we likely cannot aim to be fully equal in our treatment of citizens under such a policy. Consider the issue of airline security. If we want an efficient, equitable policy for screening passengers, it is difficult to think of a way to fully accomplish both. Instead, we need to aim for the most efficient equitable policy.

As a result, perhaps there is a better way to examine the question. We have seen throughout our policy history that we are able to balance different values; yet, we seem less willing to discuss whether all policies need to espouse all values. Perhaps there are policies that merely need to be equitable without concern for efficiency or vice versa. By viewing this question in this way, the debate regarding efficiency and equity becomes a more important topic for government as a whole.

Additional Resources

Bardach, E., *A Practical Guide for Policy Analysis: The Eightfold Path to More Effective Problem Solving* (Washington, DC: CQ Press, 2008)

Bardach's book offers clear instructions for policy managers when attempting to determine which criterion to use for evaluating policies. Since these decisions can ultimately shape the outcome of the analysis, only by understanding the values from the beginning are we able to properly assess the impact of varying public policies.

Blank, Rebecca, M. (2002). Can equity and efficiency complement each other? Adam Smith Lecture, European Association of Labour Economists, September 15, 2001, Jyväsklylä, Finland. Retrieved September 15, 2011, from www.fordschool.umich.edu/research/papers/PDFfiles/02-001.pdf

Blank examines the so-called "leaky bucket" effect that emerges when redistributive transfers increase equity while causing losses in efficiency. She attempts to demonstrate ways that equity and efficiency can be more clearly understood to be aligning with one another.

Durlauf, S.N. (2005). "Racial Profiling As a Public Policy Question: Efficiency, Equity, and Ambiguity." *The American Economic Review* (95, 2): 132–136

Durlauf highlights the role played by conflicting values in shaping racial policies in the United States. By examining racial profiling, we can begin to clearly see how values such as efficiency and equity are important to consider when looking at policy.

Lawrence, M.F. and T. Kornfield (1998). "Transportation Subsidies, Economic Efficiency, Equity, and Public Policy." *Natural Resources Research* (7, 2): 137–142

Lawrence and Kornfield examine the public debate over transportation subsidies from the context of efficiency and equity. The article is useful for students as it looks at the applicability of each value in an actual policy debate.

Weimer, D.L. and A.R. Vining, *Policy Analysis: Concepts and Practice* (New York: Longman, 2010)

Weimer and Vining offer an overview of the policy process and include deep discussions of how efficiency and equity can both be used to measure policy outcomes. By doing so, they demonstrate the complexity of these concepts and suggest ways to incorporate both into determining which policies are most likely to work and why.

ISSUE 5

Do Bureaucrats Have More Influence on Public Policy Than Other Branches of Government Do?

YES: U.S. House of Representatives, from "A Failure of Initiative: Final Report of the Select Bipartisan Committee to Investigate the Preparation for and Response to Hurricane Katrina" (2006)

NO: Douglas J. Amy, from "The Case FOR Bureaucracy," *Government Is Good: An Unapologetic Defense of a Vital Institution* (2007)

Learning Outcomes

After reading this issue, you should be able to:

- Describe the role of bureaucracy in public policymaking.
- Discuss the ability for bureaucrats to alter the written intentions of public policy.
- Gain an understanding of the complex relationships between bureaucrats, legislators, and presidents.
- Define the appropriate level of influence bureaucrats should have on shaping policy.
- Understand the potential ramifications of bureaucratic behavior on policy outcomes.
- Understand how bureaucracy impacted recovery efforts in the wake of Katrina.

ISSUE SUMMARY

YES: The U.S. House of Representatives argues that the Federal Emergency Management Agency was unprepared to respond successfully to the effects of Hurricane Katrina. While acknowledging the difficulties posed by the magnitude of the storm, it becomes clear that the House places more blame on the bureaucrats than the legislators who were largely responsible for funding and monitoring the agency.

NO: Douglas J. Amy argues that the failures of Katrina are more directly related to a lack of financial support from the president and

Congress to assure that bureaucrats are in a position to successfully carry out their assigned tasks. The stereotypes of modern bureaucracy, in his eyes, are undeserved given the effort put forth by today's public servants.

At the constitutional convention, all parties were concerned about ensuring a real separation of powers made possible through a rather elaborate system of checks and balances. The framers worked hard to maintain a real separation between the legislative, executive, and judicial branches. Yet, in the initial framing, our Founding Fathers barely uttered more than a few statements regarding the individuals who would ultimately carry out the actions of government. Even those brief mentions occurred in the context of presidential powers over the administrative state. Our Constitution—as drafted in 1787—was not intended to govern a bureaucratic nation, but that is what it ultimately helped to create. Without bureaucracy or public administration being more explicitly interwoven into the framework of our nation, we have been left to establish its appropriate role and place through basic trial and error over the years. Each branch seemingly has some control over how and when bureaucracy will function, yet the lines are not as clear as they are between Congress, the president, and the Supreme Court. As such, it is not always easy to tell whether bureaucracy has more say over public policy than the three branches.

Before discussing how bureaucracy and public administration impact and influence public policy, it is essential to understand how the other three branches do so. Congress—most clearly—impacts public policy through the writing of laws. This is the most direct influence that any branch possesses. The president—charged with executing the laws passed by Congress—has the ability to refuse policy recommendations via the veto power. Further, executive orders and signing statements can present as policy. Executive orders can take effect without the authorization of Congress and remain on the books until another president chooses to discontinue the order. Signing statements are messages attached to signed legislation by which the president explains to bureaucrats how she or he wishes for parts of the legislation to be interpreted. These tools were relatively unknown to the general public prior to a signing statement President George W. Bush added to the 2005 Detainee Treatment Act. In the statement, Bush alluded to his Commander in Chief power as allowing him to permit the questioned methods of interrogation to continue in the name of national security. Lastly, the Supreme Court impacts policy by declaring laws unconstitutional and adjudicating cases regarding aspects of legislation at varying levels of government.

So how does the power of bureaucracy compare? First, bureaucracy has the power of rulemaking. When Congress passes a law, it can be quite vague. Even the most explicit of bills will have questions regarding implementation that are left to be answered by bureaucratic agencies and employees. Through rulemaking, bureaucrats can help shape the actual effects of policy by taking the vague, nebulous ideas and turning them into concrete policies to be implemented. Further, rulemaking is a fairly democratic mechanism given the increased ability for citizens to comment on proposed rules through online submissions. Although scholars and practitioners will always question if these public comments are seriously considered, it still allows for an essential element of transparency.

Second, while rulemaking gives bureaucrats some power, actual implementation does even more. When a member of Congress proposes a law, they are aware that they will not be individually carrying out the law. Instead, that power falls to what Michael Lipsky originally referred to as street-level bureaucrats. In his eyes, only those individuals who implement policy really have true power. Let us consider some examples. If the state government passes a law that the speed limit is 55 miles per hour on state highways, the assumption is that they intend for anyone going over 55 miles per hour to be subject to being ticketed for their offense. Yet, these state legislators will not be sitting in a car with a radar gun assigning tickets. If a state trooper opts not to pull anyone over who is going less than 65 miles per hour, the policy has been altered based on the discretion of the bureaucrat charged with actually implementing the policy. The example extends beyond safety service individuals. Individuals like welfare case workers, food pantry staff, and those who determine unemployment benefits all hold the power to coach potential clients or bend the rules to assist people against the letter of the policy. Even on your college campus, street-level bureaucrats impact your daily life. The individual writing parking tickets can give you a break and simply not write the ticket. Your instructor can round up the 78.9 to a B− instead of the C+ policy says you deserve. Your resident assistant can bend some mundane policy to allow the dorm to have some more fun. Street-level bureaucrats are everywhere— determining the ultimate meaning of policy.

As we have demonstrated here, bureaucrats and public administrators play a great role in shaping public policy outcomes despite having no defined powers within the governing document in our country. Their informal powers, as a result, are oftentimes forgotten when we think about how an individual legislator's idea eventually becomes a law. It is difficult to pinpoint what branch of government ultimately has the most power. Without Congress, there is nothing to be implemented. Without the president's signature, there are no policies. If the Supreme Court deems a policy unconstitutional, it disappears (at least for a period of time). And if bureaucrats decide to implement policy in a manner different than what is written, they have made an impact. In the readings that follow, we will further examine the question of whether bureaucrats have more impact over policy than other branches. In the YES selection, the report from the U.S. House of Representatives on Hurricane Katrina shows how legislators ultimately blame bureaucracy for what occurred as Katrina ravaged New Orleans and surrounding regions. By placing this blame, the members of the House show the impact public administrators can have. In the rebuttal in the NO selection, Douglas J. Amy argues that a lack of funding from Congress and the president led to bureaucracy being unable to perform its assigned tasks.

A Failure of Initiative: Final Report of the Select Bipartisan Committee to Investigate the Preparation for and Response to Hurricane Katrina

DHS and the States Were Not Prepared for this Catastrophic Event

Summary

It is clear the federal government in general and the Department of Homeland Security (DHS) in particular were not prepared to respond to the catastrophic effects of Hurricane Katrina. There is also evidence, however, that in some respects, FEMA's response was greater than it has ever been, suggesting the truly catastrophic nature of Hurricane Katrina overwhelmed a federal response capability that under less catastrophic circumstances would have succeeded.

Nevertheless, DHS' actual and perceived weaknesses in response to Katrina revived discussion of the value of incorporation of FEMA into DHS. Many experts and Members of Congress debated the policy and operational ramifications of bringing FEMA into DHS during consideration of the Homeland Security Act of 2002 (HSA).

The HSA transferred FEMA functions, personnel, resources, and authorities to the DHS Emergency Preparedness and Response (EP&R) Directorate. The emergency management community has complained since 2003 that FEMA was being systematically dismantled, stripped of authority and resources, and suffering from low morale, in part because of the Department's focus on terrorism. Others have said that FEMA's placement in DHS enabled the Secretary of Homeland Security to augment FEMA's resources with other DHS personnel and assets, all within an integrated command structure.

The cycle of emergency management begins with preparedness and mitigation, flows into response, and ends with recovery. The four cornerstones to comprehensive emergency management—preparedness, response, recovery, and mitigation—are interdependent and all vital to successful emergency management.

U.S. House of Representatives, 2006.

Preparedness encompasses those pre-disaster activities that develop and maintain an ability to respond rapidly and effectively to emergencies and disasters. All levels of government need to be prepared to respond to disasters. International Association of Emergency Managers President Dewayne West described preparedness as "what emergency managers do every day in order to be able to respond." Emergency management officials at different levels of the government expressed concerns that distancing preparedness efforts from response, recovery, and mitigation operations could result in an ineffective and uncoordinated response.

Following Hurricane Katrina, emergency management professionals in the Gulf coast region have questioned whether DHS and state preparedness for catastrophic events has declined over the past years due to organizational changes within DHS and a shift in programmatic priorities. In particular, the decline in preparedness has been seen as a result of the separation of the preparedness function from FEMA, the drain of long-term professional staff along with their institutional knowledge and expertise, and the diminished readiness of FEMA's national emergency response teams.

In the Gulf coast region, emergency managers expressed the view that FEMA's disaster response capabilities had declined since its inclusion in DHS, in part due to subsequent organizational changes within DHS and FEMA. The emergency management community has suggested that FEMA's readiness for a large disaster has declined despite extensive preparedness initiatives within the federal government, pointing to the separation of preparedness functions from response, recovery, and mitigation.

Additionally, the tremendous damage and scale of Hurricane Katrina placed extraordinary demands on the federal response system and exceeded the capabilities and readiness of DHS and FEMA in a number of important areas, particularly in the area of staffing. The response to Hurricane Katrina required large numbers of qualified personnel at a time when FEMA's professional ranks had declined. FEMA response officials in both Mississippi and Louisiana testified that the department's inability to field sufficient numbers of qualified personnel had a major impact on federal response operations. In addition, FEMA had lost, since 2002, a number of its top disaster specialists, senior leaders, and experienced personnel, described as "FEMA brain drain." Many emergency management professionals had predicted this 'drain' would have a negative impact on the federal government's ability to manage disasters of all types.

In addition, emergency management professionals said the degraded readiness of FEMA's national emergency response teams reduced the effectiveness of the federal response to Hurricane Katrina. The diminished readiness of the national emergency response teams has been attributed to a lack of funding for training exercises and equipment. Emergency management professionals note the need for trained people, who have experience working together with their federal colleagues and state counterparts prior to a disaster, as a part of national emergency response teams. Emergency responders should not meet each other for the first time right before or after a major catastrophe. A decline in the readiness of these teams along with appropriate staffing added to an ineffective response.

Finding: While a Majority of State and Local Preparedness Grants Are Required to Have a Terrorism Purpose, This Does Not Preclude a Dual Use Application

The "all hazard" versus "just terrorism" debate plays out in the interpretation of permissible uses for homeland security grant funding and efforts to make equipment purchases and exercise scenarios fit terrorism-related criteria while still being of some general use in day-to-day emergency response. For example, funding to exercise response capabilities for WMD-related scenarios might be used to test evacuation planning and other "all hazard" response functions, with the WMD element little more than pretext.

This concern is evident at the local level. Alabama conducts or participates in approximately 50 training exercises each year ranging from "table top," classroom-like discussions to full scale exercises involving all members of the emergency management community, including federal, state, and local officials. According to Alabama officials, federal DHS funding restrictions dictate that almost all of these exercises involve a terrorism-based threat or scenario, despite the fact that all emergencies largely involve the same set of procedures—evacuations, loss of power, communications difficulties, need for shelter, food, and water, and inter-governmental coordination.

State officials also voiced a concern that in the post-9/11 environment undue emphasis is placed on terrorism-based hazards. Alabama's hazard risk profile includes terrorism, but state emergency management officials believe natural disasters pose a much more likely, perhaps inevitable, risk. Although lately, hurricanes have hit the state with some regularity, Alabama is susceptible to a wide variety of other natural disasters, including earthquakes, tornadoes, floods, and droughts. With nuclear facilities located within the state, Alabama Emergency Management Agency (AEMA) officials are also on alert for nuclear-related emergencies. Special plans and precautions have also been funded to prepare for risks posed by an Army chemical weapons storage and incineration facility.

According to Colonel Terry Ebbert, the Director of Homeland Security & Public Safety for the City of New Orleans, DHS' all hazards focus is unsubstantiated.

> [T]he Office of Domestic Preparedness restricted any use of grant funding for preparing, equipping, training, and exercising to enhance the preparedness of first responders operating in a potential WMD environment. Most allowable expenditures under the UASI program remain closely linked to the WMD threat to the exclusion of many other forms of enhanced readiness.

When Ebbert submitted a request to purchase a number of inexpensive, flat-bottomed, aluminum boats to equip his fire and police departments, with the intent of having them available to rescue people trapped by flooding, the request was denied. Ebbert concluded that the rules on what is permitted and reimbursable are unaltered while the newly stated focus on an "all hazards" approach to preparedness remains "elusive." Ebbert recommended that "existing limitations imposed on the availability of Federal preparedness funding should be broadened."

DHS officials are particularly sensitive to the charge that the agency has stopped state and local governments from purchasing equipment not exclusively suited to terrorism preparedness. Former Office of Domestic Preparedness (ODP) Director Suzanne Mencer stressed the dual use capability of many grants: "The grants don't prohibit a city from buying equipment for use in a natural disaster if it can also be used in a terrorist attack." Mencer said some locals see the WMD wording and think it prohibits items, such as radios, that could also be used in a natural disaster: "They can still meet their needs in almost all instances if they look at the broader picture and not [just] the wording in the grant." When asked about state and local complaints in Alabama and elsewhere, former director of ODP's Preparedness Programs Division, Tim Beres, noted that in fiscal 2004, grants paid for more than $1 billion worth of dual-use equipment, including $925 million for interoperable communications equipment and $140 million in chemical protection suits.

DHS continues to develop and refine its guidelines to states and localities, in accordance with Presidential Directives, which require grants to be used in support of catastrophic events regardless of their cause. Although a July 2005 Government Accountability Office (GAO) report found many state preparedness officials and local first responders believed DHS planners focused excessively on anti-terrorism criteria in their grant, training, and exercise programs, the auditors concluded that 30 of the 36 essential capabilities first responders need to fulfill the critical tasks generated by the department's 15 catastrophic emergency planning scenarios would apply to both terrorist and non-terrorist incidents. The GAO auditors concluded that DHS planning supported an all hazards approach. Indeed, according to GAO auditors, in response to state and local complaints that DHS required too much emphasis on terrorism-related activities, DHS increasingly promoted flexibility to allow greater dual usage within the grant program requirements for fiscal year 2005.

DHS' growing dual use flexibility is reflected in its most recent grant guidelines. Specifically, the FY2006 guidance points out the numerous dual-use target capabilities (identified in the National Preparedness Goal) to be attained through DHS grant funding. The guidance further states:

> [f]unding remains primarily focused on enhancing capabilities to prevent, protect against, respond to, or recover from CBRNE [Chemical, Biological, Radiological, Nuclear and Conventional Explosives], agriculture, and cyber terrorism incidents. However, in light of several major new national planning priorities, which address such issues as pandemic influenza and the aftermath of Hurricane Katrina, the allowable scope of SHSP [State Homeland Security Program] activities include catastrophic events, provided that these activities also build capabilities that relate to terrorism.

Finding: Despite Extensive Preparedness Initiatives, DHS Was Not Prepared to Respond to the Catastrophic Effects of Hurricane Katrina

As a result of various changes within DHS and FEMA, the emergency management community suggested FEMA's preparedness and readiness for a large disaster would decline despite extensive preparedness initiatives within the federal government. For example, during an April 2005 House Subcommittee hearing on DHS preparedness efforts, Dave Liebersbach, then President of the National Emergency Management Association (NEMA), expressed his fear that DHS' de-emphasis of hazards other than terrorism would result in FEMA's inability to respond to a major disaster:

> My concern is we are not going to be able to maintain [capabilities]. I honestly believe . . . that if the hurricane scenario of September 2004 that occurred in the Southeastern U.S., [happens] five years from now, we will fail the way we are going, because the success of that response, of that hurricane season, was based on the programs that had come before . . . . As we are moving forward, that legacy is going to drop if we don't pay attention to dealing with that.

Similar issues were raised during the establishment of the department by various first responder professional associations and think tanks, Members of Congress from both political parties, the Government Accountability Office, and the Congressional Research Service.

One of the primary reasons for creating FEMA in 1979 was to closely link preparedness, response, and mitigation within one organization. During consideration of the Homeland Security Act in 2002, the President proposed that all terrorism preparedness functions be consolidated into FEMA's Office of National Preparedness and be managed within the Emergency Preparedness and Response Directorate (EP&R) of the proposed department.

The intention was to provide a one-stop shop for state and local governments and achieve a unified approach to disaster response. Instead Congress opted to split preparedness functions between the Office of Domestic Preparedness (ODP), which was to be transferred to DHS from the Justice Department, and EP&R (or FEMA). The goal was to place terrorism preparedness in an organization, ODP, with a strong law enforcement background and relationship with that community.

In late 2003, the debate over the need for a one-stop shop for first responder grants and to unite preparedness with the other functions of comprehensive emergency management continued. When DHS Secretary Tom Ridge proposed to transfer most state and local grant programs to ODP, the emergency management community again cautioned the capabilities of state and local governments and FEMA to respond to all disasters would suffer. Ridge and his aides "believed FEMA should be a response and recovery agency, not a preparedness agency. In an age of terrorism, they argued, preparedness needed a law enforcement component, to prevent and protect as well as get ready to respond."

The proposal prompted then FEMA Director Michael Brown to urge Ridge not to further distance preparedness from response as it "can result in an ineffective and uncoordinated response . . . [would] shatter agency morale and would completely disconnect the Department's response functions from the responders and governments they are supposed to support." Brown was overruled and the programs were transferred to ODP, which was then incorporated into the newly created Office of State and Local Government Coordination and Preparedness (SLGCP).

The controversy over how to manage disaster preparedness increased with incoming Secretary Michael Chertoff's Second Stage Review. Chertoff argued the federal government's preparedness efforts needed to be enhanced, particularly for catastrophic disasters, and that could be best achieved by consolidating the department's preparedness functions into a new Preparedness Directorate. In a letter opposing the move, NEMA criticized the department's "total lack of focus on natural-hazards preparedness" and argued that separating preparedness from response and recovery would break emergency management's cycle of continuous improvement and result in disjointed and ineffective response operations.

While Brown agreed with the need to increase catastrophic planning (FEMA had originally proposed the catastrophic preparedness program that funded the Hurricane Pam process), he strongly disagreed with Chertoff's recommended solution of removing FEMA's remaining preparedness functions and transferring them to ODP, which would then be elevated to a Preparedness Directorate. Instead, Brown drafted a 13-page memo to Chertoff urging the consolidation of all preparedness functions into the Emergency Preparedness & Response Directorate, as originally proposed by President Bush, in order to "ensure that capabilities and procedures trained will be identical to the capabilities and procedures actually applied during a real event." As Brown described it, "These recent organizational changes [the transfer of several FEMA preparedness programs to ODP in Secretary Tom Ridge's reorganization plan of September 2003] have divided what was intended to be one, all-hazards preparedness mission into two artificially separate preparedness categories of terrorism and natural disasters."

Some experts do, however, endorse the consolidation of preparedness efforts. Last December, the Center for Strategic and International Studies and the Heritage Foundation released a joint study called "DHS 2.0," in which the authors suggested adding a new undersecretary for preparedness with direct access to the secretary. Such a move, they said, would speed preparedness decisions past layers of bureaucracy. And in a September 1, 2005 *Washington Post* article, at the height of the Katrina response effort, Paul C. Light, an authority on government operations at New York University, also endorsed Chertoff's proposed reforms.

In a December 7, 2005 report entitled "The Truth About FEMA: Analysis and Proposals," Heritage Foundation homeland security expert James Carafano and the Hudson Institute's Richard Weitz argued that Chertoff's proposed reorganization would address many of the shortfalls created by placing FEMA within DHS. At the same time, they said it would preserve the advantages of having most major federal disaster-related preparedness and response activities, for both man-made and natural disasters, concentrated in one department. The authors pointed out that in the event of large-scale disasters, FEMA could be reinforced by other assets from within DHS."

In testimony before the Select Committee, Chertoff explained his rationale for integrating the Department's existing preparedness efforts in to a single directorate for Preparedness:

> Preparedness is not just about response and recovery—rather, it must draw on the full spectrum—from prevention through protection to response. Our preparedness directorate will rely on the expertise of FEMA, but it will also integrate the experience of the Coast Guard, our Infrastructure Protection division, our intelligence units, and our other operational assets . . . FEMA will become a direct report to the Secretary, allowing it to focus on response and recovery while partnering with the new preparedness directorate to increase our overall capabilities . . . FEMA must also continue to function as an all-hazards agency, leveraging entities within the preparedness directorate, including Infrastructure Protection, the Office of Domestic Preparedness, and State and Local Government Coordination.

Although many in the emergency management community opposed Chertoff's preparedness consolidation, many first responder groups support it. For example, in a press release issued immediately following the release of Chertoff's Second Stage Review, the International Association of Fire Chiefs applauded the proposal, particularly the creation of a Preparedness Directorate.

Finding: DHS and FEMA Lacked Adequate Trained and Experienced Staff for the Katrina Response

Brown's memorandum also identified budget cuts and organizational changes he believed were harming FEMA's ability to perform its statutory responsibility of leading the federal government's response to all disasters, including terrorist attacks. For example, Brown claimed FEMA's operational budget baseline (for non-Stafford Act disaster funding) had been permanently reduced by 14.8 percent since joining DHS in 2003. In addition to the permanent baseline reduction, he claimed FEMA lost $80 million and $90 million in fiscal years 2003 and 2004 respectively from its operating budget. Brown argued these budget reductions were preventing FEMA officials from maintaining adequate levels of trained and ready staff.

Brown also said FEMA no longer managed numerous functions that were essential to meeting its statutory responsibilities, and therefore did not have the tools to successfully accomplish its mission. For example, the National Response Plan is a fundamental element of coordinating the federal government's response to disasters. Given FEMA's response mission, the Homeland

Security Act of 2002 specifically assigned FEMA responsibility for "consolidating existing Federal Government emergency response plans into a single, coordinated national response plan." However, instead of assigning this function to the organization responsible for executing the plan during a disaster (i.e. FEMA), the department initially assigned it to the Transportation Security Administration, which then relied on an outside contractor.

When some in the first responder community reacted negatively to the contractor's draft plan, the department transferred the NRP's development to another area of the department, the Integration Staff within the Secretary's office. The resulting plan made a number of departures from the existing Federal Response Plan, including the introduction of the Incident of National Significance (INS), the Principal Federal Official (PFO), the Interagency Incident Management Group (IIMG), the Homeland Security Operations Center (HSOC), and the Catastrophic Incident Annex (NRP-CIA). The emergency management community expressed concerns about each of these newly created structures, which ultimately proved problematic or experienced difficulties achieving their intended purposes during the response to Hurricane Katrina.

Brown also identified what he believed were the most important goals for achieving FEMA's mission of leading the federal government's response to disasters. Several of the issues he identified for improvement proved to be critical problem areas in the Katrina response. The requirements he identified in March 2005 included the following:

1. Improve logistics capability and asset visibility.
2. Implement a comprehensive and integrated multi-year catastrophic planning strategy.
3. Establish a National Incident Management System Integration Center to improve command and control capabilities at the federal, state, and local levels.
4. Recruit, train, credential, deploy and retain a disaster workforce with the appropriate skill mix and management structure to support the operational requirements of all disaster related functions.
5. Ensure appropriate numbers, skills, and grades of employees to support current and long-term mission needs.

Senior DHS and Office of Management and Budget officials vigorously dispute the claim that FEMA's budget has been cut at all. They argue that any transfers from the FEMA budget reflect the transfer of functions carried out by DHS for FEMA, start up costs of the Department, and the use of unobligated funds. According to Andrew Maner, Chief Financial Officer for DHS, the core of the budget adjustments cannot be classified as permanent reductions to FEMA's base budget, as Brown claims. For example, Maner said the transfer of $30.6 million was a transfer of unobligated balances from the 2002 Olympic Games to help fund the start-up of the new Department. The transfer of such unobligated balances was authorized by Congress in H.J. Res. 124, which became law on November 23, 2002 (P.L. 107–294), to pay for "the salaries and expenses associated with the initiation of the Department." Also, Maner noted the $28 million transfer to ODP reflects efforts to complete the transfer of funds accompanying former FEMA functions that have been assumed by other DHS entities.

Regardless of the impact, if any, of these budget adjustments on FEMA capabilities, the tremendous damage and scale of Hurricane Katrina placed extraordinary demands on the federal response system and exceeded the capabilities and readiness of DHS and FEMA in a number of important areas, including staffing. Hurricane Katrina consisted of three separate major disaster declarations, three separate statewide field operations, two directly-affected FEMA regional operations, and the full activation of national level resources such as the National Response Coordination Center (NRCC), the HSOC, and the IIMG. In addition, most FEMA regional offices were actively supporting Katrina operations or assisting their regions receive Gulf Coast evacuees. These operations required large numbers of qualified personnel from what had become a relatively small agency of approximately 2,500 positions.

FEMA response officials in both Mississippi and Louisiana testified that the department's inability to field sufficient numbers of qualified person-nel had a major impact on federal response operations. The Federal Coor-dinating Officer (FCO) in Mississippi, Bill Carwile, described how managing the personnel shortfall was perhaps his most difficult challenge. While he was able to deploy division supervisors to the coastal counties, he needed similar qualified employees for the devastated cities of Gulfport, Biloxi, and Pascagoula. Ultimately, FEMA officials turned to federal agencies like the U.S. Forest Service and city firefighters from across the country to staff FEMA positions in the state.

Despite those measures, Carwile stated, "We never had sufficient person-nel to meet requirements." According to Scott Wells, Deputy FCO for Louisiana, a 90-person FEMA regional office "is woefully inadequate" to perform its two primary disaster functions, operating a regional response coordination center and deploying people to staff emergency response teams in the field. "You cannot do both. Pick one," he said. Wells added, "We had enough staff for our advance team to do maybe half of what we needed to do for a day shift. . . . We did not have the people. We did not have the expertise. We did not have the operational training folks that we needed to do our mission."

In addition to having an inadequate number of qualified personnel, FEMA had lost a number of its top disaster specialists, senior leaders, and most experienced personnel. Both critics and supporters of FEMA's merger with DHS have acknowledged "FEMA brain drain" in recent years and its negative impact on the federal government's ability to manage disasters of all types. Since 2003, for example, the three directors of FEMA's preparedness, response, and recovery divisions had left the agency, and departures and retirements thinned FEMA's ranks of experienced professionals. At the time Hurricane Katrina struck, FEMA had about 500 vacancies and eight out of its ten regional directors were working in an acting capacity.

At least two factors account for FEMA's loss of seasoned veterans. First, like other government agencies, many of FEMA's long-term professionals are reaching retirement age. And second, job satisfaction was second to last in

2005, according to the Partnership for Public Service, a nonprofit group that promotes careers in federal government. Regardless of the reasons for the exodus, Brown and senior DHS officials were unable to maintain their ranks of disaster professionals, through employee retention, development, or recruitment, and this failure hindered the response to Hurricane Katrina.

The disastrous effect of this manpower shortage was compounded in Hurricane Katrina by the difficulty of getting federal workers where they needed to be because of security concerns. In Louisiana, media reports and rumors of violence and general lawlessness delayed the deployment and placement of federal response workers. The Governor's Chief of Staff Andy Kopplin said there were approximately 1,000 FEMA employees deployed and on their way to New Orleans Wednesday, August 31, 2005, many of whom turned back due to security concerns.

Finding: The Readiness of FEMA's National Emergency Response Teams Was Inadequate and Reduced the Effectiveness of the Federal Response

One of the most critical links in the federal response system is the team of FEMA personnel that deploys to a disaster site to establish a unified command with state officials and directs federal operations. These national emergency response teams are the conduits through which federal disaster assistance is requested by and delivered to a state. They are intended to be on call and deploy at a moment's notice, since many disasters provide no advance warning. In prior years, according to Carwile, "We were then able to build a team to about 125 individuals, hand picked, from around the country, and we were able to routinely exercise that team because we had the funding in place to do so on the plan, against several scenarios." The team had a robust operational plan, was sent to the Winter Olympics in Salt Lake City, and received dedicated satellite communications equipment. It appeared to be a well-equipped, well-trained team at a high state of readiness.

Carwile testified that by 2004, the readiness of FEMA's emergency response teams had plummeted dramatically. Funding for the teams dried up after 2002. They lost their dedicated communications equipment. Teams were split up into ever smaller units. Team training and exercises ceased.

In a June 30, 2004 memorandum, FEMA's top disaster response operators, the cadre of Federal Coordinating Officers, warned then FEMA Director Brown that the national emergency response teams were unprepared because no funding was available for training exercises or equipment. In a few short years, FEMA's emergency response teams had been reduced to names on a roster. It appears no actions were taken to address the problems identified in the memorandum.

Asked whether or not implementing the recommendations would have made a difference in Katrina, Carwile responded, "I felt very fortunate because many of my colleagues with me in Mississippi had been with me on a national team in years past. It was kind of coincidental . . . but I can't help but believe that trained and ready teams, people who have worked together, would not have made some difference in a positive way." Wells described the situation in Louisiana in this way: "We need to really train together as a team. We need to work as a team. What you have with this National Response Plan in the field is we have no unity of command."

The requirement for trained people, who have experience working together with their federal colleagues and their state counterparts, is a constant theme of federal, state, and local emergency professionals. Numerous officials and operators, from state and FEMA directors to local emergency managers told the same story: if members of the state and federal emergency response teams are meeting one another for the first time at the operations center, then you should not expect a well-coordinated response.

Conclusion

For years emergency management professionals have been warning that FEMA's preparedness has eroded. Many believe this erosion is a result of the separation of the preparedness function from FEMA, the drain of long-term professional staff along with their institutional knowledge and expertise, and the inadequate readiness of FEMA's national emergency response teams. The combination of these staffing, training, and organizational structures made FEMA's inadequate performance in the face of a disaster the size of Katrina all but inevitable.

Douglas J. Amy

NO

The Case FOR Bureaucracy

Most criticisms of government bureaucracy are based more on myth than reality. These agencies actually play a valuable and indispensable role in making our society a better place to live.

We all know the case *against* bureaucracy. Just say the word to yourself and consider the images it evokes. Massive waste. Inefficiency. Poor service. Ever-growing organizations. Mindless rules. Reams of useless forms. The term "bureaucrat" also comes loaded with a whole host of negative connotations: lazy, hostile, overpaid, imperious, and inflexible. In short, bureaucracy and bureaucrats are unmitigated bad things—with absolutely no redeeming qualities.

Conservatives like to play on this popular prejudice by constantly equating government with bureaucracy. The comments of Charlton Heston are typical: "Of course, government is the problem. The armies of bureaucrats proliferating like gerbils, scurrying like lemmings in pursuit of the ever-expanding federal agenda testify to that amply." Once government is thought of as "bureaucracy," the case for reducing it becomes obvious. Who could complain if Republicans want to reduce these "armies of bureaucrats"? Everyone knows that we would all be better off with less bureaucracy and fewer bureaucrats in our lives. So when conservatives want to make shrinking government sound attractive, they say they are cutting "bureaucracy"—not "programs." Most people value government programs—especially in the areas of education, health and the environment—and do not want to see them reduced; but everyone hates bureaucracy. Using the term "bureaucracy" in this way is a rhetorical sleight-of-hand that obscures the real costs of cutting back on government programs.

But while disparaging and attacking government bureaucracy has become a very effective tactic for anti-government activists, it is based more on mythology than reality. Much of what we think is wrong with bureaucracy—and what conservatives keep telling us—is highly exaggerated and often simply mistaken. This article takes a careful look at bureaucracy and finds that there is little evidence to support most of the common criticisms of these administrative agencies. Studies show that bureaucracy and bureaucrats are not nearly as bad as we usually think they are. We will also consider the case *for* bureaucracy—that these much-maligned organizations and the public servants that work in them are actually playing many valuable and indispensable roles in our society. Many of the significant achievements of modern democratic government would in fact not be possible without the large bureaucracies that oversee and implement them. It turns out that government bureaucracies are actually good.

Myth No. 1: Bureaucracies Are Immensely Wasteful

A few years ago, local officials in my town were holding a public meeting to promote a referendum that would raise taxes to pay for vital city services. A man in the audience rose to object to the tax increase, arguing that instead the city should first get rid of all the waste in the city bureaucracy. The mayor explained that after years of cutbacks in city government, there really was no "fat" left to cut from the budget, and then asked the man what specific cuts he was suggesting. The man said that he didn't know much about the city budget, but that he "knew" that there "had to be" some waste that could be cut out instead of raising taxes.

Such is the strength of the notion that government bureaucracies are inherently wasteful. Even if we don't know much about government, we are absolutely certain that government agencies are wasteful. In fact, waste is the number one citizen complaint about government—and bureaucracy usually takes most of the blame for this. Seventy percent of Americans agree that when something is run by government, it is usually wasteful and inefficient. And conservatives never tire of taking advantage of this view to lambaste the government. As two conservative economists have explained: "As every tax-payer knows, government is wasteful and inefficient; it always has been and always will be." Cutting bureaucratic waste has become a constant theme of conservatives, and it has become a major rationale for cutting taxes. They argue that we can have the best of both worlds: we can reduce taxes and also not cut back on needed government programs. How? By simply cutting out all the "fat" in government.

In the public's view, government agencies are not only wasteful, they are *enormously* wasteful. Surveys reveal that Americans believe that 48 cents of every tax dollar going to bureaucracies like the Social Security Administration are wasted. Yet investigations by the Government Accounting Office and various blue-ribbon commissions have found that waste amounts to only a small fraction of that figure. Al Gore's National Performance Review, conducted when he was vice-president, examined the federal bureaucracy in great detail and discovered that waste consisted of less than two cents of every tax dollar. Of course we should be ever vigilant about waste and try to eliminate it wherever we can find it, but it seems clear that the extent of this problem is being highly exaggerated by conservative critics of government. As one set of scholars who examined a wide variety of the studies on government waste concluded: "There is . . . little evidence to support the widespread impression that government inefficiency squanders huge amounts of money."

People tend to think there is a large amount of waste in government in part because of the loose way this term is used. For instance, some conservative critics of government count as waste those programs they simply don't like—such as the Legal Services Corporation, the National Endowment for the Arts, Americorp, and subsidies for public television. But to use the term "waste" in this way makes it entirely a political judgment and renders it essentially meaningless. Normally the term "government waste" refers to the inefficient use of funds because of overstaffing, poor productivity, etc. But conservatives are not opposed to the National Endowment for the Arts because that agency is inefficient; they oppose it on ideological grounds. They wouldn't support the NEA no matter how "lean and mean" it was. It is a misleading, then, to use the term "waste" in this way.

Another problem is that critics of bureaucracy often lump together "fraud" and "abuse" with "waste" to come up with high figures for government losses. But does it really make sense to blame government when doctors defraud the Medicare program, criminals scam the food stamp system, or private contractors cheat the Pentagon? We usually don't consider it the fault of business that they lose over $15 billion a year to employee theft and $10 billion to shoplifting. Most people blame the thieves for these losses and few consider these thefts to be an indication of something inherently wrong with capitalism. Similarly, it is unfair to consider the problems of fraud and abuse of government programs to be a product of inherently "wasteful" bureaucracies. Naturally, government should do everything it can to reduce these losses, but we should not be blaming the victim.

Myth No. 2: Business Is Always Better Than Bureaucracy

Another of the more persistent myths about bureaucracy is that "business is better"—that businesses are always more efficient than government efforts. Since government bureaucracies don't have to produce a profit and they are not subject to market competition, it is argued, they have much less incentive to be cost-efficient in their management and delivery of services. The assumed superiority of business has become so commonsensical that it is hardly ever questioned at all. This notion has also become an important argument for conservatives in their effort to reduce government and to privatize many of its functions. But are public agencies always less efficient than businesses? A careful look at this issue casts doubt on this common belief.

There have been many empirical studies examining the efficiency of government bureaucracies versus business in a variety of areas, including refuse collection, electrical utilities, public transportation, water supply systems, and hospital administration. The findings have been mixed. Some studies of electric utilities have found that publicly owned ones were more efficient and charged lower prices than privately owned utilities. Several other studies found the opposite, and yet others found no significant differences. Studies of other services produced similar kinds of mixed results. Charles Goodsell is a professor of Public Administration and Public Affairs at Virginia Polytechnic Institute and State University who has spent much of his life studying bureaucracy. After examining these efficiency studies, he concluded: "In short, there is much evidence that is ambivalent. The assumption that business always does better than government is not upheld. . . . When you add up all these study results, the basis for the mantra that business is always better evaporates."

Further evidence that business is not always superior to government bureaucracy can be found in the area of health care. This is a critical issue today and it is well worth examining in some detail the question of whether market-based health care is superior to government run programs. Conservatives constantly warn us that adopting "socialized" medicine would put health care in the hands of government bureaucracies, which would be a recipe for incredible waste and inferior care. But is this really the case? We can answer this question by comparing the performance of public versus private health care systems. Every other developed country has some form of universal health care with a substantial amount of public funding and administration. In contrast, while the U.S. has a few programs like Medicare and Medicaid, most of our health care system is privately funded and administered. According to conservative mythology, this market-based system should produce better health care and do so more cheaply. But neither of these claims hold up when we look at studies of the actual performance of public and private approaches to providing health care.

First, studies have found that the U.S. health care system is by far the most expensive in the world. We spend 13.6% of our gross domestic product on health care—the highest in the world. The average for the other 13 industrialized countries in the OECD is 8.2%. We also rank number one in terms of health care expenditures per capita, with U.S. spending $4,090 a year for every citizen. The highest figures for other industrialized nations are $2,547 per year for Switzerland, $2,339 for Germany, $2,340 for Luxembourg, and $2,095 for Canada. But while we clearly have the most expensive health care system in the world, it does not always deliver the best health care nor does it provide health care in the most efficient way.

Research has shown that the U.S. ranks poorly compared to many other countries in terms of some common measures of health. For example, we rank 26th among industrialized countries for infant mortality rates. We also do much less well in terms of life expectancy. In one typical study, the World Health Organizations (WHO) looked at "disability adjusted life expectancy"— the number of years that one can expect to lead a healthy life. The U.S. came in a disappointing 24th on this measure. As one WHO official concluded: "The position of the United States is one of the major surprises of the new rating system. . . . Basically, you die earlier and spend more time disabled if you're an American rather than a member of most other advanced countries." Moreover, an article in the *Journal of the American Medical Association* in 2000 noted with concern the results of a comprehensive study that compared how 13 industrialized nations were ranked on 16 different measures of health. The U.S. ranked an average of 12th—second to last.

Why do Americans spend so much on health care but not get superior care? There are several reasons. One is that doctors tend to make more in the U.S. than in other countries, and another is that governments in other countries negotiate better deals with pharmaceutical companies on drug prices. But the other major reason is that our private, multi-payer system is much less efficient than the public single-payer systems in other countries. Consider this: the *New England Journal of Medicine* estimates that administrative costs take 31 cents out of every health care dollar in the U.S., compared to only 17 cents in Canada. Why is this the case? Private insurance companies spend much more on paperwork and administrative overhead. The sheer number of people that are working in these private insurance bureaucracies far outstrips those required in government-funded programs. In Massachusetts alone, Blue Cross/Blue Shield employs 6,682 workers to cover 2.7 million subscribers. This is more people than work in *all* of Canada's provincial health care plans, which cover over 25 million people. Why do insurance companies need so many workers? One reason, as Paul Krugman explains, is that millions of health insurance personnel in the U.S. are employed not to help deliver health care at all, but to try to get someone else to pay the bills instead of their company.

Another source of administrative inefficiency in our private multi-payer health care system is the enormous amount of overlap between companies. Each insurance company must maintain its own records and develop its own billing processes. This is much more expensive than using a single government administrative structure. Moreover, our multi-payer system drives up the administrative costs for doctors and hospitals. They must deal with dozens of different insurance plans, each with their own coverage, payment rules, etc. We then need to add to all of this excessive overhead the need for private insurers to make a profit—something that government needn't do. This makes our private system become more expensive. It has been estimated that higher overhead and the need for profit together add from 15% to 25% to the costs of private insurance plans, while the overhead for the government-run Medicare program is a mere 3%. Given all this, it should not come as a shock to find that a 2004 study by researchers at Harvard Medical School and Public Citizen concluded that the U.S. could save up to $286 billion a year on paperwork if we switched to a single-payer, national health insurance program. This money saved from eliminating the private health care bureaucracy would be more than enough to offset the costs of extending coverage to the millions of Americans who now have no health insurance at all. (Unfortunately, this single-payer plan was blocked by Republicans and conservative Democrats in the 2010 health care reform bill.)

To sum up, government-funded universal health care plans provide better care to more people at a lower cost. This one example by itself should be enough to explode the myth that business and privatization are always better than government bureaucracy in providing vital services to the public.

Myth No. 3: We Want the Government to Act Like a Business

The astronaut John Glenn tells a story about his first trip into space. As he sat in the capsule, waiting nervously on the launching pad, he couldn't stop thinking about the fact that NASA had given the contract for the rocket to the lowest bidder. This raises another important point about government bureaucracies: we don't always want them to act like businesses. Conservatives are constantly saying that we would all be better off if government were run like a business. But would we? Businesses are obsessed with their bottom lines and are always looking for the cheapest way to make a product or deliver a service. But in many cases, we don't want government services to be as cheap as possible. Often, with government, the main concern is the quality of the service, not its costs. For example, do we really want to spend the least amount of money possible on our air traffic control system? Obviously not—the main goal should be maximizing the safety of the aviation system. Also, do we want the cheapest possible workforce in charge of security at our airports? Again, of course not—and this point was even acknowledged by Republicans when they agreed to abandon private security companies in favor of a federalized system in the wake of the 9/11 tragedy. Private security had certainly cost less, but it is clearly better to have a federal program that spends more money on training personnel and pays higher salaries to attract employees who are more capable.

Similarly, we don't really want the cheapest system for dispensing justice in our society. We could certainly save a lot on court costs if we didn't pay for lawyers for those who can't afford them and if we got rid of jury trials and lengthy appeal processes. But this would undermine the main goal of providing justice. The point here is clear: unlike businesses, public agencies are not just concerned with the bottom line. We expect our government organizations to pursue a wide variety of important goals, and often cost is not the most important consideration. In this sense, it is unfair to expect many government bureaucracies to be as cheap to run as businesses.

Myth No. 4: Bureaucracy Is a Major Cause of Government Growth

Conservatives also like to charge that bureaucracy is one of the main causes of government growth. They argue that government bureaucracies have an inherent tendency to expand. The reason is this: agency officials bent on their own career advancement are always pushing to increase their power and their budgets. Thus, bureaucracies—like cancer—inevitably become ever-growing entities with ever-increasing destructive effects. Bureaucracies are constantly eating up more tax-payer dollars and imposing more and more rules on American citizens.

This criticism of bureaucracy seems plausible, but is it really true? The evidence suggests that it is not. Consider, for example, the assumption that we are plagued by an ever-growing federal bureaucracy. Figures show that federal agencies have not been growing at an alarming rate. If we go back to 1970, we find that 2,997,000 civilians worked for the federal government at that time. By 2009, that figure had actually gone down—to 2,804,000. So much for the constantly expanding federal bureaucracy.

Second, it is not clear at all that bureaucrats are always seeking to expand their agencies and their budgets. This budget-maximizing thesis was directly contradicted by a study conducted by Julie Dolan. She compared the views of members of the federal senior civil service to those of the general public when it came to whether we should be spending more or less in a wide variety of policy areas, including education, healthcare, defense, welfare, environment, college financial aid, AIDS research, homelessness, etc. She found that in most areas the public was willing to support increased spending much more than the agency administrators. And in most cases, a majority of these administrators did not support increased budgets. This was due, she believed, to administrators having a more realistic and sophisticated knowledge of these issues and programs. Her conclusion: "In sum, the budget-*minimizing* tendencies of federal administrators reported here suggest that self-interest is not as powerful a motivator as previously believed, and they suggest we should revise our theories about self-interested bureaucrats inflating government budgets for their own gain."

Another theory of bureaucratic expansion suggests that the government grows because once an administrative agency is established, it will stick around even when its program is no longer needed. In short, the bureaucracy never shrinks, it only grows. However, studies have shown that the conservatives are just plain wrong when they claim that outmoded programs are rarely purged from government. Robert Stein and Kenneth Bikers completed a study in which they examined the number of federal programs that were eliminated between 1971 and 1990. During that twenty-year span, an average of thirty-six federal programs were terminated each year. A pretty amazing figure. The commonly held notion that bureaucracies never die is clearly false.

The Real Causes of Government Growth

Ironically, during the last several decades, as right-wing complaints about ever-increasing government have escalated, little growth has actually occurred in the federal government. However, if we look back over a longer historical period, say to the early 1900s, there is no denying that the size and scope of the federal and state governments have grown considerably. Our governments have much greater responsibilities in regulating corporations and the economic system, and we have many more programs in areas like health care, education, and the environment. But the question is whether this kind of historical growth in government has been caused by the inherent tendency of bureaucracies to expand. The answer is no. As one political scientist, Max Neiman, who studied this question extensively, has concluded, "Bureaucratic imperialism, by which public agencies generate an autonomous force for government growth, seems fairly insignificant as a cause of growing government size." But if this is true, what has driven the historical expansion of government in the United States?

One important clue can be found by identifying those periods in which government has expanded the most. For example, 70% of the growth in federal regulatory agencies occurred during three decades, the 1930s, the 1960s, and the 1970s. What these decades have in common is that they were times of enormous economic and social upheaval and increased political activism. In other words, *government responsibilities increased because the public demand for social programs and economic regulation increased.* During those eras, mass-based social movements—including the labor movement, the civil rights movement, and the environmental movement—insisted that the government address a wide variety of pressing social and economic problems.

We have big government today primarily because citizens have realized that large-scale public programs are necessary to solve big problems—economic depressions, an elderly population mired in poverty, widespread racism, growing environmental degradation, a health care crisis, etc. As Nieman has concluded, "A substantial source of growth in government activity in democratic societies is driven . . . by citizens and other groups using government to improve their life-chances." So it makes little sense to argue that growth in government has been something forced onto the American people by power-hungry bureaucrats. Government has grown mainly because we have wanted it to grow—something conservatives seem unable to admit. Growth in government is primarily a product of democracy at work, and so it should be something that is celebrated, not condemned.

Myth No. 5: Bureaucracies Usually Provide Poor Service

Yet another common criticism of government bureaucracies is that they routinely provide very poor service to the public. Unlike businesses, where the rule is "the customer is always right," public agencies seemed to adhere to the rule that "it's my way or the highway." Many people have stories of at least one frustrating encounter with a government worker where they received rude or inadequate service.

But how frequent are these bad experiences? How widespread is dissatisfaction with government workers and the services they provide? Studies show that negative experiences are not nearly as common as many think and that most people's encounters with government workers actually turn out well. For example, when a survey was done in Virginia about the quality of the services provided by local government workers, the results were surprisingly positive. Over 80 percent of citizens said that the services they receive from the fire department, EMS service, police department, public library, and parks and recreation were either "excellent" or "good." An average of a mere 2.7 percent of citizens rated these public services as "poor." Pretty impressive figures for any organization.

Perhaps more surprisingly, surveys show high citizen evaluations for most large *federal* agencies as well. The Pew Research Center conducted a survey in 2000 of citizens and businesspeople who used the services of the Social Security Administration, the Environmental Protection Agency, the Food and Drug Administration, the Internal Revenue Service, and the Federal Aviation Administration. Predictably, only 47.6 percent had a favorable view of the IRS. But 84.5 percent had favorable views of the FDA. For the Social Security Administration that figure was 72.0; for the FAA, 69.3; and for the EPA, 68.0. What makes these strong favorable ratings all the more impressive is that they include the views of people from businesses being regulated by these agencies—respondents who are going to naturally feel some hostility toward these bureaucracies.

Of course, to really evaluate the quality of services being provided by public sector bureaucracies, we need to compare them to services provided by the private sector. Such a study was done by Theodore Poister and Gary Henry, who conducted a survey of citizen satisfaction with both public and private services in Georgia. They compared satisfaction with public services like the police, public health clinics and trash collection, to that of private doctor's offices, fast-good restaurants, banks, etc. As they explained their findings: "Given the conventional wisdom about the poor quality of services provided by government and the general superiority of the private sector in delivering services, the private services included in this survey might have been expected to receive consistently higher ratings than the public services. But this was clearly not the case." . . . Both public and private service providers received consistently high scores from people who had recently used their services. On a scale of 0–100, the public agencies averaged a score of 73.5 for customer satisfaction, while the private businesses averaged 73.9—a negligible difference. Clearly, people's actual experiences and evaluations of public agencies runs directly contrary to the negative stereotype that government organizations consistently provide inferior service to that available in the private sector.

This is not to suggest that people don't sometimes have bad encounters with government bureaucracies—we all have. The point here is that these encounters are not the rule, and we usually get pretty good service from our public agencies. It is also worth keeping in mind that bad encounters with bureaucrats are not limited to the public sector. Who hasn't had a horrible time trying to get approval for a drug or a medical procedure from the rigid bureaucrats in private health insurance companies? And who hasn't wandered through seemingly endless phone trees and spent hours on hold just trying to get some technical help from large computer and software companies? Instances of poor service are hardly confined to government bureaucracies. . . .

Bureaucracy Is Good

So far, we've seen that government bureaucracies are not nearly as bad as conservative critics and popular mythology make them out to be. However, there is a much more *positive* case that can be made here—the case for bureaucracies actually being a good thing. It is not a difficult case to make. It begins with a simple fact: the modern state as we know it cannot exist without large bureaucratic agencies to implement its programs. Modern democratic governments are necessarily bureaucratic entities. And if this is true, then the successes of modern government have to also be considered the successes of government bureaucracies as well. The fact that Social Security has dramatically reduced poverty among the elderly should be counted as an achievement of this agency's bureaucracy. The Environmental Protection Agency should also get much of the credit for our being able to breathe cleaner air and drink safer water.

In short, if government is good, then government bureaucracies are good. If government programs have had many enormously positive impacts on the lives of every Americans, some of the credit for this has to go to the agencies that make these programs work. Without bureaucracy, modern democratic governments could not possibly fulfill all the crucial roles it plays in society—including creating more economic security, curing diseases, caring for the environment, dispensing justice, educating our children, and protecting us from a variety of harms.

Most of us also know, on some level, that public agencies are primarily there to help us, and that they often do so reasonably well. That is why we keep asking for more of them. Kevin Smith and Michael Licari are two political scientists who have written a textbook about public administration. They have noticed a curious fact: that even those of us who say we don't like government are usually more than willing to demand and accept a new bureaucracy if it will make our lives better off. Even people who live in that notoriously anti-government state of Texas. As Smith and Licari explain:

> Rural Texans tend to be an independent bunch. The stereotypical image is a politically conservative business owner, farmer, or rancher, raised on the myth of rugged individualism and a strong supporter of property rights. Not the sort of people, in other words, who favor big government programs. Or even small ones. Surely such citizens are the least likely group to start agitating for more government bureaucracy. So what does a conservative, small-government group like this do to help spur economic development and advocate for their issues? Well, it asks for a bureaucracy. And it gets one: the Office of Rural Community Affairs (ORCA). Created in 2001 by the Texas legislature, ORCA annually spends tens of millions of . . .

So if you feel that America is a good place to live, at least part of the credit for that must be given to government bureaucracies. Literally, the good life as we know it in the United States could not exist without the numerous and various essential tasks being performed by these public agencies on all levels of government.

Bureaucrats or Public Heroes?

If we should be thankful for government bureaucracies, we should also be thankful for the people—the "bureaucrats"—who work in them. Yet they are one of the most maligned groups in our society. They are constantly the butt of jokes and are stereotyped as being lazy, rude, rigid, arrogant, and controlling. Of course, some are like that. But you find these kind of people in every organization, including business bureaucracies. Moreover, studies have found that government bureaucrats are much like all other Americans and that there is no credible evidence supporting the charge that a pathological "bureaucratic mentality" is prevalent among government workers.

On the whole, our civil servants are hard workers dedicated to serving the public and improving our lives. There are times when this point is made in such dramatic way that no one can deny it. In the wake of the 9/11 tragedy in New York, there was an outpouring of public praise and appreciation for the incredibly brave and self-sacrificing actions taken by numerous police officers and firefighters. What we tend to forget is that for these public employees this was not unusual—they are putting their lives and health on the line every day, not just during terrorists attacks.

And we also tend to forget that police officers and firefighters are not the only heroes working for the government. Our government bureaucracies are full of "everyday heroes"—public servants who labor away in anonymity to protect us from harm and to make our lives better. As Robert Kuttner has observed:

> [We] should not let a week go by without celebrating a public hero, and not just the firefighters and the veterans. The civil servant at the Food and Drug Administration who fights drug-industry pressure and keeps a harmful drug off the market is a public hero. So is the SEC auditor who busts a corporate thief so a million people don't lose their pensions, and the Environmental Protection Agency scientist who safeguards our water from some scofflaw mogul.

Or consider the government workers of the National Highway Traffic Safety Administration. These are the people who do automobile crash tests, evaluate child safety seats, initiate recalls of defective cars, and so on. The motto of the agency is, appropriately enough, "People Saving People." They will never meet you or know your name, but they are working week in and week out to protect your health and safety. Unfortunately, we rarely celebrate these kinds of public servants—instead they must put up with the public disdain leveled at everyone who works for the government. This is the reward they get for choosing to work for the government and to promote the public interest. It is no wonder that many of our best young people are discouraged from taking on these kinds of public service jobs.

The Role of Reform

Let me be clear: I am not suggesting that we look at bureaucracy and bureaucrats through rose-colored glasses—or ignore their shortcomings. There are some inherent problems that can afflict government bureaucracies—most notably corruption and waste. And a hundred years ago, these were rampant problems. The enormously corrupt political machines that existed in many large cities during the early part of the twentieth century are examples of how badly bureaucracies can go wrong. But decades of reform efforts have greatly reduced these problems. We have rooted out large-scale corruption and are increasingly minimizing the amount of bureaucratic inefficiency, excessive paperwork, etc. These problems have not completely disappeared, and we must continue to try to improve the performance of our administrative institutions. A good example of this on-going effort was Vice-President Al Gore's project, called the National Performance Review, which sought to reduce excess federal workers. Between 1993 and 2000, the number of civilian employees in the executive branch was reduced by 193,000. But while we must be vigilant about pursuing these kinds of reform efforts, we must not exaggerate the extent of the problems in our administrative agencies. And we should not allow the occasional failures of government bureaucracies to overshadow their achievements. A more realistic and accurate view of these institutions recognizes that on the whole they are working well and they continue to play a crucial role in administering vital programs that are improving the lives of all Americans.

The Real Lessons from Katrina

And yet, what are we to make of the kind of massive bureaucratic failure that occurred when hurricane Katrina when it hit New Orleans in the fall of 2005? The Federal Emergency Management Agency's response was too little too late, and the agency was harshly criticized for its inadequate and bungling efforts. This fiasco seemed merely to confirm many peoples' worst assumptions about the problems of bureaucracy.

However, it would be a mistake to use the failures of FEMA to paint a negative picture of government bureaucracies. FEMA failed in New Orleans not because of something inherently wrong with government bureaucracies, but because of a policy of neglect by the Bush administration. First, the administration appointed Michael Brown to head the agency, a political crony with no experience in emergency response management and who was fired from his previous job for mismanagement. The agency was then downgraded and folded into the Department of Homeland Security, where its mission was re-oriented toward fighting acts of terrorism. Finally, FEMA's budget was slashed, with Bush officials arguing that "Many are concerned that federal disaster assistance may have evolved into an oversized entitlement program. . . ." As the *Washington Monthly* concluded, "FEMA was deliberately downsized as part of the Bush administration's conservative agenda to reduce the role of government." In the end, then, FEMA's failure in New Orleans was in large part a result of a conservative administration that had only contempt for the role of government in society and had little interest in ensuring the wellbeing of vital government agencies.

Ironically, the real problem with many public bureaucracies today is not that they are bloated institutions who are over-staffed and spend too much money, but that they are understaffed and don't have the funds to do their jobs. The continuing right-wing attack on government has left many agencies in a weakened state, unable to vigorously pursue their missions. There are not enough mine inspectors to protect mineworkers. The IRS lacks the personnel to detect and retrieve the billions of dollars lost every year from individuals and corporations that cheat on their taxes. Many school districts lack the teachers to keep their class size down to a reasonable level. In many cases, we have gone way past cutting "fat" out of these bureaucracies and we have begun to cut into flesh and bone. The main threat to the public interest posed by government bureaucracies these days is not that they are wasting huge amounts of our money, but that many are not healthy enough to do their job of promoting and protecting our collective wellbeing. To make matters worse, the very right-wing forces who are starving these vital agencies then turn around and cite any poor performance by these debilitated organizations as evidence of the ineptness of government.

When President Obama was elected in 2008, he was committed to revitalizing important federal agencies. For example, he worked to enable the FDA to have enough inspectors to ensure that our foods are safe to eat; and the Democratic Congress acted to increase the funding for the Consumer Product and Safety Commission. These were important steps in the right direction, but much more needs to be done to strengthen the numerous bureaucracies that serve our vital public interests. Unfortunately, the Republican takeover of the House of Representatives in 2010 threatens to undermine any systematic efforts to reinvigorate many federal agencies.

Beyond the Bureaucratic Stereotypes

The negative stereotypes of bureaucracy that we have looked at in this article contribute to a political atmosphere that legitimizes the right-wing attack on government. The problem with these stereotypes is not simply that they are exaggerated and mistaken, but that conservatives and libertarians are able to exploit these misperceptions to justify their attempts to defund and hamstring the public sector. The more Americans believe that bureaucracies are bad, the more likely they are to agree with efforts to slash taxes and gut government programs. That is why it is increasingly important that we begin to see that most of the criticisms of government bureaucracy are based more on myth than reality, and that these administrative agencies play a central role in promoting the important missions of a modern democratic government.

EXPLORING THE ISSUE

Do Bureaucrats Have More Influence on Public Policy Than Other Branches of Government Do?

Critical Thinking and Reflection

1. What role does bureaucracy and public administration play in policymaking? Do you think they should play more or less of a role?
2. How are bureaucrats able to shape and/or alter the written intention and meaning of public policy? Do bureaucrats have too much ability to impact policy outcomes?
3. How would you describe the separation of powers between bureaucrats, legislators, and presidents? How could the relationships become less complex and more easily managed?
4. What are the ramifications of bureaucratic behavior on policy outcomes? Is there a way to ensure a more positive relationship?
5. In what ways did bureaucracy impact the recovery efforts in wake of Hurricane Katrina? How did it help and hurt efforts?

Is There Common Ground?

American media likes to paint pictures of overreaching bureaucrats altering the meaning of statutes and laws against the wishes of legislators and executives alike. By examining policy enforcement from a street-level perspective, it is difficult to argue that bureaucrats lack the ability to shape public policy in their own ways. For example, if the speed limit is 35 miles per hour and you are going 39 and a police officer opts not to pull you over for speeding, she has exercised her personal discretion in an effort to meaningfully enforce the spirit of the law. In this way, there is no denying the power of bureaucrats to influence public policy.

When we think about the ability bureaucrats have to influence public policy compared to legislators and executives, it is difficult to ascertain if any one group possesses more power than any other. Through the separation of powers, our Founding Fathers successfully created a governmental framework that provides equal opportunities for different branches of government to impact policy. Even the courts have a sizeable ability to alter the language and meanings of public policy. With this framework firmly in place, perhaps the better avenue to pursue is what to do when bureaucrats overstep their bounds and ultimately enforce laws in a manner relatively inconsistent with legislative intent.

Additional Resources

Arnold, R.D., *Congress and the Bureaucracy: A Theory of Influence* (New Haven, CT: Yale University Press, 1980)

Arnold discusses the relationship between Congress and bureaucracy in American politics. Of interest to the question at hand are the sections that examine the exertion of power of one branch over the other.

Gormley, W.T. and S.J. Balla, *Bureaucracy and Democracy: Accountability and Performance,* 2nd ed. (Washington, DC: CQ Press, 2007)

Gormley and Balla look at the relationship between democracy and bureaucracy. In doing so, they look at areas where bureaucracy works as intended and others where their behaviors do not align with the goals of policy. The authors look at the give-and-take between decision makers, managers, elected officials, organized interests, and individuals.

Lipsky, M., *Street Level Bureaucracy: Dilemmas of the Individual in Public Service* (New York: Russell Sage Foundation, 1983)

Lipsky examines policy implementation from the lens of the street-level bureaucrat. Rather than having the ability to frame policy, these tireless workers are the individuals charged with implementing the goals of statutes and legislation.

Riccucci, N., *How Management Matters: Street-Level Bureaucrats and Welfare Reform* (Washington, DC: Georgetown University Press, 2005)

Riccucci examines how street-level bureaucrats can choose which aspects of policies they ultimately choose to enforce with their actions. When considering welfare reform, the author shows how these bureaucrats have great powers in shaping policy outcomes for involved citizens.

Stillman III, R., *The American Bureaucracy: The Core of Modern Government,* 3rd ed. (New York: Wadsworth, 2003)

Stillman's introductory book contains sections that clearly discuss the relationship between bureaucrats and members of the legislative branch. Further, the book explains the ramifications of bureaucracy being technically considered as part of the executive branch and how that classification impacts relationships.

ISSUE 6

Is It Possible to Coordinate Federal, State, and Local Governments in a Way That Allows Policy Making to Be More Efficient?

YES: Jenna Bednar, from "The Political Science of Federalism," *Annual Review of Law and Social Science* (December 2011)

NO: Thomas Birkland and Sarah Waterman, from "Is Federalism the Reason for Policy Failure in Hurricane Katrina?" *Publius: The Journal of Federalism* (Fall 2008)

Learning Outcomes

After reading this issue, you should be able to:

- Understand the nature of American federalism.
- Discuss how our federal system impacted recovery in the wake of Katrina.
- Describe the benefits of a federal system to efficient policy making.
- Describe the costs of a federal system to efficient policy making.
- Gain an understanding of the potential inefficiencies of federalism to policy making.
- Understand ways in which coordination can improve between different levels of government in America.

ISSUE SUMMARY

YES: Jenna Bednar argues that federalism can be an effective government format to help ensure that policies are ultimately efficient. Through successful coordination of federal, state, and local governments, it is possible to make implementation less costly and more effective for citizens.

NO: Thomas Birkland and Sarah Waterman argue that a lack of co-ordination contributed significantly to the outcomes of Hurricane Katrina. Without being coordinated from the beginning, policy had no chance of being carried out smoothly in a time of crisis. The more we attempt to coordinate, the less efficient policy outcomes are likely to be.

Despite Publius' appeals to grand design and political theory, much of the structure of the United States Constitution was the product of compromise. The authors of the Federalist Papers present one normative argument after another, justifying decisions regarding government structure with references to higher ideals. In reality, many of the major decisions reveal pragmatism and compromise. For most discussions, the elephant in the room was the existence of states. States were formed in the aftermath of the revolution from the remnants of colonial governments. Delegates of states composed the Articles of Confederation, the first attempt at a written constitution, which tilted the balance of power heavily toward the states and away from the national government. Delegates at the Constitutional Convention created something less like a confederation and more like a federal system. With a fundamental recognition that more power must be ceded to the national government, delegates disagreed as to the extent.

Most major constitutional decisions, including virtually all of the measures discussed in an introductory American civics course, reveal the existence and influence of states. A bicameral Congress, with one house based on population and the other based on equal representation of states, is clearly the product of compromise. Apportionment of seats in the House of Representatives was affected by the three-fifths compromise, a measure that allowed states to count five slaves as three members of population. The election of the American president, for which states determine many of the election rules and for distributing electoral votes, also reveals an appeal to states. The process of ratification, both of the Constitution itself and of constitutional amendments, requires the approval of states. Underlying all of these decisions is the notion of federalism.

Federalism is a system of government characterized by the existence of a national government and some subnational government. The United States and Mexico refer to the subnational governments as states, while Canada's subnational governments are called provinces. The question of why the United States has federalism is hardly the classic, nebulous chicken/egg debate. The states existed first. The delegates of states participated in the design of the national government and federal system. When faced with the option of self-preservation or self-abolition, the states ceded some power to the national government but maintained significant autonomy. The subsequent history of American federalism is one of dynamic change in the balance of power between the national government and the states. The term "intergovernmental relations" certainly indicates some level of interaction between government levels. However, cooperation and coordination are hardly guaranteed.

The American federal system is inherently fragmented. One national government exists atop 50 sovereign state governments. Although the national government has expanded in size and scope since the founding, especially since the dramatic changes of the New Deal, states maintain considerable autonomy. The Constitution says relatively little about states. Article IV, which encourages state comity and makes allowances for the admission of new states, demands that states operate under the terms of representative government. No additional requirements are provided, making it all the more surprising that the states are as similar as they are. Nevertheless, states exhibit major differences, both in political culture and government structure. These differences help to explain disparate preferences and incentives that lead to or hinder effective coordination.

The post New Deal period of American federalism is often characterized by scholars as cooperative, or marble cake, federalism. As the national government expanded the scope of responsibility, the states were encouraged to be partners through the grant system. Federal grants are national government priorities established by the U.S. Congress that encourage participation of subnational governments by funding (or partially funding) the activity. Of course, the money typically comes with conditions stipulating the terms of how the money is to be spent and how the program is to be administered. In what constitutes a classic principal-agent relationship, the states surrender autonomy and adopt the national priorities in exchange for benefits, which in this case is a desire to serve citizens while being subsidized to the national government. However, subnational governments occasionally refuse to cooperate with federal initiatives, as was the case recently when Ohio Governor John Kasich turned down money to establish a high-speed rail between Cleveland, Columbus, and Cincinnati.

The issue of coordination of the levels of the American federal system took a stark turn on September 11, 2001, when terrorists hijacked four airplanes, crashing them into the World Trade Center in New York, the Pentagon in Washington, D.C., and a field in rural Pennsylvania. In each instance, the immediate response was local. Emergency responders in Pennsylvania arrived to find widely scattered wreckage and debris and little in the way of recovery. The impact on the Pentagon was dire, but more contained and comparably more manageable than the situation in New York City. In New York, city fire and police and Port Authority officials responded immediately to what initially seemed like an accidental crash into one of the twin towers. As the scope of the disaster intensified, and it became clear that this was a terrorist attack, U.S. government involvement increased. Later analysis shows that the officials knew the planes had been hijacked, but communication between the Federal Aviation Administration, the U.S. military, and the Federal Bureau of Investigation was fractured. Since no party had complete information, coordination prior to the attack was extraordinarily difficult, if not impossible. By the time the second plane crashed into the World Trade Center, chaos increased dramatically, making coordination between levels of government even more difficult.

In the YES selection, Jenna Bednar explains how federalism can be effectively coordinated to make policy making more efficient. By coordinating, levels of government can reduce waste and redundant activity. In contrast, in the NO selection, Thomas Birkland and Sarah Waterman argue that a lack of coordination contributed significantly the aftermath of Hurricane Katrina. Although the authors acknowledge coordination is difficult in the wake of crisis, they still believe mistakes were made that further inhibited the potential for meaningful synchronization of information.

YES

Jenna Bednar

The Political Science of Federalism

The literature reviewed in this section treats the purposeful adoption of federalism as a means to achieve a socially desirable end. Attempts to develop a general theory of federalism and its potential flourished in the 1960s. Global trends including decolonization in Africa and the growing strength of smaller nations in the United Nations turned political science's attention to regime construction. The decision to federate is inherently risky. Whether federation means greater decentralization, in transformations from unitary states, or greater centralization, when formerly independent states band together, federation presents risks to the status quo power. Perhaps because of this risk, often theories of federal origins emphasize security enhancement. In addition to improved security, most benefits are economic or political. Many goals are competing, so that sometimes we need to have tradeoffs; Kincaid suggests that federalism, with the flexibility of power-sharing, can manage these competing priorities well.

Many of the economic and political claims about federalism rely on two principles: the Tiebout Hypothesis of citizen mobility and Oates' Decentralization Theorem, a prescription for subsidiarity that follows from Tiebout. Tiebout applies the theory of firm competition to government. Just as firm competition drives prices down, governments will be more efficient—deliver better services for lower taxes—when they are put in competition with one another. Voting artificially constrains citizens to a single district; entrenchment of party politics may trap the citizen into a set of unsatisfactory policies. The mobile citizen votes with her feet, locating in a community that offers a combination of services and taxes that better suits her preferences. Competition for mobile citizens encourages governments to operate more efficiently as well as to specialize.

The Tiebout Hypothesis of beneficial intergovernmental competition leads to a principle for assignment of authority between national and subnational governments: subsidiarity. It is captured in the fiscal federalism literature as Oates' Decentralization Theorem: in the absence of cost-savings from centralization, or interjurisdictional externalities, policy should be decentralized. Subsidiarity is politically popular in Europe and elsewhere because a principled preference for decentralization promotes local (member state) authority. While most justifications for subsidiarity are normative, in order for the Tiebout forces to work, policy must be decentralized, factors must be mobile, and externalities must not be problematic.

From *Annual Review of Law and Social Science,* December 2011. Copyright © 2011 by Annual Reviews, Inc. Reprinted by permission.

With these two principles—intergovernmental competition and beneficial decentralization—in hand, scholars claim that decentralized policy provision enhances governmental honesty, efficiency, and gives governments the chance to innovate, rather than adopting a common policy. These forces lead directly to a belief in efficiency, policy specialization, and a reduction in corruption. Corrupt leaders will tend to be inefficient and will not survive the local competition against their more efficient, less exploitative neighbors. Decentralized states—although not necessarily all federal—do seem to exhibit less corruption but other evidence contradicts this claim. Cai and Treisman theorize that federalism might boost corruption if subnational governments are able to shield local firms from central taxation or regulation; in these cases, internal competition corrodes the state, rather than having the beneficial effects posited by Tiebout. Cai and Treisman illustrate their claims with examples from Russia, China, and the United States. Bohara, Mitchell, and Mittendorff suggests that the electoral mechanism is an important interacting variable: when the public is more involved in elections, the relationship between federalism and corruption becomes insignificant. Myerson offers a twist, recalling arguments made by Madison in *Federalist* 10: as politicians seek higher office they will be put in competition with one another and seek to build a reputation for honesty. Unitary governments lack this advantage, as any leader elected to succeed a corrupt leader has every incentive also to be corrupt.

As citizens settle into communities that match their own preferences, at the local level the sorting produces homogeneity, while at the regional level, communities will be heterogeneous. Subnational governments can specialize, tailoring public policy to meet local demands. When governments develop unique policies they become laboratories of democracy, as Justice Brandeis described the public policy experimentation that decentralization makes possible. When subnational governments innovate, successful solutions can diffuse to other subnational states with similar preferences and problems; although the evidence may be misleading. With sufficient learning, aggregate national welfare is improved, when compared to a centralized solution.

However beneficial, meaningful state experimentation may not be common. In a cross-national study of the development of social welfare systems, Pierson 1995 finds that the effect of federalism interacts with other variables such as the nature of the party system, reminding us that experimentation depends heavily on the capacity and competence of subnational leaders. Policy innovation implies risk, an assumption that Crémer and Palfrey rely on to show that moderates prefer centralization because centralization reduces risk. In a nuanced model assessing the likelihood that politicians assume the risk associated with innovative politics, Rose-Ackerman casts doubt on the claim that federalism would generate useful innovative project, given the risk associated with true innovation. However, politicians may engage in low-risk "demonstration" projects. Institutional design might encourage experimentation: for example, Kollman argues that the rotating presidency of the European Union introduces fresh policy agenda each six months, so that the union explores new mixtures of polices.

Local governments also may not be more efficient; the infamous "fly-paper effect" is a strong caveat against universal preference for transferring federal funds to local governments. When a government receives an unconditional grant it can choose to keep spending at the same level and reduce taxes (that is, transfer the money to the citizens) or it can increase its spending, holding taxes at the same level. At levels much higher than predicted, the government chooses to spend the money rather than transfer it to the citizens. This effect is known as the flypaper effect: money "sticks where it hits." One explanation is the voter ignorance hypothesis; either the voter does not know how much the government received in transfer, or the voter keeps different mental accounts of her own privately-held money and public money. The voter ignorance hypothesis lacks empirical support, and Knight and Inman suggest that the problem is simply politics: elected politicians are eager to please their constituents by providing services, and will spend the money to boost their electoral success.

Paying close attention to the assignment of authorities, some scholars suggest that federalism promotes economic growth, a potential that Weingast identifies as market-preserving federalism. Centralized governments face a commitment problem: when governments are strong enough to be able to enforce contacts, they are strong enough to exploit their position of power, and can expropriate rents from the society. Federalism is a commitment mechanism: the central government maintains authority over monetary policy and contract enforcement, but fiscal policy is decentralized to the states. One potential problem with decentralization is that the states might run up budget deficits in hopes that the federal government will bail them out. When interstate competition is potent, with high factor mobility, coupled with centralized control over monetary policy, the incentives to bail out individual states is lowered, creating a hard budget constraint and encouraging the states to practice prudent fiscal policy. The lack of corruption and pro-growth institutions encourage foreign direct investment. The theory has been fruitfully applied to China, India, Russia, the European Union and the United States, but other research bears more disappointing results. Rodden warns of the complexity of decentralized government and the resulting difficulty in inferring fiscal responsibility from government finance data, and Wibbels warns that states ought not be included in federal-level monetary policy-making: with their divergent interests, states make structural adjustments more difficult because they block the adoption of effective policies.

Using the same principles of beneficial intergovernmental competition and decentralization, federalism is often claimed to improve political outcomes, such as respect for individual rights, group autonomy and preservation, and improved representation. The hypotheses themselves are structured essentially identically to the economic models. For example, rights-preserving federalism, claiming that individual rights, from civil to property, are better protected in a federal system than a unitary system, relies on Tiebout forces. When citizens or capital can exit the system, their ability to exit reduces a sovereign's capacity to exploit them. States would not violate individual rights because citizens would simply move.

Just as with economic claims based on Tiebout forces, the theory of rights-preserving federalism is limited by the extent to which voters are mobile. When mobility is obstructed, whether legally, or informally—through preferences (ethnic clustering or strong community bonds, for example)—the competitive forces that drive some of federalism's benefits will not develop. If only a categorical portion of the population is immobile—the poor, or ethnic minorities—then outcomes are even worse; governments compete for the wealthiest and are free to ignore these minority categories. Gibson and Mickey describe rights-violating states as "subnational autocracies"—places, like the racially-charged era in the American southern states, where disrespect for civil rights is so significant that one cannot consider the state to be a true democracy. Riker famously derided federalism as great if you're a racist.

The potential for states to discriminate against some citizens prompts some to suggest that rights should be provided at the national level where they might be protected by federal courts. Shapiro offers a challenging countertesis: full and unique provision of rights by the central government is an overreaction. Instead, by sharing rights-providing authority, the protection and extension of rights can benefit from the multiplicity of views expressed at state and federal levels, thus harnessing federalism's diversity in the rights arguments. It may be the best hope for the creation of new rights, such as recognition of same-sex marriages, where a skeptical national majority could learn from state experimentation.

Madison believed that federalism might rescue democracy; poor legislative representation could be improved with a hierarchy of elections as citizens gained experience with their representatives. Ineptitude would be recognized and voted out of office in local elections, failing to advance up the political hierarchy. Experience with elections alone may be sufficient to develop democratic skills, and one advantage of federalism is that the public has more political offices to fill, and so more elections. Democratic outcomes improve with higher participation, and participation is boosted when one's vote is likely to be pivotal, more likely to be true in smaller scale elections. The more authority held by the local government, the more voters will sense it important enough to participate.

Federalism may improve electoral accountability if voters are more likely to get accurate information about their local politicians, but other institutional factors such as electoral rules muddle the improvement. Inman and Rubinfeld report initial empirical analysis of 73 matched cases (federal/unitary) suggesting that federalism, when paired with effective democracy, protects the property, civil, and political rights of its citizens better than unitary states. Frey and Stutzer find a measurable increase in well-being from participation in direct democracy and local electoral participation.

The principles of Tiebout sorting and subsidiarity from Oates suggest that federalism would be a fine resolution to ethnic tension, and many scholars do argue for "peace-preserving federalism." At the same time, by organizing political boundaries around ethnic groups, tensions are made more salient and differences are equipped with the institutional capacities to make demands that the rest of the union cannot tolerate, leading to conflict or secession. Hale suggests that the problems arise when one core ethnic state is dominant, a position that Horowitz obliquely confirms with his emphasis on drawing federal boundaries to encourage cross-cutting cleavages. The debate is far from settled, and will likely need to wait until the technologies of data collection and analysis have advanced. Enlisting spatial data is critical. One promising project maps ethnic groups; the data have been employed to examine the coincidence of political and ethnic boundaries, the correlation between wealth inequality and ethnic conflict, and the likelihood of federal adoption.

. . .

   Concern for the distribution of authority will remain focal to the federalism literature. We will continue to want to understand how best to distribute authority in order to achieve societal goals, but the research going forward will take into account what is feasible, given the inherent tendency toward opportunism. To defend the boundaries of federalism, research on safeguards will continue, but increasingly it will recognize a broad array of safeguards, and consider how those safeguards complement one another to defend the boundaries. And finally, perhaps the most revolutionary research shift moving forward is to develop a theory of the dynamics of federalism's boundaries. Doing so means reviving the detailed understandings of intergovernmental relations that been diverted to public administration scholarship; the process of federal evolution is bottom-up, decentralized, many-actored, and responsive to cultural patterns. In moving beyond equilibrium-based theories and adopting a model of complex adaptive systems, the micro-processes leading to federal constitutional change might be soon understood. The modern science of federalism focuses on the interaction between safeguarding institutions, imperfect agents, and how those interactions shape the evolution of federalism.

**Thomas Birkland and
Sarah Waterman**

 **NO**

Is Federalism the Reason for Policy Failure in Hurricane Katrina?

As the most expensive natural disaster in American history and one of the deadliest in recent memory, Hurricane Katrina has been seared in the American psyche unlike any other natural disaster. Of particular note is the extent to which the response to Katrina has been cast as a failure of federal initiative and organization, notwithstanding the inherently intergovernmental nature of disaster preparedness, response, recovery, and mitigation in the US. The criticism has been particularly heated given the reforms occasioned by another "focusing event": The September 11 attacks and the concomitant focus on "homeland security," to the detriment of preparedness for and response to natural hazards. Since August 2005, Americans, their elected representatives, and the news media have pointedly asked, "If the federal government cannot prepare for something like Katrina, how can it prepare for a major act of terrorism?" Of course, the mantra of failure, reinforced by media coverage of the supposed overall failure of response to Katrina, failed to consider the things that worked in Katrina. Martha Derthick includes the pre-storm evacuation and the search and rescue function as success stories that involved considerable intergovernmental coordination. But Derthick also notes the failure of flood protection, another intergovernmental function.

The broader failure of disaster mitigation, preparedness, and response was manifest in Katrina. The nature of federalism and intergovernmental relations, particularly post-September 11, has been implicated in these failures. This article explores potential explanations for governmental failure during Hurricane Katrina, including federalism, policy, and administrative failures. The creation of the Department of Homeland Security (DHS) led to substantial changes in the nature of the federal–state–local relationship in emergency management. These changes appear to have validated fears raised by critics before Hurricane Katrina that the reorganization designed to respond to terrorism would undermine the nation's ability to respond to natural disasters. The important question, then, is this: Were the failures in Hurricane Katrina a result of federalism or of a particular *style* of federalism that characterizes disaster policy in the US? Or did these failures simply reflect the inherent difficulties in preparing for, responding to, and recovering from catastrophes?

Although former eras of federalism were conceptualized as cooperative or competitive, *coercive federalism* and *opportunistic federalism* are two terms that

From *Publius: The Journal of Federalism*, Fall 2008, pp. 692–695, 705–710. Copyright © 2008 by Oxford University Press Journals. Reprinted by permission via Rightslink.

might be profitably applied to homeland security and issues raised in Hurricane Katrina. Coercive federalism describes how federal regulations, federal mandates imposed on the states, and federal preemption of state authority seek to compel state and local governments to comply with federal standards in the pursuit of national goals. Many states have claimed that post-September 11 policy is coercive in that it attaches strings to federal preparedness aid.

But *coercive federalism* is potentially misleading for at least two reasons. First, it is difficult to make as strong a case for coercion in disaster policy as one can make in transportation policy [the uniform drinking age mandates, tied to federal funding] or in education [No Child Left Behind]. These are relatively high-salience issues, with rather clear linkages between state and local behavior and their receipt of federal funds. Natural hazards policies are much lower salience to most people, except on rare occasions, which makes disaster policy the province of technical experts more than political leaders. The failure of local governments to follow mandates related to natural hazards, then, is likely to be unaccompanied by much citizen attention. The one exception may be in the flood insurance program, where communities that fail to take certain mitigation steps will make themselves ineligible for highly subsidized federal flood insurance. Even then, what undermines the coercion argument is the political utility of disaster aid for the president and members of Congress, all of whom enjoy claiming credit for funneling money to local governments after disasters. After September 11, there was some coercion in tying various forms of aid to adoption of the National Incident Management System (NIMS) and adherence to the National Response Plan (NRP), now known as the National Response Framework (NRF). But this mild coercion is accompanied by generous federal funding for "homeland security" activities. This funding is basically redistributive (pork) spending rather than spending based on a risk or needs assessment, making such funding an attractive way to spend federal money locally.

Second, while many programs look like coercion, state and local governments have rather willingly ceded leadership and funding to federal authority, particularly given the promise of vast funding flowing from Washington to the states under the "homeland security" rubric, as well as the desire to be seen as doing their share.

A potentially more satisfactory model of federalism, which avoids the assumed heavy handedness of coercion and the sometimes naïve assumption of shared goals, is called *opportunistic federalism*, which Conlan defines as

> a system that allows—and often encourages—actors in the system to pursue their immediate interests with little regard for the institutional or collective consequences. For example, federal mandates, policy preemptions, and highly prescriptive federal grant programs tend to be driven by opportunistic policy makers who seek to achieve their own policy and political goals regardless of traditional norms of behavior or boundaries of institutional responsibility

This idea of opportunistic federalism is entirely consistent with the "opportunistic" and episodic nature of nearly all disaster policy, since disaster and crisis policy is almost entirely event-driven, decisions are made rapidly, and policies are often adopted without considering their long-term influence on fundamental constitutional and institutional arrangements. This is an excellent description of federal disaster policy since September 11. In the process of creating the DHS, Congress, with the president's assent, moved FEMA into the new agency without regard for its existing organizational and intergovernmental relationships. Furthermore, homeland security "experts" (many of whom had little experience in this new field) made policy in nearly complete ignorance of the vast amounts of knowledge accumulated by social scientists and practitioners on how people and organizations behave in disasters. The creators of the new homeland security establishment were driven by political and policy goals—in particular, the need to act quickly to bolster "homeland security"—rather than by a desire to understand whether the entire disaster preparedness, response, and recovery system really needed to be overhauled at all, or whether small parts needed reform to work better.

The creation of the DHS as it eventually emerged laid the shaky foundation for intergovernmental response that had been partially built before Katrina. This foundation, to be sure, was not undermined solely by opportunistic federalism, but by a patchwork of relationships between and among governments that combined features of coercion and cooperation in ways that were not yet well established after September 11. These relationships reveal challenges of network governance at least as much, if not more, than they reveal problems with the federal nature of disaster policy and practice.

. . .

Explanations for Perceived Federal Policy Failure

The normative question raised by the above analysis is this: Why do people blame the federal government more than they do state and local government for the apparent failures in Hurricane Katrina? Potential explanations for the Katrina policy failures reveal a great deal about policy design within and across various levels of government. These explanations are neither definitive nor mutually exclusive. We can define the policy failure as the inability of federal, state, and local governments to take the appropriate steps to mitigate, prepare for, and respond to Hurricane Katrina. The successful application of these aspects of disaster policy leads to disaster-resilient communities that can "bounce back" from disasters. New Orleans, just on population figures alone, cannot be said to have returned to its pre-Katrina state. On these measures, policy failure is clear. What is not yet clear is precisely how and why these policies failed, given the interconnected nature of communities and of cascading failures.

The Federal Government Objectively Failed

One reason why many people thought that the federal government failed in its perceived duties is because there is evidence that the federal government did fail in fundamental ways. FEMA's response was slow, and then FEMA director Michael Brown was portrayed as being foolish and out of touch. Later analyses suggested that he was significantly constrained by higher ups in the DHS (Cooper and Block 2006), and major questions were raised about why the federal government lacked essential supplies and equipment in staging areas much nearer to New Orleans and the Gulf Coast.

Additional questions were raised about the nature of the new NRP, the main federal guidance document that supplanted the former Federal Response Plan (FRP). The NRP was clearly written with catastrophic terrorism in mind, and in the views of most state emergency managers it had significant problems. The plan, adopted in early 2005, muted these objections. The final draft of the NRP was even worse than the one first promulgated; it sought to centralize nearly *all* disaster response in the federal government, a model that turned the entire emergency management system, and the profession itself, on its head.

Furthermore, the NRP was a lengthy document—over 400 pages long, including various annexes—and many parts of it were unintelligible to local responders and other federal agencies. The NRP was drafted with relatively little FEMA and state and local participation, and the roles that all actors would take in emergency response, in particular, were unclear. In essence, the NRP tore asunder long-standing institutional relationships that worked reasonably well before Katrina. The controversies over the creation of the NRP, and its obvious practical shortcomings, contradicted DHS claims that FEMA and the DHS would continue to pursue an "all hazards" approach to both terrorism and natural disasters.

The Storm Was So Overwhelming That Any Response Would Fail, No Matter Who Was in Charge

Another reason for the fixing of blame on the federal government recognizes that the hurricane's damage was so profound that it quickly overtaxed the ability of Orleans Parish, the neighboring parishes, and the State of Louisiana to effectively respond. One can then make one of two arguments. First, the federal government was inevitably overwhelmed by this catastrophic event, just because the disaster was very big, affecting the Gulf Coast from south-central Louisiana through Mississippi to Mobile, Alabama. The second "causal story" is that the federal government was overwhelmed because, despite assurances to the contrary, it was ill equipped and unable to respond to a disaster of this magnitude. While this has substantially disturbing consequences—if the federal government cannot respond to Hurricane Katrina, how could it handle an act of catastrophic terrorism?—this is less a question of federalism than it is of preparedness organization within the national government. After all, the provision of aid to communities that have been overwhelmed by catastrophic events is at the very heart of the federal role in the emergency management system, and the possibility of a catastrophic event is exactly why the NRP was created.

Conflicting Federal and Local Policy Goals

Another candidate explanation for failure is the classic conflict in federal systems: the conflict between federal and state goals. The state and local emergency managers, even after September 11, took the "all hazards" approach much more seriously than the federal government did. The *National Strategy for Homeland Security,* which still focuses on the "war on terrorism," speaks for itself; meanwhile, the state and local governments have consistently recognized that they are much more likely to have to address a range of natural and technological hazards and disasters as well as terrorism. The federal government's focus on civil defense is therefore neither orthogonal to nor congruent with state and local goals. This stands in rather sharp contrast to the situation during the 1990s, when there was considerably more cooperation between the federal, state, and local governments. One can therefore say that federal policy, on the one hand, and state and local policy, on the other, have been significantly divergent since 2001.

Beyond the question of response, however, one must consider the federal role in facilitating development in hazardous areas, and the intergovernmental role in persuading people that they were probably safer than they really were. Ray Burby calls these the "safe development" and the "local government" paradoxes. In the first, Burby argues that the federal government, through many subsidies and incentives, including flood insurance, levees, tax deductions for casualty losses, and generous disaster relief, encourages development in areas that would not otherwise be developed if the risk profile of the area were undistorted by these incentives. People whose risk perceptions are altered in this way are said to be susceptible to "moral hazard," in which people take risks they would not ordinarily assume because they believe that the additional risk is attenuated by the protection provided by government. Of course, these decisions may well be distorted by perceptions: Building behind a levee may provide the illusion of safety, but the probability of the levee's failing because of poor design, poor construction, poor maintenance, or exceeding the "design flood" (that is, the maximum flood level assumed in the design) are not often considered in the risk calculation. One can certainly argue that vulnerable areas are "safer" from routine events, such as "nuisance flooding," but whether an area is truly "safe" is a matter of probability just like any other risk.

The local government paradox suggests that even when the federal government wants to more aggressively address hazards, the state and local governments must implement federal ideas for mitigation. Students of intergovernmental relations and policy implementation know that designing such policies is very difficult; Malcolm Goggin and his colleagues argued in 1990 that intergovernmental policy implementation is more likely to be successful when credible policy designers communicate clear and credible signals to capable implementers whose interests are congruent with those of the policy originator. Unfortunately, the interests of the federal government are not clear, inconsistent, and not clearly communicated. Even when an incentive, such as the Hazard Mitigation Grant Program, is provided, it may not be taken up by the local governments, or their ideas of what constitutes sound mitigation may not be congruent with those of federal policymakers.

At the same time, the paradox of local development is also at work. The costs of nearly all effective preparedness and mitigation measures are borne by state and especially local governments in at least two ways: In the funds that have to be expended to execute these plans, and in the loss of tax revenue and other economic activity that accompanies allowing for land development. The promise of increased revenues was what induced the Orleans Parish levee board to use levees more as a way of creating new developable land than as a hazard mitigation measure. This problem is not unique to New Orleans; all manner of communities, particularly those running out of the safest land on which to build, experience the same pressures, and given that local property tax revenues are the major source of municipal revenue, and that urban "growth machines" work with civic leaders to promote development in unsafe areas.

Excessive Policy Demand

While the government at many levels failed in Katrina, it is also possible that citizens' expectations are too great, particularly in relation to their apparent unwillingness to take self-protective measures. One reason for policy failure is "excessive policy demand." That is, some citizens and their leaders call on government to do more than it is able to as a function of resource constraints, limits on governmental authority, or limits on political feasibility. In the first instance, while the federal government has vast resources at its disposal, these resources are not unlimited and often are the object of competition for other needs. Furthermore, at least theoretically, there are limits to what government can do in terms of the usurpation of state and local functions, the role of law enforcement officials, and the like. And some obvious responses to disasters, such as forced evacuations or forced expropriation of land in hazardous areas, are simply incongruent with our political culture and the expectations of most citizens.

One might be tempted to attribute excessive policy demand to state and local officials and their citizens, who, in the classic economic definition of efficiency, want as many services as possible for the least amount of taxes or other costs. Under this conception, state and local governments are simply seeking to offload responsibility for protecting their citizens to the federal government. On the other hand, it is equally plausible that excessive policy demand has been created and stoked by the federal government, in large part because of FEMA's apparent competence in the 1990s. Much of this demand was created in the 1990s, when the Clinton administration and James Lee Witt realized that disasters are prime political opportunities to be generous with relief. Thus, the number of declared disasters and the amount of relief distributed during the Clinton administration was the greatest in history. In the 2004 hurricane season, President Bush and his staff realized that they needed to effectively respond to overcome yet another Florida debacle on the scale of Hurricane Andrew; they were largely successful in using generous disaster relief both to help victims and as a political tool to shore up their standing in a key state in the 2004 elections.

The promises that the federal government made in the 1990s were carried forward into the 2000s, even though, beginning in 2003, the executive branch gutted FEMA to the extent that the agency was unable to perform the way it had under Witt. Major programs such as hazard mitigation were cut, funds were stripped from FEMA to pay for sometimes dubious DHS expenditures, and a key FEMA function—disaster preparedness—was taken from the agency and placed in the Office of Domestic Preparedness. Hurricane Katrina did induce the reversal of this trend. But the continued focus on homeland security in the DHS raises important questions about FEMA's location within the federal bureaucracy, and whether and to what extent it should be more directly accountable to the president, particularly since the DHS secretary, at least in this case, has taken a minimal interest in natural disasters, focusing on other, far less immediate issues such as immigration.

Finally, the problems of FEMA and the DHS were exacerbated, particularly at FEMA, by the administration's initial use of that agency as a place to put third-rate party loyalists in positions of responsibility.

Conclusion: Federalism Prospects in Emergency Management

Surprisingly, while September 11 triggered wholesale change in federal-state relationships in emergency management, Hurricane Katrina, a truly catastrophic event, has done little to change federal attitudes about the division of responsibilities. Indeed, the public pronouncements from FEMA and the DHS suggest that it will continue its pre-2001 mission of response to natural disasters using a post-2001 model of how the world works.

Perhaps the most obvious evidence of frustration with the system is, as Gerber notes, the federal response to implementation problems with the NRP. The NRP is lengthy, unwieldy, and in some places unclear; in any case, the new plan was sufficiently unfamiliar to the responders at all levels in Hurricane Katrina to serve as effective guidance document (it was released in late 2004). Given the manifest problems with the NRP, and also given the other problems cited above, including federal creation of excessive policy demand, one would assume that the federal government might revisit the NRP and its successor, the NRF, in hopes of both simplifying the plan and making it more usable by all stakeholders in disaster management, while simultaneously bringing the states and local partners into a *partnership* with the federal government rather than a subordinate role.

This is not what the federal government has done. Instead, the federal government has sought to replace the complex and difficult-to-use NRP with a new NRF. The shift from a plan to a framework was not accompanied by any change in federal attitudes toward centralizing emergency management; in particular, professional groups such as the National Emergency Management Association (NEMA) claimed that their role in shaping the framework was minimal, and the focus remains on terrorism. Furthermore, the president of the International Association of Emergency Managers (IAEM) noted that a "framework is not a plan," and bemoaned the fact that the new seventy-one page "framework," which had the hallmarks of an executive summary, not a real plan, was drafted without consultation with state and local emergency managers. In short, the homeland security establishment remains ascendant, local input is still devalued, centralizing tendencies continue, and evidence of any learning from Hurricane Katrina is tenuous at best.

It is therefore not "federalism" that explains the failure of government initiative but rather the *style* of federalism evidenced during Hurricane Katrina. The tendencies described in this article suggest a two-fold problem: The centralization of the broader direction of homeland security policy in the federal government and, at the same time, the creation of plans and organizations that are, if history is any guide, doomed to fail during times of "normal" natural disasters, in which the state and local governments still retain considerable responsibility and powers both under the Constitution and under relevant legislation and regulation. Cutting out the state and local governments has deprived the federal government of a considerable body of expertise and has undermined the traditional idea of "defense in depth" for natural disasters, with state and local governments responding first and then seeking federal assistance. If the federal government continues to dominate, state and local capacity could very well be eroded, as it was in Katrina, where capacity to plan for and respond to a Katrina-sized storm was not built in large part because of the federal government's reassignment of resources from natural disaster preparedness to homeland security "needs."

In the end, we cannot have much faith that another catastrophic disaster like Hurricane Katrina will greatly influence federal tendencies to centralize the direction of emergency management policy in Washington. After all, Katrina should have taught the folly of that approach. Rather, it is likely that only change in administration in Washington, akin to the change in 1992 that led to FEMA's reform, is likely to result in change. As long as emergency management is valued by the president and the executive branch primarily as a facet of "homeland security" or "national security," it is unlikely that the federal government will relinquish its domination of this domain, regardless of this stance's actual influence on governmental performance.

EXPLORING THE ISSUE

Is It Possible to Coordinate Federal, State, and Local Governments in a Way That Allows Policy Making to Be More Efficient?

Critical Thinking and Reflection

1. What are the major benefits and potential costs of a federal system?
2. What is the nature of contemporary American federalism?
3. How could coordination have been improved to better manage the government response to Hurricane Katrina?
4. What are the alternatives to federalism and would the alternatives be better able to handle a disaster such as Hurricane Katrina?
5. In the wake of disasters such as Hurricane Katrina and the September 11 attacks, why has coordination not advanced further than it has?

Is There Common Ground?

In the wake of unconscionable disasters such as Hurricane Katrina and the September 11 attacks, media analysis focused on questions of accountability and responsibility. Much of the coverage of Katrina highlighted the failure of the Federal Emergency Management Agency in responding to the disaster in an efficient, effective manner. However, later analysis contrasted the relative failure of the Louisiana state and local governments' response to Katrina with the relative success of the response in Mississippi. Of course, the scale of destruction in Louisiana was massive compared to Mississippi. Nevertheless, evidence has shown that established disaster management plans in New Orleans were not executed fully, contributing to the instability of the situation. The terrorist attacks of September 11, 2001, provide mixed evidence of effective communication. The immediate response of local authorities, including New York City emergency responders and Port Authority officials, suggests a reasonable level of communication. However, as the full scale of the disaster unfolded, officials at all levels of government joined the response effort. Subsequent studies suggest that coordination between the FAA, U.S. military officials, and the White House could have been improved in the immediate aftermath of the disaster. As discussed by Bednar, there are established benefits to a federal system. However, a federal system is inherently fragmented, contributing to the coordination problems discussed by Birkland and Waterman. The evidence might lead us to question whether the potential benefits of a federal system outweigh the challenges of operating government at three levels in an effective manner.

Additional Resources

Buxbaum, J. (2010). Opportunities and recommendations for state-federal coordination to improve health system performance: A focus on patient safety. *National Academy for State Health Policy.* Retrieved September 19, 2011, from http://www.nashp.org/publication/opportunities-and-recommendations-state-federal-coordination-improve-health-system.

A policy brief posted on the Internet that discusses the recommendations of a roundtable discussion of state and national health policy officials. Buxbaum outlines ways officials at different levels of government might reduce redundant effort and improve patient safety.

Cooper, C. and R. Block, *Disaster: Hurricane Katrina and the Failure of Homeland Security* (New York: Holt Paperbacks, 2007)

A book that discusses Hurricane Katrina and the role of the national government in the disaster response. The authors frame Hurricane Katrina as a homeland security issue.

National Commission on Terrorist Attacks Upon the United States. (2004). *The 9-11 Commission Report.* Retrieved on September 19, 2011, from http://govinfo.library.unt.edu/911/report/index.htm.

The 9-11 Commission Report is an in-depth policy analysis discussing the events and response to the September 11 Attacks. The report provides critical analysis of government coordination.

O'Toole, Jr., L., *American Intergovernmental Relations,* 4th ed. (Washington, DC: CQ Press, 2006)

O'Toole's edited volume brings together a series of powerful essays examining many aspects of intergovernmental relations in the American context.

United States Government Accountability, *Homeland Security: Effective Intergovernmental Coordination Is Key to Success* (Washington, DC: BiblioGov, 2011)

This volume looks at testimony presented before the subcommittee on government efficiency, financial management, and intergovernmental relations, committee on government reform in the House of Representatives.

Internet References . . .

Reason Foundation, Privatization

Reason produces rigorous, peer-reviewed research and directly engages the policy process, seeking strategies that emphasize cooperation, flexibility, local knowledge, transparency, accountability, and results. Through practical and innovative approaches to complex problems, Reason seeks to change the way people think about issues, and promote policies that allow and encourage individuals and voluntary institutions to flourish.

http://reason.org/areas/topic/privatization

Office of Government Contracting and Business Administration

The Office of Government Contracting and Business Administration's mission is to help enhance the effectiveness of small business programs by working with Government Contracting and Business Development program offices and others to develop policies, regulations, and statutory changes.

http://www.sba.gov/about-offices-content/1/2467

USAJOBS

USAJOBS is the U.S. Government's official system/program for Federal jobs and employment information. USAJOBS delivers a service by which Federal agencies meet their legal obligation (5 USC 3327 and 5 USC 3330) providing public notice of Federal employment opportunities to Federal employees and U.S. citizens.

http://www.usajobs.gov/

Political Activity (Hatch Act)

This site examines the elements of the Hatch Act and how it is applied. The site is housed with the U.S. Office of Special Counsel.

http://www.osc.gov/hatchact.htm

United States Merit System Protection Board

The Merit Systems Protection Board is an independent, quasi-judicial agency in the Executive branch that serves as the guardian of Federal merit systems. The Board was established by Reorganization Plan No. 2 of 1978, which was codified by the Civil Service Reform Act of 1978 (CSRA), Public Law No. 95-454.

http://www.mspb.gov/

The Politics–Administration Dichotomy

Although bureaucracy and public administration are unquestionably influenced by politics, they are both designed to perform optimally in a nonpartisan setting. The political side of policy is expected to take place in the halls of legislatures and at the desks of appropriate executives. Once the policy is created, however, it is supposed to be implemented and enforced in an equitable, effective manner. Yet, as we know in our nation, politics infiltrates all aspects of policy, creating the politics–administration dichotomy. In this unit, we will look at issues related to the dichotomy—focusing on neutrality and the appropriate roles and processes of government.

- Do Bureaucrats Need to Be Politically Neutral to Be Effective?
- Should Government Be Run Like a Business?
- Should Governments Use the Private Sector to Deliver Public Services?

ISSUE 7

Do Bureaucrats Need to Be Politically Neutral to Be Effective?

YES: David E. Lewis, from "Testing Pendleton's Premise: Do Political Appointees Make Worse Bureaucrats?," *The Journal of Politics* (November 2007)

NO: William F. West, from "Neutral Competence and Political Responsiveness: An Uneasy Relationship," *Policy Studies Journal* (May 2005)

Learning Outcomes

After reading this issue, you should be able to:

- Discuss the reasons why neutrality is assumed to be necessary for bureaucrats to be effective.
- Understand the conditions under which neutrality can work against effectiveness.
- Define what is meant by political neutrality.
- Describe the conflict between neutrality and responsiveness.
- Gain an understanding of the differences between career managers and political appointees.
- Understand how the interests of presidents are better served by nonneutral bureaucrats.

ISSUE SUMMARY

YES: David Lewis argues that federal programs administered by politically appointed bureau chiefs perform less effectively than those run by bureau chiefs drawn from the civil service. Career managers have more direct bureau experience and longer tenures in office. Both factors are believed to lead to better performance.

NO: William West argues that nonpartisan objectivity within the career bureaucracy does not necessarily serve the interests of presidents and other members of government. If bureaucrats must be neutral, many scholars believe they are unable to be fully responsive, thus potentially limiting their ultimate effectiveness.

When Andrew Jackson was elected president in 1829, he ushered in an era of change to the White House. He was the first southerner to be elected president. He came from modest roots (especially compared to the previous six presidents) and aimed to represent all of the citizens of our nation, not just those of privilege and wealth. And since George Washington he was the first president to have military experience. But the biggest change that accompanied Jackson's arrival on Pennsylvania Avenue was his belief in patronage politics. Jackson saw the ability to appoint friends and supporters to key positions in his administration as a perk of winning office. Neutrality played little role in his thinking as he preferred to surround himself with individuals that would be devoted to him more than individuals that would necessarily be the best fit for the job.

Fast forward some fifty years. On July 2, 1881, the 20th president of the United States of America—James Garfield—was assassinated in Washington, D.C. by a man named Charles Guiteau. While any assassination is tragic, Garfield's was particularly so as he lost his life at the hands of a pistol-wielding scorned bureaucrat. Guiteau had been a relative failure in life. He had failed in law and bill collecting. He was no better at theology. In 1880 when Garfield was nominated by the Republican Party to be president, Guiteau wrote a speech—Garfield v. Hancock—which he never orated and instead simply printed for individuals to read. When Garfield narrowly defeated Winfield Hancock, Guiteau took credit for the victory and sought a patronage position as his reward. He became psychotic in his quest for the consulship in Paris, asking the president, the party, the State Department, and Garfield's Cabinet for assistance in gaining the job. He owned one set of clothes and eventually was banned from the White House.

When this occurred, Guiteau's idea changed. No longer was he seeking a position in the administration. Instead, he believed he had been ordered to kill an ungrateful Garfield. He borrowed money and purchased a handgun that he believed would look nice in a museum after he killed the country's leader. Yet this was not simply a callous assassination. Guiteau sent letters warning Garfield and asking for Stephen Blaine (Garfield's Secretary of State who had been particularly nonunderstanding with Guiteau) to be fired; and he wrote to Commanding General William Sherman wanting protection. Perhaps most bizarrely Guiteau even went to the city jail so he could see what his new surroundings would be like. On July 2, 1881, Guiteau walked up to Garfield in the Baltimore and Potomac Railroad Station and shot Garfield at point blank range, eventually leading to his death. Andrew Jackson's belief in patronage politics had carried throughout the proceeding five decades and convinced citizens that there were potential rewards for work done on behalf of candidates. When Garfield and his staff refused Giteau's advances, he fell victim to a want to be bureaucrat scorned.

143

In response to Garfield's assassination, our nation moved quickly to assure new standards in bureaucracy. Through the Civil Service Reform Act (or Pendleton Act) we began a fast transition toward a merit system where qualifications and performance would play more of a role in the awarding of administrative positions throughout the federal government. The hope was to prevent future presidents from having to deal with individuals like Guiteau by adding a buffer (in this case merit) between the two. Further attempts to neutralize the bureaucracy came with the Hatch Act of 1939. In this federal act (formerly referred to as An Act to Prevent Pernicious Political Activities) the government prohibited civil servants in the executive branch from engaging in partisan political activity.

Questions of neutrality never fully disappeared from political debates, however. Presidents have always maintained an ability to appoint hundreds of positions upon being elected after all. There are positive and negative aspects of both approaches. Allowing presidents to have the ability to appoint patronage positions provides a great opportunity for them to reward loyal supporters and surround themselves with individuals they hold in high esteem and trust. On the negative side, however, patronage can lead to inept individuals being appointed and possibly damaging citizen trust and faith in government. We need not look much further than Hurricane Katrina to see a prime modern example of this.

George W. Bush tabbed Joe Allbaugh to run the Federal Emergency Management Association in January of 2001 after being elected. Allbaugh had successfully run Bush's campaign. As Allbaugh's first action, he turned and hired Michael Brown to be General Counsel for the agency. Prior to this position, Brown had served as Judges and Stewards Commissioner for the International Arabian Horse Association. He quickly advanced within the organization, becoming acting Deputy Director in September 2001 (before being formally nominated for the position in March 2002). When Allbaugh quit after the creation of the Department of Homeland Security, Bush turned to Brown to run FEMA. This is how Brown found himself in charge of the federal government's response to Hurricane Katrina in August and September of 2005. When the federal response was deemed to be too slow and inappropriate given the gravity of the situation, it was Brown who caught all of the flak. Katrina showed how truly unprepared and unqualified Brown was for his position. Despite Bush's continued backing (Brownie's doing a heck of a job) he eventually resigned as director on September 12, 2005. While presidents had long appointed far less qualified individuals for key positions in government, none had been forced to perform in the spotlight of every media outlet in the world like Michael Brown.

With individuals like Guiteau and Brown in our country's history, we can see clearly why the merit/patronage debate has had such a profound impact. In the following readings, we will examine the idea of neutrality further to see how it impacts bureaucratic performance in government. After all, if appointed individuals are as effective as members of the civil service, it raises new questions to consider when discussing how we should staff government agencies. David Lewis argues that programs administered by appointed individuals perform less effectively than those led by civil servants. He believes that the entrenched bureau experience and longer time in office lead to the better performance. William West, on the other hand, argues that nonpartisan objectivity does not serve the interests of presidents or members of government. He stresses the loss of responsiveness as a key cost of the push for neutrality.

YES

David E. Lewis

Testing Pendleton's Premise: Do Political Appointees Make Worse Bureaucrats?

In the aftermath of Hurricane Katrina major national newspapers and numerous public officials questioned whether the large number of political appointees in the Federal Emergency Management Agency (FEMA) contributed to the poor handling of this natural disaster.[1] By almost any count, the agency has a large number of appointees for its size and critics have argued that FEMA's appointee-laden management structure created numerous management problems. The FEMA example raises the important question of how political appointments influence management not only in FEMA but across the federal government. Questions about whether appointees or careerists are best for government performance go back at least to the late 1800s in the United States. One of the primary motivations for the 1883 passage of the Pendleton Act was to ensure competent administration of federal programs by creating a merit-based civil service system. Reformers like Woodrow Wilson believed that federal program administration would improve if it was inhabited by professional civil servants hired, fired, and promoted on the basis of merit rather than political appointment. Those objecting to its passage lamented not only the loss of valuable patronage but also worried that those employees covered under the system would become less responsive to political direction either because civil service would entrench opposition party workers or create an unresponsive aristocratic class.

Apart from helping us understand FEMA's disastrous response to Hurricane Katrina and resolve historical debates about civil service versus political appointments, there are two additional reasons for studying the relationship between appointees and performance. First, scholars have noted an increase in the number of political appointees not only in the United States but also in a number of different countries including Australia, Britain, Finland, France, Germany, Japan, and Spain. Research on the relationship between appointees and performance can inform debates about reducing the number of appointees and the likely impact of increases in appointments in different contexts.[2]

Second, a widely cited literature shows how different strategies for political control hurt agency performance. For example, when preferences between legislatures and agencies diverge, legislatures generally reduce agency discretion

From *The Journal of Politics,* November 2007, pp. 1073–1077, 1086. Copyright © 2007 by the Southern Political Science Association. Reprinted by permission of Cambridge University Press.

by writing more specific statutes, strengthening administrative procedures, and monitoring more carefully. Efforts to restrict discretion can reduce incentives for bureaucrats to develop and use expertise.[3] Studying the relationship between appointees and performance can test whether another means of securing responsiveness—political appointees—also diminishes performance.

Despite the importance and the duration of this topic, no consensus exists on whether appointees or careerists (or some combination of the two) are best for federal management. This is partly due to difficulties defining and measuring performance across agencies. In this paper I use a new numerical measure of federal program performance—the Bush Administration's Program Assessment Rating Tool (PART) scores—to analyze the relationship between political appointees and management. I find that programs administered by politically appointed bureau chiefs get systematically lower PART evaluations than programs run by bureau chiefs drawn from the civil service. I find that career managers have more direct bureau experience and longer tenures, and these characteristics are significantly related to performance. Political appointees have higher education levels, more private or not-for-profit management experience, and more varied work experience than careerists, but these characteristics are uncorrelated with performance. I argue that concerns about the relationship between appointees and performance articulated in the original debates about civil service reform and illustrated in FEMA's poor response to Hurricane Katrina are justified. Efforts to enhance political control can sometimes reduce overall bureaucratic competence. I conclude that reducing the number of appointees or increased sensitivity to appointee selection based upon certain background characteristics could improve federal bureau management.

Competing Views About Appointees and Management Performance

There are competing views about whether presidential appointees or career executives are better for performance. On the one hand, a long tradition argues that political appointees drawn from outside the civil service bring needed energy and responsiveness to federal management. According to this view, low public sector wages and the lack of pay-for-performance salary structures push the best and the brightest workers into the private sector. Civil service rules and regulations that stymie efforts to recruit, train, and retain good managers only lessen the attractiveness of federal work for potential employees. As a consequence of these factors, appointees drawn from the private sector arguably have higher levels of human capital than their careerist counterparts.

The distinct means of appointment and prior background experience create systematic differences between the two populations of federal executives. Appointees and careerists have different perspectives on the policy world (generalist vs. specialist) and a different relationship to political stakeholders (superior vs. inferior knowledge of political stakeholders' preferences). Career executives are more likely to start low in a bureau's hierarchy, work a significant portion of their career in that agency, and be a substantive expert in the policy area they manage. Appointees are less likely to be specialists, less likely to see the world through the bureau's eyes, be more attuned to the preferences of elected stakeholders, and better able to do the political work necessary for successful program implementation.

On the other hand, an impressive literature has lauded the management advantages of career executives. Indeed, the historical intellectual motivation for the career merit system itself was to establish a more competent, professional administration of government. According to this view, career executives have subject area expertise, public management skills, and longer tenure. Each of these characteristics are said to improve management. Subject area expertise and experience with the bureau being administered reduces information asymmetries between the manager and staff and facilitates monitoring and program implementation. Careerists are more likely to have *public* management experience. Many generic management skills are difficult to transfer from the private sector due to the important differences between the two work environments. Even in cases where political appointees have comparable experience and expertise, agencies administered by appointees experience higher turnover. Increased turnover creates leadership vacuums, mixed signals about agency goals, an inability to credibly commit to reform, and generally poorer performance. Turnover also disrupts working relationships among functionally related agencies and programs.

Related to the question of whether appointees or careerists are better for management is the question of whether some combination of appointees and careerists in a management team is best for performance. A number of works examine how appointees and careerists can work creatively and productively together. Indeed, the right balance of appointees and careerists may allow appointees to correct the biases that characterize careerist decision making and vice versa.

Testing Competing Views

It has been difficult to evaluate competing views about the relationship between appointments and performance empirically, and as a consequence we know strikingly little about this important issue systematically. A number of excellent works detail how appointees in specific administrations did or did not influence administrative policy and performance in specific agencies. Research which examines a broader set of agencies and isolates the influence of appointee management on performance, however, is scarce. One major difficulty is that it is hard to define good performance objectively and in a manner acceptable to different stakeholders. Is a count of enforcement actions a good measure of performance? How about the number of patents issued or the number of lawsuits filed per dollar? For administration officials a definition of good performance must include responsiveness to the president's policy agenda. For members of Congress, clients of the agency, or other interested parties, the definition of good performance is likely to differ.

A second difficulty is that it is hard to compare executives and agencies against each other since agencies have different mandates, operating environments, and constraints. Doing a comparative study of executive performance is an awesome task. It requires an acceptable definition of good performance, an identification of the universe of federal bureau chiefs, an acceptable grading scheme, willingness on the part of federal executives to participate, and an approach that is sensitive to differences among federal programs. Given these constraints, it is no surprise that large-N evaluations of comparative management performance have been difficult to execute.

The large-N evidence that seeks to examine objective performance focuses primarily on agencies engaged in macroeconomic forecasting or does not adequately distinguish appointees from careerists. The literature examining macroeconomic forecasting finds at the state level that forecasting agencies with either appointed directors and careerist employees or careerist directors and at-will employees produce the most accurate forecasts. At the federal level the evidence suggests that there is no difference in current-year forecast performance among agencies based upon differences in agency design. There is, however, some evidence which suggests that the more politicized Office of Management and Budget is systematically more optimistic in some of its future-year forecasts than the less politicized Social Security Administration, although the optimism appears unrelated to changing politicization levels within each agency over time. It is unclear, however, whether the findings are generalizable to other types of agencies.

Gilmour and Lewis use the Program Assessment Rating Tool (PART) scores described below to compare the performance of federal programs run by managers in the Senior Executive Service (SES) with programs administered by Senate-confirmed appointees. They find that federal programs administered by Senate-confirmed appointees get systematically lower PART scores but do not distinguish between appointed and careerist members of the SES or explain what it is about Senate-confirmed appointees that leads to poorer program performance.

Using the PART for Evaluating Management Performance

The Bush Administration's PART system provides a useful means of overcoming the substantial difficulties described above with measuring performance. The PART system is a grading scheme used by the Office of Management and Budget (OMB) to evaluate the performance of federal programs numerically. It was developed through the Federal Advisory Commission Act process in cooperation with the President's Management Council, the National Academy of Public Administration, and other interested parties from the administration, Congress, and the nonprofit sector. Four categories of performance receive grades from 0 to 100 based upon a series of 25–30 yes/no questions filled out jointly by agencies and OMB examiners.[4] The four categories are:

- Program Purpose & Design (weight = 20%): to assess whether the program design and purpose are clear and defensible;
- Strategic Planning (weight = 10%): to assess whether the agency sets valid annual and long-term goals for the program;

- Program Management (weight = 20%): to rate agency management of the program, including financial oversight and program improvement efforts; and
- Program Results (weight = 50%): to rate program performance on goals reviewed in the strategic planning section and through other evaluations.[5]

These raw scores are weighted and combined for a total numerical score (0–100) and overall categorical grade—ineffective, results not demonstrated, adequate, moderately effective, and effective.[6] The Bush Administration graded 234 programs (20%) for the FY 2004 budget, 176 more for the FY 2005 budget, and 206 programs for FY 2006. The remaining federal programs were scheduled to be graded in the FY 2007–2008 budgets.[7] There is quite a bit of variation in the total scores. For the cohort graded in the FY 2006 budget, the average score is 62.78 and the minimum and maximum are 13.82 and 96.7, respectively. The lowest scoring programs for FY 2006 were programs in the Bureau of Indian Affairs (Department of the Interior), the Office of Elementary and Secondary Education (Department of Education), and the Office of Post-secondary Education (Department of Education).[8] The highest scoring programs were in the Secret Service (Department of Homeland Security), National Science Foundation, and the Bureau of Educational and Cultural Affairs (Department of State).[9]

The PART is a measure of *program* performance and is useful for comparing management performance for two reasons. First, as indicated above, the way that program performance is evaluated is largely through the presence or absence of good *management* practices and performance. Second, good program performance is partly a product of management performance. If one controls for program-specific characteristics, then the impact of appointee or careerist management on program performance can be isolated.

Potential Problems with Using PART Scores

There are a number of potential objections to the use of PART scores to make inferences about management performance. First, there are different definitions of good management, and PART scores may not measure all of the aspects of these different definitions that we care about. No measure of program or management performance—including PART—is going to be able to account for all of these definitions. The PART comprises only one measure of good performance, but it has a number of advantages. Specifically, the evaluations are subject to public scrutiny, the PART is applied across more than 600 federal programs, and the instrument is comprised of generally agreed upon aspects of good performance.

A second potential difficulty with using PART scores is that there may be irregularities in the way that PART is applied across programs since programs face different legal, budgetary, and resource constraints, examiners vary in competence and experience, and data availability and quality varies. Even if there is error in the application of the PART, however, the scores can still be useful for evaluating program performance provided that the grades correlate somewhat with real performance and statistical analysis is conducted carefully.[10]

Evaluated program performance is a function of factors (both program-specific and manager-specific) that add up to true performance and some error, either a little or a lot. This error is not a problem for making comparisons between different types of managers unless the error is nonrandom and not only nonrandom, but also correlated with whether or not a program is run by a political appointee or careerist. If the error in PART scores is purely random, say a few extra points here and a few less there for all the grades, this will increase the size of standard errors (increase inefficiency). This makes it *less* likely that any statistically significant relationship between appointment authority and performance emerges and implies that the statistical tests using PART scores will be relatively conservative.

Of course, there is still the possibility of a third problem, that the grades are biased, that the errors in applying PART occur in nonrandom and pernicious ways. For example, it is possible that all programs created by Democratic presidents or all programs administered by small bureaus are graded systematically worse than programs created by Republican presidents or programs in large bureaus. While not an admirable grading scheme, this would not cause problems for inference so long as Democratic and Republican programs and programs in large and small bureaus were equally likely to be run by political appointees or careerists. That is, if the errors in grading are uncorrelated with the variable of interest (political appointee vs. careerist), we are on solid ground using the PART evaluations to make inferences about program performance and, thus, management performance.

In the worst case scenario for inference, there is error in the grading of federal programs that is correlated with whether the program is administered by a careerist or appointee. If this is the case one can prevent inferential errors by controlling for the source of bias. For example, if our concern is that all programs created by Democratic presidents or all programs in small bureaus are being graded down, we can estimate statistical models that allow us to control for precisely these program-specific and bureau-specific factors.

It is important to note that if such bias in the grading existed, the errors would likely favor political appointees. If the administration wanted to favor one group of managers over another, they would favor appointees over careerists since appointees were selected by the administration and their performance can more directly be tied to the president. In total, if used thoughtfully and with the appropriate caveats, the PART scores provide a unique opportunity to analyze the relationship between appointees and federal program performance.

. . .

This research has used the Bush Administration's Program Assessment Rating Tool (PART) scores to evaluate the relationship between appointees and federal program performance. The use of PART scores and the collection of biographical information on bureau chiefs provides a useful way of evaluating systematically two important questions in political science, namely *Are appointees or careerists better for federal management? What differences between appointees and careerists matter for management performance?* This analysis demonstrates that appointees get systematically lower performance grades than careerists. Previous bureau experience and longer tenure in management positions explain why careerist-run programs get higher grades. The advantages that appointees tend to have over careerist bureau chiefs such as higher levels of education, private management experience, and work in other departments outside the bureau are not significantly related to total PART score. Public affairs experience, however, does seem to help on one aspect of public management which is translating political wishes into a clear program purpose and design.

The systematic results demonstrating the appointee-careerist management gap have implications for our understanding the federal government's response to Hurricane Katrina, the historical justification for the merit system, current debates about reducing the number of appointees, and democratic theory. They suggest that the negative influence of appointees on FEMA performance is generalizable to other programs and agencies. These results add weight to what civil service reformers like George Pendleton believed, namely that a merit-based civil service system would lead to lower turnover in the federal workforce and the cultivation of useful administrative expertise.

One implication of this research is that reducing the number of political appointees or stemming the increase in the United States and other countries may be one means of improving performance. It appears that the need for bureaucratic control and historical demands for patronage have pushed the number of appointees beyond the numbers optimal for performance in the United States. Putting federal program management in the hands of careerist managers might help remedy that imbalance. Generally, finding the right mix of appointees and careerist can improve performance and more research needs to be conducted to find this "sweet spot" in the balance between appointee and careerist management.

Short of reducing the number of appointees, this research suggests other means of improving performance. Presidents could keep or increase the number of appointees provided they ensure the competence of the people they select or focus on selecting people who are willing to serve longer than most appointees do. The president and Congress could improve performance as measured by PART by recruiting managers from the career service and recruiting appointees who are "in-and-outers," executives who have served in previous administrations in similar positions.

In total, the research highlights how securing democratic control of the bureaucracy can erode competence. To be effective the modern administrative state needs a corps of professional, continuing personnel who are competent at what they do. Creating a corps of professional administrative officials, however, can make administrative officials more autonomous. Making government democratic requires solving the difficult problem of both establishing a competent government and reining in the autonomy that comes from making it competent.

Notes

1. Hsu, Spencer S. 2005. "Leaders Lacking Disaster Experience," *Washington Post,* September 9, 2005, p. A1; James, Frank, and Andrew Martin. 2005. "Ex-officials Say Weakened FEMA Botched Response," *Chicago Tribune,* September 3, 2005 (on-line edition).

2. For calls to reduce the number of appointees see Gruber, Amelia, "Three Former Officials Call for Fewer Political Appointees," *Government Executive Magazine,* March 6, 2003 (on-line edition); Feingold, Kenneth, "Deficit Reduction—Reducing the Number of Political Appointees" (http://feingold .senate.gov/issues_appointees.html).

3. Efforts at political control can also make it *less* likely that bureaucrats will do what politicians want if bureaucracies cannot do what politicians ask and will be punished in any case.

4. The instrument is adjusted for the type of program (regulatory, block grant, research and development, etc.). . . . Some examples of PART questions can be found at http://www.whitehouse.gov/omb/expectmore/partquestions.html.

5. U.S. Office of Management and Budget.

6. Disagreements between OMB and agencies are resolved by appeals up the OMB hierarchy. Appeals first go to the OMB branch chief then to the division director and program associate director, if necessary.

7. The administration claims a loosely stratified sampling scheme was used to select the first cohort. When asked to describe the initial sampling scheme, Marcus Peacock, Program Associate Director, Office of Management and Budget, called the approach a stratified sampling scheme. He said OMB tried to get a diverse group of programs, large and small, programs with a history of good management and bad management, and programs with different missions and functions. Comments made at Program Performance and the FY 2004 Budget Process, June 13, 2003, 2247 Rayburn House Office Building, Washington, DC.

8. The programs are the LWCF Land Acquisition program (13.82), Impact Aid Payments for Federal Property (22), and the B.J. Stupak Olympic Scholarship Program (23).

9. The programs are Protective Intelligence (95.18), Polar Tools, Facilities, and Logistics (95.29), and the Global and Cultural Exchanges program (96.17).

10. Evidence from interviews with OMB and agency officials involved in the PART process indicates that both the bureau chiefs being evaluated and budget examiners doing the evaluating believe that the scores measure variance in true management quality.

William F. West

 **NO**

Neutral Competence and Political Responsiveness: An Uneasy Relationship

Neutral competence has retained a good deal of currency in the public administration literature despite the realization that politics and administration are intertwined. Although the concept has been developed, it's modern version is based most explicitly by scholars lamenting the politicization of the Office of Management and Budget (OMB) and other organizations within the Executive Office of the President (EOP). Their argument is that the president is best served by nonpartisan institutions and dispassionate civil servants that will furnish the expertise and continuity essential for effective governance and that will also be responsive to his political needs.

Notwithstanding the appeal of neutral competence, the modern version of the concept is based on facile assumptions about the compatibility between nonpartisan objectivity and political responsiveness. This tension is reflected in the ambiguity of the concept, itself—at least as articulated by its leading exponent, Hugh Heclo. In a related vein, empirical arguments by students of public administration and political science suggest two, competing challenges to the doctrine of neutral competence as a viable prescription for presidential management. One is the oft-noted tendency of bureaucrats to pursue agendas that differ from those of their political principals. The other, implied by two recent studies of OMB, is that bureaucrats must become politicized in order to be responsive.

The intent here is not to argue that neutral competence is an irrelevant value for bureaucracy. It brings important qualities to the administrative process, especially in those contexts where political responsiveness raises ethical issues or where it might result in unsound policy. Although such functional distinctions are not always clear-cut, these might respectively include the application of policy in individual cases and the provision of analysis for use by policy makers. The narrower point of this essay is simply that it may not be realistic to expect that bureaucratic agents charged with accomplishing the policy objectives of the president and other political executives can do so by remaining nonpartisan and objective.

From *Policy Studies Journal,* May 2005, pp. 147–154, 156–158. Copyright © 2005 by Policy Studies Organization. Reprinted by permission of Wiley Blackwell via Rightslink.

The Doctrine of Neutral Competence: Old and New

Like other administrative values, the doctrine of neutral competence is grounded in interrelated normative and empirical assumptions about the role of bureaucracy in government. It was originally conterminous with the idea that public administration could and should be technical as opposed to political in nature. As this neat distinction broke down, scholars sought to redefine neutral competence in an effort to reconcile nonpartisanship and objectivity with responsiveness to politically based control. A discussion of the concept's evolution provides a useful basis for understanding its limitations and ultimately its ambiguity as currently employed.

The Traditional Model

The term "neutral competence" is most closely associated with the "traditional school" of public administration. As is frequently recited, the foundation of the traditional model was the assumption that politics and administration were conceptually distinct and practically separable activities. The former had to do with articulating the will of the state and was infused with value judgments. In our democratic system, it was the province of elected institutions—especially legislative assemblies. In contrast, the administrative process had to do with "getting things done." As such, it was the province of the bureaucracy. In so far as it existed, the pure form of the traditional model envisioned little intrusion by politicians and bureaucrats into each others' functional domains.

It followed from this simple dichotomy that administration should be as objective and efficient as possible. Whether or not Woodrow Wilson's 1887 essay had much influence in its time, the general thrust of scholarship during the next several decades was consistent with his thesis that administration was a technical enterprise. A closely related premise was that bureaucrats, themselves, should be competent and should not be motivated by partisan concerns. The latter prescriptions were reflected in several Progressive-era reforms, including the independent commission form of regulatory agency and the city manager form of local government. The most important institutional manifestation of the doctrine of neutral competence was the merit system of personnel administration. A reaction to the alleged corruption and incompetence associated with patronage, one purpose of civil service reform was to recruit and promote capable bureaucrats through the use of objective, job-related examinations. Another was to insulate bureaucrats from inappropriate political pressures by creating a career civil service protected by due process.

The appeal of the traditional model could be explained in part by its neat reconciliation of the administrative process with the American constitutional principles of representative democracy and separation of powers. As is also frequently recited, however, its underlying assumption about the character of public administration could not withstand the growth of bureaucracy and of delegated authority that occurred during the New Deal and afterwards. In fact, the leading scholars of the traditional era never embraced the politics/

administration dichotomy in anything approaching absolute terms. To some, perhaps, it was a premise that was sufficiently realistic to serve as a basis for prescriptive theory. At least to some of its later adherents, it also provided a convenient rationalization for addressing the constitutional, normative, and political issues (including the inter-branch tensions) surrounding the expansion of delegated authority and of executive power more generally. This was almost certainly true of the authors of the Brownlow Report, as one notable illustration. In any case, students of bureaucracy in the late 1930s and 1940s explicitly began to emphasize the fact that administration was infused with politics.

Although few today would contend that administration can be divorced from politics, a coherent and widely accepted doctrine has not emerged to replace the traditional model. Rather, political and administrative values have come to enjoy an uneasy coexistence. On the one hand, we want bureaucracy to be responsive to those who are affected by its decisions. This goal is reflected, not only in academic writing but in institutional arrangements such as notice-and-comment rulemaking, the expansion of standing in the administrative process, and the requirement that agencies consult with advisory committees. Yet on the other hand, traditional norms of objectivity and rationality are clearly evinced in administrative institutions such as cost-benefit analysis and the requirement that agencies base policy decisions on evidence in a record.

If it is schizophrenic in terms of its underlying assumptions about the character of administration, the simultaneous pursuit of political and traditional values is also easy enough to understand. In fact, administration combines technical and political elements. To the extent that it rests on the latter, moreover, many remain uncomfortable with the exercise of political discretion by non-elected officials.

Reframing Neutral Competence

The unsettled state of administrative doctrine affords a useful context for understanding the fate of neutral competence as a prescription for bureaucratic behavior. Although many have stressed the fact that civil servants (especially high-ranking ones) must operate within political environments, even some of the same observers have stressed the need for careerists to be nonpartisan and objective. Among the latter, perhaps the most explicit and certainly the most influential is Hugh Heclo. Although Heclo is much too sophisticated to conceive of administration as purely a technocratic process, he reframes the norm of neutral competence essentially by distinguishing between the roles of career bureaucrats and the political executives they serve. He contends that the former can effectively promote the interests of the latter, much as senior careerists in Great Britain are loyal to whatever government is in power without sacrificing their objectivity to partisanship. As he describes it:

> Neutral competence does not mean the possession of a direct-dial line to an overarching, non-partisan conception of the public interest. Rather it consists of giving one's cooperation and best independent judgment

of the issues to partisan bosses—and of being sufficiently uncommitted to do so for a succession of partisan leaders. The independence entailed in neutral competence . . . exists precisely in order to serve the aims of partisan leadership.

Heclo develops his thesis through an historical evaluation of the Office of Management and Budget (OMB). Drawing a comparison with its more wholesome predecessor, the Bureau of the Budget (BoB), he argues that OMB's effectiveness has suffered as the result of its politicization. This has occurred in part through a layering of presidential appointees at the top of the organization. In a related vein, it has also occurred through the destabilization of OMB's structure and personnel, and through the evolution of an organizational culture and incentive system that encourages partisan behavior by its career staff. Heclo observes that OMB's politicization has resulted from the president's need for political responsiveness, but that it has ironically undermined the agency's usefulness to the presidency by compromising values critical to effective governance. Among them are the career bureaucracy's objective expertise, its institutional memory, its networks of communication, and its knowledge of governmental procedures and folkways.

Other scholars have offered similar assessments of OMB, of other units within the Executive Office of the President (EOP), and of the bureaucracy more generally. Implicitly or explicitly, the common theme of their arguments is not that policy implementation is apolitical, but that objectivity can effectively be put to the service of political goals. Their common prescription is for politicians to place more trust in bureaucrats and established institutions.

In a sense, the revised version of neutral competence has moved the institutional boundary separating politics from administration. Again, these functions respectively coincided with the legislative and administrative processes under traditional doctrine as a way of improving bureaucracy's performance and of reconciling its role in government with a simple (or perhaps simplistic) conception of separation of powers. As a concession to the reality of delegated authority and to the president's corresponding need to shape policy through the bureaucracy, they are now defined by a distinction between the roles of political appointees and career civil servants within the administrative process.

Challenges to Neutral Competence: Reexamining OMB

Notwithstanding its influence within the public administration community as a prescription for improving executive management and bureaucratic performance, the doctrine of neutral competence may not be compatible with the president's need for political responsiveness. At least as articulated by Heclo, the concept, itself, is vague or inconsistent in this regard. On the one hand, for example, Heclo describes neutral competence as "the best independent judgment of the issues" and as a "fine disregard for the political bearing of who believes what at a given time." On the other, he describes it as "partisanship that shifts with the changing partisans."

There would seem to be little difference between the latter characterization of neutral competence and its undesirable antithesis, politicization. If one defines the concept in the former terms of nonpartisan objectivity, however, studies of the administrative presidency present two additional questions concerning its relationship to political responsiveness in the Executive Office. The first, raised most forcefully by Terry Moe and by Moe and Scott Wilson, is whether established institutions staffed by career bureaucrats can be responsive to the president and other political executives. The second, which is implied by the inconsistency of Heclo's definition, is whether such responsiveness (in so far as it occurs) can be apolitical or nonpartisan under any reasonable constructions of those terms.

The Principal-Agent Problem

Although the doctrine of neutral competence holds that politicians can trust career bureaucrats and established institutions to respond to their wishes, a passing familiarity with the literature in political science reveals that this is hardly a foregone conclusion. Many have argued that bureaucrats have their own policy preferences that are grounded in their organizations' routines and sense of mission, in their professional orientations, or in their allegiances to specific clientele groups. Moreover, bureaucrats' ability to pursue their own goals is allegedly reinforced by their tenure and by their technical expertise, by their control over relevant information, and by other "asymmetries of knowledge" that inhibit oversight and control by politicians.

Moe and others have argued in these respects that the explanation for presidents' unwillingness to rely on civil servants and established institutions is simple: Given its inertial character and the environment within which it operates, bureaucracy is not sufficiently responsive to their political agendas. Moe feels that this is true even of organizations within the Executive Office. The difficulty of controlling bureaucracies has arguably posed more and more of a dilemma for chief executives as the growth of delegated authority has rendered control over the administrative process increasingly critical to their success in office. In marked contrast to the criticisms and prescriptive conclusions of Heclo and others, Moe feels that presidents have adopted ad hoc, centralized, and politicized management strategies because neutral competence does not adequately serve their need for "responsive competence."

Moe adds that the institutional needs of the presidency are, themselves, different from the neo-Brownlowian premises (my interpretation) that inform the analyses of Heclo and others. Although presidents are strongly driven to exercise policy leadership through the administrative process as well as the legislative process in Moe's view, and although this is a (much needed) source of governmental cohesiveness in a broad sense, chief executives care little about economy and efficiency as ends in themselves. Moreover, Moe feels that an essential quality of the presidency is its incumbents' short-term orientation. In light of these facts, presidents do not place a high premium on the continuity and other managerial values that Heclo associates with neutral competence.

Politicized Responsiveness

The second challenge to the doctrine of neutral competence is in a sense the inverse of Moe's thesis. It is the contention that bureaucrats and established organizations within the EOP *can* be responsive to the wishes of politicians precisely because they are willing to engage in politicized behavior. This possibility is suggested by two recent studies. One challenges the assertion that the Bureau of the Budget (BoB) was characterized by nonpartisan objectivity during its supposed golden age; the other observes politicized responsiveness by career bureaucrats in the modern OMB's oversight of agency policy making.

Again, Heclo argues that the BoB of the 1940s and 1950s served presidents well without being excessively politicized. As he notes:

> Neutral competence has always been a somewhat fragile growth in American government, and the old (post 1939) Bureau of the Budget was one of the few places where it was nourished and took root. Talk with the veterans of that institution and they harken back to a golden age when "the old Bureau was really something special." The Bureau was a place where the "generalist ethic was admired and defended," a place where you were "you were both a representative for the President's particular view and the top objective resource for the continuous institution of the presidency."

The ambiguity that runs throughout Heclo's conception of neutral competence is evident in the tension between representing the "President's particular view" and serving as an "objective resource." In any case, a study by Dickinson and Rudalevige leaves little doubt that the former role was prominent in BoB under Harry Truman. Based on an extensive analysis of internal memoranda and other archival data, their study concludes that "BoB [career] personnel did more than identify the president's legislative priorities: they were actively involved in shaping those priorities into legislation, and tracking the legislation as it worked its way through Congress." In so doing, they were "clearly expected to respond to the president's political needs."

Although Dickinson and Rudalevige take exception with Heclo's characterization of BoB's golden age, they attempt to salvage a distinction between the roles of bureaucrats and political advisors. Thus, they note that, in addition to promoting the president's short-term political interests, BoB careerists of the Truman era demonstrated a sensitivity to the needs of the presidency as an institution. This included a concern with issues of bureaucratic freelancing and inter-organizational coordination. Whether or not such issues can truly be differentiated from the interests of particular incumbents to govern effectively, however, the authors also note that the functions of OMB officials and White House aides were so closely intertwined that there was often little distinction between the two. Moreover, careerists performed activities as overtly political in nature as writing speeches in support of policies and collecting information on the attitudes of interest groups, the media, state and local officials, and the general public concerning actual and contemplated policy initiatives by the president.

Similar patterns of politicized responsiveness by career bureaucrats are evident in my study of regulatory oversight by OMB's Office of Information and Regulatory Affairs (OIRA). OIRA is an organization of about 60 individuals that reviews the roughly 500–700 "significant" rules developed by federal agencies each year. The purposes of regulatory review are to ensure that agency policies are based on sound cost-benefit analysis *and* that they are otherwise consistent with the president's agenda. As Stuart Shapiro argues in an insightful paper, the latter of these goals almost always takes precedence over the former when the two come into conflict.

OIRA has only one presidential appointee, and its organizational structure and key personnel have been remarkably stable since the early 1980s. Thus, although it is the most significant extension of centralized executive influence over the bureaucracy in recent decades, it bears little resemblance to the personalized management strategies that presidents are alleged to prefer by both their critics and their defenders. Nevertheless, OMB clearance of agency rule has adapted readily from a confrontational, anti-regulatory posture under Ronald Reagan and George H.W. Bush, to a more cooperative, consultative approach under Bill Clinton, and back to a more aggressive orientation under George W. Bush. It has done so in part by internalizing the political agendas of different incumbents. This process, which has been facilitated by communications with White House staff, has included developing a sensitivity to the actual and probable reactions of the current administration and its most important constituents to agency initiatives. To the latter end, some OIRA staffers have kept their ears to the ground by subscribing to trade journals and by monitoring other media coverage of regulatory issues in their areas of responsibility.

Neither Dickinson and Rudaleviage nor I disconfirm the argument that neutral competence can effectively serve the president's political interests: We only demonstrate that this has not happened in the cases we examine. Still, our studies suggest a fundamental limitation of efforts to reconcile neutral competence with responsiveness. Heclo's prescription for rendering "the best independent judgment . . . to partisan bosses" is reasonable enough as far as it goes. To the extent that bureaucrats are required to make *independent decisions* in implementing policy, however, and to the extent that those decisions involve political discretion, then civil servants must in some manner take up the partisan concerns of their bosses in order to be responsive.

Dickinson and Rudaleviage demonstrate that career BoB officials were expected to exercise discretion as agents of the president under Harry Truman, and that they did so in a variety of ways. As many have remarked, OMB has become increasingly important as a centralized instrument for achieving presidential policy objectives in the intervening decades. This has allegedly occurred in response to chief executives' frustration in their efforts to affect policy change through the line bureaucracy. Whether the institutionalization of regulatory review in terms of its organizational continuity and its reliance on a stable cadre of career personnel is anomalous as a strategy or technique for centralized control is an interesting question. In any event, it would be impossible for OIRA's lone political executive to weigh in intelligently on all or even a sizeable proportion of the political issues that arise in the oversight process. Indeed, these issues are sometimes resolved most effectively through informal give and take between OIRA analysts and agency staff as regulatory proposals are being developed (and before they are formally submitted for review). The former must exercise independent initiative in promoting the president's interests.

The Limitations and Uses of Neutral Competence

In brief, neutral competence may never have been so neutral at the old BoB, and responsiveness in the performance of at least one important function by the current OMB has occurred through the political sensitization of its career staff. Whether such responsive competence has been truly competent or whether it has diminished OMB's managerial capacity in the ways that Heclo, Wyszomirski, Rourke, and others associate with politicization is a question that will have to wait for another day. (The conduct of regulatory review is not lacking for either its defenders or its critics on this and other scores, for example.) The point is that neutral competence—at least defined as nonpartisan objectivity—may not be a viable prescription for OMB given the president's demands for political responsiveness. Or at least it may not be for those OMB activities invested with agency and requiring political discretion.

Although the concept of neutral competence has been explicated most fully as it relates to the OMB and other units within the EOP, it obviously has broader implications. Certainly, there are those who criticize its decline throughout government as a symptom of politicians' misguided distrust of the bureaucracy. It may be useful, therefore, briefly to speculate in broader institutional terms about the compatibility of neutral competence with political responsiveness in other contexts, as well as about its role within the administrative process more generally.

. . .

The Importance of Objectivity

One should hasten to reiterate, however, that this latter version of neutral competence is hardly neutral. What of its more straightforward definition as nonpartisanship and objectivity? To note the uneasy relationship between these values and political responsiveness, as this essay has, it not to say that neutral competence is unimportant. The enduring appeal of objectivity as an administrative value reflects a tension between representative democracy and delegated authority that is not eliminated by the practical necessity of the latter.

Under any type of regime, moreover, neutral competence can enhance the fairness and effectiveness of government. As Weimer argues, for example, it may be an especially valuable quality in developing nations, where bureaucracy's corruption and lack of technical capacity have often prevented governments from addressing critical human needs. Beyond the effective provision of services and infrastructure, the legitimacy or confidence in government inspired by neutral competence may help provide the necessary medium for the development of democratic institutions.

An important observation from a doctrinal perspective is that administration is hardly monolithic. Often slighted by political scientists, the fact that agencies perform different functions within different technical and political task environments has profound implications for the process values that are both possible and desirable. As Emmette Redford argues, for example, neutral competence may be especially desirable as a constraint on individual or "micro level" decisions, such administrative adjudication or those involving discretion to prosecute, where the qualities of objectivity, accuracy, and consistency from one case to the next are of paramount importance. Even administrative policy decisions are typically based in large part on empirical premises about means-ends relationships that should be evaluated as dispassionately and expertly as possible. If they often succumb to political temptations in practice, for example, policy analysts should arguably strive for objectivity in providing advice to decision makers.

Of course, such distinctions are not always straightforward. As anyone familiar with administrative law knows, bureaucratic actions are often difficult to place into neat functional categories such as rulemaking, or adjudication, or the exercise of executive discretion. Even when they can be, decisions are often based on different kinds of premises that ideally call for different qualities in the decision maker. As just one illustration, decisions applying the law in individual cases can have policy and political implications that far transcend the parties immediately affected. If bureaucrats must ultimately sort all of this out, however, perhaps adopting different role orientations for different kinds and dimensions of decisions, they can at least do so more intelligently by being able to relate doctrine to context. This has important if sometimes neglected implications for public affairs education.

Conclusion

The overarching point, then, is that a tension exists between the need for objectivity and the need for political responsiveness within the administrative process that cannot be neatly resolved. This tension, which has long bedeviled normative administrative theory, lies at the heart of Heclo's inconsistency in defining neutral competence. It also underlies various other efforts to reconcile traditional administrative values with bureaucracy's need to accommodate competing interests and respond to its political masters. For example, at least part of the popularity of policy analysis as a constraint on bureaucracy lies in its apparent reduction of political issues to objective terms. As another illustration, Martin Shapiro argues (disapprovingly) that the influence of "post-consequentialist ethics" in administrative law reflects the desire to arrive at objectively correct answers to social or political issues through dialectical processes.

The irony, or course, is that the greater the delegation, the more desirable and the less realistic neutral competence becomes. Yet the tension between objectivity and political responsiveness is not unhealthy—at least for those who can continue to function while retaining contradictory ideas in their heads. The devil is in the context, and this is why scholars such as Paul Appleby observed long ago that, especially at the highest levels, public administration is an art that does not lend itself to simple formulas or coherent prescriptive doctrines. Recognizing the limitations as well as the applications of neutral competence in some ways renders it a more viable concept for scholars and for public servants alike.

EXPLORING THE ISSUE

Do Bureaucrats Need to Be Politically Neutral to Be Effective?

Critical Thinking and Reflection

1. Why do classic public administration theorists—such as Weber—argue that neutrality is necessary for bureaucracy?
2. Is there a relationship between neutrality and effectiveness? Under what conditions can neutrality work against effectiveness?
3. How do career managers differ from political appointees? Who is assumed to be less neutral and why?
4. Why is it assumed that presidents can benefit more from nonneutral bureaucrats? What are they able to do that neutral managers are not?
5. What is meant by neutrality? How can neutrality be measured? Why does the American public seem to call for neutrality in government?

Is There Common Ground?

Neutrality has long been considered a necessity for effective bureaucrats given their ability to do as they believe they are supposed to rather than as someone wishes under this condition. Nonneutral bureaucrats are assumed (rightly or wrongly) to be more worried about pleasing a particular individual or organization than in fulfilling the spirit of a particular law or statute. For career bureaucrats, such a stance makes logical sense. They are members of the bureaucracy and should, under that condition, be responsible for implementing policy as intended. For political appointees, however, their direct allegiance is typically to the individual who has brought them into bureaucracy. Their stay will oftentimes last only as long as their appointer's. Under this circumstance, one could argue that it is nearly impossible to expect complete neutrality from these bureaucrats.

Most important for the question at hand, however, is how we can best measure effectiveness. If effectiveness means getting citizens what they want, one can wonder if neutrality actually matters. If, on the other hand, effectiveness means upholding the spirit of policy, it seems that neutral workers will be more likely to do so. Hence, we are left with a need to better define concepts such as effectiveness if we wish to determine the category of bureaucrat that is best-suited to meet that definition. For as long as interested parties get to continue spinning their own meaning of effectiveness, we can be sure that their chosen category will be the most effective.

Additional Resources

Asmerom, H.K. and E.P. Reis, *Democratization and Bureaucratic Neutrality: Experience from the Developed and Developing Countries* (New York: Palgrave Macmillan, 1996)

The book focuses on the mutual implications of bureaucratic neutrality and democracy from the perspective of societies formerly under authoritarian regimes.

Carpenter, D., *The Forging Bureaucratic Autonomy: Reputations, Networks, and Policy Innovation in Executive Agencies, 1862–1928* (Princeton, NJ: Princeton University Press, 2001)

Carpenter takes a historical look at the growth of bureaucratic autonomy in federal executive agencies and attempts to show why the basic assumptions of public administration are challenged by this growth.

Huber, G.A., *The Craft of Bureaucratic Neutrality* (Boston: Cambridge University Press, 2007)

This book reconciles the apparent contradiction between political understandings of bureaucracy, in which interest groups and elected officials shape how the law is enforced, and accounts in public administration and elsewhere about the neutral and consistent implementation of the law.

Huber, J.D. and C.R. Shipan, *Deliberate Discretion? The Institutional Foundations of Bureaucratic Autonomy* (Boston: Cambridge University Press, 2002)

Huber and Shipan examine the role of bureaucracy in shaping legislation by focusing on how implementation differs depending on the level of detail put into a law when it is drafted and adopted.

Lewis, D.E., *The Politics of Presidential Appointments: Political Control and Bureaucratic Performance* (Princeton, NJ: Princeton University Press, 2008)

In this book, David Lewis examines why presidents tend to rely on political appointees to staff bureaucracies rather than career civil servants.

ISSUE 8

Should Government Be Run Like a Business?

YES: **Julia Beckett,** from "The 'Government Should Run Like a Business' Mantra," *American Review of Public Administration* (June 2000)

NO: **Jim Powell,** from "The Disaster of Government-Run Businesses," *Campaign for Liberty* (July 2010)

Learning Outcomes

After reading this issue, you should be able to:

- Understand the difference between government-run businesses and the use of private business techniques in the public sector.
- Describe the arguments in favor of running government like a business.
- Describe the arguments against running government like a business.
- Gain an understanding of how America has attempted to run public businesses in various policy areas.
- Discuss examples of different forms of business and their applicability to public administration and policy.
- Discuss the potential justifications for governments running businesses.

ISSUE SUMMARY

YES: Julia Beckett argues that the government-as-business metaphor can be effectively utilized, although judicious application is encouraged. She focuses on three forms of business—the sole proprietor, the partnership, and the corporation—and analyzes the appropriateness of each to government operation.

NO: Jim Powell argues that government-run businesses are at best ineffective and potentially catastrophic. He examines both international and domestic cases, citing Britain's National Health System and Amtrak, Fannie Mae, and Medicare as American examples of government-run corporate entities that produce unintended consequences.

A t a fundamental level, many citizens anticipate the arrival of the mail. Occasionally, a birthday package or greeting card finds its way through the junk mail, bills, and unsolicited catalogs. Article I, Section 8, Clause 7 of the U.S. Constitution has been interpreted to bestow upon the United States Postal Service a legal monopoly over the delivery of greeting cards and other first-class mail. However, advances in Internet technology, which allow citizens to communicate efficiently and pay most bills online, have dramatically reduced the amount of first-class mail collected by the Postal Service. These developments offer citizens a choice between paying a bill instantaneously with no fee or paying 44 cents and waiting several days for delivery. Furthermore, various private sector organizations provide competitive prices on package delivery and express mail. Rapid changes in technology and communication, combined with increased competition from the private sector, have conspired to drastically reduce the revenue collected by the Postal Service, leading some to question its utility.

The Postal Service was created in 1775, naming Benjamin Franklin as its first postmaster general. By 1792, the Post Office Department was enshrined as a Cabinet-level agency. The Postal Reorganization Act of 1970 established the U.S. Postal Service, an independent agency of the U.S. government. A critical difference between the Post Office as a Cabinet-level executive agency and the U.S. Postal Service as an independent agency is how the latter organization operates and generates revenue. Rather than function as part of the government, funded and operated under taxpayer revenue, the U.S. Postal Service was designed by law to be a self-sustaining enterprise, supporting itself by selling products and services to consumers. As a result, the U.S. Postal Service sells various levels of postal delivery services. In addition to stamps, many post offices also sell stamp collecting products and greeting cards. Fundamentally, the change from government agency to independent agency altered the nature of a stamp, which under the former might be considered a tax or user fee. Today, stamps might be considered products, similar to the birthday cards and wrapping paper also sold at many post offices. However, if the postal service is to be self-sustaining, should it make a profit? Should it at least be revenue-neutral?

The U.S. Postal Service regularly reminds citizens that it receives no taxpayer funding. Although this is not entirely true (the U.S. government subsidizes mail delivery for legally blind individuals and election ballots mailed from overseas), through the course of its existence, the Postal Service has supported itself primarily through the sale of postal products and services. However, contemporary technology has not been kind to the Postal Service in recent years. Furthermore, the Postal Service is struggling to fund employee pensions in the wake of a widespread, lengthy economic crisis, a problem facing many agencies at all levels of government. In 2010 and 2011, the U.S. Postal Service lost more than $8 billion annually, leading Postmaster General Patrick Donohoe to testify before Congress that the problem is not that the Postal Service is treated like a business, but that it is not treated enough like a business. Since the Constitution mandates that Congress "establish Post Offices and Post Roads," they regulate and conduct oversight of the Postal Service. Donohoe testified that the regulations established by Congress are too restrictive, requiring the Postal Service to compete in a sector against other organizations that are not similarly regulated. Donohoe told a Senate committee that "The Postal Service is in a crisis today because it operates with a restrictive business model." Essentially, the U.S. Postmaster General argued to Congress that the Postal Service would be more successful and competitive if it were less heavily regulated and treated more like a business.

Is the U.S. Postal Service government or a business? The answer is that it has characteristics of both. Certainly, the Postal Service exhibits more business-like characteristics than the Consumer Product Safety Commission, another independent agency of the U.S. government. However, unlike most business, the U.S. Postal Service is not obligated to pay taxes and is given the power to utilize eminent domain to obtain private property. Despite these advantages, the Postal Service has struggled recently, prompting the Postmaster General to ask for some flexibility regarding days of delivery and loosening of regulations regarding employee benefits. Even if the proposed changes allowed the Postal Service to be more competitive and able to survive, some might still wonder whether it serves a useful purpose. Since the 1970s, the Postal Service has supported itself through the sale of postage and postage services. However, technology has allowed us to communicate more efficiently with the transitions from mail to telegraph to telephone to e-mail. If the Postal Service sells less of what financially sustains it, should it do something else or should it cease to exist?

The national government no longer operates a bank in the sense debated in *McCulloch v. Maryland* (1819). Does the fact that the Constitution instills Congress with the power to establish a post office mandate that they do so? Is there an overriding public policy goal met by the Postal Service? Some communities administer services, such as public transportation, that hemorrhage money year after year. In these instances, it seems that service to the community overrides cost effectiveness. Fundamentally, a decision must be made regarding the goal of the Postal Service. If collection and delivery of first class mail is considered to be core function of the national government, a decision must be made regarding administration of that function. Should Congress decide that the service greatly outweighs cost, postage would once again be considered a tax or user fee rather than a product. If cost effectiveness is a competing primary or even a secondary objective, then perhaps the recommendations of Postmaster General Donohoe should be considered. Would treating the Postal Service more like a business improve its organizational effectiveness?

In the YES selection, Julia Beckett explains how business forms can be effectively applied to government to improve performance. Of course, government is not business and not all areas of government can be managed with business techniques, but Becket argues that some business techniques can be effectively applied. In contrast, in the NO selection, Jim Powell argues that government-run businesses produce unintended and often destructive consequences. National and international examples are utilized.

YES

Julia Beckett

The "Government Should Run Like a Business" Mantra

> The business of America is business.
>
> —Calvin Coolidge

> What others see, and we often do not, is that business has an unusually powerful influence on the behavior, the attitudes, the beliefs and the perceptions of all Americans. Business is central to our lives. We have an extensive business mythology: businesses, business people, the fortunes made from business figure largely in the stories we tell of American heroes and heroines. Business has a central role in our interpretations of our national past.
>
> —James Oliver Robertson (1985)

In our age of sound bites and video clips, a well-turned familiar phrase can be influential. Many American images and phrases reflect business influences, or, as Robertson calls it, "business mythology." *Government should run like a business* is a phrase that evokes powerful images and ideas. Government and business have long been compared, but it seems the current iteration is a mantra. Although a common phrase can carry meaning that is open to interpretation and extrapolation, it seems that the focus of the current government-business comparison has shifted.

The mantra is now found in the popular press and in politics. It seems that if the mantra, "government should run like a business," is said often enough and sincerely enough, then a transformation will occur. In discussions of market management, business ideas are extracted, adopted, and applied to government. Concepts are substituted; for example, owner replaces citizen and customer replaces client. The idea of taxpayer is supplanted with the notion that government services are exchanged for value. Governments are urged to be entrepreneurial or engage in partnerships. What underlies many of these comparisons and writings is the foundational government-business metaphor.

The mantra is associated with the widespread, enduring, new public management (NPM) political reforms. These reforms, calling for managerial or business-type approaches to government, are connected to origins in both the

From *American Review of Public Administration,* June 2000, pp. 185–192, 200–201. Copyright © 2000 by Sage Publications. Reprinted by permission via Rightslink.

Thatcher and Reagan administrations. Some give 1979 as the start date of this political reform, which continues to dramatically change governance, public administration, and public management throughout many nations.

The mantra has also entered the study of public administration theory and practice, where it is most often connected to the NPM movement. This academic movement is a broad approach to governance, based in part on a rejection of public administration and bureaucracy and in part of finding better methods to manage practical problems of governance. The public management movement aspires to "'making a difference' in public affairs;" this is true of the political reforms. Countries that have instituted NPM reforms and techniques include Britain, New Zealand, Australia, Canada, Israel, Finland, and Sweden. Kettl calls it a "global revolution in public management."

The mantra has been used in the past to elicit reforms. During the municipal reform movement era (1895–1910) and the Progressive era (1910–1920), the phrase was also evoked. The purpose of the mantra in the Progressive era was to increase community political action by encouraging citizens to consider themselves active owners of the municipal corporation (Schachter, 1997; Stillman, 1974). The mantra is associated anew with political reforms of the global NPM—but perhaps modern viewpoints on the government-business comparison have changed its meaning.

"Government should run like a business" is both a phrase and a metaphor. Common phrases contain layers of connotations, and they tacitly include values transmitted and received. The fact that a phrase evokes multiple ideas is part of its power. Morgan has demonstrated how metaphor is intrinsic in our understanding of organizations. Lakoff and Turner note how, in cognitive linguistics, metaphors are essential to understanding but can also lead to misunderstanding. Further, in the political and social realm, there may be fundamental misunderstandings of common images based on individuals' conservative or liberal worldview. Metaphors, symbols, and phrases are both abstractions and social convention; therefore, it is worthwhile to consider a phrase in common use.

The analysis of the mantra begins with breaking it into parts and focusing on different meanings of government and business. Government includes federal, state, and local government systems and structures. As a starting point, business means a firm, company, or economic entity that produces or provides goods or services for profit. But this definition of business seems to cover broad categories. There must be ways to refine and clarify. The word *should* is distinctive and imperative; it is a directive. The simile *should run like* is not a simple comparison. Instead, it makes business an exemplar. There are a multitude of definitions and imagery for *run*, including to go fast, to compete, to operate, or to have a certain form. The mantra makes business an exemplar for government, and this article analyzes this business identity.

Government and business have been compared and contrasted throughout public administration literature. To trace this connection would involve tracing the history of public administration. This article suggests that variations exist in what is meant by business in classic public administration literature. Current public management writings also have variations on what business means, and the critiques challenge whether the business comparison is appropriate. However, it appears that language in current writings reveals a shift in the comparison regarding business forms; this includes references to partnerships and entrepreneurs. Accordingly, this article will explore the conceptual frame of business forms, rather than production management or executive control, to discuss what it means to run like a business. The three general types of business forms—the sole proprietor, the partnership, and the corporation—will be analyzed. During the discussion of these structural types of business, the expectations of business will be compared to expectations of government.

Classic American Theme

Tracing the comparison of business and government would be to trace the history of public administration. Linking government administration to business-like practices was present in works of Wilson, Goodnow, and White in the early orthodox era of public administration (1880–1920). The "government should run like a business" mantra can be seen as a continuation and slight variation of a classical theme that stressed adopting business-like approaches to government to provide economy, efficiency, and professional administration.

The approach of "administration as the business of government" deals more with business being an activity of organizing resources in order to produce and distribute goods and services of society. The operational commonality between government and business is a foundation of organization theory. Organization theory as it has developed, whether generic, systemic, or humanistic, has tended to look at large entities and consider the administrative and managerial aspects of production or the executive power aspects of decisions.

In most discussions, the organizational entity is assumed to be a business. It is typically called the organization, but other nomenclature for the entity includes "industry;" "body corporate;" "enterprise" and "firm." The entity is assumed to produce goods or services. The entity is assumed to produce goods or services. Often the value measure of how good the organization is is either control or efficiency. In discussions, the term *business* is generically abstracted and normatively idealized. It is not clear that businesses really have the attributes ascribed to them.

Public administration theorists have questioned the generic approach and have asserted a distinctive role for government. As a generic approach to organization was being proposed, public administration writers, even the early progressive reformers, enunciated their views of "citizenship, common good, [and] institutional legitimacy." Public interest elements make government distinctive. Comparing government with all other forms of social action, Appleby concluded that government is different because it was the public's business. Works comparing and contrasting government and business shifted the terminology to public and private. As captured in Sayre's dicta, "Public and private management are alike in all unimportant respects."

Competition and Change

The "government should run like a business" mantra can be interpreted as an extension of the classic generic contrast of business and government, but this is incomplete. Political economy and public choice theories also juxtapose business and government. Sometimes in political economy discussions, these comparisons of business and government regard participation and resources. Often these comparisons do not differentiate government as a distinctive actor, but just another entity in the marketplace.

Public choice applies business ideas of exchange and self-interest to government. The economic assumptions of the market draw attention to and compare revenue and profits. Comparing fiscal resources between business and government does not translate well. Businesses raise capital as investments, with expected profitable returns; governments raise revenues through taxing powers to pursue activities for the public good. These revenue categories of business exchange and sales are equated with government revenue from fees for services. The revenue sources, although they are often contrasted, are not evenly paired. Efficiency is a further comparison, but business or economic firms ideally have net efficiency, and this is rare for government. Efficiency in business is focused on maximizing profits or the bottom line, and efficiency in government has focused on minimizing costs.

The "government should run like a business" mantra is associated with market economics in both strands, the political reform and academic studies, of NPM writings. Although the mantra seldom is advocated as such, it is worth considering whether the meaning of the term business has shifted in this area. Works clustered under the public management movement are varied and diffuse, but many of them adopt the view that competition, business competition in the market, is the basis of comparison between government and business. Within the NPM, works connected to reforming the national government advocate government change by reinventing, reengineering, and privatization. The initial point is often that the classic bureaucratic model needs to be changed. The fact that the classic politics-administration dichotomy and classic Weberian bureaucracy have long been challenged and discredited is often irrelevant.

Some interpret the mantra to mean that government should compete like business. In this view, competition is viewed as a catalyst for business. Customers are better served by competition. Innovations and improvements in services, techniques, and products come from competition. Obsolete and inefficient products and services are disclosed and superseded through competition. In this viewpoint, competition is a causal agent for progress; government should compete like successful businesses and reap similar rewards. Although these are the popular exhortations, the more recent works are more measured.

The need to change and improve government performance and results has been considered essential; this is the message of the *National Performance Review*. The 5th-year report card indicates that there are improvements but that there is much to be done. To achieve the change in performance and results, the comparison again is government and business. Models and ideas for the NPM have come from business and business literature, but rather that an idea of business being a firm or a corporation, it is business practices and techniques that are examined. Foremost is the elevation of the place of the market and the idea of competition and exchange. Thus, the beginning point is less the structure and interorganizational relation of business and more a consideration of business as a seller and supplier in the marketplace. A critique of this approach holds that it ignores the constitutional basis of our government.

The ideas of successful market exchange and competition are part of the change in the view of business to which government is compared. NPM is based on "enterprise economics," which considers commercialism, competition, and risk taking as beneficial. This focus in public management has been called market-driven management. The NPM is bolder when it posits that the current models and practices are outmoded, and new models and new approaches are essential to adjust to present and future demands. The questions of input, output, and measurement are central in searches for efficient performance and results, but the measure and emphasis should be on results.

Another view is that the grounding for NPM literature is eclectic, catholic, and varied but still the predominant theoretical grounding coming from economic or political economy paradigms. It emphasizes market exchange language, measures, and mechanism, where ideas reflecting the sentiment that "government should compete or get out of the way" are studied under categories of privatization and of deregulation within government. It emphasizes new techniques invented or adapted to fit the situation through reengineering or innovation. As part of these discussions, business entrepreneurships and partnerships are included as practices and techniques for improvement. This inclusion of other business forms departs from, and perhaps expands, the meanings of the business entity.

The nature of the comparisons between government and business and its implications has also been questioned as a paradigm shift. Lan and Rosenbloom have argued that a conservative political shift has led to the predominance of the economics-based approaches to governance in which business is given supremacy. Reschenthaler and Thompson argue that this approach is a new economics of organization, based more on technological advancement, in which neither form of entity, business or government, have preeminence.

> The new public managers reestablished a kinship with business management, not because business was better than government, but because managers in both sectors once again faced similar problems and opportunities and the business management literature was full of interesting ideas that seemed relevant to meeting new challenges.

Whether there is a paradigm shift or a renewed emphasis on market economics, it seems the borrowing of business ideas in the recent public management literature and NPM political reforms do place business as an exemplar.

Often, the shift in the NPM literature promotes the positive attributes of business, particularly the aggressive, risk-taking entrepreneurial businesses.

These enterprises are viewed as high achievers through innovation and low-ered costs. This view of competition seeks victory over limits. One writer sug-gested that government administrators should just ignore the rules and laws that constrain them: "Indeed, inertia is the most serious malady plaguing pub-lic organizations. As a result, achieving success often involves circumventing or subverting political and institutional obstacles to innovation."

This NPM literature has gathered serious attention and pointed criti-cism. Privatization is criticized for incomplete application of economic theory, often emphasizing benefits without recognizing the cost. One criticism from Rosenblum relates to defining values: "The NPM [new public management] would remake public administration in the image of business, apparently without recognizing the degree to which the Constitution places substantive, procedural, and organizational constraints on government that simply do not apply to private enterprise." Other critiques of these writings involve govern-ment and public interest considerations—administrators' responsibility to the public, their duty to enforce the laws, and the necessity to work within the system to improve practices or provide redress.

Other public management writers analyze critically the general claims to business predominance in certain situations. DiIulio begins his discussion of deregulation with the following:

> The nation's federal, state, and local public service is in deep trouble. Many government agencies cannot attract and retain first-rate exec-utives, managers, and line staff. Most do not operate in a way that inspires public confidence. In reaction, some observers say "privatize everything" others deny that serious problems exist, and still others chant "run government like a business."

But DiIulio's next sentence is, "All three responses are misguided." Behn cautions, "In the United States it has become fashionable to worship the tech-niques of business management and seek to implement them in government." Then, Behn analyzes innovation based on the purpose of improving govern-ment agencies' performance, not just the innovation of anecdotal business success. The NPM brings in different business ideas and practices than the clas-sic comparisons; in addition to suggesting management techniques, additional business forms—entrepreneurs and partners—are part of the discussions. This public management literature also raises tensions about business.

What Kind of Business?

A literal interpretation of the "government should run like a business" man-tra builds on the assumptions that business is good and government is lack-ing. This is the part of the slogan where somehow business has become the benchmark and standard. Perhaps this is a victory of public relations skills, or perhaps it is romantic idealism. Saying that government should run like a busi-ness may indicate a popular understanding of business as efficient, productive, and profitable, but it was not so long ago that business, or at least big American business, was suspect. What, then, is meant by business?

What is presented as proofs that business runs well? Reports of the success and failure of businesses are often selective or anecdotal. Current data paint broad pictures roughly indicating that for each 2 business starts, 1 business fails; the ratio for 1994 was 1 failure per 2.63 starts, and the ratio for 1995 was 1 failure per 2.36 starts. What is not clear is why these businesses fail. Many business management books start with the premise that there is considerable room for improvement in most businesses; Japanese management and Demming methods promote the improvement of established business practices. There are many prescriptions in the business management literature, but what is common or acceptable business practice? Modeling government after individual examples may not translate well, the exhortations continue.

Whatever reasons there are behind the preeminence of business, government is compared to it. But it is not clear what is meant by business. The term business is used in a multitude of ways, shapes, and forms. Big business, or corporate business, often is distinguished from farmers, small businesses, and entrepreneurs. The large corporations—in power and impact on the national economy—are commonly cited as evidence of the dominance of business.

In many discussions, not only are organizations generic but the "generic" business type is assumed to be a large corporation. This presents problems.

> Earlier, the large corporation was described as the characteristic institution of our market economy. So it is, but it is hardly the representative one: the typical business is not organized as a corporation, but rather as an individual proprietorship or a partnership. In 1990, the latest year for which statistics are published, a total of 20.0 million nonfarm businesses reported to the tax authorities: 16.3 million proprietorships and partnerships, 3.7 million corporations. The corporations accounted for 90 percent of the sales and receipts reported by all business firms. The were some seven thousand corporations with assets of $250 million or more, the largest class demarcated. These accounted for more than half (51 percent) of the total sales and receipts of all businesses. Large corporations were most dominant in manufacturing (2,602 with 74 percent of sales), utilities and transportation (716 with 76 percent of sales), and finance and real estate (1,503 with 71 percent of sales).

Recent works considering corporate businesses have analyzed these entities with criteria constituting ownership and control. Without distinguishing by the structure or type of business form, Benn and Gaus analyzed private and public organizations using constructs of agency, interests, and access. The definitions of these constructs is worth noting: Agency indicates on whose behalf a person is acting; interest relates to who is affected or who benefits; and access denotes openness of activities and information. Bozeman used criteria of economic power, political power, and social constraints to compare public and private organizations. A recent twist of the generic organization approach is in

Bozeman's argument that all organizations are public, but again, the business structure or form was implicitly corporate.

What is lacking in many of the government and business comparisons is consideration of either defining what a business is and in differentiating forms of business entities.

Defining the terms to evaluate "What is business?" is a significant inquiry. "The questions we ask about business are how to do it, or how to control it. Not where did it come from or why do we have it." The how to do business and how to control business are adapted in the classic view of a business-like public administration.

. . .

This article begins by quoting Robertson's description of business mythology in American life. Not only is our business mythology positive and heroic, it is projected onto government. Business and government comparisons are common in public administration, but the definition of these concepts has varied over time. The current popular iteration of the business myth is expressed in the "government should run like a business" mantra.

The business mythology that affects the beliefs and the perceptions of Americans is expressed in phrases. Ideas expressed by clichés, slogans, phrases, and mantras may be more than just words or phrases. The pervasive use of the mantra "government should run like a business" suggests that it is more than an idiom and that it may be a paradigm. Yanow explained the following:

> [Some] use the word paradigm in the Kuhnian sense, to mean something akin to a religious conviction that organizes one's perception of the world. Paradigms are no more interchangeable or ephemeral than convictions of other sorts. They are "ways of seeing" or *weltanschauungen* (world views), conditioned by family and community backgrounds, education, training, experience and so forth—but that cannot be removed or replaced like a pair of eyeglasses.

Discussion or analysis of a phrase that reflects the business mythology is problematic, especially if it involves ways of seeing or organizing perceptions about government. What can be done is to provide information as grounds for comparison and consideration. This article considered the three major forms of business structures—the sole proprietorship, the partnership, and the corporation. There are expectations that go to the essence of what business is, and for all three, the broad generalizations hold the following: Business is expected to be self-interested and self-supporting. Business is expected to take chances and bear the risks and rewards. Business is expected to keep secrets. Business rights are based on property, ownership, and control.

The mantra projects business as the exemplar for government to follow, but business expectations are not basic to government. Discussions of government may address the responsibilities of the executive and the management, but they go beyond this to consider the public. Analyses and discussions of government denote the responsibility to the populous as part of the descriptive hierarchy and interactive systems in government. New public administration and the Blacksburg group directed attention to democratic expectations of citizen participation. The role of citizens in a democratic society is a fundamental and constant concern.

The mantra comparing government to business reflects the influence of the business mythology. It idolizes and projects attributes onto business. It places business on a pedestal and makes it larger, bigger, and better than life. Thus, business is an allegory. It is not real and it does not have to be real. When government is compared to mythic business, it pales. Although we may have our myths and we may need our myths, we need to separate the ideal from the real. Government can certainly learn from some business practices and procedures, but caution and care are essential. In comparing business and government, we should be selective in our choices and clear in our concepts.

Jim Powell

The Disaster of Government-Run Businesses

Part 1

Barack Obama defied experience everywhere when he stubbornly claimed he could make a government-run health program work. The standard practice of any government-run business is to provide favored interest groups with something for nothing, forcing other people to pay for it, and there always seem to be complications.

If Obama really wanted to see how nationalizing health care was likely to turn out, all he had to do was look across the Canadian border. Canadian governments gained control of the health-care business so they could give voters subsidized health-care benefits, but that led everybody to want more, which bid up health-care prices, which then led officials to try to control soaring health-care prices with health-care rationing and below-market compensation for doctors.

Not surprisingly, doctors began fleeing the country, and patients formed long waiting lines for the care they needed. In 2004—more than four decades after a national government-run health-care system was under way—Canadian officials seem to have acknowledged the problem. They introduced a "Wait Times Project . . . to make timely access to quality care a reality for all Canadians."

Waiting lines aren't the only issue, however. Because Canada's government-run health system is a monopoly financed by taxpayers whether they like it or not, it lacks incentives to provide competitive service. The Vancouver-based Fraser Institute reported, "Canada is currently operating far too many older, outdated, and possibly unreliable medical technologies"— even though "Canada maintains one of the developed world's most expensive universal access health care systems." According to the *New York Times,* many Canadians either seek treatment in the United States or violate Canadian laws by going to a private clinic.

Waiting in the UK

Britain became a pace-setter for nationalized health care in July 1948. Publisher Cecil Palmer recalled that

> for months and months prior to the inauguration of the National Health Service [NHS], the government went propaganda mad. The

radio, the pulpit, the platform, and the press were all used. The public believed that it was being offered the finest medical service in the world for next to nothing. We were to have more and better hospitals, more and better clinics. Doctor and patient were invited to enter paradise.

Yet from the beginning, the British National Health Service spent more and provided less than promised. The NHS became well known for its long waiting lines. In 1992 the NHS Management Executive pledged that long waiting lines would be a thing of the past. As economist Catherine Pope explained, "Not only would the backlog of patients who had waited for more than two years be cleared, but the right of future patients to be admitted for treatment within two years would henceforth be guaranteed by the patients' charter."

The NHS increased staffing only to find that the number of people seeking health care increased. Since people didn't have to pay directly for health care, naturally they wanted more of it. The Department of Health established a Waiting List Initiative Fund of about £30 million per year to do something about waiting lines, but since that was a comparatively small amount of money, it was used for small fixes, such as making more operating rooms available for knee replacements. That and other initiatives to resolve the waiting-list problem were soon abandoned, apparently because they didn't seem to do much good. Pope observed, "The emphasis of policy has been on finding out why the queue doesn't move rather than explaining how it occurred."

The length of the NHS waiting lines often became a political issue, and the party in power sometimes manipulated numbers to make the situation look better. For instance, the North East Thames Regional Health Authority abolished the most embarrassing waiting lines, such as the one for varicose-vein surgery. Other tricks included making a waiting line for hospitalization shorter by making a line for an outpatient visit longer; suspending a patient's admission; or directing patients back to a general practitioner (rather than advancing them through a maze of referrals). In 1984, the London-based College of Health, a charity, published a *Guide to Waiting Lists* (about 50 pages), but unfortunately they gave up the project in 1991 when about a million people were on NHS waiting lists.

Reforms

During the 1980s and early 1990s, Conservative governments reorganized the National Health Service with some market-oriented reforms, but they didn't go very far. In the late 1990s, Labor governments reorganized the NHS again, reintroducing more central control. According to Julian Le Grand at the London School of Economics, endless reorganizing isn't likely to help much, since Britain has a shortage of acute-care hospital beds. There's a shortage of nursing-home beds, limiting the ability of hospitals to discharge elderly patients—and further delaying the admission of new patients. Britain has a chronic shortage of doctors and nurses—fewer per 1,000 population, for example, than Australia, Canada, France, or the United States. The NHS has tried recruiting doctors from overseas, without evident success. In an effort to control costs, Britain's National Institute for Health and Clinical Excellence (NICE) has prevented patients from gaining access to life-saving drugs.

When economists Stephen Martin and Peter G. Smith analyzed the NHS in 2002, there were still about a million people waiting. The authors reported,

> Although H.F. Sanderson quite reasonably assumed that the length of a wait is likely to be related to levels of resources, others have claimed that there is no relationship between resources and waiting times. Some have interpreted these results as implying that increased funding would ultimately have little effect on waiting times and would merely induce greater demand.

As of March 31, 2009, 916,175 people were reported to be on a NHS waiting list for a first outpatient appointment following a referral from a general practitioner. So a decade after the NHS Management Executive vowed to banish the notorious waiting lists, they were still about as long as ever.

Chronic problems with government-run health care systems cannot be fixed by health-care experts. Problems are inevitable whenever government tries to provide something for nothing by squeezing taxpayers for subsidies—regardless what industry a government-run business happens to be in.

This has been the situation for a very long time. The Industrial Revolution, which ushered in the modern world, was to a significant degree a breakaway from government-run businesses. As Harvard economic historian David S. Landes explained,

> The state of the seventeenth and eighteenth centuries was incapable of planning development nationally or allocating resources efficiently. The state promoted monopoly, when nothing could have been more harmful for long-run development. State assistance was more often than not an encouragement to laxity and a cover for incompetence. With some notable exceptions, privileged enterprises were sloppily managed and required repeated transfusions of royal capital. Often they turned out an inferior product that could be disposed of only to captive customers, like army regiments.

Part 2

In the 1870s, the Japanese had many government-run businesses—among them, mining, shipbuilding, railways, and silk production. According to economic historians Johannes Hirschmeier and Tsunehiko Yui, they "were a heavy burden on government finance, and on the whole were running in the red." The government couldn't even make money with silk production, something the Japanese had a lot of experience with. Hirschmeier and Yui wrote,

> The much promoted Tomioka Filiature was a failure as far as management was concerned. In spite of the good export market for raw silk, the administrators prevented visitors from entering lest their inefficiency be exposed.

In 1881, guided by finance minister Matsukata Masayoshi, the government began phasing out subsidies and selling its mismanaged businesses for whatever they would fetch, which often wasn't much. For example, in 1885 the entrepreneur Furukawa Ichibei paid 338,000 yen for the Ani Copper Mines, where the government had spent 1.7 million yen. The government had spent 2.4 million yen at the Kamaishi iron mine, but the results were so bad that it was shut down. In 1887 the entrepreneur Tanaka Chobei bought the abandoned property for 12,600 yen.

Private Japanese entrepreneurs outperformed subsidized, government-run businesses. For example, in 1870 Yataro Iwasaki founded Mitsubishi, a shipping company that proved to be more efficient and less expensive than the government-run Nippon Postal Steamship Company. "While the Postal Steamship Company makes use of government protection and is boastful and overbearing," Iwasaki declared, "we of the Mitsubishi strengthen our internal controls and go out of the way to please the people." Nippon Postal Steamship Company subsequently went out of business. As a result, those who used shipping services—not the taxpayers—paid for them and got better service. Japan's rise as an industrial power began as it opened up, sold off government-run businesses, and phased out subsidies.

British Socialism

Although the Allies won World War II, socialists came to power throughout Western Europe and promoted nationalization of major industries. In Britain, for instance, the Labour Party won the July 1945 elections. Prime Minister Clement Atlee told the House of Commons, "In matters of economic planning, we agree with Soviet Russia."

Coal mines—about 800—were nationalized first. Labourites insisted that only government could make the mines bigger and more modern. This, it was presumed, would result in greater efficiency. But efficiency never happened. The new National Coal Board drove out private managers and technical people, which delighted the coal miners. The National Union of Mineworkers gained big wage concessions, and there were coal shortages. The National Coal Board blamed consumers. For instance, its 1953 report stated that "changes in consumption are required to overcome the shortage of coal." The British government lavished more capital on the coal mines than any other nationalized industry, but because officials didn't need to perform to get their hands on taxpayers' money, it was squandered. During the 1950s, absenteeism went up, miners were given more time off, and the cost of producing coal soared. Thousands more unionized coal miners were hired, and their pay increased, but coal output went down, and coal shortages persisted.

In its most ambitious effort, Parliament established the British Transport Commission and gave it responsibility for transportation by railroads, trucks, highways, and water. This involved nationalizing some 3,800 businesses. Here again, the assumption was that by combining all these different operations into a big monopoly, it would become more efficient. But nobody could agree on exactly how everything was to be combined, and the bigger the monopoly became, the harder it was to manage. The British Transport Commission established a central bureaucracy that was supposed to be dynamic, but that turned out to be impossible. The leading lights of British nationalization didn't have any idea how they would find capital to upgrade the facilities, how they would operate the services to achieve greater efficiency, or how they would improve labor relations. Meanwhile, unionized employees won generous pay raises, none of them could be fired, and deficits of the various government-run businesses skyrocketed.

Nationalizations of electricity (about 550 businesses), gas (about 1,000 businesses), and steel (217 businesses) caused more problems. Incredibly, many people imagined that the best bet would be more government intervention. Atlee introduced forced labor. By the end of 1947, as University of Manchester economist John Jewkes noted,

> No man between the ages of 18 and 50 years and no woman between the ages of 18 and 40 years could change his or her occupation at will. Every such change had to be registered at the Employment Exchange, and the Minister of Labour had the power to direct workers changing their jobs to the employment he considered best in the national interest.

Despite all the harm done, it was politically almost impossible to get rid of government-run businesses because they were aggressively defended by labor unions, and people had lived so long with big government that they couldn't imagine how the economy would function without it. In 1950, the Labour Party wanted more government-run businesses. The Liberal Party wanted to keep some and sell off others. Conservatives didn't want any more government-run businesses, but they were concerned that selling them off might be risky. They privatized only the steel and trucking industries. The economy deteriorated for three more decades until the "British disease" (strikes, taxes, inflation, stagnation) became bad enough that there was public support for unloading government-run businesses and liberating the private sector.

The Soviet Union and the United States

If there were any doubt about the folly of government-run businesses, surely the experience of the Soviet Union ought to have resolved it. Consider the Samarkand Refrigerator Factory, which received many awards for meeting its Five-Year Plan production quotas. Paul Craig Roberts and Karen LaFollette reported the refrigerators

> were of such dismal quality that most were eventually sent back to the plant—this rejection was in a country where consumers pounce on goods of even sub-minimal quality. More surprising: every year that factory has asked for and received a higher level of subsidy from the government to produce junk refrigerators nobody wants.

This case was typical. Roberts and LaFollette noted that

> new roads collapse, heat pipelines burst in cold weather, floors in new houses look like washing boards, and TVs spontaneously catch fire. Western visitors have reported the astonishing sight of nets extended between the first and second stories of new buildings to catch debris falling from above.

Since the economy had nothing but government-run businesses, it was no wonder the Soviet Union collapsed and vanished from the map.

Meanwhile, American taxpayers are stuck with many money-losing government-run businesses. Next year, for instance, Amtrak will mark its 40th consecutive year of losses. Amtrak was started in 1970 to save the jobs of unionized employees whose featherbedding and gold-plated benefits had done much to drive passenger railroads into bankruptcy.

Taxpayers are stuck, too, with the Federal National Mortgage Association (Fannie Mae) and the Federal Home Loan Mortgage Corporation (Freddie Mac), government-sponsored enterprises that had special privileges, including a line of credit at the U.S. Treasury. By channeling several trillion dollars into subprime mortgages, Fannie and Freddie did more than anyone else to cause the housing bubble that burst in 2008. Thus far, the government has committed American taxpayers to cover as much as $400 billion of Fannie's and Freddie's losses.

The most costly government-run business is Medicare "insurance" which has an estimated $36 trillion of unfunded liabilities. That's how much would have to go into an interest-bearing account now to generate enough income, on top of future Medicare payroll taxes, to cover benefits seniors have been promised in perpetuity. Medicare is generating enormous pressure for higher taxes, and it seems certain there will be an epic political battle between the rapidly growing numbers of seniors who demand their Medicare benefits and younger Americans who are staggering under the burden of ever higher Medicare payroll taxes. It's possible that when enough younger taxpayers adopt so many tax-avoidance strategies that tax revenues fall short, the government will churn out stupendous amounts of paper money for paying Medicare as well as Social Security benefits, and America will be devastated by runaway inflation.

What to say the next time somebody has a bright idea for another government-run business? Never again!

EXPLORING THE ISSUE

Should Government Be Run Like a Business?

Critical Thinking and Reflection

1. In what ways is government similar and different to a business?
2. What services that are currently not government offered do you believe could be more efficiently provided by government?
3. What are the main arguments made against government operating like a business?
4. What government offered services do you think administrators need to do a better job of handling? Why? How could government improve?
5. What is the ultimate goal of government corporations: service or profit? Why?

Is There Common Ground?

At the core, government and private businesses share many things in common. There are clients, products, and services. Managers oversee workers and aim for efficiency. However numerous the similarities, there are even greater differences. Government aims to provide services to citizens that they are statutorily expected to. They are responsible to the citizenry rather than a board of directors or the bottom line. They are more easily able to act inefficiently if it ensures greater equity and effectiveness in service offerings. And they are not expected to make decisions strictly through the lens of profit. Today, we hear regularly about concerns with the U.S. Postal Service as it attempts to break even and still provide first-class mail service to citizens despite competition in other products from larger private companies. Yet, instead of asking whether government should be run like a business, perhaps we would better enrich policy outcomes in our country if we tried to figure out exactly what aspects and characteristics of business we want to see implemented in public agencies and programs. With that information, we could then make the needed adjustments to remain public entities that simply utilize the best practices of the private sector in directly applicable ways.

Additional Resources

Amtower, M., *Selling to the Government: What It Takes to Compete and Win in the World's Largest Market* (Hoboken, NJ: John Wiley & Sons, 2011)

United States government business—from federal and state to local institutions—is the largest market in the world. Regardless of economic trend or national and international conditions, it's a market everyone wants to get into. But in the convoluted and complex U.S. government market, it can be tough to get an "in"—and there are few shortcuts a business can take.

Cooper, P., *Governing by Contract: Challenges and Opportunities for Public Managers* (Washington, DC: CQ Press, 2002)

Is the public getting a good deal when the government contracts out the delivery of goods and services? Phillip Cooper attempts to get at the heart of this question by exploring what happens when public sector organizations—at the federal, state and local levels—form working relationships with other agencies, communities, nonprofit organizations, and private firms through contracts.

Downs, G. and P.D. Larkey, *The Search for Government Efficiency: From Hubris to Helplessness* (Philadelphia, Temple University Press, 1996)

Downs and Larkey examine the need for government to be efficient and how some business practices can help us achieve this goal.

Price, M.,W. Mores, and H.M. Elliotte, *Building High Performance Government through Lean Six Sigma: A Leader's Guide to Creating Speed, Agility, and Efficiency* (New York: McGraw-Hill, 2011)

No corner of the government or public sector has been spared from budget turmoil in recent years. Among budget cuts, increased requirements, and new threats and challenges, governments typically balance the scales through (1) increased funding and/or (2) rationalizing services or service levels. This book gives you a third option. It is called high performance, and it has been implemented in the private sector—with great success—for more than two decades.

Teeuwen, B., *Lean for the Public Sector: The Pursuit of Perfection in Government Services* (New York: Productivity Press, 2010)

Written specifically to address the application of Lean practices in government and the public sector, this how-to workbook gives you the wherewithal to combat the "We don't make widgets" mentality. Providing the tools to manage the entire Lean transformation process, the book helps you immediately integrate the Lean way of thinking and its tools into your improvement program.

ISSUE 9

Should Governments Use the Private Sector to Deliver Public Services?

YES: Leonard C. Gilroy, from "Local Government Privatization 101," *Reason Foundation Policy Brief* 86 (2010)

NO: Paul R. Verkuil, from *Outsourcing Sovereignty: Why Privatization of Government Functions Threatens Democracy and What We Can Do About It* (Cambridge University Press, 2007)

Learning Outcomes

After reading this issue, you should be able to:

- Define privatization.
- Discuss appropriate ways to privatize.
- Gain an understanding of the benefits of privatization.
- Gain an understanding of the costs of privatization.
- Describe how privatization can work in opposition to basic democratic principles.
- Gain an understanding of when privatization can be best utilized.

ISSUE SUMMARY

YES: Leonard C. Gilroy argues that, although caution must be utilized, privatization of public services is an effective way to improve overall performance and cut costs to the taxpayer. He uses data and case examples to establish the conditions under which privatization is best used.

NO: Paul R. Verkuil argues that privatization has the potential to damage government effectiveness and employee morale. He appeals to constitutional and statutory limits to privatization.

A stroll through most public universities would likely generate evidence of privatization in the public sector. University food service is often delivered by private companies who were selected through a competitive bidding process. Other universities contract with private companies for printing and copying, building maintenance and cleaning, and security. The difference between a cheeseburger assembled by a state employee and one prepared by a private food service firm is likely negligible to the median college student. However, the university seeking the private contract has relinquished control of a non-essential function for some practical purpose, usually improved performance or cost savings. This distinction between what constitutes an appropriate division between public and private organizations seems increasingly blurry. Strictly public organizations, in other words, government organizations, tend to deliver public goods. However, some public organizations compete directly with private organizations delivering the same service or product. One major example is higher education.

Public goods are both nonrival and nonexcludable. Nonrival means that consumption of the good does not deplete it to the extent that others cannot enjoy it. A good is nonexcludable if people cannot be prohibited from consuming the good. Because a morning cup of coffee has a cost, which excludes others unable or unwilling to pay, and is completely depleted once consumed, it is a private good. The playground slide at a city park, which is free to use and can be repeatedly enjoyed by all, is a public good. A city park is publicly funded for the enjoyment and use of all citizens. Governments make policy decisions that exhaust taxpayer resources, providing services that are too expensive or too broad in scope for other sectors to produce. The interstate highway system is extraordinarily expensive, making it unlikely that any private entity could adequately fund and maintain it. In contrast, first-class mail, for which the national government has monopolistic control, could be delivered by the private sector. Elementary and secondary education are both considered public goods in the United States. What about higher education?

Since the costs of public elementary and secondary education are borne by all taxpayers, American children can attend school for no direct cost. However, American universities, whether public or private, carry direct costs to students. Since many private universities receive various forms of government aid, particularly in the form of student financial aid, the distinction between public and private universities is hardly tidy. Fundamentally, students at private universities pay a larger share of their direct educational costs, while students at public universities are more heavily subsidized by the citizenry. In this case, it appears that the public good offered by a public university is not the education itself, but the subsidy provided that increases access by lowering the barrier to higher education. Higher education delivered by a public university operates more like a club or toll good, which is a good that is nonrival but is excludable, such as a public golf course or a section of a highway that requires a toll.

All 50 U.S. states operate and fund universities. The California State University system consists of 23 four-year campuses and the University of California system operates 10. The state university system competes with dozens of private universities scattered throughout the state. Meanwhile, California faces severe financial stress. As a result, the state university system faced a $1 billion cut in 2011. Recent years have seen University of California system schools cutting the number of in-state students to recruit both out-of-state and foreign students. Both classes of students pay sharply higher tuition than in-state students. This change has led critics to label the change the "privatization" of the UC system (public interest). Another study indicated that as of 2007, a student with a family income in the top 20 percent was 2.31 times as likely as a student with a family income in the bottom 20 percent to attend one of the 50 flagship state universities in the United States, further suggesting that public universities increasingly exhibit characteristics of private universities (college affordability).

The essential question, then, revolves around the nature of the service provided by public and private universities. Students at public and private universities enroll in comparable courses taught by similarly qualified instructors utilizing the same textbooks. If both sectors provide equivalent experiences, why is the service offered by both? Some city governments collect residential solid waste, while others contract with private organizations. However, it is unlikely that a local government would assume the responsibility and develop the infrastructure to collect residential waste while offering citizens the option to buy waste collection from a private sector firm. In the case of first class mail, the Congress has required by law that the U.S. Postal Service maintains a monopoly. For universities, no such monopoly exists. Public universities compete directly with private universities. Evidence suggests that public universities increasingly appear to be private, either in delivery of services or the consequences of state funding and recruiting decisions. If evidence suggests that privatizing public universities would ease fiscal stress in difficult economic times by cutting costs and improving performance, should this be done? Is higher education an essential service of states, a public good that should be delivered no matter the cost?

In the YES selection, Leonard C. Gilroy argues that privatization of public services can be effectively utilized. He discusses the circumstances under which privatization is most appropriate and when caution must be used to ensure that the taxpayer resources and trust are best protected. In contrast, in the NO selection, Paul R. Verkuil suggests that privatization often produces unintended negative consequences. He recommends that legal and constitutional limits be applied to any public function to determine whether privatizing it would violate public trust.

YES
Leonard C. Gilroy

Local Government Privatization 101

Introduction

"It is not a government's obligation to provide services, but to see that they are provided."

—former New York Governor Mario Cuomo

"Privatize everything you can."

—Chicago Mayor Richard Daley (advice to an incoming mayor)

Over the last half century, governments of all political complexions have increasingly embraced privatization—shifting some or all aspects of government service delivery to private sector provision—as a strategy to lower the costs of government and achieve higher performance and better outcomes for tax dollars spent. Recent decades have seen privatization shift from a concept viewed as radical and ideologically based to a well-established, proven policy management tool. Indeed, local policymakers in many jurisdictions in the U.S. and around the world have used privatization to better the lives of citizens by offering them higher quality services at lower costs, delivering greater choice and more efficient, effective government.

In the 21st century, government's role is evolving from service provider to that of a provider *or* broker of services, as the public sector is increasingly relying far more on networks of public, private and non-profit organizations to deliver services. Virtually every local government service—from road maintenance, fleet operations and public works to education, corrections and public health services—has been successfully privatized at some point in time somewhere in the world.

This trend is not confined to any particular region, or to governments dominated by either major political party. The reason for the widespread appeal of privatization is simple: it works. Decades of successful privatization policies have proven that private sector innovation and initiative can do certain things better than the public sector. Privatization also boosts the local economy and tax base, as private companies under government contract pay taxes into government coffers and offer employment to communities.

Privatization—sometimes referred to as contracting out, outsourcing, competitive sourcing or public-private partnerships—is really an umbrella

From *Reason Foundation Policy Brief,* no. 86, 2010. Copyright © 2010 by Reason Foundation. Reprinted by permission.

term referring to a range of policy choices involving some shift in responsibility from the government to the private sector, or some form of partnership to accomplish certain goals or provide certain services. It covers everything from simple contracting to asset sales and joint ventures (see textbox below on common forms of privatization). Though often involving governments partnering with for-profit firms to deliver services, privatization can also involve partnering with non-profit organizations or volunteers.

All forms of privatization are simply *policy tools*—they can be effective when used well and ineffective when used incorrectly. The reason privatization works is simple: it introduces competition into an otherwise monopolistic system of public service delivery. Governments operate free from competitive forces and without a bottom line. Thus, program structures and approaches often stagnate, and success is not always visible and is hard to replicate. Worse, since budgets are not linked to performance in a positive way, too often poor performers in government get rewarded as budget increases follow failure.

Competition done right drives down costs and incentivizes performance. Private firms operating under government contracts have strong incentives to deliver on performance—after all, their bottom line would be negatively impacted by the cancellation of an existing contract or losing out to a competitor when that contract is subsequently re-bid. On the government's side, applying competition forces management to identify the true cost of doing business, and, with efficiency as a goal, compels an agency to use performance measurement to track and assess quality and value. At its root competition promotes innovation, efficiency and greater effectiveness in serving the shifting demands of customers. Oftentimes, this allows contractors to provide comparable or even superior wages and benefits while reducing service costs and improving service levels.

COMMON GOALS OF PRIVATIZATION

Government managers use privatization to achieve a number of different goals:

Cost Savings: Competition encourages would-be service providers to keep costs to a minimum, lest they lose the contract to a more efficient competitor. Cost savings may be realized through economies of scale, reduced labor costs, better technologies, innovations or simply a different way of completing the job. A review of over 100 studies of privatization showed that cost savings ranged between 5 and 50 percent depending upon the scope and type of service; as a conservative rule of thumb, cost savings through privatization typically range between 5 and 20 percent, on average.

Improved Risk Management: Through contracting and competition, governments may be better able to control costs by building cost containment provisions into contracts. In addition, contracting may be used to shift major liabilities from the government (i.e., taxpayers) to the contractor, such as budget/revenue shortfalls, construction cost overruns, and compliance with federal and state environmental regulations.

Quality Improvements: Similarly, a competitive process encourages bidders to offer the best possible service quality to win out over their rivals.

Timeliness: Contracting may be used to speed the delivery of services by seeking additional workers or providing performance bonuses unavailable to in-house staff.

Accommodating Fluctuating Peak Demand: Changes in season and economic conditions may cause staffing needs to fluctuate significantly. Contracting allows governments to obtain additional help when it is most needed so that services are uninterrupted for residents without permanently increasing the labor force.

Access to Outside Expertise: Contracting allows governments to obtain staff expertise that they do not have in-house on an as-needed basis.

Innovation: The need for lower-cost, higher-quality services under competition encourages providers to create new, cutting-edge solutions to help win and retain government contracts.

FORMS OF PRIVATIZATION

While there are many different forms of privatization, some of the most common are:

Contracts: The most common form of privatization in local governments occurs when governments contract with private sector service providers, for-profit or nonprofit, to deliver individual public services, such as road maintenance, custodial services, fleet maintenance and water system operations and maintenance. Local governments also routinely contract with private firms to provide administrative support functions, such as information technology, accounting and human resources. Local governments are also increasingly using "bundled" service contracts that integrate more functions or responsibilities into a single contract, such as a contract to outsource an entire city public works department.

Franchises: In a franchise arrangement—also referred to as a lease or concession—government typically awards a private firm an exclusive right to provide a public service or operate a public asset, usually in return for an annual lease payment (or a one-time, upfront payment) and subject to meeting performance expectations outlined by the public sector. As an example, in many jurisdictions common utility services—such as telecommunications, gas, electricity and water—are provided through long-term franchise agreements. Franchise-based privatization initiatives may involve the privatization of an existing government asset, such as a toll road, water/wastewater plant or airport, though similar arrangements can be used to finance, build and deliver new infrastructure assets as well. Chicago's $1.8 billion lease of its Chicago Skyway toll road, $1.15 billion

(Continued)

lease of its downtown parking meter system, and $560 million lease of four downtown parking garages are recent examples of the franchise approach.

Divestiture: Some forms of privatization involve governments getting out of a service, activity or asset entirely, often through outright sales. Local governments routinely sell off aging or underutilized land, buildings, and equipment, returning them to private commerce where they may be more productively used. For example, in the late 1990s New York City sold off two city-owned radio stations and a television station, and Orange County, California raised more than $300 million through real asset sales and asset sale-leaseback arrangements over the course of 18 months to help recover from collapse into bankruptcy in 1995.

Where Can—Or Can't—Local Governments Apply Privatization?

Local policymakers often ask a very simple question: "where can we apply privatization?" However, the answer is somewhat more complicated.

One obvious place to start is examining what other local governments are doing. The International City-County Management Association (ICMA) conducts a survey of alternate service delivery by local governments every five years, measuring service delivery for 67 local services across more than 1,000 municipalities nationwide. The 2007 survey shows that public delivery is the most common form of service delivery at 52 percent of all service delivery across all local governments on average (see Figure 1). For-profit privatization

Figure 1

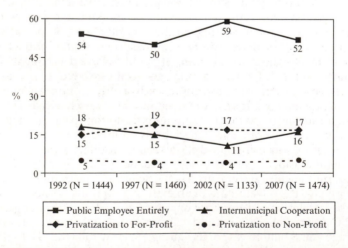

Local Privatization Trends in the United States

Source: Warner and Hefetz, *Trends in Public and Contracted Government Services: 2002–2007.*

at 17 percent and intergovernmental contracting at 16 percent are the most common alternatives to public delivery. Non-profit privatization is next at 5 percent, and franchises, subsidies and volunteers collectively account for less than 2 percent of service delivery, on average.

Trends in levels of for-profit privatization and non-profit contracting have remained relatively steady over the last two decades (though the 2007 survey would not capture the likely uptick in local government privatization in the wake of the 2008–2009 recession and subsequent proliferation of state and local fiscal crises).

Table 1 shows the percentages of surveyed local governments using privatization across a range of public services. Among the most frequently privatized local government services are waste collection (residential and commercial), waste disposal, vehicle fleet management, hospitals, vehicle towing, electric utilities, drug programs and emergency medical services.

Those services are just a start; one privatization expert at the City University of New York identified over 200 city and county services that have been contracted out to private firms (including for-profit and non-profit). Some of the most prevalent areas of local government privatization include:

- Accounting, financial and legal services;
- Administrative human resource functions (e.g., payroll services, recruitment/hiring, training, benefits administration, records management, etc.);
- Core IT infrastructure and network, Web and data processing;
- Risk management (claims processing, loss prevention, etc.);
- Planning, building and permitting services;
- Printing and graphic design services;
- Road maintenance;
- Building/facilities financing, operations and maintenance;
- Park operations and maintenance;
- Zoo operations and maintenance;
- Stadium and convention center management;
- Library services;
- Mental health services and facilities;
- Animal shelter operations and management;
- School construction (including financing), maintenance and non-instructional services;
- Revenue-generating assets (garages, parking meters, etc.), and
- Major public infrastructure assets (roads, water/wastewater systems, airports, etc.).

This is but a partial list. But more important, the question of "what can local governments privatize" is in many ways the wrong question to ask, as privatization is a policy tool that should be considered in most instances.

A better question is "where *can't* local governments apply competition or privatization?." Virtually every service, function and activity has successfully been subjected to competition by a government somewhere around the world at some time. When asked what he wouldn't privatize, former Florida Governor Jeb Bush replied: ". . . police functions, in general, would be the

Table 1

Use of Alternative Service Delivery Forms by Metro Status

Service	% Use 2007			% Point Change 2002–2007		
	Metro	Suburb	Rural	Metro	Suburb	Rural
For-Profit Contracting						
Res. Waste Collection	29.0%	57.3%	39.3%	−4.6%	10.4%	10.0%
Comm. Waste Collection	39.2%	63.8%	52.7%	−2.1%	14.5%	18.9%
Waste Disposal	35.3%	51.9%	30.4%	−1.7%	8.0%	0.8%
Hazardous Materials	32.4%	29.1%	36.5%	−10.1%	−9.0%	2.5%
Airport	17.1%	14.7%	9.0%	−6.2%	−15.8%	−5.3%
Electric Utility	42.6%	56.7%	36.8%	26.0%	16.4%	19.6%
Vehicle Towing	57.1%	68.4%	65.4%	−22.3%	−13.1%	−9.3%
Daycare	39.0%	53.8%	64.9%	1.1%	13.8%	33.1%
Child Welfare	8.7%	10.9%	8.9%	−6.1%	−2.4%	4.6%
Transit Services	24.4%	17.7%	13.3%	−0.4%	−3.4%	−0.7%
Job Training	9.2%	7.4%	2.6%	−5.2%	−3.0%	−5.6%
Welfare Eligibility	1.0%	3.0%	0.8%	−1.3%	1.7%	−2.5%
Hospitals	35.3%	38.6%	43.2%	24.2%	8.6%	11.6%
Insect Control	14.8%	24.6%	19.3%	1.7%	3.5%	8.9%
Drug Programs	23.6%	17.0%	22.0%	1.1%	−1.7%	10.1%
Emergency Medical	16.1%	16.6%	18.3%	1.4%	3.9%	8.0%
Museums	3.0%	4.3%	4.1%	−0.8%	−0.4%	−0.8%
Fleet Management	23.6%	28.6%	22.3%	−15.3%	−11.2%	−8.4%

Source: International County and City Management Association, Alternative Service Delivery Surveys, 2002, 2007; Washington DC. Service average is the percentage based on number answering each question where the denominator varies with each service. This is consistent with ICMA's reporting method in the *Municipal Yearbook*.

first thing to be careful about outsourcing or privatizing. This office. Offices of elected officials . . . and major decision-making jobs that set policy would never be privatized." Governor Bush used competitive sourcing more than 130 times, saving more than $500 million in cash-flow dollars and avoiding over $1 billion in estimated future costs.

Privatizing City Hall: Sandy Springs and the New Georgia Contract Cities

What may surprise many local policymakers is the extent to which other communities have embraced privatization, extending the boundaries far beyond what's seen in most jurisdictions. For example, over the last four years, five new cities serving over 200,000 residents have incorporated in metropolitan Atlanta, Georgia as "contract cities." These newly incorporated cities opted to contract out virtually all of their non-safety related government services to private firms, dramatically reducing costs and improving services along the way.

Sandy Springs, Georgia was the first. Fed up with high taxes, poor service delivery and a perceived lack of local land use control, 94 percent of Sandy Springs' nearly 90,000 people voted to incorporate as an independent city in 2005. What makes Sandy Springs interesting is that instead of creating a new municipal bureaucracy, the city opted to contract out for nearly all government services (except for police and fire services, which are required to be provided directly by the public sector under Georgia's state constitution).

Originally created with just four government employees, the city's successful launch was facilitated by a $32 million contract with CH$_2$M-Hill OMI, an international firm that oversees and manages day-to-day municipal operations. The contract value was just above half what the city traditionally was charged through taxes by Fulton County. The city maintains ownership of assets and maintains budget control by setting priorities and service levels. Meanwhile the contractor is responsible for staffing and all operations and services. According to Sandy Springs Mayor Eva Galambos, the city's relationship with the contractor "has been exemplary. We are thrilled with the way the contractors are performing. The speed with which public works problems are addressed is remarkable. All the public works, all the community development, all the administrative stuff, the finance department, everything is done by CH$_2$M-Hill," Galambos said. "The only services the city pays to its own employees are for public safety and the court to handle ordinance violations."

Sandy Springs recently successfully rolled out its own police and fire departments. Counting police and fire employees, the city of 90,000 has only 196 total employees. Nearby Roswell, a city of 85,000 has over 1,400 employees. Furthermore, Sandy Springs' budget is over $30 million less, and by most accounts provides a higher level of service.

The "Sandy Springs model" seems to be gaining steam. The city's incorporation was perceived as such a success that four new cities—Johns Creek, Milton, Chattahoochee Hills and Dunwoody—have been formed in Georgia since 2006 employing operating models very similar to Sandy Springs (though severe revenue shortfalls in 2009 prompted the two smallest to scale back their contracts). And in 2008, city officials in the recently incorporated Central, Louisiana (population 27,000) hired a contractor to deliver a full range of municipal services—including public works, planning and zoning, code enforcement and administrative functions—as part of a three-year, $10.5 million contract.

Sandy Springs and other contract cities demonstrate something very powerful from a public administration standpoint: there's hardly anything that local governments do that can't be privatized, so there's no reason policy-makers shouldn't think big on privatization.

Myths vs. Facts on Privatization

Privatization is a complex subject, and one that is commonly misunderstood. Three of the most prevalent myths include:

Myth: Privatization is partisan.

Fact: Privatization is not the domain of any one political party or ideology. In the U.S., privatization is used by leaders of both major political parties, and they have demonstrated that not only can politicians at all levels successfully privatize public services, but they can get re-elected after doing so.

For example, former Indianapolis Mayor Stephen Goldsmith, a Republican, identified $400 million in savings and opened up over five dozen city services—including trash collection, pothole repair and wastewater services—to competitive bidding. Chicago Mayor Richard Daley, a Democrat, has privatized more than 40 services and, since 2005, has generated over $3 billion in privatization deals for the Chicago Skyway toll road, four downtown parking garages, and the city's downtown parking meter system. And when Democrat Ed Rendell, governor of Pennsylvania, was mayor of Philadelphia, he saved $275 million by privatizing 49 city services, including golf courses, print shops, parking garages and correctional facilities.

Myth: Privatization involves a loss of public control.

Fact: This myth involves a fundamental misunderstanding of the nature of privatization—that government loses control of an asset or service once it is privatized since the public sector is no longer providing that service. In well-structured privatization initiatives the government and taxpayers gain accountability. In fact, the legal foundation of a privatization initiative is a contract that spells out all of the responsibilities and performance expectations that the government partner will require of the contractor. No detail is too small for the contract. Any failure to meet the performance standards specified in the contract could expose the contractor to financial penalties, and in the worst-case scenario, termination of the contract.

So government never loses control—in fact, it can actually *gain more control* of outcomes—in well-crafted privatization arrangements. For example, state officials in Indiana have testified that they were able to require higher standards of performance from the concessionaire operating the Indiana Toll Road than the state itself could provide when it ran the road, precisely because they specified the standards they wanted in the contract and can now hold the concessionaire financially accountable for meeting them.

Myth: Privatization hurts public employees.

Fact: Privatization tends to encounter opposition from public employee unions who view it as a threat to their jobs and influence. Well-managed privatization initiatives need not put undue burden on public employees, however. Comprehensive examinations of privatization initiatives have found that they tend to result in few, if any, layoffs—those not retained by the new contractor usually either retire early or shift to other public sector positions—and that public employees can actually benefit in the long term when hired on by contractors, as private companies often present greater opportunities for upward career advancement, training and continuing education, and pay commensurate with performance, for example.

Nevertheless, it is important that management communicate early and often with the public employee unions regarding privatization initiatives. In the event that city employee jobs are at risk, the city should develop a plan to manage public employee transitions.

The Bottom Line

1. Privatization is a nonpolitical, nonpartisan tool used by Republicans and Democrats.
2. Privatization does not lead to less control but gains more control of outcomes.
3. Privatization can benefit employees through better opportunities, education, pay, promotion and advancement.

Best Practices and Lessons Learned in Local Government Privatization

As is the case in all types of contracting, privatization can be implemented well or can be implemented poorly. A successful privatization process will ensure transparency, accountability and the delivery of high-performance services through a strong, performance-based contract. By using best practices and lessons learned from the experiences of other governments, the likelihood of achieving those results is greatly enhanced. Among them:

Rethink the status quo, and ask the "make or buy" question: Taking a page from management guru Peter Drucker, every "traditional" service or function should have to prove its worthiness and proper role and place within government. Contract cities like Sandy Springs were able to start with a blank slate and ask fundamental questions about what role government should play, such as "if we weren't doing this yesterday, would we do it today?" Once they whittled the list down to those core functions deemed necessary, they then asked whether they should "make or buy" those services, opting to contract out as many services as possible to the private sector to get the best value for taxpayers. Traditional cities should not hesitate to ask these same questions regarding existing services.

Think big: Sandy Springs and the other contract cities prove that the central question on the subject of outsourcing should not be "what can we privatize?" but, rather, "what can't we privatize?" Outside of public safety services, the courts and policymaking functions, the private sector has proven repeatedly in the contract cities that there is nothing in the routine operations of government—those things that citizens interface with most directly—that cannot be privatized.

Bundle services for better value: Local governments may find greater economies of scale, cost savings and/or value for money through bundling several—or even all—services in a given department (e.g., public works) or departmental subdivision (e.g., facility management and maintenance) into an outsourcing initiative, rather than treat individual services or functions separately. There have been several instances of governments moving toward this approach since 2008. Centennial, Colorado privatized all of its public works functions in 2008. Bonita Springs, Florida privatized all of its community development services (planning, zoning, permitting, inspections and code enforcement) that same year, and Pembroke Pines, Florida privatized its entire building and planning department in June 2009. Also, the state of Georgia signed a large-scale outsourcing contract for the management and maintenance of numerous secure-site facilities held by the Department of Corrections, Department of Juvenile Justice and Georgia Bureau of Investigation.

Focus on building procurement and contract management expertise: Successful privatization initiatives require good contract negotiation, management and monitoring skills on the part of city managers. The more that local governments use privatization, the greater the degree to which the city manager's role will center on contract administration—monitoring and enforcing contracts to ensure that the contractor's performance lives up to his contractual obligations. Staff must be properly trained in contracting best practices and, in particular, how to build specific service standards into agreements and monitor provider performance, in order to avoid possible ambiguities, misunderstandings and disputes.

Establish a centralized procurement unit: Governments should maintain an expert team of procurement and competition officials to guide individual departments in developing their privatization initiatives. This central unit will help to break down the "silos" that departments sometimes operate within and identify city-wide or enterprise-wide competition opportunities that might not otherwise be considered.

Apply the "Yellow Pages Test" through regular commercial activity inventories: Local government managers should regularly scour all government agencies, services and activities and classify each as either "inherently governmental" (i.e., services that should only be performed by public employees) or "commercial" (i.e., services offered by private sector vendors) in nature. This famous "Yellow Pages Test" helps government concentrate on delivering core, "inherently governmental" services while partnering with the private sector for commercial activities. In other words, undertaking a commercial activities inventory helps identify those areas in which government is engaged in the business of business, effectively competing against private sector business and undermining free enterprise and economic development.

The results of commercial activity inventories can be illuminating, especially with regard to the extent to which some governments compete against private enterprise to provide services. For example, Virginia's first commercial activity inventory in 1999 identified 205 commercial activities being performed by over 38,000 state employees, accounting for nearly *half* of all state workers.

Utilize performance-based contracting: It is crucial that local governments identify good performance measures to fairly compare competing bids and accurately evaluate provider performance after the contract is awarded.

Performance-based contracts should be used as much as possible to place the emphasis on obtaining the results the city wants achieved, rather than focusing merely on inputs and trying to dictate precisely how the service should be performed. Performance standards should be included in contracts and tied to compensation through financial incentives.

Establish guidelines for cost comparisons: Local governments should establish formal guidelines for cost comparisons to make sure that all costs are included in the "unit cost" of providing a service, so that an "apples-to-apples" comparison of competing bidders may be made. This is especially important in situations in which public employees may bid against private sector firms to provide a given service, as the public and private sectors operate under different rules.

Utilize "best value" contracting: Initiatives that are considered best practices for government procurement and service contracting utilize "best value" techniques where, rather than purchasing based on cost or "lowest bid" alone, governments choose the best mix of quality, cost and other factors in selecting a service vendor. Many privatization failures are linked to a low-cost selection where the allure of increased cost savings negatively impacted service quality.

Ensure contractor accountability through rigorous monitoring and performance evaluation: Regular monitoring and performance evaluations are essential to ensure accountability, transparency, and that the local government's management and the service provider are on the same page. This can help address any problems that might arise early, before they become major setbacks.

Conclusion

Just moments after taking her oath of office in 2005 after the city's incorporation, Sandy Springs Mayor Eva Galambos said, "We have harnessed the energy of the private sector to organize the major functions of city government instead of assembling our own bureaucracy. This we have done because we are convinced that the competitive model is what has made America so successful. And we are here to demonstrate that this same competitive model will lead to an efficient and effective local government."

Local policymakers should periodically ask fundamental questions about how their governments operate and whether there is a better way. The experiences of Sandy Springs and the thousands of other local governments around the country—and indeed, around the world—that have embraced privatization demonstrate that there is another way to govern. When implemented with care, due diligence and a focus on maximizing competition, privatization is an approach that puts results, performance and outcomes first to deliver high-quality public services at a lower cost.

Paul R. Verkuil  **NO**

Outsourcing Sovereignty: Why Privatization of Government Functions Threatens Democracy and What We Can Do About It

Conclusions (Wherein the Principal Instructs Her Agents)

. . . The Founders were not greatly concerned with the line between private and public. During the revolutionary period, they were delighted to receive help from wherever it originated, as the Marquis de Lafayette's presence at Washington's side testifies. But the Constitution was more careful. It might be read as endorsing private contractors in only one instance, the Marque and Reprisal Clause, which authorized the long-ago repudiated practice of employing privateers to do the work of the Navy. But that Clause, even if revived, would support the arguments advanced here because it requires Congress to initiate privatizing actions. It does not leave it to the Executive or the states to do so unilaterally.

Other delegations in the Constitution by the Principal to her agents are made directly, under the assumption that those agents would themselves be the ones to act or at least would devolve their significant duties to other public officials. These are the persons generally charged with forming the administration, a concept familiar to the Founders. As Hamilton also emphasized, ". . . the true test of a good government is its aptitude and tendency to produce a good administration."

The Constitution was careful about placing responsibility in the hands of public officials. These officials are not only required to be confirmed, but they swear oaths to uphold the Constitution. The Principal (the People) as well as the president or Congress (who are both agents and principals) have the right and duty to instruct these agents. Whether at the time of the Constitution's framing or anytime since the subject of outsourcing government functions has been discussed, what might the People say to each of the branches? Here are some thoughts drawn from the arguments in this book.

To the Executive and the Agents

Article II comes first. Most outsourcing or privatization decisions are initiated by the Executive Branch, since it is the branch that forms the administration. In modern times, outsourcing has been accepted as a necessary part of the governing function, especially in the military context. There are many reasons why the executive has let that happen. The need for special talents not readily available in government is one reason. In addition, as a political matter, outsourcing lets the president claim to be reducing the size of government while adding to it (i.e., headcounts v. budget effect). And politics also may be a motivator when the outsourced functions devolve to loyal supporters of the president. Ultimately, although the technique has valid uses, it also can be deceptive and destructive of the common good.

On the Military Side

In Iraq, military contractors have suffered losses that are not counted as casualties; they are off the books (in a body count but not budget sense). Although there is much that private contractors can legitimately do in wartime, what they should not do is exercise force in ways that are unaccountable and even uncontrollable. The military has the ability to distinguish proper from improper use of contractors, even on the battlefield. The field commander is now the one on whom these decisions fall. That should be changed. He or she should not the one to make hard choices under the stress of combat. A commitment to inherent government functions, as RAND continues to remind the DOD, balances the commitment to competitive sourcing and moderates the use of private power.

Military commanders find it difficult to work with contractors who are not subject to the command and control system. Efforts are being made to give commanders emergency authority over contractors, but that is a less than ideal situation. If commanders are adequately staffed and supported by professional soldiers, the problems of inappropriate contractor roles would not arise. But adequate staffing is the big assumption that lies behind many of the problems that the military has faced in Iraq. The president, through the Secretary of Defense, is the one to determine how and when to use contractors in potentially compromising battlefield situations. This decision is tied into funding levels for personnel and strategic decisions about the use of force.

Moreover, market alternatives themselves may adversely affect the availability of military services. Private security companies (PSCs) are a $100 billion industry, which is growing to $200 billion. These companies buy up top-quality professionals at two to three times their military salaries and thereby reduce the availability of experienced troops. Because that demand is largely produced by the U.S. military itself, it also can be moderated by the same institution. PSCs often focus on the most highly trained members of the military (Special Forces, Seals, etc.), which are the most difficult to replace. If the military has a monopoly on force, it also has a monopoly on the market for force. The military faces competition of its own choosing and it can protect itself by reducing the desirability of nonmilitary options. P. W. Singer has urged that the DOD needs to do a careful risk based analysis on the use of military contractors "at the top of the spear." This analysis should limit and even consider eliminating the use of private contractors in roles that only the best trained military can perform.

It should decide how best to keep these forces in the public sector up to the time of their retirement. The economics of this choice must be analyzed, as maintaining a public force is now a market-driven decision. This is why the distinction between proper and improper outsourcing is so important. Support services should be market tested, but fighting forces should retain their status as a monopoly. The DOD must reconcile the use of contractors on the battlefield with the nondelegation of military functions. The Army manual recognizes the distinction, but the field commanders are often in no position to honor it. Abu Ghraib is a scar for both the military and its consultants, and should serve as a reminder and motivator.

The DOD's broader challenge, however, is in the growth of no-bid contracts. Even assuming the war in Iraq required fast decisions when it began, after five years the contracting process should have been regularized and competitive bidding restored. The embarrassments that these contracts produce should be motivation enough to contain and to monitor them. The number of contracting officers must be augmented and they, not private contractors, should be responsible for oversight of the contracting process in Iraq.

The contracting difficulties in Iraq are inexcusable. When the special auditor assigned to Iraq is sacked, both branches should be called to account. Stuart W. Bowen Jr., the head of the Office of the Special Inspector General for Iraq Reconstruction, found his job eliminated in a military authorization bill signed by the president. Mr. Bowen, a political appointee with impeccable Republican credentials, was essentially fired after successfully challenging expenditures by companies such as Halliburton, Parsons, and Bechtel. The State and Defense Department Inspector Generals tried to assure dissenting members of Congress that they will assume Bowen's duties, but, given the shortage of personnel available for contractor oversight, that is a less than reassuring response. The new Congress properly reversed this decision.

On the Civilian Side

On the civilian side of government, the Executive is faced with even greater challenges. The biggest one may be confronting the risks to government inherent in a downsizing environment. Arbitrarily set personnel limits on government positions compel the use of consultants in ways that are inimical to the best interests of government. And this problem is compounded by an increase in political appointees relative to career officials. The relative performance deficit of political appointees has only recently been exposed.

It is difficult to convince any president to reduce the number of political appointees, as has been proposed by the Volcker Commission. But, from the People's point of view, good administration requires talented civil servants, especially at the top. The Executive can begin restoring balance and competency to government by reinvigorating the SES. An analogy to ambassadorial appointments may be helpful here. Ambassadorships are coveted by the White

House as rewards for campaign contributors, but they are carefully doled out. Political appointees are sent to "safe" countries, with very strong first officers to support them. An equal effort should be made to focus career officials on those agencies where turmoil and challenge are the highest. One of the problems at DHS and FEMA was exactly this—that top flight professionals did not follow the new agency, they abandoned it. The next White House needs to send the message that public service is crucial to the proper performance of important government functions.

The agencies (the traditional Fourth Branch) are ultimately the ones who hire contractors and bear responsibility for continuing them. Agencies such as DOE that have become virtual contractor shops are the most difficult to reach in this regard. It may not be possible to convince an agency this far committed to managing contractors that sovereignty transfer is a problem it can fix. But other agencies that utilize consultants in ways that encroach on inherent powers can moderate their consumption. For example, the use of consultants to read and summarize comments submitted on a rule is a reasonable outsourcing decision. But the next step of analyzing and drafting proposed rules crosses the line. Consultants who write testimony are also coming close to the inherent function line.

Here, instructions can be given to limit these practices. If new positions are necessary to do this work in-house, they should be made available. Again, cost considerations are important but not controlling in a situation involving the performance of inherent government functions.

Agencies are the heart of the administration. Their career ranks both drive and implement policy for the executive and legislative branches. The use of contractors where they have expertise and can provide services not available in house is one thing, but a largely unchecked resort to contractors jeopardizes the effectiveness of government.

Viewed from the perspective of agency cost theory, the problem for the branches (and by extension, the People) is that of the noncomplying agency. Political control of agencies requires a variety of techniques, including political appointees and career officials who are sworn to be loyal. Consultants are less directly controlled in this regard and less easily monitored. When they act substantively, consultants are more likely to escape political and legal oversight. They cannot be called before Congress and their work is often outside the ambit of transparency devices such as FOIA. Finally, downsizing initiatives have reduced the number of government officials who can oversee contractors and hold them accountable. The limits of accountable government have been reached when contractors monitor the performance of contractors.

To the Congress

Congress, the first branch under the Constitution, has the most to lose by the excessive use of contractors. Congress already suffers an information asymmetry vis-à-vis the president and the agencies. Contractors exacerbate this deficiency because their work is often outside the usual channels of review and oversight. And, in the foreign affairs arena, executive secrecy and deliberative privileges pose further obstacles to congressional information streams.

Congress has three critical ways to hold government officials accountable—the appointment process, the budget process and oversight hearings. In the first two situations, consultants can cause a disconnect between Congress and the agency heads who appear before them. If consultants have prepared analyses relative to rules, for example, that fact is obscured from view. When Congress holds hearings with cabinet secretaries, it might like to know how much of the work presented has been produced by consultants. An opening question from the committee chair that asks "Who wrote your testimony?" is an impertinent but not irrelevant way to start the inquiry.

Expressed in agency cost theory, Congress might like to know who its agents really are before it delegates powers to them. And, if consultants are involved, it might like to see the contracts under which they operate. It does, after all, have a choice to delegate the details of legislation or specify them itself. In times of divided government, Congress does specify details of legislation more carefully. If Congress knows that an agency relies on contractors to analyze its mission, it may well feel that more direct instructions are needed. Indeed, the presence of private agents may cause Congress to retain power rather than delegate it in the first place.

The objection is not so much that the Secretary did not act personally, but that the consultants who did the work are not before the committee. Because agency testimony is vetted by the OMB or other executive officials, this problem may be manageable. Still, one purpose of oversight is to assure Congress that the agency before it is functioning properly. Proper functioning requires agency officials both to make and to understand the policy decisions before them.

To perform its role under Article I, Congress must be willing to challenge the executive. That is what the Constitution intended when it separated powers among the branches. Politically, the adversarial role of Congress is much easier when one party does not hold both houses and the presidency. As the 2006 elections show, divided government can be a source of power to the People. The quiet elimination of the Office of Special Inspector General for Iraq, for example, would likely not have occurred if the House had been in Democratic hands. Indeed, the first thing the new Congress promised was the restoration of that office. Members of Congress take oaths to uphold the Constitution, not the Executive branch. Party loyalty is understandable, but branch loyalty is also expected whenever Congress acts.

Congress has other powers with regard to the outsourcing problem that it can readily invoke. The Constitution established a legislative role whenever the Executive branch privatizes. Congress has taken advantage of this opportunity by participating actively in executive reorganization. Under the Subdelegation Act, Congress can participate in the contracting-out process. That act's limiting dimensions require Congress to approve subdelegations of significant authority to anyone who is not an officer of the United States. Congress holds the key to permitting, forbidding, or challenging delegations of government functions to private contractors.

In fact, it often uses that power wisely. When it wants to delegate choices about contracting it has done so (under the FAIR Act, for example). Surely Congress does not want to micromanage the procurement process and agency (DOD) choices in this regard should be supported. But oversight hearings on the use of private contractors are entirely appropriate and necessary. Moreover, the effectiveness of the OMB's Circular A-76 process, which the GAO has explored and the FAIR Act assumes, is another area worthy of congressional study. Attention to the inherent government function side of the ledger is something Congress can require and, with the GAO's help, can calculate the results of.

Congress also has created an oversight mechanism with the enactment of the False Claims Act. By giving private parties the power to pursue government fraud, which the DOJ can ultimately control, the FCA provides an additional check on government efforts to ferret out fraud. This is particularly relevant in the context of Iraq, where many contracts have been challenged by whistleblowers. In circumstances in which public inspectors general are stretched thin, this statute becomes an important tool of congressional oversight.

Ultimately, the Appointments Clause gives Congress, through the Senate, the power to control the exercise of inherent government functions. When powers are delegated from these executive agents, who are also agents of Congress, to others, Congress has a constitutional stake in the process. Its job is to assure the People that the work of government stays in the hands of those responsible for its execution.

To the Court

The People's expectations of the judicial branch under the Constitution are more limited. Although it is clearly the duty of the Court to say what the law (and the Constitution) means under *Marbury v. Madison,* that role has practical limitations in a democratic society. The nondelegation doctrine, when buttressed by the Due Process (*Carter Coal*) and Appointments Clauses, has precise application to outsourcing and the duty to govern. But such broad challenges to outsourcing by agencies have to be carefully justified. Few want a return to the substantive due process era characterized by the *Lochner* Court. However, it is hard to oversee delegations to private contractors without challenging current views of the constitutional role.

Moreover, this is the era of *Chevron,* where deference to the Executive has risen to the level of a counter-*Marbury* principle. *Chevron* reflects a separation of powers principle that assumes the agencies are better prepared than the courts to execute legislative policy. Under *Chevron,* principles of reasoned decision making on judicial review can be invoked to challenge delegations that transfer to private contractors the duty to analyze if not govern.

At a time when the executive seeks to deprive the Court of jurisdiction over the detention policies behind the War on Terror, building a constitutional case against outsourcing government functions may seem less daunting. And it reflects core values. The due process approach subjects private delegations to public oversight mechanisms. The Appointments Clause approach suggests that such executive branch delegations must be connected to statutory author-izations. These limitations on the Executive's powers to delegate to private hands are not preclusive. They assume that Congress can provide adequate procedures and instructions that can be administered by following established precedents like the Subdelegation Act.

On the statutory front the courts also have a role to play. Although *Chevron* and the rule of regularity tend to insulate agency action from judi-cial second guessing, these doctrines must be reconciled with existing stand-ards of judicial review. Reasoned decision making and hard-look review derive from the courts' reviewing function under the Administrative Procedure Act. If a court becomes aware that agencies use consultants to analyze and prepare (if not decide) important decisions (rulemaking, for example), a fair question becomes has the agency itself engaged in reasoned decision making. A few cases questioning these practices would likely put an end to them.

Finally, the courts have a role to play in agency implementation of A-76 practices. Since 1996, bid protests have been considered in the U.S. Court of Federal Claims. Judicial review of decisions whether to treat a government function as inherent or not can be obtained by granting plaintiffs (govern-ment officials who lost competitions and their unions) standing to challenge results under existing law. The judicial role on the merits is limited by the arbi-trary and capricious standard, so practices may not change dramatically. But, again, interest in the question by the Federal Circuit should make agencies decide the critical question of private delegation more carefully.

The People expect effective judicial review of public sector decision mak-ing. A government that operates well is a protection of citizens' interests. The Republic is better off if the courts participate in the accountability process. Contractors are vital to the provision of government services so long as they support and do not transplant the role government officials play. The courts are agents of the People, as are the two political branches. The courts can sometimes alert the other branches to institutional problems. That is one of the functions judicial review and, to a more limited extent, constitutional review serve in a democratic society.

Conclusion

The People's Constitution has spoken. As faithful agents, the branches must reply. The use of contractors to displace functions normally performed by gov-ernment officials who exercise significant authority can be a danger to the Republic; it should be curtailed in the future. Given its imbedded nature and the fuzzy lines between inherent and competitive functions, this cannot be done overnight. But what we require now, as Ted Sorensen asked for at a differ-ent but no less perilous time, are watchmen in the night: People who can help secure and preserve our public values in an era of unprecedented delegations of power to the private sector.

EXPLORING THE ISSUE

Should Governments Use the Private Sector to Deliver Public Services?

Critical Thinking and Reflection

1. Why would government rely on the private sector to deliver public services in some cases?
2. What tasks should government use private sector agencies to deliver and why?
3. What sorts of tasks should always be administered by a public entity such as government and why?
4. In what ways are the public and private sectors similar?
5. What are the arguments against the government using private sector agencies to fulfill public services?

Is There Common Ground?

Privatization is a hotly debated topic within American government. Proponents regularly argue that private sector companies would be able to more efficiently complete tasks presently undertaken by public sector agencies. On the opposite side, opponents question what the role of government even is if private sectors are able to allegedly do everything better. What the debate tells us is that privatization has become quite the politicized issue. Without question, there are inefficiencies in American government that could (and in most cases should) be corrected. Yet, continually turning toward the private sector opens a slippery slope that will be difficult to maneuver on. Although UPS and FedEx may operate from within a better business model than the national post office, do we really want this fact to be used as the basis for increasing reliance on private military contractors? In terms of common ground, what we need to do is recognize that there are inefficiencies in government today and determine ways that public administrators can operate in a different manner to increase efficiency. There is no reason, after all, why our first instinct every time government struggles should be to hand the power off to the private sector. Instead, we should be asking what needs to be done to allow government to do the job as well and as cost-effectively as their private rivals.

Additional Resources

Donahue, J.D., *The Privatization Decision: Public Ends, Private Means* (New York: Basic Books, 1991)

Donahue—in this classic work—offers early answers to the question of what government activities should be contracted out to private companies.

Written by a policy analyst, it shuns global answers and explores how to examine individual cases.

Roland, G. and J. Stiglitz, *Privatization: Successes and Failures* (New York: Columbia University Press, 2008)

Privatization: Successes and Failures provides the first broad assessment of the benefits and costs of privatization policies around the world for over the past twenty years. Privatization is an important and controversial policy issue, and unlike previous studies, this book's goal is not to champion privatization policies but rather to undertake a deep and careful evaluation of them.

Savas, E.S., *Privatization and Public-Private Partnerships* (Washington, DC: CQ Press, 1999)

Savas provides a complete guide to privatization—the background, theory, and practical reality. This book explains what, why, when, and how to privatize. Contracting services, using franchises and vouchers, divesting government-owned businesses, privatizing infrastructure through public–private partnerships, reforming education, privatizing the welfare state, and overcoming opposition to privatization are discussed in detail.

Schlar, E., *You Don't Always Get What You Pay For: The Economics of Privatization* (Ithaca, NY: Cornell University Press, 2001)

Schlar offers a balanced look at the costs and benefits of privatization of the public sector in the American context.

Verkuil, P., *Outsourcing Sovereignty: Why Privatization of Government Functions Threatens Democracy and What We Can Do About It* (New York: Cambridge University Press, 2007)

Reliance on the private military industry and the privatization of public functions has left our government less able to govern effectively. When decisions that should have been taken by government officials are delegated (wholly or in part) to private contractors without appropriate oversight, the public interest is jeopardized.

Internet References . . .

Reason Foundation, Privatization

Reason produces rigorous, peer-reviewed research and directly engages the policy process, seeking strategies that emphasize cooperation, flexibility, local knowledge, transparency, accountability, and results. Through practical and innovative approaches to complex problems, Reason seeks to change the way people think about issues, and promotes policies that allow and encourage individuals and voluntary institutions to flourish.

http://reason.org/areas/topic/privatization

Office of Government Contracting and Business Administration

The Office of Government Contracting and Business Administration's mission is to help enhance the effectiveness of small business programs by working with Government Contracting and Business Development program offices and others to develop policies, regulations, and statutory changes.

http://www.sba.gov/about-offices-content/1/2467

USAJOBS

USAJOBS is the U.S. Government's official system/program for federal jobs and employment information. USAJOBS delivers a service by which Federal agencies meet their legal obligation (5 USC 3327 and 5 USC 3330) providing public notice of Federal employment opportunities to Federal employees and U.S. citizens.

http://www.usajobs.gov/

Political Activity (Hatch Act)

This site examines the elements of the Hatch Act and how it is applied. The site is housed within the U.S. Office of Special Counsel.

http://www.osc.gov/hatchact.htm

United States Merit System Protection Board

The Merit Systems Protection Board is an independent, quasi-judicial agency in the Executive branch that serves as the guardian of federal merit systems. The Board was established by Reorganization Plan No. 2 of 1978, which was codified by the Civil Service Reform Act of 1978 (CSRA), Public Law No. 95-454.

http://www.mspb.gov/

Functions of Government Workers: Administration, Management, and Budgeting

*G*overnment employees are responsible for a myriad of activities. *Issues such as administration, management, and budgeting are regularly handled by bureaucrats and help ensure policies are implemented effectively and that the individuals analyzing policy outcomes and choices have as much information as possible. These tasks are the true work of government employees as they make policy become more than written words on a piece of signed paper. In this unit, we look at issues surrounding the functions of government bureaucrats. By examining the day-to-day tasks, we are able to gain a more complete view of the role of public administrators as practitioners.*

- Does Performance Management Lead to Better Policy Outcomes?

- Is Employment Equity Necessary?

- Is It Possible to Motivate Workers in a Manner That Increases Job Satisfaction in the Public Sector?

- Should Incrementalism Be the Guiding Budgeting Philosophy of Public Agencies?

- Do We Need More Budget Flexibility for Discretionary Spending Compared to Entitlements?

ISSUE 10

Does Performance Management Lead to Better Policy Outcomes?

YES: One Hundred Third Congress of the United States, from "Government Performance & Results Act of 1993"

NO: Robert D. Behn, from "The Psychological Barriers to Performance Management: Or Why Isn't Everyone Jumping on the Performance-Management Bandwagon?" *Public Performance & Management Review* (September 2002)

Learning Outcomes

After reading this issue, you should be able to:

- Define performance management.
- Discuss the relationship between performance management and policy outcomes.
- Gain an understanding of federal government attempts at performance management.
- Describe potential barriers to successfully implementing performance management.
- Understand the relationship between performance management and tax payer accountability.
- Describe arguments regarding why performance management fails to enhance policy outcomes.

ISSUE SUMMARY

YES: Congress and President Clinton worked in 1993 to pass the Government Performance & Results Act. They hoped the legislation would help restore America's faith in the federal government's ability to efficiently and equitably implement policy and run our nation.

NO: Robert D. Behn argues that performance management does not necessarily improve the performance of public agencies. In his view, performance management has not led to improved performance as much as scholars have simply succeeded in finding some successful agencies where these programs are in place.

In 1927, Hawthorne Works—a Western Electric factory near Chicago—commissioned a study to examine whether workers would be more productive based on the level of light in the factory. What ultimately emerged was evidence that productivity increased under any lighting scenario and dropped quickly upon the conclusion of the study. Looking back some 20 years later, Henry Landsberger identified the change in output as the Hawthorne effect. The productivity gain was attributed to the motivational effect on the workers due to being observed. Scholars tend to focus just on the illumination studies, but there were a series of other factors tested at Hawthorne Works as well. Researchers examined the effects of cleanliness, ease of maneuvering, and moving workstations. All had the same findings: As long as workers were being observed, their output increased. As such, we can see that there is a definite relationship between performance management and outcomes.

Although the Hawthorne experiments show us that performance management (or even simple performance observations) can lead to increased productivity, there are still a myriad of factors to consider with relation to the applicability to public administration and policy. The main concern is that we simply cannot afford to have someone stand over the shoulder of every bureaucrat in our country to assure they work to their maximum capabilities. Frederick Taylor's idea of time and motion studies worked well with manual labor but can only have so much impact on government work since there are not as easily discerned input behaviors. Instead, we must determine alternative, less costly mechanisms to bring out the best of public workers.

To begin this discussion, we need to determine what we mean by performance. In its most basic terms, we can consider performance to be the difference between actual and desired results. If our actual results fail to meet our desired results, we can improve performance. According to the United States Office of Personal Management, performance management consists of a system whereby work is planned and expectations are set, performance of work is monitored, staff ability to perform is developed and enhanced, performance is rated and the ratings summarized, and good performances are rewarded. Benefits for agencies may include direct financial gain, a motivated workforce, and improved management control.

More specifically, there is a recommended process on how to implement performance management in a public agency. First, organizations need to review their goals to associate preferred organizational results in terms of performance. Second, the organization needs to specify desired results for whatever element the plan focuses on and then they must ensure that the domain directly contributes to the performance of the larger organization. Next, it is essential to figure out how results will be measured. In the fifth step, the organization needs to identify the standards that will be used to assess if the desired results are being achieved. At that point, they can document a performance plan that explains all of this information in a clear, concise manner for workers. With the planning completed, the organization can then begin observing and measuring performance with an open exchange of feedback occurring throughout the process. After a set period of time, they can conduct a performance review to see if goals are being met. If they are, workers should be rewarded for their efforts. If not, then the organization must return to the plan and reassess what is needed to address the performance gap. They should then return to measuring outcomes and working through the process until performance is made acceptable.

It is not just individual organizations, however, that can strive to improve policy outcomes through performance management. In 1993, the U.S. federal government took steps toward enhancing performance in all agencies through passage of the Government Performance and Results Act. Aimed at improving project management, GPRA requires agencies to set goals, measure results, and report their progress. If they wish to remain compliant, they need to produce strategic and performance plans along with conduct gap analyses. There are three main components to GPRA. First, agencies need to create five-year plans that contain a mission statement and long-term goals based on measurable outcomes and directly related to the major functions of the organization. Secondly, agencies need to prepare annual performance plans that establish the goals for each fiscal year, a short explanation of how the goals will be accomplished, and how results will be verified. Lastly, there must be performance reports produced each year that state the agency's success or failure with relation to the stated annual goals and long-term goals. The most remarkable part of the Government Performance and Results Act is that it was based on the work of two public administration scholars—David Osborne and Ted Gaebler.

As we can see from this discussion, performance management has been relatively new to the national scene. Despite being mentioned in organizational contexts, it has only in the past two decades been considered a legitimate alternative to the status quo of assessing outputs of bureaucratic agencies. Although there are many stated benefits, it does require costs. First, it forces agencies to look at least five years in advance and risk looking bad with the public as goals will be publicly stated and citizens will be able to monitor performance on their own. Second, it requires employee buy-in to ensure that meaningful goals are set and all possible energies are exerted to assure they are met. In the Yes and NO readings, we will look at two very divergent views on the potential impact of performance management on policy outcomes. First, in the YES reading, we will look at the Government Performance & Results Act of 1993. Passed by President Clinton and Congress, the act is intended to restore America's faith in the government through efficient and equitable policy implementation. In the NO reading, Robert D. Behn, on the other hand, argues that practitioners and academics have had to selectively find cases where performance management has led to the measurable outcomes that we anticipated.

YES ⬅

Government Performance & Results Act of 1993

Begun and held at the City of Washington on Tuesday, the fifth day of January, one thousand nine hundred and ninety-three.

An Act

To provide for the establishment of strategic planning and performance measurement in the Federal Government, and for other purposes.

Be it enacted by the Senate and House of Representatives of the United States of America in Congress assembled.

Section 1: Short Title

This Act may be cited as the "Government Performance and Results Act of 1993".

Section 2. Findings and Purposes

   a. Findings.—The Congress finds that—
   1. waste and inefficiency in Federal programs undermine the confidence of the American people in the Government and reduces the Federal Government's ability to address adequately vital public needs;
   2. Federal managers are seriously disadvantaged in their efforts to improve program efficiency and effectiveness, because of insufficient articulation of program goals and inadequate information on program performance; and
   3. congressional policymaking, spending decisions and program oversight are seriously handicapped by insufficient attention to program performance and results.

   b. Purposes.—The purposes of this Act are to—
   1. improve the confidence of the American people in the capability of the Federal Government, by systematically holding Federal agencies accountable for achieving program results;

United States Congress, 1993.

2. initiate program performance reform with a series of pilot projects in setting program goals, measuring program performance against those goals, and reporting publicly on their progress;
3. improve Federal program effectiveness and public accountability by promoting a new focus on results, service quality, and customer satisfaction;
4. help Federal managers improve service delivery, by requiring that they plan for meeting program objectives and by providing them with information about program results and service quality;
5. improve congressional decisionmaking by providing more objective information on achieving statutory objectives, and on the relative effectiveness and efficiency of Federal programs and spending; and
6. improve internal management of the Federal Government.

Section 3. Strategic Planning

Chapter 3 of title 5, United States Code, is amended by adding after section 305 the following new section:

"Sec. 306. Strategic plans

"a. No later than September 30, 1997, the head of each agency shall submit to the Director of the Office of Management and Budget and to the Congress a strategic plan for program activities. Such plan shall contain—

"1. a comprehensive mission statement covering the major functions and operations of the agency;
"2. general goals and objectives, including outcome-related goals and objectives, for the major functions and operations of the agency;
"3. a description of how the goals and objectives are to be achieved, including a description of the operational processes, skills and technology, and the human, capital, information, and other resources required to meet those goals and objectives;
"4. a description of how the performance goals included in the plan required by section 1115(a) of title 31 shall be related to the general goals and objectives in the strategic plan;
"5. an identification of those key factors external to the agency and beyond its control that could significantly affect the achievement of the general goals and objectives; and
"6. a description of the program evaluations used in establishing or revising general goals and objectives, with a schedule for future program evaluations.

"b. The strategic plan shall cover a period of not less than five years forward from the fiscal year in which it is submitted, and shall be updated and revised at least every three years.
"c. The performance plan required by section 1115 of title 31 shall be consistent with the agency's strategic plan. A performance plan may not be submitted for a fiscal year not covered by a current strategic plan under this section.
"d. When developing a strategic plan, the agency shall consult with the Congress, and shall solicit and consider the views and suggestions of those entities potentially affected by or interested in such a plan.

"e. The functions and activities of this section shall be considered to be inherently Governmental functions. The drafting of strategic plans under this section shall be performed only by Federal employees.

"f. For purposes of this section the term 'agency' means an Executive agency defined under section 105, but does not include the Central Intelligence Agency, the General Accounting Office, the Panama Canal Commission, the United States Postal Service, and the Postal Rate Commission."

Section 4. Annual Performance Plans and Reports

a. Budget Contents and Submission to Congress.—Section 1105(a) of title 31, United States Code, is amended by adding at the end thereof the following new paragraph:

"29. beginning with fiscal year 1999, a Federal Government performance plan for the overall budget as provided for under section 1115."

b. Performance Plans and Reports.—Chapter 11 of title 31, United States Code, is amended by adding after section 1114 the following new sections:

"Sec. 1115. Performance plans

"a. In carrying out the provisions of section 1105(a)(29), the Director of the Office of Management and Budget shall require each agency to prepare an annual performance plan covering each program activity set forth in the budget of such agency. Such plan shall—

"1. establish performance goals to define the level of performance to be achieved by a program activity;

"2. express such goals in an objective, quantifiable, and measurable form unless authorized to be in an alternative form under subsection (b);

"3. briefly describe the operational processes, skills and technology, and the human, capital, information, or other resources required to meet the performance goals;

"4. establish performance indicators to be used in measuring or assessing the relevant outputs, service levels, and outcomes of each program activity;

"5. provide a basis for comparing actual program results with the established performance goals; and

"6. describe the means to be used to verify and validate measured values.

"b. If an agency, in consultation with the Director of the Office of Management and Budget, determines that it is not feasible to express the performance goals for a particular program activity in an objective, quantifiable, and measurable form, the Director of the Office of Management and Budget may authorize an alternative form. Such alternative form shall—

"1. include separate descriptive statements of—

"(A)(i) a minimally effective program, and

"(ii) a successful program, or

"(B) such alternative as authorized by the Director of the Office of Management and Budget, with sufficient precision and in such terms that would allow for an accurate, independent determination of whether the program activity's performance meets the criteria of the description; or

"2. state why it is infeasible or impractical to express a performance goal in any form for the program activity.

"c. For the purpose of complying with this section, an agency may aggregate, disaggregate, or consolidate program activities, except that any aggregation or consolidation may not omit or minimize the significance of any program activity constituting a major function or operation for the agency.

"d. An agency may submit with its annual performance plan an appendix covering any portion of the plan that—

"1. is specifically authorized under criteria established by an Executive order to be kept secret in the interest of national defense or foreign policy; and

"2. is properly classified pursuant to such Executive order.

"e. The functions and activities of this section shall be considered to be inherently Governmental functions. The drafting of performance plans under this section shall be performed only by Federal employees.

"f. For purposes of this section and sections 1116 through 1119, and sections 9703 and 9704 the term—

"1. 'agency' has the same meaning as such term is defined under section 306(f) of title 5;

"2. 'outcome measure' means an assessment of the results of a program activity compared to its intended purpose;

"3. 'output measure' means the tabulation, calculation, or recording of activity or effort and can be expressed in a quantitative or qualitative manner;

"4. 'performance goal' means a target level of performance expressed as a tangible, measurable objective, against which actual achievement can be compared, including a goal expressed as a quantitative standard, value, or rate;

"5. 'performance indicator' means a particular value or characteristic used to measure output or outcome;

"6. 'program activity' means a specific activity or project as listed in the program and financing schedules of the annual budget of the United States Government; and

"7. 'program evaluation' means an assessment, through objective measurement and systematic analysis, of the manner and extent to which Federal programs achieve intended objectives.

"Sec. 1116. Program performance reports

"a. No later than March 31, 2000, and no later than March 31 of each year thereafter, the head of each agency shall prepare and submit to the President and the Congress, a report on program performance for the previous fiscal year.

"b. 1. Each program performance report shall set forth the perform-ance indicators established in the agency performance plan under section 1115, along with the actual program performance achieved compared with the performance goals expressed in the plan for that fiscal year.

"2. If performance goals are specified in an alternative form under section 1115(b), the results of such program shall be described in relation to such specifications, including whether the perform-ance failed to meet the criteria of a minimally effective or success-ful program.

"c. The report for fiscal year 2000 shall include actual results for the pre-ceding fiscal year, the report for fiscal year 2001 shall include actual results for the two preceding fiscal years, and the report for fiscal year 2002 and all subsequent reports shall include actual results for the three preceding fiscal years.

"d. Each report shall—

"1. review the success of achieving the performance goals of the fis-cal year;

"2. evaluate the performance plan for the current fiscal year relative to the performance achieved toward the performance goals in the fiscal year covered by the report;

"3. explain and describe, where a performance goal has not been met (including when a program activity's performance is determined not to have met the criteria of a successful program activity under section 1115(b)(1)(A)(ii) or a corresponding level of achievement if another alternative form is used)—

"(A) why the goal was not met;

"(B) those plans and schedules for achieving the established per-formance goal; and

"(C) if the performance goal is impractical or infeasible, why that is the case and what action is recommended;

"4. describe the use and assess the effectiveness in achieving per-formance goals of any waiver under section 9703 of this title; and

"5. include the summary findings of those program evaluations completed during the fiscal year covered by the report.

"e. An agency head may include all program performance information required annually under this section in an annual financial state-ment required under section 3515 if any such statement is submit-ted to the Congress no later than March 31 of the applicable fiscal year.

"f. The functions and activities of this section shall be considered to be inherently Governmental functions. The drafting of program performance reports under this section shall be performed only by Federal employees.

"Sec. 1117. Exemption

"The Director of the Office of Management and Budget may exempt from the requirements of sections 1115 and 1116 of this title and section 306 of title 5, any agency with annual outlays of $20,000,000 or less."

Section 5. Managerial Accountability and Flexibility

a. Managerial Accountability and Flexibility.—Chapter 97 of title 31, United States Code, is amended by adding after section 9702, the following new section:

"Sec. 9703. Managerial accountability and flexibility

"a. Beginning with fiscal year 1999, the performance plans required under section 1115 may include proposals to waive administrative procedural requirements and controls, including specification of personnel staffing levels, limitations on compensation or remuneration, and prohibitions or restrictions on funding transfers among budget object classification 20 and subclassifications 11, 12, 31, and 32 of each annual budget submitted under section 1105, in return for specific individual or organization accountability to achieve a performance goal. In preparing and submitting the performance plan under section 1105(a)(29), the Director of the Office of Management and Budget shall review and may approve any proposed waivers. A waiver shall take effect at the beginning of the fiscal year for which the waiver is approved.

"b. Any such proposal under subsection (a) shall describe the anticipated effects on performance resulting from greater managerial or organizational flexibility, discretion, and authority, and shall quantify the expected improvements in performance resulting from any waiver. The expected improvements shall be compared to current actual performance, and to the projected level of performance that would be achieved independent of any waiver.

"c. Any proposal waiving limitations on compensation or remuneration shall precisely express the monetary change in compensation or remuneration amounts, such as bonuses or awards, that shall result from meeting, exceeding, or failing to meet performance goals.

"d. Any proposed waiver of procedural requirements or controls imposed by an agency (other than the proposing agency or the Office of Management and Budget) may not be included in a performance plan unless it is endorsed by the agency that established the requirement, and the endorsement included in the proposing agency's performance plan.

"e. A waiver shall be in effect for one or two years as specified by the Director of the Office of Management and Budget in approving the waiver. A waiver may be renewed for a subsequent year. After a waiver has been in effect for three consecutive years, the performance plan prepared under section 1115 may propose that a waiver, other than a waiver of limitations on compensation or remuneration, be made permanent.

"f. For purposes of this section, the definitions under section 1115(f) shall apply."

Section 6. Pilot Projects

a. Performance Plans and Reports.—Chapter 11 of title 31, United States Code, is amended by inserting after section 1117 (as added by section 4 of this Act) the following new section:

"Sec. 1118. Pilot projects for performance goals

"a. The Director of the Office of Management and Budget, after consultation with the head of each agency, shall designate not less than ten agencies as pilot projects in performance measurement for fiscal years 1994, 1995, and 1996. The selected agencies shall reflect a representative range of Government functions and capabilities in measuring and reporting program performance.

"b. Pilot projects in the designated agencies shall undertake the preparation of performance plans under section 1115, and program performance reports under section 1116, other than section 1116(c), for one or more of the major functions and operations of the agency. A strategic plan shall be used when preparing agency performance plans during one or more years of the pilot period.

"c. No later than May 1, 1997, the Director of the Office of Management and Budget shall submit a report to the President and to the Congress which shall—

"1. assess the benefits, costs, and usefulness of the plans and reports prepared by the pilot agencies in meeting the purposes of the Government Performance and Results Act of 1993;

"2. identify any significant difficulties experienced by the pilot agencies in preparing plans and reports; and

"3. set forth any recommended changes in the requirements of the provisions of Government Performance and Results Act of 1993, section 306 of title 5, sections 1105, 1115, 1116, 1117, 1119 and 9703 of this title, and this section."

b. Managerial Accountability and Flexibility.—Chapter 97 of title 31, United States Code, is amended by inserting after section 9703 (as added by section 5 of this Act) the following new section:

"Sec. 9704. Pilot projects for managerial accountability and flexibility

"a. The Director of the Office of Management and Budget shall designate not less than five agencies as pilot projects in managerial accountability and flexibility for fiscal years 1995 and 1996. Such agencies shall be selected from those designated as pilot projects under section 1118 and shall reflect a representative range of Government functions and capabilities in measuring and reporting program performance.

"b. Pilot projects in the designated agencies shall include proposed waivers in accordance with section 9703 for one or more of the major functions and operations of the agency.

"c. The Director of the Office of Management and Budget shall include in the report to the President and to the Congress required under section 1118(c)—

"1. an assessment of the benefits, costs, and usefulness of increasing managerial and organizational flexibility, discretion, and authority in exchange for improved performance through a waiver; and

"2. an identification of any significant difficulties experienced by the pilot agencies in preparing proposed waivers.

"d. For purposes of this section the definitions under section 1115(f) shall apply."

c. Performance Budgeting.—Chapter 11 of title 31, United States Code, is amended by inserting after section 1118 (as added by section 6 of this Act) the following new section:

"Sec. 1119. Pilot projects for performance budgeting

"a. The Director of the Office of Management and Budget, after consultation with the head of each agency shall designate not less than five agencies as pilot projects in performance budgeting for fiscal years 1998 and 1999. At least three of the agencies shall be selected from those designated as pilot projects under section 1118, and shall also reflect a representative range of Government functions and capabilities in measuring and reporting program performance.

"b. Pilot projects in the designated agencies shall cover the preparation of performance budgets. Such budgets shall present, for one or more of the major functions and operations of the agency, the varying levels of performance, including outcome-related performance, that would result from different budgeted amounts.

"c. The Director of the Office of Management and Budget shall include, as an alternative budget presentation in the budget submitted under section 1105 for fiscal year 1999, the performance budgets of the designated agencies for this fiscal year.

"d. No later than March 31, 2001, the Director of the Office of Management and Budget shall transmit a report to the President and to the Congress on the performance budgeting pilot projects which shall—

"1. assess the feasibility and advisability of including a performance budget as part of the annual budget submitted under section 1105;

"2. describe any difficulties encountered by the pilot agencies in preparing a performance budget;

"3. recommend whether legislation requiring performance budgets should be proposed and the general provisions of any legislation; and

"4. set forth any recommended changes in the other requirements of the Government Performance and Results Act of 1993, section 306 of title 5, sections 1105, 1115, 1116, 1117, and 9703 of this title, and this section.

"e. After receipt of the report required under subsection (d), the Congress may specify that a performance budget be submitted as part of the annual budget submitted under section 1105."

Section 7. United States Postal Service

Part III of title 39, United States Code, is amended by adding at the end thereof the following new chapter:

"CHAPTER 28-STRATEGIC PLANNING AND PERFORMANCE MANAGEMENT
  "Sec.
  "2801. Definitions.
  "2802. Strategic plans.
  "2803. Performance plans.

"2804. Program performance reports.

"2805. Inherently Governmental functions.

"Sec. 2801. Definitions

"For purposes of this chapter the term—

"1. 'outcome measure' refers to an assessment of the results of a program activity compared to its intended purpose;

"2. 'output measure' refers to the tabulation, calculation, or recording of activity or effort and can be expressed in a quantitative or qualitative manner;

"3. 'performance goal' means a target level of performance expressed as a tangible, measurable objective, against which actual achievement shall be compared, including a goal expressed as a quantitative standard, value, or rate;

"4. 'performance indicator' refers to a particular value or characteristic used to measure output or outcome;

"5. 'program activity' means a specific activity related to the mission of the Postal Service; and

"6. 'program evaluation' means an assessment, through objective measurement and systematic analysis, of the manner and extent to which Postal Service programs achieve intended objectives.

"Sec. 2802. Strategic plans

"a. No later than September 30, 1997, the Postal Service shall submit to the President and the Congress a strategic plan for its program activities. Such plan shall contain—

"1. a comprehensive mission statement covering the major functions and operations of the Postal Service;

"2. general goals and objectives, including outcome-related goals and objectives, for the major functions and operations of the Postal Service;

"3. a description of how the goals and objectives are to be achieved, including a description of the operational processes, skills and technology, and the human, capital, information, and other resources required to meet those goals and objectives;

"4. a description of how the performance goals included in the plan required under section 2803 shall be related to the general goals and objectives in the strategic plan;

"5. an identification of those key factors external to the Postal Service and beyond its control that could significantly affect the achievement of the general goals and objectives; and

"6. a description of the program evaluations used in establishing or revising general goals and objectives, with a schedule for future program evaluations.

"b. The strategic plan shall cover a period of not less than five years forward from the fiscal year in which it is submitted, and shall be updated and revised at least every three years.

"c. The performance plan required under section 2803 shall be consistent with the Postal Service's strategic plan. A performance plan may not be submitted for a fiscal year not covered by a current strategic plan under this section.

"d. When developing a strategic plan, the Postal Service shall solicit and consider the views and suggestions of those entities potentially affected by or interested in such a plan, and shall advise the Congress of the contents of the plan.

"Sec. 2803. Performance plans

"a. The Postal Service shall prepare an annual performance plan covering each program activity set forth in the Postal Service budget, which shall be included in the comprehensive statement presented under section 2401(g) of this title. Such plan shall—
   "1. establish performance goals to define the level of performance to be achieved by a program activity;
   "2. express such goals in an objective, quantifiable, and measurable form unless an alternative form is used under subsection (b);
   "3. briefly describe the operational processes, skills and technology, and the human, capital, information, or other resources required to meet the performance goals;
   "4. establish performance indicators to be used in measuring or assessing the relevant outputs, service levels, and outcomes of each program activity;
   "5. provide a basis for comparing actual program results with the established performance goals; and
   "6. describe the means to be used to verify and validate measured values.

"b. If the Postal Service determines that it is not feasible to express the performance goals for a particular program activity in an objective, quantifiable, and measurable form, the Postal Service may use an alternative form. Such alternative form shall—
   "1. include separate descriptive statements of—
      "(A) a minimally effective program, and
      "(B) a successful program,
      with sufficient precision and in such terms that would allow for an accurate, independent determination of whether the program activity's performance meets the criteria of either description; or
   "2. state why it is infeasible or impractical to express a performance goal in any form for the program activity.

"c. In preparing a comprehensive and informative plan under this section, the Postal Service may aggregate, disaggregate, or consolidate program activities, except that any aggregation or consolidation may not omit or minimize the significance of any program activity constituting a major function or operation.

"d. The Postal Service may prepare a non-public annex to its plan covering program activities or parts of program activities relating to—
   "1. the avoidance of interference with criminal prosecution; or
   "2. matters otherwise exempt from public disclosure under section 410(c) of this title.

"Sec. 2804. Program performance reports

"a. The Postal Service shall prepare a report on program performance for each fiscal year, which shall be included in the annual comprehensive statement presented under section 2401(g) of this title.

"b. 1. The program performance report shall set forth the performance indicators established in the Postal Service performance plan, along with the actual program performance achieved compared with the performance goals expressed in the plan for that fiscal year.

"2. If performance goals are specified by descriptive statements of a minimally effective program activity and a successful program activity, the results of such program shall be described in relationship to those categories, including whether the performance failed to meet the criteria of either category.

"c. The report for fiscal year 2000 shall include actual results for the preceding fiscal year, the report for fiscal year 2001 shall include actual results for the two preceding fiscal years, and the report for fiscal year 2002 and all subsequent reports shall include actual results for the three preceding fiscal years.

"d. Each report shall—

"1. review the success of achieving the performance goals of the fiscal year;

"2. evaluate the performance plan for the current fiscal year relative to the performance achieved towards the performance goals in the fiscal year covered by the report;

"3. explain and describe, where a performance goal has not been met (including when a program activity's performance is determined not to have met the criteria of a successful program activity under section 2803(b)(2))—

"(A) why the goal was not met;

"(B) those plans and schedules for achieving the established performance goal; and

"(C) if the performance goal is impractical or infeasible, why that is the case and what action is recommended; and

"4. include the summary findings of those program evaluations completed during the fiscal year covered by the report.

"Sec. 2805. Inherently Governmental functions

"The functions and activities of this chapter shall be considered to be inherently Governmental functions. The drafting of strategic plans, performance plans, and program performance reports under this section shall be performed only by employees of the Postal Service."

Section 8. Congressional Oversight and Legislation

a. In General.—Nothing in this Act shall be construed as limiting the ability of Congress to establish, amend, suspend, or annul a performance goal. Any such action shall have the effect of superseding that goal in the plan submitted under section 1105(a)(29) of title 31, United States Code.

b. GAO Report.—No later than June 1, 1997, the Comptroller General of the United States shall report to Congress on the implementation of this Act, including the prospects for compliance by Federal agencies beyond those participating as pilot projects under sections 1118 and 9704 of title 31, United States Code.

Section 9. Training

The Office of Personnel Management shall, in consultation with the Director of the Office of Management and Budget and the Comptroller General of the United States, develop a strategic planning and performance measurement training component for its management training program and otherwise provide managers with an orientation on the development and use of strategic planning and program performance measurement.

Section 10. Application of Act

No provision or amendment made by this Act may be construed as—

1. creating any right, privilege, benefit, or entitlement for any person who is not an officer or employee of the United States acting in such capacity, and no person who is not an officer or employee of the United States acting in such capacity shall have standing to file any civil action in a court of the United States to enforce any provision or amendment made by this Act; or
2. superseding any statutory requirement, including any requirement under section 553 of title 5, United States Code.

Section 11. Technical and Conforming Amendments

a. Amendment to Title 5, United States Code.—The table of sections for chapter 3 of title 5, United States Code, is amended by adding after the item relating to section 305 the following:

"306. Strategic plans."

b. Amendments to Title 31, United States Code.
   1. Amendment to chapter 11.—The table of sections for chapter 11 of title 31, United States Code, is amended by adding after the item relating to section 1114 the following:
   "1115. Performance plans.
   "1116. Program performance reports.
   "1117. Exemptions.
   "1118. Pilot projects for performance goals.
   "1119. Pilot projects for performance budgeting."
   2. Amendment to chapter 97.—The table of sections for chapter 97 of title 31, United States Code, is amended by adding after the item relating to section 9702 the following:
   "9703. Managerial accountability and flexibility.
   "9704. Pilot projects for managerial accountability and flexibility."

c. Amendment to Title 39, United States Code.—The table of chapters for part III of title 39, United States Code, is amended by adding at the end thereof the following new item:

"28. Strategic planning and performance management 2801".

Speaker of the House of Representatives.

Vice President of the United States and President of the Senate.

Robert D. Behn

The Psychological Barriers to Performance Management: Or Why Isn't Everyone Jumping on the Performance-Management Bandwagon?

Everyone is in favor of performance management? Just ask them: "Are you in favor of improving the performance of government?" Do you know anyone who thinks improving the performance of public agencies is truly a bad idea?

Indeed, our formal institutions of government, as well as our informal institutions, are all in favor of performance management. The United States Congress (P.L. 103–62) and the General Accounting Office favor performance management. The National Academy of Public Administration, the International City/County Management Association, and the Urban Institute all love performance management.

Performance management goes by many names, is defined in a variety of ways, and includes an array of concepts. It has been called results-driven government, performance-based management, outcome-oriented management, reinventing government, the new public management, the new managerialism, and marketization. It includes, for example, the ideas espoused by David Osborne and Ted Gaebler in *Reinventing Government,* by Prime Minister Margaret Thatcher's Finance Management Initiative and her Next Steps agencies, by Vice President Gore's National Performance Review, and now by President Bush's Management Agenda. Performance management covers a variety of concepts from performance pay for public employees to the privatization of public services.

Yet, all of these concepts, strategies, tactics, initiatives, and labels are motivated by the same, single purpose: To improve the performance of public agencies; to enhance the results and value produced by government. The objective is to move from rule-driven management to results-driven management. No longer will the efforts of public managers and public employees be focused on following the rules. Under performance management, they will focus on improving performance, producing results, and adding value.

For example, President George W. Bush has offered "a bold strategy for improving the management and performance of the federal government."

This "management agenda" is "results-oriented," says the President. "What matters most is performance." Sounds very much like the National Performance Review—but without any little red book.

But can public managers really use the concepts of performance management (whatever they might be) to actually improve the performance of their organizations—to get them to produce more and better results? It isn't clear that the research that praises various (and usually isolated) examples of performance management isn't—in George Frederickson's famous phrase—simply "painting bull's eyes around bullet holes." Given the large number of public agencies and the stochastic nature of organizational behavior, we should expect that some agencies would perform better than others, that some of those that performed better would appear to be employing some of the concepts of public management, and that a few public-management scholars might stumble across them.

Still, it isn't as if concepts of performance management are completely a theoretical. Many are descended from some distinguished theoretical pedigrees. Behind many of the ideas of internal management—for example, how to motivate improved performance by employees inside an organization—lie a variety of ideas from social-psychology—many of which have been employed by private-sector organizations to improve performance. And the ideas of marketization—using market incentives to motivate improved performance—have a long and distinguished ancestry in economics.

Yes: There are questions about how these ideas ought to be applied in democratic government, and how such applications might mesh or clash with both the fundamental principles and operational realities of our democracy. But such concerns may not trouble the individual public manager who is under real and explicit pressure to improve performance (however such improvement might be defined). Public managers everywhere have an incentive to employ the ideas of performance management—or, at least, to pretend that they are employing them.

And, indeed, the rhetoric of performance management (e.g., "steer don't row") has been widely echoed by practitioners at all levels of government. Many public managers report that they are aggressively engaged in performance management. Many do collect and publish all sorts of performance measures. But do they really use these measures in any way that might actually feed back to create improved performance. If you examine closely what public managers are actually doing, it often looks more like a hoop-jumping exercise than a real adaptation of even a few of the basic ideas of performance management to the challenge of actually producing more and better results in their particular circumstance.

Performance management has not swept the world; it lives more in rhetoric than reality. Most public managers, for example, still row more than they steer. If performance management is so promising—if it has worked well, if in particular circumstances—why has its impact on government been primarily rhetorical rather than behavioral? Why isn't everyone doing it? Why haven't public managers been intelligently and tenaciously adapting the concepts of performance management to the particular performance challenges faced by their own agencies?

Possible Explanations for the Failure of Performance Management to Sweep the World

Why haven't public managers been aggressively employing the concepts of performance management? As with most such questions about public management, this one has no universal answer. Rather, there exist a variety of possible explanations, some of which provide more insight in some situations while, in other circumstances, different explanations may prove more edifying.

The first, and most obvious, explanation is practical: performance management doesn't work. And, indeed, there are numerous skeptics among both scholars who are paid to be cynical and managers who are paid to be careful. Performance management isn't a coherent set of proven ideas, say the pessimistic academics. Performance management won't work in my organization say the prudent practitioners. And, of course, even if performance management does work, it can have, as Peter Smith of the University of York reports, "unintended consequences." Still, even if both the scholars and the practitioners of public management agreed that the concepts of performance management could (if deployed thoughtfully) produce significant—if not dramatic—increases in performance, there are a variety of reasons why these concepts might not be adopted by managers throughout the public sector.

The second possible explanation is political: Performance management isn't politically useful. It doesn't win election—or reelection—for anyone. Yes, it doesn't get anyone defeated either. No one campaigns against an incumbent president, governor, or mayor on a platform promising to eliminate any form of performance management. No one campaigns against a U.S. representative, state legislator, or city councilor by denouncing the incumbent for promoting performance management. In our frequent and various campaigns for public office, neither candidates, journalists, opinion leaders, nor voters pay much attention to the performance of public agencies—let alone to the specifics of performance management. And if elected officials don't care about performance management, why would we expect political or career managers to care?

A third possible explanation is managerial: Performance management is damn hard. The leaders of a public agency can't just open the performance-management cookbook, use the index to find the recipe that applies to their agency, and follow the instructions. It's not easy to ratchet up the performance of a single public agency, let alone a large collection of many public agencies: Which of the many (and perhaps even contradictory) concepts of public management will work in this particular situation?

In any effort to produce bigger and better results, the leadership team of any government organization faces a variety of challenges. For example, they must operate within the confines of a large number of significant constraints. They can't simply deploy their dollars and people so as to maximize results or public value. They must cope with a variety of overhead agencies, internal regulators, and stakeholder organizations who possess the formal or informal authority to tell them: "No. You can't do that." Still, these political and regulatory constraints, which make performance management (and public management in general) so difficult, do not appear to be the sole reason why so many public executives have not jumped on the performance-management bandwagon.

A fourth possible explanation is psychological: The explicit use of performance measures—which is inherent to almost all forms of performance management—creates some valid fears: "If my organization starts measuring performance, what might happen?" Many of the possible consequences of attempting to measure performance are not positive. The repercussions of any effort to measure performance are not necessarily positive for the individuals in the organization or for the organization itself. Little wonder that many public employees harbor some very legitimate fears of performance measurement.

A fifth possible explanation is also psychological: Performance management requires a variety of people—from the leaders of a public agency to legislators and citizens—to think differently about the overall responsibilities of government, about the responsibilities of individual public employees and teams of employees, about the responsibilities of each of the three branches of government, and about the responsibilities of citizens. And to change the thinking of these different people—and thus to change their behavior—will be difficult.

As is usually the case when multiple explanations for human behavior are possible, no single one is valid for all individuals or circumstances. Rather, in every situation, the real explanation is some unique combination of the various possibilities. Thus, when sorting out cause and effect, and when attempting to modify such linkages, it is important to understand each potential explanation. The first three explanations—the practical, political, and managerial explanations—have been analyzed extensively, and thus I will not discuss them here. The fourth explanation—the fears of the consequences of creating and using performance measures—will have to wait for a future analysis. Here, I will focus on the fifth explanation—the mental reorientation that performance managers requires of so many people.

Thinking (and Rethinking) About Performance

This last, psychological explanation for the failure of performance management to sweep the public-management world may not have been carefully examined or even explicitly defined. Yet a lack of scholarly, analytical attention to this barrier, which involves the implicit thinking of numerous people—does not mean that public managers have failed to recognize it. After all, public managers are "trained"—not in the formal sense but in the on-the-job sense—to identify potential problems. That's how they moved up the organizational hierarchy—by keeping a succession of units out of trouble. They mastered rule-driven management, figuring out how to abide by the formal regulations created by the overhead units of personnel and procurement and learning how to adjust to the unofficial norms enforced by journalists, legislators, and stakeholders. And once a public manager realizes, if only implicitly, that performance management will require a lot of people to think (let alone act) very differently, he or she can simply choose to focus on something less risky than attempting to employ an entire set of new ideas.

After all, the shift from traditional, rules-based management to results-oriented management involves more than the mere replacement of one set of managerial tools with another. It requires a complete mental reorientation. And it is not just the public managers who have to think differently. Citizens, legislators, and others in the executive branch all need to reorient their thinking, and much of the thinking that inhibits the shift to performance management is strictly implicit.

In particular, how citizens, legislators, public employees, policy makers, and politically-appointed executives think about performance and results creates some real barriers to their ability to focus on outcomes and value. Indeed, until each of these groups begins to think differently about what government should and should not do, the concepts performance management may remain primarily a set of theoretical ideas that are used only occasionally by a few, independently wealthy mavericks who need not worry about society's ability to punish their heresies or failures.

Citizen Thinking

When citizens think about government performance, they naturally emphasize personal results rather than societal results. This kind of thinking is inherently human.

It may be presumptuous to suggest that all citizens employ the same mental framework when they think about government performance. (Indeed, it might be presumptuous to suggest that many citizens ever think about government performance or that they actually employ any consistent framework when they do.) Nevertheless, the what's-in-it-for-me framework does have a distinguished heritage.

Still, it is not easy for citizens to employ even this traditional, framework. After all, to do so, a citizen has to figure out three different things: (1) What components of this governmental activity might affect me? (2) How might these components affect me? (3) How do I evaluate the net effect of the collection of personal consequences that these potential impacts will have on me? And, although we tend to think that such "rational" thinking is both common and easy, it isn't necessarily either.

But using the new, performance framework is even more difficult. Again, citizens have to figure out three different things, but these three things are more complicated and require much more thought. (1) What components of this government activity might affect what parts of society? (2) How might these components affect these different parts of society? (3) How do I evaluate the net effect of the consequences that these potential impacts will have on these parts of society? Clearly it is much more challenging to analyze the impacts of a governmental activity on all of society than it is to think about the impacts on me.

But it isn't just the analytical challenge that makes this new kind of performance thinking difficult for citizens. The fundamental shift is psychological—from what's in it for me to what's in it for society. When the performance measures for the state's school districts are published on the front page of the papers, what performance numbers do citizens look at and care about? Those for the state as a whole, or those for their local district? Even those citizens whose children have graduated from high school care more about their local district's performance—because that performance affects their property values. And when citizens think about the steps that should be taken to improve school performance, are they more worried about the resources needed in their own district or about the change in educational institutions and pedagogical strategies statewide?

Performance management requires a set of macro strategies that can change operational behavior at the service-delivery level. It requires macro strategies that can improve the performance of every unit. It requires an expectation that every unit—for example, every school in the state—with improve its performance. Thus, it requires an set of macro strategies designed to improve the performance of every unit up to the state-wide standard.

Legislative Thinking

When legislators think about the "results" of government's efforts, they tend to place more emphasis on where the inputs are immediately deployed than on what outcomes might be eventually achieved. After all, the ultimate consequences might not be realized for years while the inputs can be distributed (or, at least, announced) tomorrow. And the legislators may have to stand for reelection before the outcomes are realized but not before the inputs are distributed. Indeed, the legislators may have to stand for election several times before it becomes the least bit obvious whether the inputs that have been distributed are producing anything close to the outcomes that have been promised.

An obvious example is K-12 education. The new funds for more teachers to reduce the size of classes can be distributed this year. But the outcomes about which we as a society really care—students who grow up to be productive employees and responsible citizens—cannot be evaluated for years. As we decide whether to vote for our incumbent state legislator or the challenger, we can't evaluate the incumbent by examining the value that our local schools have added to our children's and society's future; but we can evaluate this incumbent by checking on the number of new teachers that he or she convinced the state to allocate to our town—or even to our neighborhood school.

By establishing that the terms our legislators (and other elected officials) will serve will last just two or four years, we citizens have implicitly told them to worry about the short term. And when we impose term limits on legislators, we have implicitly reenforced this message: Ignore any consequences that will occur after your legal ability to be reelected has expired.

Elected chief executives—presidents, governors, and mayors—can also engage in this "legislative thinking." When they stand for reelection, we will evaluate them by looking at what they have produced over the previous four (or, in a few cases, two) years. Nevertheless, an elected chief executive has more of an opportunity to establish a reputation based on the government's performance in the years after he or she leaves office. As he retired after two decades as chief executive officer of General Electric, Jack Welch observed: "You should measure my success eventually by how well GE does in the next five years."

The same could and should be said for an elected chief executive. If a governor or a mayor sought to apply the concepts of performance management to a state's or city's school system, we citizens would realize that this executive's impact on the outcomes produced by these schools would not be fully realized for years or even decades. An elected chief executive does (or can) exercise significant personal influence over future governmental performance by defining (or redefining) the nature of real performance, by establishing some explicit measures to drive that performance, by developing talent, and by fostering an explicit culture of performance.

For example, President Clinton promised to wage a war on international terrorists, yet did very little; now citizens are remembering both his personal, televised commitment and his administration's failure to create any long-term strategy. Because both the president and what the president says are so visible, we citizens often measure his success by how well the nation does in the years after he leaves office.

The same, however, applies to only a few legislators. Those who are able to accumulate expertise, prestige, and authority—for example, the speaker of the house, or the chairman of the senate finance committee—are able to have some visible, long-term impact on their government's performance in some policy areas. But we don't really expect our individual legislator to have very much impact on the government's long-term performance. We do, however, recognize that our legislator can definitely have an short-term impact on how many new resources are allocated to our community. Given these institutional arrangements, we should not be surprised that, when it comes to the performance of government, legislators necessarily employ a very high discount rate and emphasize inputs over outcomes.

Public-Employee Thinking

When public employees think about the consequences of their work, they are more concerned about avoiding mistakes that will produce certain punishment than about producing successes that might generate a little praise. This kind of thinking is the direct result of the accountability and reward system that we Americans have created for our public officials (from top executives to front-line workers). As I have written elsewhere, all public employees recognize how this accountability system works: "When they do something good, nothing happens. But when they screw up, all hell can break loose." That is: "Accountability means punishment."

This implicit but very real system of punishment makes rule-driven management so attractive. If you simply follow the rules—if you fill out all the forms completely and adhere to the letter of every prescribed process—you can't make a mistake. And if you can't make a mistake, you can't get punished. Following the rules is the only rationale response to our traditional system of incentives. Indeed, to even worry about results—to steal time from an assiduous attention to satisfying all of the myriad rules—is irrational. After all, the performance of any organization—public or private—depends not only upon internal leadership and management but also upon a variety of exogenous forces; thus, any failure of performance to match expectations can be explained by some of these unforeseen, unforeseeable, and uncontrollable forces.

Like legislators, public employees pay attention to the incentives that we citizens create for them. Not that we have written into every legislator's oath of office a sentence that explicitly says: "I promise to focus on the short-term distribution of inputs to my constituents and to ignore the long-term performance of government agencies and the long-term value that they might create for society." Not that we have written into every civil servant's oath of office a sentence that explicitly says: "I promise to take no action that might possibly be interpreted by someone as being a procedural, legal, or political mistake and to avoid wasting any of my time on trying to improve my organization's performance." We need not require legislators or civil servants to take this kind of pledge. We have already created a easy-to-understand and easy-to-implement reward structure that has precisely the same consequence.

Policy Thinking

When many people reflect on the challenge of improving the work of government, they focus on creating better policy rather than on managing better within the existing policy framework. This kind of thinking reflects the persistent ascendency of policy over management.

Management is the mundane, grunt work of getting existing organizations and existing systems to work better so as to achieve existing purposes. Policy is the grand, exhilarating work of inventing new organizations and new systems to achieve new or (at least) refined purposes. Policy thinking suggests that people who really want to make a big difference should focus their energies on crafting visible, innovative policies that will dramatically effect the behavior of all the existing organizations and systems or—even better—concocting visible, innovative policies that require the creation of new (visible and innovative) organizations and systems.

In his introduction to his "management agenda," President Bush noted that "Goverment likes to begin things—to declare grand new programs and causes." Moreover, he noted that Congress faces "an understandable temptation to ignore management reforms in favor of new policies and programs." But it is not just Congress that is tempted to devote its attention to new policies and programs. Legislators at all levels are so tempted. So are scholars in universities and think-tanks, analysts in policy and budget shops, and executive-branch managers at all levels of government. This "understandable temptation" is a direct consequence of policy thinking.

The appeal of policy over management seems unaffected by the accumulation of evidence suggesting that policy innovations without competent (and, perhaps even, innovative) management will accomplish little. Yet as long as making public policy appears to be more exciting and more consequential than managing public organizations, performance management will not attract the attention, the resources, or the talent that it requires to produce meaningful improvements. Policy thinking drains talented people away from the important work of improving the operational performance of government agencies.

Assistant-Secretary Thinking

When ambitious political appointees consider what they can accomplish while in office, they tend to choose to craft a new policy innovation rather than to improve their organization's capacity to perform. After all, most political appointees serve for only a brief period of time; the average tenure of an assistant secretary in the federal government continues to hover around two years. And in two years as the head of any organizational unit, public or private, most people can make progress on a very limited number of fronts.

And this law of limited managerial accomplishment applies not just to appointed managers but to elected ones as well. Every two years, the National Governors' Association holds its "Seminar for New Governors" during which veteran governors offer their new colleagues the wisdom they have gained. And one important lesson that they frequently impart is: "Limit your agenda." And with only two exceptions, the nation's governors serve four-year terms. And with only one exception, the nation's governors can seek reelection for a second, consecutive term. Yet, even governors who can hold office for eight years—subject to only one, intervening performance review—feel compelled to limit their agenda. Certainly the same rule ought to apply to less powerful public executives who might serve only two years.

Moreover, when they accept their position, many political appointees well recognize that they will be in the position for only a short time. Thus when they begin their tour as a political executive, such individuals need to think seriously about what they might possibly achieve during their limited time, about what they might feel proud of accomplishing during this time, about what they might do to establish a reputation during this time. Consequently, even if political appointees have not already fallen captive of "policy thinking," their implicit recognition that their time horizon is necessarily short will encourage them to focus on policy rather than management.

In twenty-four months, an assistant secretary can design a new policy initiative and get it authorized (be that through legislation, executive order, or internal fiat). In contrast, improving the management of the organization—in particular, improving the performance of the organization—will take much longer. Sure, the assistant secretary could within 24 months make significant improvements in the organization's capacity to perform better. But the actual performance consequences of this capacity-building effort might not become obvious or measurable until well after the assistant secretary has returned to the private sector—or been promoted to another job. And because their job is a lot less visible than Jack Welch's, few assistant secretaries can expect that any improvements in their organization's future performance will ever be credited to their work.

Many political executives think the way David Stockman did in 1981 when he was President Reagan's director of the Office of Management and Budget: "I'm just not going to spend a lot of political capital solving some other guy's problem in 2010." Assistantsecretary thinking is driven by the much longer time necessary to lead an organization to a higher level of performance than to initiate a new policy.

Assistant-secretary thinking can reflect a self-indulgent lust to enhance one's personal reputation. Alternatively, assistant-secretary thinking can reflect an altruistic assessment about how best to maximize one's contribution to society subject to a (very real and very short) time constraint. Or, it can reflect some combination of these motives. Regardless—whether a new political appointee is attempting to maximize personal benefits or societal benefits—he or she is apt to conclude that it makes more sense to concentrate on creating a new policy innovation than on fixing the organization's capacity to perform.

Big-Picture Thinking

When many people think about the challenge of improving government performance, they are so overwhelmed with the enormity of the task, that they are blinded to the opportunity to create some meaningful improvement through a series of individually small, but collectively significant actions. Rather, they observe big problems and conclude that they can only be attacked with big solutions. Moreover, to get society to pay attention to the problem, to convince society to devote some of its limited resources to attacking the problem, people feel compelled to portray the problem as a big one.

Such big-picture thinking causes people to overlook the possibility of making progress by slowly but steadily ratcheting up the performance of the organizations responsible for dealing with the problem. Rather they think that their big problem necessarily requires a big solution—with big policy changes and the allocation of significant resources. (In this way, big-picture thinking contributes to policy thinking.) But if big policy changes can not be negotiated through the requisite authorizing channels and the significant resources (in either high-level attention or dollars) can not be obtained, big-picture thinking produces little progress and much frustration.

In his classic article outlining a "strategy of small wins," Karl Weick of Cornell University observes that "people often define social problems in ways that overwhelm their ability to do anything about them." As a society, we have reached a general "agreement" that our social problems are "big problems," he writes. "And that's the problem."

Weick argues that we should "recast larger problems into smaller, less arousing problems" that will give people an opportunity to "identify a series of controllable opportunities of modest size that produce visible results." Producing visible results is, of course, the purpose of performance management. But who will listen to the advocate of a small-wins, performance-management strategy that promises not to solve a big problem but, instead, as Weick suggests will "call a problem minor rather than serious"—even though, as he argues, to do so is "appropriate if people don't know what to do or are unable to do it."

Who, however, will be motivated to work on a "minor" problem when there are so many "serious" problems that merit the serious attention of serious people. This is the logic of bigpicture thinking.

Self-Interested Thinking and Societal Thinking

These six different kinds of thinking can be divided up another way—into two categories based on their motivation:

    a. Self-interested thinking. Citizens, legislators, public employees, and assistant secretaries think in terms of their personal self-interest.
    b. Societal thinking. "Policy thinking" and "big-picture thinking" are not derived from the particular incentive structures under which specific individuals must live or work. Rather, they reflect societal attitudes— views that have been shaped indirectly and that manifest themselves only subtly.

And this taxonomy might help us think about how we might influence such thinking. Adjusting the design of our political institutions could influence some forms of self-interested thinking. Societal thinking, however, is more likely to be influenced by information and education.

For example, it might be possible to alter some of the self-interested thinking—and thus the self-interested behavior that it produces—by altering the incentives that our current institutions of government create. To lengthen the time horizon of legislators and encourage them to worry about the outputs and outcomes of policy as well the distribution of the inputs, we could give legislators longer terms (rather than imposing term limits which exacerbate short-term, legislative thinking). To encourage assistant secretaries to think more about management and less about policy, we could ask these political appointees to make a four-year (or even eight-year) commitment to a specific position and a specific performance task, and ask elected officials to keep their political appointees in a single position for at least one full term. To encourage public employees to worry more about improving performance and less about avoiding mistakes, we could reward them as much as we punish them, recognizing individual and team contributions to improved performance while imposing fewer and less severe penalties on those who make minor and "honest" mistakes.

It is difficult to imagine, however, what me might do (even if we thought it was a good idea) to change the incentive structure of individual citizens, to get them to worry less about personal results and more about societal results. After all, citizen thinking has not been created by our form of government. Self-interested citizen thinking simply exists—prior to and independent of government. And although some argue that all self-interested thinking is genetically based, the behavior that self-interested thinking encourages in legislators, public employees, and assistant secretaries is also a function of institutional design. Not so for citizen thinking.

We might, however, get citizens to pay a little more attention to societal outcomes if we gave them more outcome data more frequently. After all, citizens have a wide variety of informal ways to get information about the educational performance of their local school or the results produced by the state environmental protection agency in cleaning up their nearby river. They have many fewer sources of information about state-wide or nation-wide performance (and, indeed, are most likely to infer such state-wide or nation-wide performance from the local performance that they themselves observe). So some additional information on performance on a broader scale might help to broaden citizens' thinking.

Altering the two kinds of "societal thinking" will also be difficult—both conceptually and operationally. For, again, this thinking is not a function of the kind of political institutions we created but of the kind of humans we are. And, even if we thought we could figure out what kind of cognitive frameworks might best supplant both "policy thinking" and "big-picture thinking," we would still face the challenge of getting people to modify their subconscious mental habits. Still some educational efforts might mitigate some of the consequences of policy and big-picture thinking. For example, Liner and his Urban Institute colleagues report:

> most legislators seem less than enamored with performance data and do not seek them out. Nevertheless, from the little evidence available, it appears that when agencies provide clear and meaningful outcome data (such as information on infant mortality, traffic injuries, juvenile delinquency, and numbers of fish kills caused by pollution), these data will get legislators' attention.

These six modes of thinking—and the barriers that they create to performance management—are not about to disappear. Intellectually, people may even accept that the improving the performance of public agencies is essential and that we need to think differently about how we should design public institutions to foster such performance. But such an intellectual epiphany will not eliminate the six psychological barriers.

If performance management is to live up to its promise to improve the consequences of governmental action, we will need to figure out some way to cope with these six psychological barriers. Maybe we can change some incentives by redesigning our existing institutioins. Maybe we can lower some through information and education. Maybe public managers can ignore a few and evade others. None, however, are apt to be torn down or disappear.

Congratulations, public managers: As you strive to improve performance, as you seek to cope with yet one more set of demands on your time, energy, and resources, here are six more things that you have to worry about.

EXPLORING THE ISSUE

Does Performance Management Lead to Better Policy Outcomes?

Critical Thinking and Reflection

1. How is performance management linked to policy outcomes? What impact can each have on the other?
2. How has the federal government attempted to implement performance management? Has it been successful? Why or why not?
3. Why can it be difficult to implement performance management in public agencies? Are there ways to make implementation easier? How?
4. What is the relationship between performance management and accountability? Does performance management lead to a more direct link between taxpayers and bureaucrats? Why or why not?
5. Can performance management enhance policy outcomes? Why or why not?

Is There Common Ground?

Few Americans would argue that performance management is a flawed idea in theory. When we consider that performance management in the public sector can include evaluations of organizations, departments, employees, and processes, it seems to be a desirable undertaking. However, any type of formal evaluation carries with it significant costs. Further, individuals within public agencies worry about the results of performance management studies as any signs of inefficiency are likely to be greeted by public outroar and questions from elected politicians. When considering the costs and benefits, it appears outsiders are more likely to call for performance management to be present in public sector agencies without considering the costs of such efforts.

Although the debate on whether to instill performance management is worthy of discussion, so too is the question of what effects we can expect performance management to have on outcomes. In an ideal world, performance management would lead to more efficient bureaucracies and ultimately better policy outcomes. Yet, we are aware that no single factor can by itself increase the merits of American policy. Instead, it takes myriad of variables being comprehensively considered and factored to create truly effective outcomes. Perhaps by spending more time creating thorough performance management mechanisms, we can more easily devote time to these other essential variables.

Additional Resources

de Lancer Julnes, P., *Performance-Based Management Systems: Effective Implementation and Maintenance* (Boca Raton, FL: Auerbach Publications, 2008)

This book supports practical efforts to build and maintain performance management systems in public organizations, explaining obstacles to measurement efforts and providing guidance on how to overcome them.

Ellig, J., M. McTigue, and H. Wray, *Government Performance and Results: An Evaluation of GPRA's First Decade* (Boca Raton, FL: CRC Press, 2011)

The book documents the current state of the art in federal performance reporting, measures the extent of improvement, compares federal performance reports with those produced by state governments and other nations, and suggests how GPRA has affected management of federal agencies and resource allocation by policymakers.

Keehley, P. and N.N. Abercrombie, *Benchmarking in the Public and Nonprofit Sectors: Best Practices for Achieving Performance Breakthroughs*, 2nd ed. (San Francisco, CA: Jossey-Bass, 2008)

Keehley and Abercrombie take a step-by-step approach to benchmarking techniques, differentiating between them and then providing a new approach to solution-driven benchmarking that requires less time and fewer resources.

Moynihan, D.P., *The Dynamics of Performance Management: Constructing Information and Reform* (Washington, DC: Georgetown University Press, 2008)

Moynihan illustrates how governments have emphasized some aspects of performance management—such as building measurement systems to acquire more performance data—but have neglected wider organizational change that would facilitate the use of such information.

van Dooren, W., G. Bouckaert, and J. Halligan, *Performance Management in the Public Sector* (New York: Routledge, 2010)

The book examines performance management by situating performance in the current public management debates, discussing the many definitions of performance, looking at ways to measure performance, and exploring potential future avenues.

ISSUE 11

Is Employment Equity Necessary?

YES: John F. Kennedy, from *Executive Order 10925: Establishing the President's Committee on Equal Employment Opportunity* (March 1961)

NO: Anthony Kennedy, from "Majority Opinion," *Ricci v. DiStefano* (June 2009)

Learning Outcomes

After reading this issue, you should be able to:

- Define employment equity.
- Discuss the historical reasons for why employment equity exists in the United States.
- Gain an understanding of America's initial efforts to ensure employment equity.
- Describe how employment equity has been viewed differently by the Supreme Court in recent years.
- Define affirmative action.
- Discuss the positive and negative elements of employment equity.

ISSUE SUMMARY

YES: President John F. Kennedy argued that government contractors needed to take action to ensure applicants are considered without regard to any characteristic such as race, color, or nationality. In 1964, his arguments led to the creation of the Equal Employment Opportunity Commission through the Civil Rights Act.

NO: Justice Anthony Kennedy argues that tests that are vetted properly can be used for merit promotion even if there are apparent racial divides within the results. In this light, affirmative action should be devoted to ensuring that minorities are equally prepared for tests, not in assuring actual equity.

The historic debate over employment equity in our country strangely begins on a Louisiana streetcar in July 1892. At that time, the New Orleans

Comité des Cityones arranged for Homer Plessy to board a whites-only car of the East Louisiana Railroad in New Orleans. The car was designated for only white patrons under accordance of Louisiana state law. The Comité des Cityones planned the act of civil disobedience in hopes of having the court (at any level) rule that separate but equal was not an acceptable policy when considering segregation. To show how difficult it can be to enforce racial segregation, the Comité des Cityones chose Plessy, who was born free and only one-eighth black. Under a state law from 1890, he was still considered to be black and was supposed to sit in that car. After the conductor was made aware of Plessy's race, he was asked to move to the proper car. When he refused, he was removed and arrested.

The Supreme Court was not sympathetic to Plessy, ruling 7-1 that the Louisiana law did not in any way violate the 14th amendment. Going even further, the Court found that the law did not suggest the inferiority of blacks, but instead asked for the races to be separated as a matter of public policy. Justice Brown, writing for the majority of the Court, stated "We consider the underlying fallacy of the plaintiff's argument to consist in the assumption that the enforced separation of the two races stamps the colored race with a badge of inferiority. If this be so, it is not by reason of anything found in the act, but solely because the colored race chooses to put that construction upon it." If anyone felt inferior as a result of the law's presence, it was due to their own perceptions rather than what the letter of the law asked for and mandated.

It would take until 1954, when a mother grew tired of watching her daughter ride by a white-only school seconds from her home to drive miles away to the school for African-Americans in Topeka, for the Supreme Court to return back to the question of separate but equal. In *Brown v. Board of Education of Topeka, Kansas*, the Supreme Court deemed separate but equal was no longer an acceptable doctrine and set out to ensure equality more completely. The next year the Court ordered segregated districts to integrate with "all deliberate speed."

Although the previous discussion has not explicitly focused on employment equity, it presents the necessary background to understand the content of the nation in 1961. We have witnessed a long period of "separate but equal" guiding our race decisions and then a quick transformation to "separate but equal" being deemed unconstitutional. It was in this context that President John F. Kennedy issued Executive Order No. 10925 in 1961. In this, he established the concept of affirmative action by requiring projects financed through federal monies to take affirmative action to ensure that hiring and employment practices are free of any sort of racial bias. Since then, affirmative action has become a hotly debated political topic within our country's borders with numerous arguments being advanced in support and opposition to Kennedy's idea.

Much like the federal program, many states have ordered the prohibition of discrimination and outline affirmative action requirements with regard to a host of variables at the state level. These include race, color, religion, national origin, age, gender, disability status, and sexual orientation. Proponents believe that the system does more than just protect racial minorities as a result. Deirdre Bowen conducted a study to examine the impact of being a minority student. Bowen finds that these students experience greater hostility and internal and external stigma in states where affirmative action is banned. Likewise, the University of Chicago found in a 2003 study that individuals with black-sounding names are almost half as likely to be interviewed for a job when compared with people who have white-sounding ones. With these figures and studies in mind, we can more easily see why many Americans believe that employment equity is still a necessary goal in our country.

Arguments against affirmative action begin with the idea of class inequality. Many Americans find that middle- and upper-class African and Hispanic Americans benefit from affirmative action rather than lower class members who actually struggle to compete for jobs and opportunities within our country. Even more importantly, the idea of class-based inequality suggests a place for white individuals in the affirmative action debate. A study in 2005 found that African-American students received the equivalent of 250 SAT points due to their race when applying for college. Asians actually lost the equivalent of 50 points due to their ethnic background. What this shows is the disparity between how our system traces people of different backgrounds. The more political debate focuses on the idea that affirmative action is reverse discrimination. If affirmative action asks us to take steps to ensure that different minorities are not discriminated against, does that lead to the majority groups facing the same discrimination we are working to prevent? If the answer is yes, affirmative action could be viewed as counter-productive and perhaps even harmful to society. Other concerns include whether affirmative action leads to unprepared applicants being accepted into schools or positions that they are not necessarily well-qualified for. In these instances there is a strong possibility of long-term failure—which may be even worse for society as a whole than not accepting the individual in the first place. Others worry that affirmative action lowers the bar—preventing individuals from obtaining a true sense of achievement through their own efforts and merit.

Showing how employment equity remains a highly politicized issue, consider that many states now specifically prohibit affirmative action. California, Washington, Michigan, and Nebraska have all passed laws banning the use of affirmative action within their states based on many of the criticisms we described earlier. Likewise, California, Michigan, Texas, Florida, and Washington all ban the use of race or sex when determining college admissions. In the following section, we will look more closely at employment equity and attempt to determine if it is still needed today. To begin, in the YES selection, we will look at President John F. Kennedy's Executive Order 10925, which first introduced the concept of employment equity to our country. On the opposite side, in the NO selection, we will read Anthony Kennedy's majority decision from the 2009 case *Ricci v. DiStefano* in which he argues that tests that are vetted properly can be used for merit promotion in public agencies even if there are apparent racial divides within the results. In the eyes of the Court, affirmative action should ensure minorities are prepared to take the test in an equal manner to their counterparts—but not guarantee equal outcomes.

YES

John F. Kennedy

Executive Order 10925: Establishing the President's Committee on Equal Employment Opportunity

WHEREAS discrimination because of race, creed, color, or national origin is contrary to the Constitutional principles and policies of the United States; and 13 CFR 1960 Supp.

WHEREAS it is the plain and positive obligation of the United States Government to promote and ensure equal opportunity for all qualified persons, without regard to race, creed, color, or national origin, employed or seeking employment with the Federal Government and on government contracts; and

WHEREAS it is the policy of the executive branch of the Government to encourage by positive measures equal opportunity for all qualified persons within the Government; and

WHEREAS it is in the general interest and welfare of the United States to promote its economy, security, and national defense through the most efficient and effective utilization of all available manpower; and

WHEREAS a review and analysis of existing Executive orders, practices, and government agency procedures relating to government employment and compliance with existing non-discrimination contract provisions reveal an urgent need for expansion and strengthening of efforts to promote full equality of employment opportunity; and

WHEREAS a single governmental committee should be charged with responsibility for accomplishing these objectives:

NOW, THEREFORE, by virtue of the authority vested in me as President of the United States by the Constitution and statutes of the United States, it is ordered as follows:

Part I—Establishment of the President's Committee on Equal Employment Opportunity

SECTION 101. There is hereby established the President's Committee on Equal Employment Opportunity.

SECTION 102. The Committee shall be composed as follows:

From *Executive Order 10925: Establishing the President's Committee on Equal Employment Opportunity,* March 1961.

(a) The Vice President of the United States, who is hereby designated Chairman of the Committee and who shall preside at meetings of the Committee.

(b) The Secretary of Labor, who is hereby designated Vice Chairman of the Committee and who shall act as Chairman in the absence of the Chairman. The Vice Chairman shall have general supervision and direction of the work of the Committee and of the execution and implementation of the policies and purposes of this order.

(c) The Chairman of the Atomic Energy Commission, the Secretary of Commerce, the Attorney General, the Secretary of Defense, the Secretaries of the Army, Navy and Air Force, the Administrator of General Services, the Chairman of the Civil Service Commission, and the Administrator of the National Aeronautics and Space Administration. Each such member may designate an alternate to represent him in his absence.

(d) Such other members as the President may from time to time appoint.

(e) An Executive Vice Chairman, designated by the President, who shall be ex officio a member of the Committee. The Executive Vice Chairman shall assist the Chairman, the Vice Chairman and the Committee. Between meetings of the Committee he shall be primarily responsible for carrying out the functions of the Committee and may act for the Committee pursuant to its rules, delegations and other directives. Final action in individual cases or classes of cases may be taken and final orders may be entered on behalf of the Committee by the Executive Vice Chairman when the Committee so authorizes.

SECTION 103. The Committee shall meet upon the call of the Chairman and at such other times as may be provided by its rules and regulations. It shall (a) consider and adopt rules and regulations to govern its proceedings; (b) provide generally for the procedures and policies to implement this order: (c) consider reports as to progress under this order; (d) consider and act, where necessary or appropriate, upon matters which may be presented to it by any of its members; and (e) make such reports to the President as he may require or the Committee shall deem appropriate. Such reports shall be made at least once annually and shall include specific references to the actions taken and results achieved by each department and agency. The Chairman may appoint subcommittees to make special studies on a continuing basis.

Part II—Nondiscrimination in Government Employment

SECTION 201. The President's Committee on Equal Employment Opportunity established by this order is directed immediately to scrutinize and study employment practices of the Government of the United States, and to consider and recommend additional affirmative steps which should be taken by executive departments and agencies to realize more fully the national policy of nondiscrimination within the executive branch of the Government.

SECTION 202. All executive departments and agencies are directed to initiate forthwith studies of current government employment practices within their responsibility. The studies shall be in such form as the Committee may prescribe and shall include statistics on current employment patterns, a review of current procedures, and the recommendation of positive measures for the elimination of any discrimination, direct or indirect, which now exists. Reports and recommendations shall be submitted to the Executive Vice Chairman of the Committee no later than sixty days from the effective date of this order, and the Committee, after considering such reports and recommendations, shall report to the President on the current situation and recommend positive measures to accomplish the objectives of this order.

SECTION 203. The policy expressed in Executive Order No. 10590 of January 18, 1955 (20 F.R. 409) with respect to the exclusion and prohibition of discrimination against any employee or applicant for employment in the Federal Government because of race, color, religion, or national origin is hereby reaffirmed.

SECTION 204. The President's Committee on Government Employment Policy, established by Executive Order No. 10590 of January 18, 1955 (20 F.R. 409), as amended by Executive Order No. 10722 on August 5, 1957 (22 F.R. 6287), is hereby abolished, and the powers, functions, and duties of that Committee are hereby transferred to, and henceforth shall be vested in, and exercised by, the President's Committee on Equal Employment Opportunity in addition to the powers conferred by this order.

Part III—Obligations of Government Contractors and Subcontractors

Subpart A—Contractor's Agreements

SECTION 301. Except in contracts exempted in accordance with section 303 of this order, all government contracting agencies shall include in every government contract hereafter entered into the following provisions:

"In connection with the performance of work under this contract, the contractor agrees as follows:

"(1) The contractor will not discriminate against any employee or applicant for employment because of race, creed, color, or national origin. The contractor will take affirmative action to ensure that applicants are employed, and that employees are treated during employment, without regard to their race, creed, color, or national origin. Such action shall include, but not be limited to, the following: employment, upgrading, demotion or transfer; recruitment or recruitment advertising; layoff or termination; rates of pay or other forms of compensation; and selection for training, including apprenticeship. The contractor agrees to post in conspicuous places, available to employees and applicants for employment, notices to be provided by the contracting officer setting forth the provisions of this nondiscrimination clause.

"(2) The contractor will, in all solicitations or advertisements for employees placed by or on behalf of the contractor, state that all qualified applicants will receive consideration for employment without regard to race, creed, color, or national origin.

"(3) The contractor will send to each labor union or representative of workers with which he has a collective bargaining agreement or other contract or understanding, a notice, to be provided by the agency contracting officer, advising the said labor union or workers' representative of the contractor's commitments under this section, and shall post copies of the notice in conspicuous places available to employees and applicants for employment.

"(4) The contractor will comply with all provisions of Executive Order No. 10925 of March 6, 1961, and of the rules, regulations, and relevant orders of the President's Committee on Equal Employment Opportunity created thereby.

"(5) The contractor will furnish all information and reports required by Executive Order No. 10925 of March 6, 1961, and by the rules, regulations, and orders of the said Committee, or pursuant thereto, and will permit access to his books, records, and accounts by the contracting agency and the Committee for purposes of investigation to ascertain compliance with such rules, regulations, and orders.

"(6) In the event of the contractor's non-compliance with the nondiscrimination clauses of this contract or with any of the said rules, regulations, or orders, this contract may be cancelled in whole or in part and the contractor may be declared ineligible for further government contracts in accordance with procedures authorized in Executive Order No. 10925 of March 6, 1961, and such other sanctions may be imposed and remedies invoked as provided in the said Executive order or by rule, regulation, or order of the President's Committee on Equal Employment Opportunity, or as otherwise provided by law.

"(7) The contractor will include the provisions of the foregoing paragraphs (1) through (6) in every subcontract or purchase order unless exempted by rules, regulations, or orders of the President's Committee on Equal Employment Opportunity issued pursuant to section 303 of Executive Order No. 10925 of March 6, 1961, so that such provisions will be binding upon each subcontractor or vendor. The contractor will take such action with respect to any subcontract or purchase order as the contracting agency may direct as a means of enforcing such provisions, including sanctions for noncompliance: Provided, however, that in the event the contractor becomes involved in, or is threatened with, litigation with a subcontractor or vendor as a result of such direction by the contracting agency, the contractor may request the United States to enter into such litigation to protect the interests of the United States."

SECTION 302. (a) Each contractor having a contract containing the provisions prescribed in section 301 shall file, and shall cause each of its subcontractors to file Compliance Reports with the contracting agency, which will be subject to review by the Committee upon its request. Compliance Reports shall be filed within such times and shall contain such information as to the practices, policies, programs, and employment statistics of the contractor and each subcontractor, and shall be in such form, as the Committee may prescribe.

(b) Bidders or prospective contractors or subcontractors may be required to state whether they have participated in any previous contract subject to the provisions of this order, and in that event to submit, on behalf of themselves and their proposed subcontractors, Compliance Reports prior to or as an initial part of their bid or negotiation of a contract.

(c) Whenever the contractor or subcontractor has a collective bargaining agreement or other contract or understanding with a labor union or other representative of workers, the Compliance Report shall include such information as to the labor union's or other representative's practices and policies affecting compliance as the Committee may prescribe: Provided, that to the extent such information is within the exclusive possession of a labor union or other workers' representative and the labor union or representative shall refuse to furnish such information to the contractor, the contractor shall so certify to the contracting agency as part of its Compliance Report and shall set forth what efforts he has made to obtain such information.

(d) The Committee may direct that any bidder or prospective contractor or subcontractor shall submit, as part of his Compliance Report, a statement in writing, signed by an authorized officer or agent of any labor union or other workers' representative with which the bidder or prospective contractor deals, together with supporting information, to the effect that the said labor union's or representative's practices and policies do not discriminate on the grounds of race, color, creed, or national origin, and that the labor union or representative either will affirmatively cooperate, within the limits of his legal and contractual authority, in the implementation of the policy and provisions of this order or that it consents and agrees that recruitment, employment, and the terms and conditions of employment under the proposed contract shall be in accordance with the purposes and provisions of the order. In the event that the union or representative shall refuse to execute such a statement, the Compliance Report shall so certify and set forth what efforts have been made to secure such a statement.

SECTION 303. The Committee may, when it deems that special circumstances in the national interest so require, exempt a contracting agency from the requirement of including the provisions of section 301 of this order in any specific contract, subcontract, or purchase order. The Committee may, by rule or regulation, also exempt certain classes of contracts, subcontracts, or purchase orders (a) where work is to be or has been performed outside the United States and no recruitment of workers within the limits of the United

States is involved; (b) for standard commercial supplies or raw materials; or (c) involving less than specified amounts of money or specified numbers of workers.

Subpart B—Labor Unions and Representatives of Workers

SECTION 304. The Committee shall use its best efforts, directly and through contracting agencies, contractors, state and local officials and public and private agencies, and all other available instrumentalities, to cause any labor union, recruiting agency or other representative of workers who is or may be engaged in work under Government contracts to cooperate with, and to comply in the implementation of, the purposes of this order. SECTION 305. The Committee may, to effectuate the purposes of section 304 of this order, hold hearings, public or private, with respect to the practices and policies of any such labor organization. It shall from time to time submit special reports to the President concerning discriminatory practices and policies of any such labor organization, and may recommend remedial action if, in its judgment, such action is necessary or appropriate. It may also notify any Federal, state, or local agency of its conclusions and recommendations with respect to any such labor organization which in its judgment has failed to cooperate with the Committee, contracting agencies, contractors, or subcontractors in carrying out the purposes of this order.

Subpart C—Powers and Duties of the President's Committee on Equal Employment Opportunity and of Contracting Agencies

SECTION 306. The Committee shall adopt such rules and regulations and issue such orders as it deems necessary and appropriate to achieve the purposes of this order, including the purposes of Part II hereof relating to discrimination in Government employment.

SECTION 307. Each contracting agency shall be primarily responsible for obtaining compliance with the rules, regulations, and orders of the Committee with respect to contracts entered into by such agency or its contractors, or affecting its own employment practices. All contracting agencies shall comply with the Committee's rules in discharging their primary responsibility for securing compliance with the provisions of contracts and otherwise with the terms of this Executive order and of the rules, regulations, and orders of the ommittee pursuant hereto. They are directed to cooperate with the Committee, and to furnish the Committee such information and assistance as it may require in the performance of its functions under this order. They are further directed to appoint or designate, from among the agency's personnel compliance officers. It shall be the duty of such officers to seek compliance with the objectives of this order by conference, conciliation, mediation, or persuasion.

SECTION 308. The Committee is authorized to delegate to any officer, agency, or employee in the executive branch of the Government any function of the Committee under this order, except the authority to promulgate rules and regulations of a general nature.

SECTION 309. (a) The Committee may itself investigate the employment practices of any Government contractor or subcontractor, or initiate such investigation by the appropriate contracting agency or through the Secretary of Labor, to determine whether or not the contractual provisions specified in section 301 of this order have been violated. Such investigation shall be conducted in accordance with the procedures established by the Committee, and the investigating agency shall report to the Committee any action taken or recommended.

(b) The Committee may receive and cause to be investigated complaints by employees or prospective employees of a Government contractor or subcontractor which allege discrimination contrary to the contractual provisions specified in section 301 of this order. The appropriate contracting agency or the Secretary of Labor, as the case may be, shall report to the Committee what action has been taken or is recommended with regard to such complaints.

SECTION 310. (a) The Committee, or any agency or officer of the United States designated by rule, regulation, or order of the Committee, may hold such hearings, public or private, as the Committee may deem advisable for compliance, enforcement, or educational purposes.

(b) The Committee may hold, or cause to be held, hearings in accordance with subsection (a) of this section prior to imposing, ordering, or recommending the imposition of penalties and sanctions under this order, except that no order for debarment of any contractor from further government contracts shall be made without a hearing.

SECTION 311. The Committee shall encourage the furtherance of an educational program by employer, labor, civic, educational, religious, and other nongovernmental groups in order to eliminate or reduce the basic causes of discrimination in employment on the ground of race, creed, color, or national origin.

Subpart D—Sanctions and Penalties

SECTION 312. In accordance with such rules, regulations or orders as the Committee may issue or adopt, the Committee or the appropriate contracting agency may:

(a) Publish, or cause to be published, the names of contractors or unions which it has concluded have complied or have failed to comply with the provisions of this order or of the rules, regulations, and orders of the Committee.

(b) Recommend to the Department of Justice that, in cases where there is substantial or material violation or the threat of substantial or material violation of the contractual provisions set forth in section 301 of this order, appropriate proceedings be brought to enforce those provisions, including the enjoining, within the limitations of applicable law, of organizations, individuals or groups who prevent directly or indirectly, or seek to prevent directly or indirectly, compliance with the aforesaid provisions.

(c) Recommend to the Department of Justice that criminal proceedings be brought for the furnishing of false information to any contracting agency or to the Committee as the case may be.

(d) Terminate, or cause to be terminated, any contract, or any portion or portions thereof, for failure of the contractor or subcontractor to comply with the nondiscrimination provisions of the contract. Contracts may be terminated absolutely or continuance of contracts may be conditioned upon a program for future compliance approved by the contracting agency.

(e) Provide that any contracting agency shall refrain from entering into further contracts, or extensions or other modifications of existing contracts, with any non-complying contractor, until such contractor has satisfied the Committee that he has established and will carry out personnel and employment policies in compliance with the provisions of this order.

(f) Under rules and regulations prescribed by the Committee, each contracting agency shall make reasonable efforts within a reasonable time limitation to secure compliance with the contract provisions of this order by methods of conference, conciliation, mediation, and persuasion before proceedings shall be instituted under paragraph (b) of this section, or before a contract shall be terminated in whole or in part under paragraph (d) of this section for failure of a contractor or subcontractor to comply with the contract provisions of this order.

SECTION 313. Any contracting agency taking any action authorized by this section, whether on its own motion, or as directed by the Committee, or under the Committee's rules and regulations, shall promptly notify the Committee of such action or reasons for not acting. Where the Committee itself makes a determination under this section it shall promptly notify the appropriate contracting agency of the action recommended. The agency shall take such action and shall report the results thereof to the Committee within such time as the Committee shall provide.

SECTION 314. If the Committee shall so direct, contracting agencies shall not enter into contracts with any bidder or prospective contractor unless the bidder or prospective contractor has satisfactorily complied with the provisions of this order or submits a program for compliance acceptable to the Committee or, if the Committee so authorizes, to the contracting agency.

SECTION 315. Whenever a contracting agency terminates a contract, or whenever a contractor has been debarred from further Government contracts, because of noncompliance with the contractor provisions with regard to nondiscrimination, the Committee, or the contracting agency involved, shall promptly notify the Comptroller General of the United States.

Subpart E—Certificates of Merit

SECTION 316. The Committee may provide for issuance of a United States Government Certificate of Merit to employers or employee organizations which are or may hereafter be engaged in work under Government contracts, if the Committee is satisfied that the personnel and employment practices of the employer, or that the personnel, training apprenticeship, membership, grievance and representation, upgrading and other practices and policies of the employee organization, conform to the purposes and provisions of this order.

SECTION 317. Any Certificate of Merit may at any time be suspended or revoked by the Committee if the holder thereof, in the judgment of the Committee, has failed to comply with the provisions of this order.

SECTION 318. The Committee may provide for the exemption of any employer or employee organization from any requirement for furnishing information as to compliance if such employer or employee organization has been awarded a Certificate of Merit which has not been suspended or revoked.

Part IV—Miscellaneous

SECTION 401. Each contracting agency (except the Department of Justice) shall defray such necessary expenses of the Committee as may be authorized by law, including section 214 of the Act of May 3, 1945, 59 Stat. 134 (31 U.S.C. 691): Provided, that no agency shall supply more than fifty per cent of the funds necessary to carry out the purposes of this order. The Department of Labor shall provide necessary space and facilities for the Committee. In the case of the Department of Justice, the contribution shall be limited to furnishing legal services.

SECTION 402. This order shall become effective thirty days after its execution. The General Services Administration shall take appropriate action to revise the standard Government contract forms to accord with the provisions of this order and of the rules and regulations of the Committee.

SECTION 403. Executive Order No. 10479 of August 13, 1953 (18 F.R. 4899) together with Executive Orders Nos. 10482 of August 15, 1953 (18 F.R. 4944), and 10733 of October 10, 1957 (22 F.R. 8135) amending that order, and Executive Order No. 10557 of September 3, 1954 (19 F.R. 5655), are hereby revoked, and the Government Contract Committee established by Executive Order No. 10479 is abolished. All records and property of or in the custody of the said Committee are hereby transferred to the President's Committee on Equal Employment Opportunity, which shall wind up the outstanding affairs of the Government Contract Committee.

Majority Opinion, *Ricci v. DiStefano*

J ustice Kennedy delivered the opinion of the Court.

In the fire department of New Haven, Connecticut—as in emergency-service agencies throughout the Nation—firefighters prize their promotion to and within the officer ranks. An agency's officers command respect within the department and in the whole community; and, of course, added responsibilities command increased salary and benefits. Aware of the intense competition for promotions, New Haven, like many cities, relies on objective examinations to identify the best qualified candidates.

In 2003, 118 New Haven firefighters took examinations to qualify for promotion to the rank of lieutenant or captain. Promotion examinations in New Haven (or City) were infrequent, so the stakes were high. The results would determine which firefighters would be considered for promotions during the next two years, and the order in which they would be considered. Many firefighters studied for months, at considerable personal and financial cost.

When the examination results showed that white candidates had outperformed minority candidates, the mayor and other local politicians opened a public debate that turned rancorous. Some firefighters argued the tests should be discarded because the results showed the tests to be discriminatory. They threatened a discrimination lawsuit if the City made promotions based on the tests. Other firefighters said the exams were neutral and fair. And they, in turn, threatened a discrimination lawsuit if the City, relying on the statistical racial disparity, ignored the test results and denied promotions to the candidates who had performed well. In the end the City took the side of those who protested the test results. It threw out the examinations.

Certain white and Hispanic firefighters who likely would have been promoted based on their good test performance sued the City and some of its officials. Theirs is the suit now before us. The suit alleges that, by discarding the test results, the City and the named officials discriminated against the plaintiffs based on their race, in violation of both Title VII of the Civil Rights Act of 1964, 78 Stat. 253, as amended, 42 U. S. C. §2000e et seq., and the Equal Protection Clause of the Fourteenth Amendment. The City and the officials defended their actions, arguing that if they had certified the results, they could have faced liability under Title VII for adopting a practice that had a disparate

Supreme Court of the United States, June 2009.

impact on the minority firefighters. The District Court granted summary judgment for the defendants, and the Court of Appeals affirmed.

We conclude that race-based action like the City's in this case is impermissible under Title VII unless the employer can demonstrate a strong basis in evidence that, had it not taken the action, it would have been liable under the disparate-impact statute. The respondents, we further determine, cannot meet that threshold standard. As a result, the City's action in discarding the tests was a violation of Title VII. In light of our ruling under the statutes, we need not reach the question whether respondents' actions may have violated the Equal Protection Clause.

I

This litigation comes to us after the parties' cross-motions for summary judgment, so we set out the facts in some detail. As the District Court noted, although "the parties strenuously dispute the relevance and legal import of, and inferences to be drawn from, many aspects of this case, the underlying facts are largely undisputed." 554 F. Supp. 2d 142, 145 (Conn. 2006).

A

When the City of New Haven undertook to fill vacant lieutenant and captain positions in its fire department (Department), the promotion and hiring process was governed by the city charter, in addition to federal and state law. The charter establishes a merit system. That system requires the City to fill vacancies in the classified civil-service ranks with the most qualified individuals, as determined by job-related examinations. After each examination, the New Haven Civil Service Board (CSB) certifies a ranked list of applicants who passed the test. Under the charter's "rule of three," the relevant hiring authority must fill each vacancy by choosing one candidate from the top three scorers on the list. Certified promotional lists remain valid for two years.

The City's contract with the New Haven firefighters' union specifies additional requirements for the promotion process. Under the contract, applicants for lieutenant and captain positions were to be screened using written and oral examinations, with the written exam accounting for 60 percent and the oral exam 40 percent of an applicant's total score. To sit for the examinations, candidates for lieutenant needed 30 months' experience in the Department, a high-school diploma, and certain vocational training courses. Candidates for captain needed one year's service as a lieutenant in the Department, a high-school diploma, and certain vocational training courses.

After reviewing bids from various consultants, the City hired Industrial/Organizational Solutions, Inc. (IOS) to develop and administer the examinations, at a cost to the City of $100,000. IOS is an Illinois company that specializes in designing entry-level and promotional examinations for fire and police departments. In order to fit the examinations to the New Haven Department, IOS began the test-design process by performing job analyses to identify the tasks, knowledge, skills, and abilities that are essential for the lieutenant and captain positions. IOS representatives interviewed incumbent captains and lieutenants and their supervisors. They rode with and observed other on-duty officers. Using information from those interviews and ride-alongs, IOS wrote job-analysis questionnaires and administered them to most of the incumbent battalion chiefs, captains, and lieutenants in the Department. At every stage of the job analyses, IOS, by deliberate choice, oversampled minority firefighters to ensure that the results—which IOS would use to develop the examinations— would not unintentionally favor white candidates.

With the job-analysis information in hand, IOS developed the written examinations to measure the candidates' job-related knowledge. For each test, IOS compiled a list of training manuals, Department procedures, and other materials to use as sources for the test questions. IOS presented the proposed sources to the New Haven fire chief and assistant fire chief for their approval. Then, using the approved sources, IOS drafted a multiple-choice test for each position. Each test had 100 questions, as required by CSB rules, and was written below a 10th-grade reading level. After IOS prepared the tests, the City opened a 3-month study period. It gave candidates a list that identified the source material for the questions, including the specific chapters from which the questions were taken.

IOS developed the oral examinations as well. These concentrated on job skills and abilities. Using the job-analysis information, IOS wrote hypothetical situations to test incident-command skills, firefighting tactics, interpersonal skills, leadership, and management ability, among other things. Candidates would be presented with these hypotheticals and asked to respond before a panel of three assessors.

IOS assembled a pool of 30 assessors who were superior in rank to the positions being tested. At the City's insistence (because of controversy surrounding previous examinations), all the assessors came from outside Connecticut. IOS submitted the assessors' resumes to City officials for approval. They were battalion chiefs, assistant chiefs, and chiefs from departments of similar sizes to New Haven's throughout the country. Sixty-six percent of the panelists were minorities, and each of the nine three-member assessment panels contained two minority members. IOS trained the panelists for several hours on the day before it administered the examinations, teaching them how to score the candidates' responses consistently using checklists of desired criteria.

Candidates took the examinations in November and December 2003. Seventy-seven candidates completed the lieutenant examination—43 whites, 19 blacks, and 15 Hispanics. Of those, 34 candidates passed—25 whites, 6 blacks, and 3 Hispanics. 554 F. Supp. 2d, at 145. Eight lieutenant positions were vacant at the time of the examination. As the rule of three operated, this meant that the top 10 candidates were eligible for an immediate promotion to lieutenant. All 10 were white. Ibid. Subsequent vacancies would have allowed at least 3 black candidates to be considered for promotion to lieutenant.

Forty-one candidates completed the captain examination—25 whites, 8 blacks, and 8 Hispanics. Of those, 22 candidates passed—16 whites, 3 blacks, and 3 Hispanics. Ibid. Seven captain positions were vacant at the time of the

examination. Under the rule of three, 9 candidates were eligible for an immediate promotion to captain—7 whites and 2 Hispanics. Ibid.

B

The City's contract with IOS contemplated that, after the examinations, IOS
would prepare a technical report that described the examination processes
and methodologies and analyzed the results. But in January 2004, rather than
requesting the technical report, City officials, including the City's counsel,
Thomas Ude, convened a meeting with IOS Vice President Chad Legel. (Legel
was the leader of the IOS team that developed and administered the tests.)
Based on the test results, the City officials expressed concern that the tests had
discriminated against minority candidates. Legel defended the examinations'
validity, stating that any numerical disparity between white and minority candidates was likely due to various external factors and was in line with results of
the Department's previous promotional examinations.

Several days after the meeting, Ude sent a letter to the CSB purporting
to outline its duties with respect to the examination results. Ude stated that
under federal law, "a statistical demonstration of disparate impact," standing
alone, "constitutes a sufficiently serious claim of racial discrimination to serve
as a predicate for employer-initiated, voluntar[y] remedies—even . . . race-
conscious remedies."

App. to Pet. for Cert. in No. 07-1428, p. 443a; see also 554 F. Supp. 2d, at
145 (issue of disparate impact "appears to have been raised by . . . Ude").

1

The CSB first met to consider certifying the results on January 22, 2004. Tina
Burgett, director of the City's Department of Human Resources, opened the
meeting by telling the CSB that "there is a significant disparate impact on
these two exams." App. to Pet. for Cert. in No. 07-1428, at 466a. She distributed lists showing the candidates' races and scores (written, oral, and composite) but not their names. Ude also described the test results as reflecting "a very
significant disparate impact," id., at 477a, and he outlined possible grounds for
the CSB's refusing to certify the results.

Although they did not know whether they had passed or failed, some
firefighter-candidates spoke at the first CSB meeting in favor of certifying the
test results. Michael Blatchley stated that "[e]very one" of the questions on
the written examination "came from the [study] material. . . . [I]f you read the
materials and you studied the material, you would have done well on the test."
App. in No. 06-4996-cv (CA2), pp. A772–A773 (hereinafter CA2 App.). Frank
Ricci stated that the test questions were based on the Department's own rules
and procedures and on "nationally recognized" materials that represented the
"accepted standard[s]" for firefighting. Id., at A785–A786. Ricci stated that
he had "several learning disabilities," including dyslexia; that he had spent
more than $1,000 to purchase the materials and pay his neighbor to read them
on tape so he could "give it [his] best shot"; and that he had studied "8 to
13 hours a day to prepare" for the test. Id., at A786, A789. "I don't even know

if I made it," Ricci told the CSB, "[b]ut the people who passed should be promoted. When your life's on the line, second best may not be good enough." Id., at A787–A788.

Other firefighters spoke against certifying the test results. They described the test questions as outdated or not relevant to firefighting practices in New Haven. Gary Tinney stated that source materials "came out of New York. . . . Their makeup of their city and everything is totally different than ours." Id., at A774-A775; see also id., at A779, A780-A781. And they criticized the test materials, a full set of which cost about $500, for being too expensive and too long.

2

At a second CSB meeting, on February 5, the president of the New Haven firefighters' union asked the CSB to perform a validation study to determine whether the tests were job-related. Petitioners' counsel in this action argued that the CSB should certify the results. A representative of the International Association of Black Professional Firefighters, Donald Day from neighboring Bridgeport, Connecticut, "beseech[ed]" the CSB "to throw away that test," which he described as "inherently unfair" because of the racial distribution of the results. Id., at A830-A831. Another Bridgeport-based representative of the association, Ronald Mackey, stated that a validation study was necessary. He suggested that the City could "adjust" the test results to "meet the criteria of having a certain amount of minorities get elevated to the rank of Lieutenant and Captain." Id., at A838. At the end of this meeting, the CSB members agreed to ask IOS to send a representative to explain how it had developed and administered the examinations. They also discussed asking a panel of experts to review the examinations and advise the CSB whether to certify the results.

3

At a third meeting, on February 11, Legel addressed the CSB on behalf of IOS. Legel stated that IOS had previously prepared entry-level firefighter examinations for the City but not a promotional examination. He explained that IOS had developed examinations for departments in communities with demographics similar to New Haven's, including Orange County, Florida; Lansing, Michigan; and San Jose, California.

Legel explained the exam-development process to the CSB. He began by describing the job analyses IOS performed of the captain and lieutenant positions—the interviews, ride-alongs, and questionnaires IOS designed to "generate a list of tasks, knowledge, skills and abilities that are considered essential to performance" of the jobs. Id., at A931-A932. He outlined how IOS prepared the written and oral examinations, based on the job-analysis results, to test most heavily those qualities that the results indicated were "critica[l]" or "essentia[l]." Id., at A931. And he noted that IOS took the material for each test question directly from the approved source materials. Legel told the CSB that third-party reviewers had scrutinized the examinations to ensure that the written test was drawn from the source material and that the oral test accurately tested real-world situations that captains and lieutenants would face. Legel confirmed that IOS had selected oral-examination panelists so that each three-member assessment panel included one white, one black, and one Hispanic member.

Near the end of his remarks, Legel "implor[ed] anyone that had . . . concerns to review the content of the exam. In my professional opinion, it's facially neutral. There's nothing in those examinations . . . that should cause somebody to think that one group would perform differently than another group."

Id., at A961.

4

At the next meeting, on March 11, the CSB heard from three witnesses it had selected to "tell us a little bit about their views of the testing, the process, [and] the methodology." Id., at A1020. The first, Christopher Hornick, spoke to the CSB by telephone. Hornick is an industrial/organizational psychologist from Texas who operates a consulting business that "direct[ly]" competes with IOS. Id., at A1029. Hornick, who had not "stud[ied] the test at length or in detail" and had not "seen the job analysis data," told the CSB that the scores indicated a "relatively high adverse impact." Id., at A1028, A1030, A1043. He stated that "[n]ormally, whites outperform ethnic minorities on the majority of standardized testing procedures," but that he was "a little surprised" by the disparity in the candidates' scores—although "[s]ome of it is fairly typical of what we've seen in other areas of the countr[y] and other tests." Id., at A1028-A1029. Hornick stated that the "adverse impact on the written exam was somewhat higher but generally in the range that we've seen professionally." Id., at A1030-A1031.

When asked to explain the New Haven test results, Hornick opined in the telephone conversation that the collective-bargaining agreement's requirement of using written and oral examinations with a 60/40 composite score might account for the statistical disparity. He also stated that "[b]y not having anyone from within the [D]epartment review" the tests before they were administered—— limitation the City had imposed to protect the security of the exam questions—"you inevitably get things in there" that are based on the source materials but are not relevant to New Haven. Id., at A1034–A1035. Hornick suggested that testing candidates at an "assessment center" rather than using written and oral examinations "might serve [the City's] needs better." Id., at A1039-A1040. Hornick stated that assessment centers, where candidates face real-world situations and respond just as they would in the field, allow candidates "to demonstrate how they would address a particular problem as opposed to just verbally saying it or identifying the correct option on a written test." Ibid.

Hornick made clear that he was "not suggesting that [IOS] somehow created a test that had adverse impacts that it should not have had." Id., at A1038. He described the IOS examinations as "reasonably good test[s]." Id., at A1041. He stated that the CSB's best option might be to "certify the list as it exists" and work to change the process for future tests, including by "[r]ewriting the Civil Service Rules." Ibid. Hornick concluded his telephonic remarks by telling the CSB that "for the future," his company "certainly would like to help you if we can." Id., at A1046.

The second witness was Vincent Lewis, a fire program specialist for the Department of Homeland Security and a retired fire captain from Michigan. Lewis, who is black, had looked "extensively" at the lieutenant exam and "a little less extensively" at the captain exam. He stated that the candidates "should know that material." Id., at A1048, A1052. In Lewis's view, the "questions were relevant for both exams," and the New Haven candidates had an advantage because the study materials identified the particular book chapters from which the questions were taken. In other departments, by contrast, "you had to know basically the . . . entire book." Id., at A1053. Lewis concluded that any disparate impact likely was due to a pattern that "usually whites outperform some of the minorities on testing," or that "more whites . . . take the exam." Id., at A1054.

The final witness was Janet Helms, a professor at Boston College whose "primary area of expertise" is "not with firefighters per se" but in "race and culture as they influence performance on tests and other assessment procedures." Id., at A1060. Helms expressly declined the CSB's offer to review the examinations. At the outset, she noted that "regardless of what kind of written test we give in this country . . . we can just about predict how many people will pass who are members of underrepresented groups. And your data are not that inconsistent with what predictions would say were the case." Id., at A1061. Helms nevertheless offered several "ideas about what might be possible factors" to explain statistical differences in the results. Id., at A1062. She concluded that because 67 percent of the respondents to the job-analysis questionnaires were white, the test questions might have favored white candidates, because "most of the literature on firefighters shows that the different groups perform the job differently." Id., at A1063. Helms closed by stating that no matter what test the City had administered, it would have revealed "a disparity between blacks and whites, Hispanics and whites," particularly on a written test. Id., at A1072.

5

At the final CSB meeting, on March 18, Ude (the City's counsel) argued against certifying the examination results. Discussing the City's obligations under federal law, Ude advised the CSB that a finding of adverse impact "is the beginning, not the end, of a review of testing procedures" to determine whether they violated the disparate-impact provision of Title VII. Ude focused the CSB on determining "whether there are other ways to test for . . . those positions that are equally valid with less adverse impact." Id., at A1101. Ude described Hornick as having said that the written examination "had one of the most severe adverse impacts that he had seen" and that "there are much better alternatives to identifying [firefighting] skills." Ibid. Ude offered his "opinion that promotions . . . as a result of these tests would not be consistent with federal law, would not be consistent with the purposes of our Civil Service Rules or our Charter[,] nor is it in the best interests of the firefighters . . . who took the exams." Id., at A1103-A1104. He stated that previous Department exams "have not had this kind of result," and that previous results had not been "challenged as having adverse impact, whereas we are assured that these will be." Id., at A1107, A1108.

CSB Chairman Segaloff asked Ude several questions about the Title VII disparate-impact standard.

"CHAIRPERSON SEGALOFF: [M]y understanding is the group . . . that is making to throw the exam out has the burden of showing that there is out there an exam that is reasonably probable or likely to have less of an adverse impact. It's not our burden to show that there's an exam out there that can be better. We've got an exam. We've got a result. . . ."

"MR. UDE: Mr. Chair, I point out that Dr. Hornick said that. He said that there are other tests out there that would have less adverse impact and that [would] be more valid."

"CHAIRPERSON SEGALOFF: You think that's enough for us to throw this test upside-down . . . because Dr. Hornick said it?"

"MR. UDE: I think that by itself would be sufficient. Yes. I also would point out that . . . it is the employer's burden to justify the use of the examination." Id., at A1108-A1109.

Karen DuBois-Walton, the City's chief administrative officer, spoke on behalf of Mayor John DeStefano and argued against certifying the results. DuBois-Walton stated that the results, when considered under the rule of three and applied to then-existing captain and lieutenant vacancies, created a situation in which black and Hispanic candidates were disproportionately excluded from opportunity. DuBois-Walton also relied on Hornick's testimony, asserting that Hornick "made it extremely clear that . . . there are more appropriate ways to assess one's ability to serve" as a captain or lieutenant. Id., at A1120.

Burgett (the human resources director) asked the CSB to discard the examination results. She, too, relied on Hornick's statement to show the existence of alternative testing methods, describing Hornick as having "started to point out that alternative testing does exist" and as having "begun to suggest that there are some different ways of doing written examinations." Id., at A1125, A1128.

Other witnesses addressed the CSB. They included the president of the New Haven firefighters' union, who supported certification. He reminded the CSB that Hornick "also concluded that the tests were reasonable and fair and under the current structure to certify them." Id., at A1137. Firefighter Frank Ricci again argued for certification; he stated that although "assessment centers in some cases show less adverse impact," id., at A1140, they were not available alternatives for the current round of promotions. It would take several years, Ricci explained, for the Department to develop an assessment-center protocol and the accompanying training materials. Id., at A1141. Lieutenant Matthew Marcarelli, who had taken the captain's exam, spoke in favor of certification.

At the close of witness testimony, the CSB voted on a motion to certify the examinations. With one member recused, the CSB deadlocked 2 to 2, resulting in a decision not to certify the results. Explaining his vote to certify the results, Chairman Segaloff stated that "nobody convinced me that we can feel comfortable that, in fact, there's some likelihood that there's going to be an exam designed that's going to be less discriminatory." Id., at A1159-A1160.

C

The CSB's decision not to certify the examination results led to this lawsuit. The plaintiffs—who are the petitioners here—are 17 white firefighters and

1 Hispanic firefighter who passed the examinations but were denied a chance at promotions when the CSB refused to certify the test results. They include the named plaintiff, Frank Ricci, who addressed the CSB at multiple meetings.

Petitioners sued the City, Mayor DeStefano, DuBois-Walton, Ude, Burgett, and the two CSB members who voted against certification. Petitioners also named as a defendant Boise Kimber, a New Haven resident who voiced strong opposition to certifying the results. Those individuals are respondents in this Court. Petitioners filed suit under Rev. Stat. §§1979 and 1980, 42 U. S. C. §§1983 and 1985, alleging that respondents, by arguing or voting against certifying the results, violated and conspired to violate the Equal Protection Clause of the Fourteenth Amendment. Petitioners also filed timely charges of discrimination with the Equal Employment Opportunity Commission (EEOC); upon the EEOC's issuing right-to-sue letters, petitioners amended their complaint to assert that the City violated the disparate-treatment prohibition contained in Title VII of the Civil Rights Act of 1964, as amended. See 42 U. S. C. §§2000e-2(a).

The parties filed cross-motions for summary judgment. Respondents asserted they had a good-faith belief that they would have violated the disparate-impact prohibition in Title VII, §2000e-2(k), had they certified the examination results. It follows, they maintained, that they cannot be held liable under Title VII's disparate-treatment provision for attempting to comply with Title VII's disparate-impact bar. Petitioners countered that respondents' good-faith belief was not a valid defense to allegations of disparate treatment and unconstitutional discrimination.

The District Court granted summary judgment for respondents. 554 F. Supp. 2d 142. It described petitioners' argument as "boil[ing] down to the assertion that if [respondents] cannot prove that the disparities on the Lieutenant and Captain exams were due to a particular flaw inherent in those exams, then they should have certified the results because there was no other alternative in place." Id., at 156. The District Court concluded that, "[n]otwithstanding the shortcomings in the evidence on existing, effective alternatives, it is not the case that [respondents] must certify a test where they cannot pinpoint its deficiency explaining its disparate impact . . . simply because they have not yet formulated a better selection method." Ibid. It also ruled that respondents' "motivation to avoid making promotions based on a test with a racially disparate impact . . . does not, as a matter of law, constitute discriminatory intent" under Title VII. Id., at 160. The District Court rejected petitioners' equal protection claim on the theory that respondents had not acted because of "discriminatory animus" toward petitioners. Id., at 162. It concluded that respondents' actions were not "based on race" because "all applicants took the same test, and the result was the same for all because the test results were discarded and nobody was promoted." Id., at 161.

After full briefing and argument by the parties, the Court of Appeals affirmed in a one-paragraph, unpublished summary order; it later withdrew that order, issuing in its place a nearly identical, one-paragraph per curiam opinion adopting the District Court's reasoning. 530 F. 3d 87 (CA2 2008). Three days later, the Court of Appeals voted 7 to 6 to deny rehearing en banc, over written dissents by Chief Judge Jacobs and Judge Cabranes. 530 F. 3d 88.

This action presents two provisions of Title VII to be interpreted and reconciled, with few, if any, precedents in the courts of appeals discussing the issue. Depending on the resolution of the statutory claim, a fundamental constitutional question could also arise. We found it prudent and appropriate to grant certiorari. 555 U. S. ___ (2009). We now reverse.

. . .

EXPLORING THE ISSUE

Is Employment Equity Necessary?

Critical Thinking and Reflection

1. What is employment equity and affirmative action? How are the ideas similar and different?
2. Why do we strive for employment equity in the United States? What are the historical reasons for this?
3. What were the initial efforts our country undertook to ensure employment equity?
4. In recent years, the Supreme Court has altered its views on employment equity. How did the view change? What are the potential long-term effects of this shift?
5. What is good about employment equity? What are the possible drawbacks? Do we need to continue ensuring employment equity? Why or why not?

Is There Common Ground?

Employment equity is a difficult subject for many Americans to publically discuss. It brings up thoughts of racism, gender bias, and employment struggles for individuals of any walk of life. At times in our country's history, there is no denying there was a clear need to ensure equity for minority job candidates. Yet, even with agreement on this basic belief, individuals argued the degree of equity that should be ensured. Would it be enough to simply ensure the same opportunities for all individuals? Or should a type of quota system be adopted to guarantee positions would be distributed across different groups?

Second-level questions involve the discrepancies in expectations between public and private hiring practices. Should private firms or businesses be exempt from equitable employment standards? If so, how can such a decision be relayed to the public? As American society has progressed, interpretations of employment equity have changed. Recent Supreme Court rulings, for example, run contrary to previous beliefs. Perhaps, though, the debate over employment equity can lead us to seriously addressing an even more pressing matter: 50 years after the civil rights movement first took hold in the United States, why have we failed to move past a point where matters like employment equity even need to be considered?

Additional Resources

Abu-Laban, Y. and C. Gabriel, *Selling Diversity: Immigration, Multiculturalism, Employment Equity, and Globalization* (Toronto, ON: University of Toronto Press, 2002)

This book examines employment equity and globalization from the Canadian perspective. It presents a different take on these policies—especially for individuals who have only considered the policies through an American lens.

Anderson, T .H., *The Pursuit of Fairness: A History of Affirmative Action* (New York: Oxford University Press, 2005)

Anderson offers a direct assessment of the history of affirmative action in the United States. By looking at the policy from pre-Roosevelt through modern times, the book allows for an examination of contextual factors and ultimately a deeper understanding of employment equity in our country.

Jain, H.C., P. J. Sloane, and F.M. Horwitz, *Employment Equity and Affirmative Action: An International Comparison* (New York: M.E. Sharpe, 2003)

In this book, Jain, Sloane, and Horwitz examine employment equity and affirmative action in a comparative context. By focusing on countries outside of the United State, the authors aim to shine new light on what we already know from our domestic experience.

Kellough, J.E., *Understanding Affirmative Action: Politics, Discrimination, and the Search for Justice* (Washington, DC: Georgetown University Press, 2006)

J. Edward Kellough brings together historical, philosophical, and legal analyses to fully inform participants and observers of the debate over affirmative action in the United States.

Kirkpatrick, J.J., R.B. Ewen, R.S. Barrett, and R.A. Katsell, *Testing and Fair Employment: Fairness and Validity of Personnel Tests for Different Ethnic Groups* (New York: New York University Press, 1968)

In this classic work, the four authors assess the validity of personnel tests for various ethnic and racial groups. One of the first studies to do so, the book looks at whether personnel tests are ultimately fair to minority employees.

ISSUE 12

Is It Possible to Motivate Workers in a Manner That Increases Job Satisfaction in the Public Sector?

YES: **James L. Perry and Lyman W. Porter**, from "Factors Affecting the Context for Motivation in Public Organizations," *The Academy of Management Review* (January 1982)

NO: **Seong Soo Oh and Gregory B. Lewis**, from "Can Performance Appraisal Systems Inspire Intrinsically Motivated Employees?" *Review of Public Personnel Administration* (June 2009)

Learning Outcomes

After reading this issue, you should be able to:

- Define public sector motivation.
- Discuss the relationship between motivation and performance.
- Gain an understanding of the relationship between motivation and job satisfaction.
- Describe different ways to motivate public workers.
- Distinguish between intrinsic and extrinsic motivation.
- Describe the difficulties in measuring motivation.

ISSUE SUMMARY

YES: James L. Perry and Lyman W. Porter examine comparative motivational contexts in public organizations to determine what can be done to increase motivation. They ultimately find out monetary incentives, goal setting, job design, and participation all have different impacts on motivation.

NO: Seong Soo Oh and Gregory B. Lewis argue that some employee motivation tools, such as performance appraisal systems, can decrease employee productivity. The authors find that this is especially true for intrinsically motivated workers.

$\mathbf{F}$rederick Taylor's contribution to public administration orthodoxy theory is the development of scientific management. Scientific principles, time and motion studies, were utilized to determine the "one best way" to complete a task, thereby improving efficiency and productivity. Taylor argued that it was the responsibility of management to design work in such a way that workers fit the job. To the extent that worker motivation was considered in scientific management, economic motives were likely predominant. By the 1930s, scholars identified with the Human Relations movement challenged Taylorism by suggesting that human beings were hardly a monolithic group, driven entirely by economic considerations and material gain. Worker motivation is the product of a complex mix of personal factors and work characteristics.

Mary Parker Follett (1926) argued that one of the great contributions of scientific management is the depersonalization of orders. However, integral to Follett's argument is the recognition of human psychology and personal needs. For example, Follett responded to a union member who reported a lack of dignity at being "a mere employee," suggesting "he can have all the dignity in the world if he is allowed to make his fullest contribution to the plant and to assume definitely the responsibility therefore." Worker dignity, and perhaps job satisfaction, is related to the contribution one makes to the firm. Follett remarked that although supervision is essential, many people object to being watched at work. This contrasts with the findings of the Hawthorne studies of the 1920s and 1930s, which reported that worker productivity declined when the workers knew that they were no longer being observed. Clearly, the work environment and the conditions of work can impact employees.

One of the major contributors to motivation theory is Abraham Maslow (1943), who incorporated social relationship factors into his hierarchy of needs. Maslow argued that people are motivated to achieve tiered needs: physiological needs, such as food and water; safety needs; love or affiliation needs; esteem needs; and self-actualization. According to Maslow, once a lower level need was met, it no longer motivated behavior. In other words, once a stable food source and shelter are acquired, an individual begins to seek safety. Once the personal lower level needs are met, people seek the more relational needs of affiliation and esteem, both of which can be potentially satisfied through work. Douglas McGregor (1957) confirmed Maslow's theory, arguing that it is in the interest of management to offer employees opportunities to meet higher level needs, as overall organization needs will be met. McGregor described a management approach called Theory X, which was largely reminiscent of scientific management. Management saw workers as unmotivated and passive. As a result, the task of management is to control workers through a system of coercion and rewards. Instead, McGregor advocated a Theory Y, encouraging management to focus on higher level needs through techniques such as delegation, job enlargement, and performance appraisal.

Frederick Herzberg's (1959) two-factor theory further elaborated Maslow's theory by collapsing needs into two categories: hygiene factors and motivators. According to Herzberg, hygiene factors, such as salary, supervision, and work conditions, will not motivate workers to perform. The perceived inadequacy of hygiene factors will lead only to dissatisfaction with one's job. Herzberg's motivators, reflective of both Maslow's higher level needs and Follett's notion of employee dignity, include recognition, achievement, and responsibility. An employee's positive perception of motivators can lead to job satisfaction. Hackman and Oldham (1976) argued that five job characteristics contribute to three psychological states that can lead to worker motivation and job satisfaction. Meaningfulness of work is affected by a worker using a variety of skills used on the job, the employee's ability to identify a task, and a belief that the task is significant to the overall work of the firm. A sense of responsibility at work is produced by worker autonomy. Finally, knowledge of outcomes is produced by providing feedback to the employee. Hackman and Oldham argue that a sense of meaningfulness of work leads to worker motivation, particularly intrinsic motivation. People are extrinsically motivated when the activity leads to a valued reward or fear of punishment or coercion. In contrast, intrinsic motivation occurs when people are motivated simply by the work itself, which Hackman and Oldham contend is more likely when employees believe the work is meaningful. Responsibility and knowledge of outcomes can contribute to the satisfaction of higher level needs of esteem and self-actualization.

One might wonder whether the application of motivation theory differs according to whether it is applied to the public or the private sector. Private sector organizations are accountable to shareholders and are cognizant of the bottom line of profit. In contrast, the shareholders of public organizations are the citizenry at large. Further, as any student of the contemporary federal budget process has noticed among increasing deficits and spiraling debt, there is no bottom line. Scholars in the 1960 began to investigate the existence of public service motivation (PSM). Empirical research suggested that public workers were less motivated by material incentives and placed higher value on task importance. More recent research has found that public sector employees were more likely to be "service oriented," and that service-oriented federal employees exhibited greater productivity. This research seems to confirm the earlier studies and provide contemporary public managers with some valuable clues regarding employee motivation.

In the YES selection, James L. Perry and Lyman W. Porter study public sector motivation across various contexts. The authors examine many of the motivation strategies generated in earlier theories, including material incentives, job design, and employee participation, finding that each strategy can contribute to employee motivation. In the NO selection, Seong Soo Oh and Gregory Lewis argue that performance appraisal, recommended by Douglas McGregor as a Theory Y motivation technique, can actually decrease employee productivity, particularly in the case of the intrinsically motivated employee.

YES

**James L. Perry and
Lyman W. Porter**

Factors Affecting the Context for Motivation in Public Organizations

. . .

The Context for Motivation

As a hypothetical construct, motivation usually stands for that which "energizes, directs, and sustains behavior." In shorthand terms, it is the degree and type of effort that an individual exhibits in a behavioral situation. However, care needs to be taken not to equate motivation simply with sheer amount of effort. It also has to do with the direction and quality of that effort.

Any comprehensive look at the motivational bases of behavior in organizational settings must of necessity focus on the several sets of variables that influence motivation. A classification system, found useful identifies four major categories of variables: (1) individual characteristics, (2) job characteristics, (3) work environment characteristics, and (4) external environment characteristics. If motivation is to be affected, one or more of these variables must be changed or affected. Let us look briefly at each category of variables and the special facets of motivational tasks in public organizations.

Individual Characteristics

Although it is obvious that certain characteristics (such as attitudes) can be changed after one joins an organization, the focus here is on individual characteristics *brought to* the work situation. Presently there is a very limited understanding of special considerations that involve the "raw materials" in public sector motivational processes. Of course, one reason for this deficiency is simply the belief that, if government is different from other management contexts, it is distinguished by the nature of work or the environment within which the work occurs, not by the individuals whom it attracts or employs. Given this prevailing belief, only a few studies provide an indication of the motivational characteristics of public employees. Guyot compared middle managers in the federal government and in business on their needs for achievement, affiliation, and power. He concluded, quite surprisingly, that both popular and academic images of civil servants were distorted. Government middle managers had higher needs for achievement and lower needs for affiliation than did their business counter-parts, but their needs for power were roughly the same.

Few researchers have attempted to replicate Guyot's results. However, two relatively recent studies by Rawls and his associates, using samples of students about to enter management careers, again uncovered differences in individual characteristics. They found that students about to enter the non-profit sector (primarily government) were significantly more dominant and flexible, had a higher capacity for status, and valued economic wealth to a lesser degree than did entrants to the profit sector. No significant differences existed between the groups on need for power and need for security. Thus, the collective findings of the three studies cited above exhibit a fairly high degree of consistency, considering the limitations on the comparisons that may be made among them, regarding the needs of public employees and how these needs differ from indivduals in other sectors.

An independent issue related to individual characteristics involves the types of individual needs that are satisfied by the activities that occur in gov-ernment organizations. Several studies indicate that public managers experi-ence significantly lower levels of satisfaction than do their counterparts in business. Among the areas in which the differences are significant is satisfac-tion with promotion. This finding can be contrasted with the strong need for achievement found among entrants to government organizations. However, these studies utilized deficiency scores to measure satisfaction; thus levels of satisfaction then could simply reflect more stringent norms or expectations among government managers.

Job Characteristics

The second major set of variables that can be changed or modified to affect motivation involve what the person *does* at work—that is, the nature of the job or the collection of tasks that comprise the job. Although the unique features of government structures are generally believed, as indicated earlier, to have little impact on individual characteristics affecting public sector motivational processes, organizational structures and goals unique to government clearly influence the design of jobs in the public sector. Yet, just as the understanding of individual characteristics is deficient, motivation-relevant characteristics of public sector jobs also are not well documented in the research literature. Among the job characteristics that have been identified to be important, how-ever, are the measurability of individual performance, degree of goal clarity, and degree of job challenge.

A frequent point of departure for many scholars attempting to identify unique aspects of public employment is the nature, both from aggregate and disaggregate perspectives, of public sector jobs. For example, Rainey, Backoff, and Levine, Newman and Wallendar, and Fottler have concluded that demands on higher level public managers to maintain constituencies, deal with com-peting external interests, and seek funding in a political environment prob-ably differentiate their roles from managers in other economic sectors. This view is reinforced by the results of a study that compared time management and task accomplishment for public and private managers. Similarly, from an aggregate perspective, government is perceived primarily as a service provider rather than a goods producer. And, in fact, government is enormously more labor intensive than are other sectors of the American economy because it is oriented toward the provision of personal services. The implications of this phenomenon are significant for the dimension of jobs that Thompson terms the *types of assessments* levied against individuals, that is, the extent to which individuals are likely to be evaluated by maximizing or satisficing criteria. Because government organizations are predominantly service providers, with additional burdens of accountability and public responsiveness, the problems of creating performance criteria and implementing evaluation schemes are complex and difficult. The difficulties place a special burden on public managers in designating what performance shall be evaluated.

A related aspect of performance appraisal in many public organizations is what Buchanan terms *goal crispness*. Buchanan argues that governmental organizations pursue diffuse and conflicting goals, quite unlike the tangible and relatively more specific goals of business organizations. Thus, public managers are usually confronted by a two-pronged dilemma with respect to the motivational properties of public sector jobs: (1) jobs for which performance criteria cannot be readily defined or measured and (2) conflicting criteria for superior performance.

Quite surprisingly, the consequences of these characteristics of governmental jobs do not appear to spill over into other job dimensions and, therefore, they do not further complicate motivational processes. For example, Rainey hypothesized that the greater vagueness and intangibility of governmental goals would lead to public middle managers expressing higher mean scores on role conflict and role ambiguity. He found, however, no significant differences between government and business managers. Thus, performance in public sector jobs generally may be more difficult to assess, and the task goals of public jobs might inherently conflict, but these phenomena apparently do not produce corresponding role-related conflicts. Managers develop means for coping with problematic job characteristics such as assessing jobs in terms of standard operating procedures that simplify and avoid the difficulties of performance measurement in public service organizations.

A recent report by the National Center for Productivity and Quality of Working Life suggests that two other job dimensions, job content and job challenge, satisfy the needs of employees relatively well. Most public employees responding to a series of attitude surveys rated the content of their jobs as good (managers—84 percent; non-managers—64 percent), and few disagreed with a statement that their jobs made good use of their skills and abilities (managers—14 percent; non-managers—23 percent). Buchanan reports results on first-year job challenge comparing business and public managers that seemingly contradict the latter result. Industrial managers in his sample scored higher, reporting significantly greater *first-year* job challenge. Buchanan focused, however, on first-year job challenge, and it is quite plausible that differences might exist between the National Commission results and his more restrictive and retrospective concept. He offers several reasons for the lower level of first-year job challenge among government managers. One reason is that bureaucratic roles, particularly at training levels, might be difficult to infuse with excitement. This could be exacerbated by the gap that exists between the routineness of the first job and the idealism that might have drawn the manager to the public service. Buchanan notes that first-year job challenge might also be negatively affected by government's efforts to assure representation and to train unemployed individuals. These policies might unwittingly contribute to overstaffing and the dilution of training positions.

Work Environment Characteristics

Variables dealing with work environment characteristics that can be changed or modified to impact motivation can be placed into two subcategories: immediate work environment characteristics and organizational actions. Clearly, the two most critical factors in an employee's immediate work environment are: the peer group and the supervisor. Organizational actions, insofar as they affect motivation, can be classified into (a) provision of system rewards, (b) provision of individual rewards, and (c) creation of an organizational climate.

More insights have been developed about important motivational aspects of the work situation in public organizations than about the preceding two categorizations of variables, individual and job characteristics. A number of these insights relate to organizational climate and emanate from Buchanan's work on organizational commitment. Among the work situation characteristics affecting motivation is the phenomenon of *goal crispness,* discussed earlier in conjunction with job characteristics. The diffuseness of, and contradictions among, public organizational goals may be viewed as work environment characteristics as well as job characteristics. In either instance, they complicate the task of developing attachments to government organizations and generating spontaneous goal directed activities.

Goal crispness is only one of several work environment characteristics relevant to motivation in the public sector. Buchanan identifies at least three other work environment characteristics that influence a manager's leverage in motivating employees: personal significance reinforcement, stability of expectations, and reference group experiences.

Personal significance reinforcement, a related aspect of goal crispness, involves the extent to which individuals perceive that they make contributions to organizational success. As Buchanan argues, it is especially difficult for many public agencies to instill employees with a sense of personal significance. One reason is that it is often difficult for public employees to observe any link between their contributions and the success of their organizations. The absence of this linkage is the result of a variety of factors, among them the sheer size of many governments, the pluralistic composition of policy implementation networks, and the lack of clear-cut performance indicators or norms. Developing the attitude among employees that they are valued members of an organization is a difficult job even in the best circumstances. However, the task becomes increasingly demanding when attitudes of personal significance must be developed within a large scale organization in which there might be little acceptance or recognition of general standards of performance. The problems of stimulating a sense of personal significance among employees are compounded by the constitutional separation of the executive and legislative branches of government, which occasionally produces legislative-administrative conflicts that destroy attitudes of personal significance.

Goal crispness and personal significance reinforcement perhaps are the most important, but not the only, work situation characteristics affecting motivation.

A third factor, stability of expectations, is directly related to the frequency with which the dominant coalitions of governments change. This variable involves whether employees perceive that their organizations have a stable commitment to the mission or programs that they pursue. Of course, even "planned" changes in political leadership seriously jeopardize the development of this stability. If the directions of programs or missions change frequently enough, employees are likely to question the need to put forth maximum effort on what they come to perceive as transitory programs. The end result of such instability is that an organization "will find it more difficult to command the same intensity of loyalty that other organizations enjoy."

Another significant work environment characteristic that influences motivation is the diversity of values and characteristics of work groups. Work or similar task related groups exercise a certain amount of control over their members' attitudes. Heterogeneous or representative groups, more typical of government than of the private sector, will, in Buchanan's terms, "rarely develop intensely favorable attitudes toward their agencies or foster climates in which commitment to the agency is a group norm." This phenomenon, by reducing cohesion and consensus within the work group, diminishes the likelihood or, at the very least, increases the difficulty of eliciting spontaneous goal directed behaviors from employees.

Another interpersonal dimension of the work situation, an aspect of the immediate work environment, with significant implications for motivation is the quality of supervision. The National Center for Productivity, drawing on a nonrandom sample of previous attitudinal studies, reported employee perceptions of lower supervisory quality in the public than in the private sector. One exception to this generalization was that, among managers, public sector supervisors were rated more highly than private supervisors on human relations skills. Public supervisors, in contrast to their private counterparts, suffered primarily in terms of their subordinates' evaluation of their technical competence. The quality-of-supervision differences reported by the National Center for Productivity might have a variety of causes. The evaluations of technical competence could reflect greater predominance of manager-professional conflicts in government organizations. They also might reflect less investment in training or less success in recruiting supervisory personnel. In any event, the quality of supervision is a critical element in motivational processes.

As a whole, these special work environment considerations in public organizations appear likely to constrain motivational levels significantly even when individual and job characteristics are conducive to employee motivation. Factors such as goal crispness and the quality of supervision are too integral to eliciting superior employee performance to argue otherwise. Although the accumulated research evidence permits some generalizations about the underlying processes, it does not offer any prescriptions for better managing these work environment characteristics.

External Environment Characteristics

The fourth major category of variable that can affect employee motivation is the external environment (or environments). In particular, it is changes or the anticipation of changes in the external environment that can have powerful impacts on individuals' behavior in work organizations. This category of variables, however, in contrast with the first three, is not one which any given organization can directly control. Nevertheless, that does not leave the organization helpless. It can monitor the external environment and, based on such monitoring, it can proceed to make changes internally within the organization that can influence employee motivation.

External environments can be usefully subdivided (arbitrarily, to be sure) into several major categories: socionormative, political, demographic, economic, and technological. Focus will be on the first two categories, because it is believed that they contain the variables that have the greatest differential effects on employee motivation in public sector organizations.

Socionormative Changes

Public sector organizations cannot help but be impacted by what Clark Kerr has termed the "fourth period of great evolutionary change" in the labor force in the United States with respect to "its composition, its character, and the rules for its conduct." The quest for personal self-fulfillment is regarded by Kerr, along with other social observers such as Daniel Yankelovich and Amitai Etzioni, as especially significant for the work environment—any work environment, including that of the public sector. As Kerr puts it, "We have a crisis of aesthetics, not ethics—tastes have changed, and the indulgence of psychic satisfactions has increased."

These broad socionormative changes can directly affect motivation, by altering the orientations of those who enter public organizations, but they also might influence motivation indirectly, by modifying the attitudes and values of those whom public organizations serve. To the extent that the general public holds unfavorable attitudes about public employment and public bureaucracies, motivation-relevant employee perceptions, such as self-worth and personal significance, can be expected to be affected. Furthermore, compounding any motivational difficulties that might be associated with society's attitudes about public employment—attitudes that tend to fluctuate widely over time—is the complexity of public attitudes about government. As Katz and his colleagues have observed, for example, there appear to be marked inconsistencies between the public's ideological and pragmatic attitudes. One manifestation of this inconsistency (so evident in the public's response to Proposition 13) is that, at an ideological level, private enterprise is perceived as more effective than government agencies, but, at a pragmatic level, government interventions into areas like pollution control and auto safety regulation are strongly supported by the public. The continued existence of these types of inconsistencies in the socionormative environment will challenge those who attempt to sharpen the goals of public organizations and may diminish managers' ability to motivate individuals who seek guidance from stable and consistent, rather than ambiguous, public expectations.

Political Changes

The implications of these changes for motivation perhaps are the most difficult to characterize because they influence motivation less directly than do socionormative or demographic changes, and, in recent years, they collectively have followed no easily discernible patterns. Some of the more long-standing political trends no doubt affect employee motivation only in very general ways. Counted among these trends might be the recent (the post-Eisenhower period) instability in the American Presidency, steadily declining public trust in major political institutions, and, perhaps partially as an outgrowth of the latter trend, increasingly frequent legislative intervention into day-to-day administrative details. Except for legislative interventionism, which actually or potentially might have an impact on the task structure of government jobs, the political changes above influence motivation primarily by altering the climate—the "psychological feel"—within an organization.

Other, more discrete political changes of recent years unquestionably will affect motivation in measurable, but yet to be explored ways. Legislative mandates for citizen participation, spanning the eras of the Great Society and New Federalism, have contributed to the dispersion of power and authority in administrative systems. This most recent manifestation and reassertion of the tenets of representative democracy most certainly has affected key variables bearing on motivation. Similar consequences could be expected to flow from other current political developments: the "new" populism (including Ralph Nader, Common Cause, and Jimmy Carter), the ebb of the electorate toward greater conservatism (often equated with less government), and an era of relative scarcity within the political economy.

Efficacy of Motivational Techniques

Most organizations employ one or more methods to elicit role compliance and goal directed behaviors from their employees. These motivational techniques usually are intended to maximize benefits to the organization, but their relative utility varies considerably. The list of motivational techniques presently used by employers is extensive: monetary incentives, goal setting, flexitime, job enlargement, job enrichment, behavior modification, participation, award and recognition plans, discipline, and counseling. However, as a recent review illustrates, most research has focused on four basic (but not mutually exclusive) motivational methods: monetary incentives, goal setting, job design, and participation. In fact, most motivational methods are derived from these basic techniques.

Monetary Incentives

Locke et al. concluded from their review of field studies of monetary incentives that significant performance improvements resulted from the use of these techniques. The median performance increase found in the field studies they reviewed was 30 percent. This median increase, however, may overestimate the value of money as an incentive, because monetary incentives typically are accompanied by some form of methods analysis, goal setting, or other technique that contributes to motivating performance. Until quite recently, monetary incentives, with the exception of output-oriented merit increases, have not been adopted widely in the public sector. A 1973 survey of 509 local governments reported that 42 percent of the respondents used merit increases, only 6 percent employed performance bonuses, and 1 percent used shared savings or piecework systems. On the basis of a very limited amount of information, government's success with monetary incentives prior to the Federal Civil Service Reform Act of 1978 (CSRA) has, at best, been mixed. For example, the National Commission on Productivity stated:

> Some reported output-oriented merit increases were, in fact longevity increases or focused more on personal characteristics rather than output. Indeed, even truly output-oriented merit increases often became routine and are taken for granted by employees after they have been in operation for a while.

It should be noted, however, that CSRA is intended to remedy these types of shortcomings associated with the use of monetary incentives in the federal government. Whether or not the reforms achieve this goal is a matter for future inquiry.

At a conceptual level, the designs of monetary incentives must clearly deal with some of the motivational considerations discussed earlier. Perhaps the most important consideration is the values of employees. As noted previously, there is some indication that individuals entering the public sector value economic wealth to a lesser degree than do entrants to the profit sector. If this is indeed true, the motivational potential of monetary incentives might be limited in contrast to experiences elsewhere. It is quite possible, however, that greater emphasis on monetary incentives will begin to attract individuals who value economic wealth more highly. This development might lessen the attraction of the public service to more idealistic types. These concerns may be moot considering that even with the addition of monetary incentives public managers probably will receive much lower monetary rewards than will managers in other economic sectors.

The successful use of monetary incentives in government also is threatened by the extent to which performance differences can be measured with precision and an equitable formula can be developed that ties rewards to performance. Definition and measurement of performance criteria obviously will affect the acceptability and results of such incentive systems. The extent to which competing goals of an agency are mirrored in performance criteria also will complicate incentive systems.

Goal Setting

Goal setting essentially involves establishing observable standards for employee performance and offering feedback to the employee about the extent to which the standards have been achieved. Techniques for goal setting, like monetary incentives, come in a variety of formats, including performance targets, management by objectives, and work standards. Goal setting techniques have been used widely in government, and the early conceptual and practical development of some techniques, like MBO, owe a great deal to governmental experience.

From their review of 17 field studies of goal setting, Locke et al. attribute a 16 percent median improvement in performance (with a range of 2 percent to 57.5 percent) as a result of goal setting. They also emphasized that feedback about progress vis-à-vis goals is essential for goal setting to regulate performance effectively. One reported use of goal setting in the Bureau of Census, which gave regular feedback about performance against work standards, achieved a 52 percent improvement in output.

The design of goal setting techniques for public organizations must take into account a myriad of considerations that might moderate their success. The most important of these obviously is the vague and conflicting nature of governmental goals. An important issue is whether goal setting techniques will encourage more concrete goal explication, or whether there are countervailing influences that assure that government goals will remain inherently vague and conflicting. Although examples supporting the belief that goal setting can indeed improve employee understanding of tasks and objectives might readily be obtained, the practical difficulty of creating concrete and precise goal statements in many situations is not altered. Also, there is the problem that attempting to make goals more concrete (crisp) may run the risk of making them more trivial. Given these considerations, it might be necessary to create highly flexible, decentralized goal setting techniques so that the task characteristics of the focal agency receive adequate attention. It also might be necessary to state goals in terms of organizational inputs or activities rather than outputs because of the difficulty of measuring achievement.

The vagueness of the goals of public organizations is perhaps the most challenging problem confronting the success of goal setting, but it is not the only issue with which public managers and policy makers must be concerned. The diversity of internal and external constituencies will increase the effort that must be devoted to goal setting and could possibly increase the likelihood of political attacks upon administrators. It may be necessary to protect administrators from these inefficiencies or risks of goal setting techniques to assure that they will fully support their use.

Although the difficulties of implementing goal setting successfully in public organizations appear substantial, these difficulties must be weighed against several considerations. First, goal setting often is an important prerequisite of effective performance appraisal and monetary incentives. Second, goal setting offers one of the primary routes to personal significance reinforcement because it creates a mechanism by which individuals can observe their contributions to organizational success. Third, goal setting is an attractive alternative to monetary incentives, which, in the long run either could fail for lack of adequate financial rewards or might detract from public interest values. Fourth, goal setting might be an efficient alternative to monetary incentives in that it offers a high rate of return for quite limited investments. This is an important factor in light of declining budgets and resource scarcity. Thus, because goal setting is an integral aspect of other motivational techniques and possibly is more efficient than other methods, it may be more likely to be incorporated effectively by public organizations.

Job Design

Job design involves the structuring of various aspects of the job content. For example, job design might involve increasing job responsibilities, the variety of tasks, or employee autonomy. Although job design has been popular since the early 1960s, the 1973 Urban Institute survey for the National Commission on Productivity reported that only 73 of 509 local government organizations had used some form of job rotation, redesign, or teamwork technique.

Evaluating the effectiveness of job design is more difficult than evaluating the effectiveness of other motivational techniques because it usually is implemented in conjunction with feedback and other structural changes. As Locke et al. suggest, if the performance contributions of the goal setting component of job design programs are controlled, job design might have no further effects on performance. Thus, the contributions of job design to public sector performance are somewhat problematic. Many cases of successful job design are described in the National Commission report, but no rigorous evaluation of applications of the technique is available. Furthermore, the primary thrust of job design has been toward changing job content, but, as already indicated, this is not a widespread source of dissatisfaction among public employees. This indicates that there might be only a selective need for job design, possibly confined to those situations in which a direct cause-effect relationship exists between satisfaction with job content and service quality or output, or in cases in which an employee is being underutilized.

Another threat to the success of job design involves the ability of managers to alter variables significantly—variables such as self-direction or responsibility—when these aspects of the job are controlled by legislators or program constituents. At the very least, this problem might restrict the applicability of job design to jobs embedded both vertically and horizontally within an organization. One selective use for which job design might clearly pay dividends is in training positions. The problem of first-year job challenge is clearly amenable to solution by the use of job design.

Participation

Participation involves some type of shared or joint decision making between superiors and subordinates at the work group, program, or organizational level. A few instances of its use in state and local governments are described in the National Commission report. Of course, collective bargaining, already widespread in the public sector, is one variant of participation.

Because of the limited understanding of the effects of participation, it is extremely difficult to judge its probable efficacy as a motivational tool in government. At a superficial level, questions might be raised about participation's consequences for "who governs," but this does not appear to be a significant impediment to the instrumental use of participation. Intuitively, one might expect that participation would contribute positively to motivational considerations like perceptions of personal significance and quality of supervision. Its utility for moderating the effects of other variables, such as work group diversity, is less clear.

Conclusions

This paper has reviewed a diverse set of topics focused around motivational processes in public organizations. Now is proposed an agenda for research, composed primarily of questions that have been raised implicitly in this paper. The issues enumerated below are illustrative of those that might be addressed.

1. The individual-organization match. Considerable research attention has been addressed to how organizations choose individuals, but much less attention has been paid to the reverse: how individuals choose organizations and how organizations attract individuals. Insufficient research attention also has been given to a related aspect of the individual-organization match: How the attitudes, beliefs, and interests that an individual brings to organizational settings impact motivation. An understanding of these questions seems particularly important in light of research evidence that indicates that public organizations attract somewhat different types of individuals than do private organizations. The practical payoff from such a line of inquiry might be to increase the extent to which individuals entering government are satisfied with their organization and the extent to which the organization is able to secure effective behaviors from its members.

2. Measurability of individual performance. One of the most immediately pressing needs for research attention involves the measurability of individual performance in typical public sector jobs. For example, it might be necessary to make some conceptual advances before a public manager's "ability to deal with competing external interests" can be adequately measured. Because the performance of many public employees probably will be measured despite the lack of availability of generally accepted criteria, research on performance appraisal methods most appropriate for such circumstances also is needed.

3. Goal clarity. A better understanding of the sources of goal clarity (or lack of it) is needed so that remedies can be designed or a certain degree of murkiness in the goals of public organizations may have to be generally accepted. It is necessary to develop a better understanding of the ways in which the political environment reduces goal crispness and displaces goal directed activity. Research on how people adapt to situations in which goals are inherently unclear might

contribute to developing methods for encouraging effective behaviors in such situations.

4. Job security. Differences between job security practices are a source of continuing, and often unfavorable, comparison between the public and private sectors. As noted earlier, the findings of several studies suggest that the security needs of public employees do not differ from those of private employees. However, knowledge about the motivational effects of the use of job security as a system wide reward in public organizations is minimal. Research might focus on developing a better understanding of the motivational "costs" and "benefits" of current public job security practices and designing alternative means for protecting political neutrality.

5. Moderators of motivation techniques. Another research issue might be the identification of key moderators of the effectiveness of the various motivational techniques. For example, Locke et al. indicated in their review that although participation had demonstrated only about a 1 percent *median* performance increase in a group of 16 field studies, half of the field experiments exhibited positive results, one as high as 47 percent. The critical research question is: Did the eight field sites in which participation was successful share characteristics that were absent in those sites where participation failed? This search for the factors that moderated the effectiveness of participation could be generalized to all the motivational techniques and should be a central concern of evaluative studies in public organizations. . . .

**Seong Soo Oh and
Gregory B. Lewis**

 **NO**

Can Performance Appraisal Systems Inspire Intrinsically Motivated Employees?

Can a performance appraisal system (PAS) elicit better performance from an intrinsically motivated workforce? By explicitly linking extrinsic rewards to performance, a PAS might actually discourage the work effort of the primarily intrinsically motivated federal workforce. Data from the 2000 Merit Principles Survey show that few federal employees believe that the PAS increases their productivity. Logit analysis confirms that intrinsically motivated employees are more skeptical of the effectiveness of PAS than are extrinsically motivated employees who are demographically similar, work in similar positions, and have similar beliefs about the fairness of the system and the probability of being rewarded for superior performance.

Results-oriented government reform efforts have made the performance appraisal system (PAS) a central part of public agencies' performance management. PAS aims to improve organizational productivity by providing developmental feedback and by linking rewards to performance. By tying pay to performance, agencies hope to increase the productivity of poor performers while maintaining or enhancing that of higher performers. Although the two largest federal departments (Homeland Security and Defense) have made the strongest efforts toward pay-for-performance systems, using pay banding to widen the gap between the pay of high and low performers, pay for performance has not been very effective in the public sector to date. Critics have largely focused on the inadequacy of the financial rewards and the shortage of incentives for public managers to implement them effectively.

The more important problem, however, may be a fundamental mismatch between PAS and a primarily intrinsically motivated workforce. Although this hypothesis is controversial, extrinsic rewards may discourage intrinsically motivated workers, and public employees place greater value on intrinsic motivators than do private sector workers. By explicitly tying extrinsic rewards to performance, PAS could potentially demotivate a large group of federal employees.

Data from the 2000 Merit Principles Survey indicate that few federal employees see the PAS as motivating them to do a better job but that the pattern is particularly dismal for the intrinsically motivated. Logit analysis confirms that more intrinsically motivated employees find fewer benefits from PASs—even

From *Review of Public Personnel Administration,* June 2009, pp. 158–161, 164–165. Copyright © 2009 by Sage Publications. Reprinted by permission via Rightslink.

holding constant demographics, hierarchical level, and agency as well as satisfaction with supervisors, skepticism about the link between performance and rewards, and beliefs about the fairness of performance standards, all important beliefs for PAS to motivate workers.

Literature Review

Intrinsically motivated employees work for the inherent satisfaction of the labor, whereas extrinsically motivated employees "engage in the work in order to obtain some goal that is apart from the work itself." Hackman and Oldham argued that strong intrinsic motivation occurs when three psychological states are created: "1) experienced meaningfulness of the work, 2) experienced responsibility for outcomes of the work, and 3) knowledge of the actual results of the work activities;" they urged organizations to restructure work to induce intrinsic motivation. Greater skill variety, task identity, and task significance increase the experienced meaningfulness of the work, autonomy raises experienced responsibility, and feedback provides knowledge of results. PAS is one means to facilitate that feedback.

Governments largely rely on "separable consequences" (e.g., pay, promotions, working conditions, and fringe benefits) to motivate employees, even though many researchers have regarded intrinsic motivation as more important. Frank and Lewis, for instance, found that intrinsic motivators are more strongly related to self-reported work effort than are extrinsic motivators. Until the 1960s, the dominant perspective was that extrinsic and intrinsic motivations were independent and that performance would be highest when they were combined. Several studies, however, suggested that extrinsic rewards can drive out intrinsic motivation, particularly when a majority of employees are intrinsically motivated. Other empirical studies, however, indicated that pay is an important motivator and that extrinsic rewards do not negatively affect intrinsic motivation.

Since Perry and Wise popularized the concept of public service motivation (PSM), several empirical studies have supported their hypotheses that public employees are more likely to be motivated by "a desire to serve the public interest, loyalty to duty and to the government as a whole, and social equity" and that high-PSM employees may be more productive workers.

PASs are used to provide extrinsic rewards to employees who perform well. Because those rewards matter less to the intrinsically motivated, who may even be discouraged by those extrinsic rewards, PAS should be less effective for them than for employees who are more extrinsically motivated. Thus, PAS may be ineffective with the largest and most productive group of federal employees.

Data

We test this possibility using data from the 2000 Merit Principles Survey, one of a series of surveys the U.S. Merit Systems Protection Board (MSPB) has conducted every 3 years or so since 1983. MSPB distributed the questionnaire to random samples of 750 full-time permanent employees in each of 23 federal agencies and got a 43% response rate—6,958 employees. Dropping those with missing values on key variables decreased our sample to 4,384, which we weighted to be representative of the full-time civil service.

Table 1 lists the question wording for our key variables. Our dependent variable is whether respondents agreed with the statement, "The performance appraisal system motivates me to do a better job." Our key independent variable measures how intrinsically motivated the employee is. Respondents were

Table 1

Survey Questions and Responses (in percentages)

	Strongly Disagree	Disagree	Neither	Agree	Strongly Agree
The performance appraisal system motivates me to do a better job.	30	28	24	15	4
The standards used to evaluate my performance are fair.	10	14	24	46	6
Overall, I am satisfied with my supervisor.	12	11	18	40	19

	Very Unlikely	Somewhat Unlikely	Neither Likely nor Unlikely	Somewhat Likely	Very Likely
If you perform better in your present job, how likely is it that you will receive more pay (e.g., bonus, promotion, cash award)?	36	16	11	27	9

Three factors that most motivate you to do a good job		Agree
Intrinsic motivators	Personal pride or satisfaction in my work	81
	Personal desire to make a contribution	56
	My duty as a public employee	23
Extrinsic motivators	Monetary award	27
	Desire to help my work unit meet its goals	21
	Increasing my chances for a promotion	18
	Availability of flexible working conditions	14
	Good working environment overall	14
	Desire to get a good performance rating	10
	Desire not to let my coworkers down	8
	Recognition from my coworkers	8
	My supervisor's encouragement	8
	Desire not to let my supervisor down	6
	Desire to make my supervisor look good	2

asked to "mark the three factors that most motivate you to do a good job" from a list of 14. Three of the top motivators are clearly intrinsic. Four out of five respondents listed "personal pride or satisfaction in my work," more than half listed "personal desire to make a contribution," and one fourth said "my duty as a public employee." The first measure captures motivation that comes directly from the work itself, whereas the latter two measure a more explicit PSM. Most of the other motivators on the list are clearly extrinsic (e.g., "monetary reward" and "increasing my chances for promotion," listed by one fourth and one fifth, respectively), though some are a mix of intrinsic and extrinsic (e.g., "desire to help my work unit meet its goals," also listed by one fifth). Our independent variable, number of intrinsic motivators, simply counts the number of the three clearly intrinsic motivators that the respondent chose.

Findings

Only 18% of federal employees agree that the PAS motivates them to do a better job, including 4% who strongly agree. In contrast, 58% disagree, including 30% who strongly disagree. Most federal employees emphasized intrinsic motivators: In all, 12% listed all three, another 44% listed two, and just 7% listed only extrinsic motivators. As hypothesized, those with higher levels of intrinsic motivation had more negative beliefs about the motivational power of PAS (see Table 2). Those who listed no intrinsic motivators were 3 times as likely as those who listed all three to agree that PAS motivated them to do a better job (30% vs. 9%). . . .

Can a well-implemented PAS make the highly intrinsically motivated federal workforce more productive? Few federal employees seem to think so. Only 18% agree that the PAS motivates them to do a better job; many more (30%) strongly disagree. The pattern is even more dismal for the intrinsically motivated: Among those who list only intrinsic motivators, only 9% believe that the PAS motivates them to do a better job, and 39% strongly disagree. This lower impact of PAS on the performance of the intrinsically motivated persists after controlling for a variety of demographic and organizational

Table 2

Level of Intrinsic Motivation and Belief That Performance Appraisal System (PAS) Motivates Them to Do a Better Job (in percentages)

	Number of Intrinsic Motivators				
	0	**1**	**2**	**3**	**Total**
Percentage who agree that PAS motivates them to do a better job	30	22	16	9	18
Number in group	326	1,599	1,917	542	4,384

variables, even though the intrinsically motivated were just as likely as the extrinsically motivated to hold other beliefs essential for PAS to succeed. Although many studies explain the ineffectiveness of PAS in the federal civil service as an implementation failure, pay for performance may simply be incompatible with the kind of workforce the federal service attracts and wants to attract.

This study suffers from all the weaknesses of relying on self-reports of motivation. Rynes et al. pointed to "discrepancies between what people say and do with respect to pay" and argued that "people are more likely to under-report than to overreport the importance of pay as a motivational factor in most situations." Employees may not realize how strongly monetary awards, promotion, and other benefits motivate them. Even if they do, they may not be willing to admit it, and those who claim all intrinsic motivators may be the least willing to acknowledge that they are responding to the PAS.

Still, our findings suggest that the federal government faces major obstacles in linking pay to performance as a means of improving government productivity and that market-oriented reform in rewards system may be a step in the wrong direction. As Perry and Wise argued, the federal government may get further by emphasizing the rewards associated with PSM. As Wright argued, involving employees in system design and administration may do a better job of motivating them, echoing the argument of Hackman and Oldham that increasing workers' experience of meaning, responsibility for outcomes, and knowledge of results will enhance their intrinsic motivation.

EXPLORING THE ISSUE

Is It Possible to Motivate Workers in a Manner That Increases Job Satisfaction in the Public Sector?

Critical Thinking and Reflection

1. What types of factors do scholars believe motivate workers in the public sector?
2. How are motivation and job satisfaction related? Is it the same in the private sector as in the public sector? Why or why not?
3. What can lead to motivation not positively increasing job satisfaction? Is there a way to overcome these blocks?
4. If motivated workers do not have higher job satisfaction, what other ways do we have for creating happier workers?
5. Do we need workers to be satisfied with their jobs to be effective public administrators? Why or why not?

Is There Common Ground?

Regardless of the job, we have long assumed that happy workers are better workers. If we take this premise as correct, it becomes important to understand how we can best motivate public employees in a way that increases job satisfaction. Studies have shown us that public employees are often underpaid and underappreciated. There are negative stereotypes everywhere they look that paint them as being lazy and incompetent. Yet, these workers perform vital tasks for everything that occurs with relation to public policy. If it is possible to motivate public employees, it is essential for scholars to devote time and energy to determining the most effective manners of motivation. If it is not, it is equally important to figure out how private sector practices can best be transferred to public workers. Increased job satisfaction, after all, is the best way to keep good government workers in the public service. Although there are somewhat limited opportunities for extravagant salaries or promotion, there are still mechanisms through which we can show public employees that we value their work and dedication. Ultimately, whether we can motivate workers in ways that increase job satisfaction or not, we still have overarching questions that are important to continue examining in order to assure are bureaucrats continue serving the American people.

Additional Resources

Denhardt, J.V. and R.B. Denhardt, *The New Public Service: Serving, Not Steering* (New York: M.E. Sharpe, 2011)

Denhardt and Denhardt trace the transition of public service from rowing to steering to listening and serving. In doing so, they discuss ways workers can be motivate to actively buy-in to the ideals of new public service.

Dukakis, M.S. and J.S. Potz, *Leader-Manager in the Public Sector: Managing for Results* (New York: M.E. Sharpe, 2010)

Dukakis and Potz examine forms of public management and how they are best able to lead to increased results within public organizations.

Martin, W.T., *Motivation and Productivity in Public Sector Human Service Organizations* (Westport, CT: Quorum Books, 1988)

Public sector human service organizations have unique problems of employee motivation and productivity, both on the professional and direct service levels. Martin examines these problems in detail and offers practical solutions based on his own extensive personal experience in the field.

Perry, J.L. and A. Hondeghem, *Motivation in Public Management: The Call of Public Service* (New York: Oxford University Press, 2008)

To paraphrase James Madison, "public servants are not angels," but neither are they self-aggrandizing opportunists. The evidence presented in this volume offers a compelling case that motivation theory should be grounded not only in rational choice models, but altruistic and prosocial perspectives as well. In addition to reviewing evidence from many disciplines, the volume extensively reviews research in public management conducted under the rubric of "public service motivation."

van Dooren, W., G. Bouckaert, and J. Halligan, *Performance Management in the Public Sector* (New York: Routledge, 2010)

Tackling the key topics of reform and modernization, this book systematically examines performance in public management systems.

ISSUE 13

Should Incrementalism Be the Guiding Budgeting Philosophy of Public Agencies?

YES: Aaron Wildavsky and Naomi Caiden, from *The New Politics of the Budgetary Process*, Third Edition (Longman, 1997)

NO: Aidan Kelly, from "An End to Incrementalism? The Impact of Expenditure Restraint on Social Service Budgets, 1979–1986," *Journal of Social Policy* (April 1989)

Learning Outcomes

After reading this issue, you should be able to:

- Gain an understanding of budgeting in public agencies.
- Define incrementalism.
- Discuss the arguments for and against incremental budgets.
- Describe alternative approaches to incrementalism.
- Understand programs for which incremental budgeting is appropriate.
- Understand how incrementalism can be used to minimize political conflict.

ISSUE SUMMARY

YES: Aaron Wildavsky and Naomi Caiden argue that incremental budgeting accurately reflects the nature of the political process in the United States. Conflict is minimized by accepting this reality and focusing on only a handful of discretionary items.

NO: Aidan Kelly argues that incremental budgeting has not been shown to occur throughout many social service departments in England. Most troubling, however, is that much of the success in the departments occurred within nonincremental budgeting frameworks.

In the 1960s, Peter Pyhrr, in his role as Division Coordinator at Texas Instruments, implemented a budgeting strategy known as zero-base budgeting (ZBB). ZBB requires that budget proposals be combined into groups called "decision packages." Upper level managers are responsible ranking the decision packages according to priority. Decision packages are selected until available revenue to fund packages is depleted. Impressed with this approach, Georgia Governor Jimmy Carter invited Pyhrr to act as budget consultant for the implementation of ZBB at the state level. During the 1976 presidential campaign, Governor Carter advocated adopting ZBB at the national level. Ultimately, ZBB was never fully implemented at the national level, leading to continued reliance on incrementalism as a budgeting strategy.

Ideally, the budget process would be rational. Rational-comprehensive decision making proceeds along a linear path. A problem is identified, decision criteria are established, alternative solutions are considered against criteria, and the "best" alternative is selected and implemented. The stepwise approach makes the process rational and selecting from among all possible alternatives is comprehensive. Unfortunately, political reality often makes a rational-comprehensive approach unlikely, if not impossible. Herbert Simon (1945) argued that human behavior is defined by bounded rationality. This includes limits on time, limited information, and cognitive limits. Simon argued that bounded rationality produces "satisficing," a situation in which a decision maker selects from among satisfactory options. Charles Lindblom (1959) further elaborated this notion, questioning the likelihood of any completely rational decision-making process. Rather than a completely rational approach, Lindblom argued that decisions tend to be made based on historical experience and a willingness to make incremental changes to current policy. Lindblom calls these incremental changes "successive limited comparisons," the term itself contrasting heavily with the rational comprehensive approach. Acknowledging the limits of time and scarce resources, a satisficer adopting a policy of making successive limited comparisons can still make acceptable decisions.

The budget process is highly political. In fact, Lynch (2004) remarks that "the political context of budgeting often forces analysts to realize that politics supersedes rationality." A government budget is a political document that allocates scarce resources for agreed-upon policies. Government budgets usually start as an executive request, containing all department and agency budget requests. Agencies compete with each other for funding, arguing to the decision makers that their program is more essential than the others. At the national level, the president utilizes the Office of Management and Budget to analyze requests and compile them into an overall budget proposal. The executive budget is submitted to a legislature for approval. At the national level, presidents tend to present budgets to Congress in the first week of February. Congress then conducts analysis of the presidential budget, with the assistance of the Congressional Budget Office. The budget committees of both houses of Congress produce a budget resolution by April 15, which does not require the approval of the president. By mid-May, appropriations committees in both houses recommend funding allocation levels. This compressed time schedule, not to mention the political nature of the process, can lend itself to incremental decision making, tempting agency heads to propose funding levels marginally different from prior years and congressional decision makers to appropriate funding in a similar manner.

Perhaps incremental budgeting is reasonable, given the limits of time, resources, and abilities. However, government budgets are made to accomplish public policy objectives, advanced in the interest of the citizenry. Spending is accomplished through the collection of revenue, taxes paid by individual citizens and organizations. Decision makers responsible for budget creation wield extraordinary power to impact citizens' lives. Does incremental budgeting, in which prior requests can weigh more heavily than current justifications, represent a method of budgeting that exhibits a reverence for the responsibility government has to protect and promote its citizens? Several budget reforms have been designed to address that question, attempting to improve the rationality of the budget process. Planning-programming-budgeting (PPB) was an approach to budgeting that called for increased use of analysis, including marginal utility analysis and cost-benefit analysis, and the grouping of government functions in to programs. In addition, PPB incorporated planning beyond the current budget year, perhaps five years. Secretary of Defense Robert McNamara implemented PPB in the Department of Defense in the 1960s, followed by President Johnson's mandate that it be used by other agencies. PPB was eventually deemed too complex for widespread use, and the Nixon administration halted its use.

A later attempt to inject rationality in the budget process is ZBB. By forcing decision makers to consider programs by ranking them, managers were required to defend program activities and costs. Although the name Zero-base budgeting suggests that every program was justified from zero each year, this was often not the case. However, managers were sometimes required to consider scenarios in which programs were funded a lower level than prior years, in order to encourage meaningful rankings and a willingness to defend hard choices. The notion of ZBB is appealing to those who seek a more rational budget process. However, in practice, ZBB exhibited numerous problems. First, the sheer amount of analysis and paperwork required by the process overwhelmed managers. The ZBB experiment in Georgia produced 10,000 decision packages. Furthrmore, Lynch (2004) argues that the effectiveness of ZBB is dependent on the programs analyzed, suggesting that applying the techniques of ZBB to government entitlement programs, the spending for which decision makers have no control, is "logically impossible." Like planning-programming-budgeting, the effectiveness of ZBB seems be contingent upon both the type of government activity and internal support for its use. Although these more rational methods may appeal to those seeking to increase budgetary responsibility, incremental budgeting allows decision makers to satisfice and produce a budget for a vast bureaucratic enterprise in a relatively timely manner.

In the YES selection, Aaron Wildavsky and Naomi Caiden argue that the use of incremental budgeting reflects the state of politics in the United States.

What it lacks in rationality, it gains in conflict resolution and expediency. In contrast, in the NO selection, Aiden Kelly uses comparative analysis to demonstrate that more rational budgeting approaches can be used effectively, providing evidence that the most successful government departments utilize nonincremental approaches.

YES

**Aaron Wildavsky and
Naomi Caiden**

The New Politics of the Budgetary Process, Third Edition

. . .

Incremental Budgeting

The largest determining factor of this year's budget is last year's. Most of each budget is a product of previous decisions. The budget may be conceived of as an iceberg; by far the largest part lies below the surface, outside the control of anyone. Many items are standard, simply reenacted every year unless there is a special reason to challenge them. Long-range commitments have been made, and this year's share is scooped out of the total and included as part of the annual budget. The expenses of mandatory programs (entitlements), such as price supports or veterans' pensions, must be met. Some ongoing programs that appear to be satisfactory are no longer challenged. Agencies are going concerns and a minimum must be spent on housekeeping (though this item is particularly vulnerable to attack because it does not appear to involve a reduction in services or benefits). Powerful political support makes including other activities inevitable. At any one time, after past commitments," are paid for, a rather small percentage—seldom larger than 30 percent, often smaller than 5—is within the realm of anybody's (including congressional and Budget Bureau) discretion as a practical matter.

Budgeting is incremental, not comprehensive. The beginning of wisdom about an agency budget is that it is almost never actively reviewed as a whole every year, in the sense of reconsidering the value of all existing programs as compared to all possible alternatives. Instead, it is based on last year's budget with special attention given to a narrow range of increases or decreases. General agreement on past budgetary decisions combined with years of accumulated experience and specialization allows those who make the budget to be concerned with relatively small increments to an existing base. Their attention is focused on a small number of items over which the budgetary battle is fought. Political reality, budget officials say, restricts attention to items they can do something about—a few new programs and possible cuts in old ones.

Budgeting Is Linked to Base and Fair Shares

Central to incrementalism is the concept of the base. The base is the general expectation that programs will be carried on at close to the going level of expenditures. Having a project included in the agency's base thus means more than just getting it in the budget for a particular year. It means the expectation that the expenditure will continue, that it is accepted as part of what will be done, and, therefore, that it will normally not be subjected to intensive scrutiny. (The word *base,* incidentally, is part of the common parlance of officials engaged in budgeting, and it would make no sense if experience led them to expect wide fluctuations from year to year, rather than additions to or subtractions from some relatively steady point.)

Linked to the concept of the base is the idea of "fair share." Fair share means not only the base an agency has established but also the expectation that the agency will receive some proportion of funds, if any, which are to be increased over or decreased below the base of the other governmental agencies. Fair share, then, reflects a convergence of expectations on roughly how much an agency is to receive in comparison to others.

The absence of a base, or an agreement on fair shares, makes it much harder to calculate what the agency or program should get. That happens when an agency or program is new or when rapid shifts of sentiment toward it take place. When times are tough, the base is subject to debate and adjustment. The base may be defined either as the "current estimate" (existing spending level of an agency) or next year's anticipated cost of maintaining programs at current levels of service (particularly important in inflationary times). In any case there will be disagreement on what constitutes the base.

Budgeting Is Consensual

There must be agreement on the general direction of public policy, at least on most past policies, or Congress would be swamped with difficult choices. Past policies would have to be renegotiated every year, a time-consuming and enervating process. Simultaneously, new programs are sure to engender controversy; without agreement that keeps the past mostly out of contention, it becomes harder to deal with the present. Consensus on policies need not be total; conflict is ever-present. Yet if disagreement encompasses too many policies, aids to calculation will not work well.

Budgeting Is Historical

One way of dealing with a problem of huge magnitude is to make rough guesses while letting experience accumulate. When the consequences of various actions become apparent, it is then possible to make modifications to avoid the difficulties. Since members of Congress usually serve for several years before getting on appropriations committees, and since they are expected to serve an apprenticeship before making themselves heard, the more influential among them typically have long years of experience in dealing with their specialties. They have absorbed the meaning of many past moves and are prepared to apply the results of previous calculations to present circumstances. In this way the magnitude of any one decision at any one time is reduced, and with it the burden of calculation.

A line-item budgetary form facilitates this historical approach. Instead of forging on various programs, as a whole, the committees usually can concentrate on changes in various items—personnel, equipment, maintenance, specific activities—which make up the program. By keeping categories constant over a number of years, and by requiring that the previous and present year's figures be placed in adjacent columns, calculations made in the past need not be gone over again completely. And though members know that the agency is involved in various programs, the line-item form enables them to concentrate on the less divisive issue of how much for each item.

Yet the past is not a foolproof guide to the future. Because so many actions are being undertaken at the same time, it is hard to disentangle the effects of one particular action compared to others. Consequently, disputes may raise about the benefits of continued support for an item. Ultimately, reliance on a theory of cause and effect to provide guidance as to what is expected to happen becomes necessary.

Budgeting Is Fragmented

Budgets are made in fragments. Agencies develop budgetary requests based on their specialized needs. These requests are then channeled to any number of the multiple levels of specialization within Congress—the House and Senate appropriations committees, their subcommittees, the subject areas within these subcommittees, the Senate Appropriations Committee appeals procedure the Conference Committee, and the authorizations functions of the substantive committees and their specialized subcommittees. Even the subcommittees do not deal with all items in the budget but will pay special attention to instances of increases or decreases over the previous year. In this way, it might be said, subcommittees deal with a fragment of a fragment of the whole.

Budgeting Is Simplified

Another way of handling complexity is to see how actions on simpler items can be indices for more complicated ones. Instead of dealing directly with the cost of a huge new installation, for example, decision-makers may look at how personnel and administrative costs, or real estate transactions with which they have some familiarity, are handled. If these items are treated properly, then they may feel better able to trust administrators with the larger ones. Unable to handle the more complex problems, decision makers may retreat to the simple ones.

Budgeting Is Social

Participants take clues from how others behave. They try to read character to reach programs. This method calls for looking at the administrative officials responsible rather than at the subject matter. To see if they are competent and reliable, officials can be questioned on a point here and there, a difficulty in this or that. One senior congressman reported that he followed an administrator's testimony to probe for weaknesses, looking for "strain in voice or manner," "covert glances," and so on.[1] Also, if an official can get people to go along, and if too many others do not complain too long and loud, then he may take the fact of agreement on something as his measure of success.

Budgeting Is "Satisficing"

Calculations may be simplified by lowering one's sights. Although they do not use Herbert Simon's vocabulary, budget officials do not try to maximize but, instead, they "satisfice" (satisfy and suffice).[2] Which is to say that the budgeters do not try for the best of all possible worlds (whatever that might be) but, in their own words, try to "get by," to "come out all right," to "avoid trouble," to "avoid the worst." And since the budget comes up every year, and deals largely with piecemeal adjustment, this is one way to correct glaring weaknesses as they arise.

Budgeting Is Treated as if It Were Nonprogrammatic

This statement does not mean that people do not care about programs; they do. Nor does it mean that they do not fight for or against some programs; they do. What it does mean is that, given considerable agreement on policy, decision makers may see most of their work as marginal monetary adjustments to existing programs so that the question of the ultimate desirability of most programs arises only once in a while. "A disagreement on money isn't like a legislative program . . . ," one appropriations committee member said in a typical statement, "it's a matter of money rather than a difference in philosophy." An appropriations committee member explains how disagreements are handled in the markup session when members retire behind closed doors to work out their recommendations. (Nowadays many such sessions are open.) "If there's agreement, we go right along. If there's a lot of controversy we put the item aside and go on. Then, after a day or two, we may have a list of ten controversial items. We give and take and pound them down till we get agreement."[3] Obviously, they did not feel too strongly about each item or they could not agree so readily.

Budgeting Is Repetitive

Decision making in budgeting is carried on with the knowledge that few problems have to be "solved" once and for all. Everyone knows that a problem may be dealt with over and over again. Hence considerations that a member of Congress neglects one year may be taken up another year, or in a supplementary action during the same year. Problems are not so much solved as they are worn down by repeated attacks until they are no longer pressing or have been superseded by other problems. Problem-succession, not problem solving, best describes what happens.

Budgeting Is Sequential

The appropriations committees do not try to handle every problem at once. On the contrary, they do not deal with many problems in a particular year, and those they do encounter are dealt with mostly in different places and at different times. Many decisions made in previous years are allowed to stand or to vary slightly without question. Then committees divide up subjects for more intensive inquiry among subcommittees and their specialists. Over the years, subcommittees center now on one and then on another problem. When budgetary decisions made by one subcommittee adversely affect those of another, the difficulty is handled by "fire-truck tactics," that is, by dealing with each problem in turn in whatever jurisdiction it appears. Difficulties are overcome not so much by central coordination or planning as by a cybernetic approach—attacking each manifestation in the different centers of decision in sequence.

These aids ease the burden of calculations that are necessary for the development of a budget. Because attention is focused on the increment rather than on the relative value of a particular program compared to others, aids to calculation also serve to moderate conflict. The specialized and apparently nonprogrammatic character of decisions enhances the appearance of the budgetary process as technical. Since decisions are simplified and are made in different arenas at different times, the chance that severe conflict will converge is reduced. In such a situation, the role of participants—agencies, appropriations committees, and the Bureau of the Budget—were clearly defined.

. . .

Notes

1. L. Dwaine Marvick, *Congressional Appropriation Politics,* Ph.D. Dissertation, Columbia University, 1952, p. 297.

2. Herbert, Simon, *Models of Man* (New York: Wiley, 1957); see also Jerome S. Bruner, Jacqueline J. Goodnow, and George A. Austin, *A Study of Thinking* (New York: Wiley, 1956), for a fascinating discussion of strategies of concept attainment useful for dealing with the problem of complexity.

3. Simon, *Models of Man.*

Aidan Kelly  **NO**

An End to Incrementalism? The Impact of Expenditure Restraint on Social Services Budgets, 1979–1986

Adrian Webb once described the process of resource allocation in social service departments as 'one of the great mysteries of social services policy making,' a situation Judge has attributed to social administration's traditional preoccupation with establishing the legitimacy of demands for social services rather than with how resources are allocated between competing demands. Since the advent of a government committed to 'rolling back' the welfare state, greater understanding of the nature and outcome of resource allocation processes within welfare agencies has become an important objective for academics and welfare professionals. Although developed largely to account for national level budget decisions, the theory of incrementalism is a useful starting point for the exploration of resource allocation processes in local authority social services departments (SSDs).

This paper aims to assess the ability of the theory of incremental budgeting to predict changes in the level of expenditure allocated to various client groups and forms of care.[1] The data used covers the period 1979 to 1986, allowing a detailed assessment of the impact of expenditure restraint on incremental budgeting in the social services. After describing the theory of incrementalism, the paper reviews the findings of previous studies of resource allocation in the social services. The problems of operationalising incrementalism are then discussed and the measures adopted defined. The following sections present findings that assess the extent to which:

1. changes in the SSD expenditure outcomes between 1978/9 and 1985/6 are consistent with the predictions of the theory of incremental budgeting;
2. SSD budgetary outcomes became more incremental as the period of expenditure restraint became more protracted; and,
3. those SSDs that experienced the greater degree of expenditure restraint were the most incremental.

The paper then proceeds to examine what expenditures have been allowed to grow or decline in the less incremental SSDs. The paper concludes with an

From *Journal of Social Policy*, April 1989, pp. 188–193, 207–209. Copyright © 1989 by Cambridge University Press. Reprinted by permission.

assessment of the implications of the findings for the development of a theory of resource allocation in welfare agencies.

Incrementalism and Budgeting in Social Service Departments

Incrementalism is a theory of budgeting that has close intellectual links with the 'muddling through' perspective developed by Charles Lindblom as an antidote to the waves of rationalisation that many public sector organisations were subjected to by management consultants and their political allies in the 1960s and early 1970s. These explicitly normative models of resource allocation suggest that budgeting should follow a comprehensive process of analysing policy objectives, prioritising competing objectives, and evaluating means. Systematic goal definition, prioritisation and means evaluation are, the rational analysts would argue, likely to result in a non-incremental switch of resources towards prioritised activities and to more cost effective means of achieving objectives.

Critics of these proposals assert that budgetary reality rarely conforms to this ideal and that financial allocations tend to reflect inherited, unanalysed commitments to produce a range of service outputs whose effects are seldom evaluated. As described by its most prominent advocate, this perspective argues that:

> Budgeting is incremental not comprehensive. The beginning of wisdom about an agency budget is that it is almost never reviewed as a whole year ... Instead it is based on last year's budget with special attention given to a narrow range of increases or decreases.

The contrast between rational comprehensive and incrementalist models of the resource allocation process are summarised in Figure 1.

Incremental budgeting is a way of describing resource allocation processes where financial allocations reflect the pursuit of marginally redefined policy goals by corresponding marginal adjustments in heads of expenditure. The incremental budgetary process scrutinises proposals for marginal changes

Figure 1

Two Models of Budgetary Processes and Outcomes

	Rational budgeting	Incremental budgeting
Processes	analysis of objectives needs/demand oriented strategic analysis forecasting/planning review base budgets	means-based 'analysis' services oriented use of decision rules retrospective defend base budgets
Outcomes	change in budget shares budgets do not change pro-rata	stable budget shares budgets change pro-rata with total expenditure

in the internal allocation of resources between various heads of expenditure and, as a consequence, budgetary outcomes tend to be small, equal additions or reductions from 'the traditional budget.' Incrementalist research on budgetary outcomes has examined changes in the size of budgets over time, drawing upon the incrementalist theory of budgetary processes in order to account for these changes.

Although they are relatively few in number, previous studies of social services expenditure have tended to support the theory of incremental budgeting. In their study of budgeting in 76 SSDs between 1979–80 and 1980–81, Ferlie and Judge found that incrementalism was 'well established.' Using Judge's terminology, the size of the cake is first determined, then more or less sliced pro-rata to produce incremental allocations to each activity. There was some room for choice in distributing 'the crumbs,' but these produced only marginal shifts of resources between the various activities. In an in-depth study of two SSDs, Glennerster *et al.* found in one authority that the aim was to preserve existing services with little analysis or review of the adequacy of this base, although some protection was extended to priority groups. In the other, there was a search for economies and savings 'across the board,' and the social services directorate was required to produce a list of cuts that would produce savings of 5 per cent and 10 per cent of the total social services expenditure. In a series of studies of aggregate SSD spending, Webb and Wistow found some evidence of 'expediency' in the decimation of the capital programme, and some evidence of rational planning in the growth of community care for the elderly, but they conclude that incrementalism was the dominant force in determining patterns of expenditure:

> . . . [the] overwhelming conclusion appears to be . . . that . . . net current expenditure . . . was very largely allocated in proportion to the historic budget shares rather than in accordance with changes in need priorities or policies to secure greater cost effectiveness. It was largely the proportionate allocation of growth to activities with different expenditure baselines which produced the appearance of changed priorities in budgeting.

More recently, however, they have noted that the situation is too complex to allow this general conclusion to stand unqualified, since many SSDs have sought to become less incremental.

In sum, however, these studies support the theory of incremental budgeting and the prediction that SSDs will have responded to expenditure restraint by implementing 'across the board' reductions in the rate of expenditure growth. Further support for this expectation is provided by the plausibility of the argument that there are intra-organisational supports for incrementalism that prevent the specification of priorities and the pursuit of cost-effectivess. These supports are of two kinds: the cognitive limits to rational policy making and the intra-organisational politics of resource allocation. This is the explanatory core of incrementalist theory and if it is plausible as a description of SSDs this would provide further grounds for predicting incremental budgetary outcomes in SSD expenditure. The next section considers the incrementalist account of intra-organisational decision making processes and its relevance to SSDs.

The Cognitive Bases of Incrementalism

March and Simon have described the way in which organisations set 'cognitive limits' on the process of policy making and implementation through their structural arrangements, information systems and socialisation patterns. The consequences are 'bounded rationality' in goal identification and means evaluation; and 'satisficing' rather than maximising in goal attainment. Incrementalism in policy making and resource allocation is supported by the culture of the organisation: 'daily routine drives out planning.' Planning and innovation are likely to occur when there is some clearly defined crisis facing the organisation.

Apart from these routine cultural supports for incrementalism in organisations, there are additional problems of implementing the comprehensive rational model in welfare agencies. Prominent amongst these are the practical difficulties involved in implementing rigorous evaluation research designs, and in the measurement of policy outcomes. Assessing the comparative cost effectiveness of alternative policies involves complex policy analysis and sophisticated research designs. Policy research, at the local authority departmental level, is often largely concerned with identifying changes in the pattern of need such as those of a demographic nature, and monitoring national-level service evaluations and policy guidelines. Departments themselves have limited resources for the application of comprehensive rational analysis of the kind required to challenge established incremental patterns of resource allocation. The need for inhouse research/policy units has become accepted. Nonetheless, in 1986 the average spent on research and development was less than half of one percent of total SSD expenditure. We know very little about the impact of policy analysis and research at the local level. In so far as policy change results from research and policy analysis, however, it is likely to be that conducted by the DHSS, the Social Work Service (now Inspectorate), Royal Commissions, client based pressure groups and other national-level agencies.

When confronted by the complexity of policy analysis and evaluation, decision makers seek 'aids to calculation' one of which is to presume the validity of the existing historical budget and not subject it to review or investigation. Incrementalism limits the search for data with which to assess the relative worth of policy options, it gives clear guides to action, and it avoids protracted conflict over budgets. These organisational supports for incremental budgeting are reinforced by the pluralistic politics of organisations.

The Political Bases of Incrementalism

Incrementalism is not simply a function of limited analytical capacity, it is also a consequence of the fact that budgetary processes are characterised by alliance building and bargaining. Organisation structures, reinforced by patterns of recruitment, often shape a complex set of horizontal and vertical interest groups with associated beliefs and values reflected in policy preferences. Local authority SSDs are a conglomeration of historically separate services that have proved resistant to attempts at integration. They have inherited patterns of provision for a wide range of service users including children and their families; the elderly;

the mentally ill; the mentally handicapped; and the disabled. These differences are reinforced by patterns of professional recruitment and by differences in the balance between professional and non-professional staff. These features would suggest that the budgetary process in SSDs is likely to be characterised by highly pluralistic bargaining between those responsible for different user groups and between those involved in different forms of care. This pluralism is of the kind often linked to incremental budgetary outcomes. The rational model of policy making tends to presume a high degree of consensus on goals and values and a strong centralised policy making body, yet the plurality of interests within SSDs makes this unlikely. The assumptions of the rational model are in sharp contrast to variations in beliefs about appropriate policy objectives, decision making arrangements and criteria of evaluation. The problems involved in translating organisation goals into measurable 'performance indicators' result in part from the fact that policy objectives are often inherently ambiguous. Thus the pluralistic politics of organisations tends to undermine the rational model of resource allocation.

In organisations where there is a lack of consensus on values and policy objectives, participants in the budgetary process seek to minimise the possible impact of any redistribution on their own areas of work by adopting the 'fair shares' principle. The proposition that each of a range of budget heads should be allocated only marginal changes is likely to attract widespread agreement between section managers, since the alternative 'rational' approach to resource allocation generates uncertainty and may lead to some services being given higher priority than others. Second, the pattern of interests and alliances encourages incrementalism since it will be easy to mobilise support for incremental change that reinforces the political status quo: pluralistic patterns of 'partisan-mutual adjustment' are usually linked to incremental policy change.

Taken together these arguments suggest there are intra-organisational conditions that place cognitive and political limits on the use of the comprehensive rational model of budgeting and that these limits are likely to operate in SSDs. Assuming these conditions to be permanent, there was little prospect for non-incremental policy change in SSDs until the late seventies when the debate was revitalised by assessments of the likely impact of expenditure restraint on resource allocation processes and outcomes. It is to these arguments that we now turn.

. . .

Incrementalism is a theory of resource allocation that resonates with much common sense experience of budgetary processes and outcomes. Its predictions are underpinned by plausible accounts of intra-agency conditions that have gained it widespread acceptance in the academic literature on public sector budgeting. Despite having long since 'passed into conventional wisdom,' there remains uncertainty as to how it should be operationalised in empirical research. The theory is not clear in defining the most appropriate measure, and the degree of support for the theory is dependent on the measure of incrementalism adopted. 'Incremental' can be taken to mean changes in budgets pro-rata with changes in the size of the agency's total budget or it can refer to the stability of the shares of the budget taken by each component activity of the agency.

In assessing the hypothesis that SSD outcomes are incremental additions and subtractions from the traditional budget, the data show that between the years 1979 to 1986 the mean percentage change in budgets was 73 per cent greater or lesser than the change in the total agency budget. In the same period, the budget shares remained stable with a mean change of only plus or minus 2 per cent. There is little support for incrementalism when it comes to pro-rata percentage changes in budgets, but some when looking at stability in budget shares. As regards the impact of expenditure restraint on the degree of incrementalism, the relationship between restraint and incrementalism is activity-specific: some activities become more incremental, some less so. The summary indices show a decline in the overall level of incrementalism and suggest that the relationship between restraint and non-incremental budgeting will tend to become stronger as the general climate of restraint continues to prevail.

Prolonged restraint leads to some non-incremental allocations in the most restrained SSDs. These non-incremental shifts in expenditure can be clearly linked to the pursuit of the community care strategy within state-provided services for children and the elderly. In the absence of data on these budgetary processes, one can only speculate as to whether the observed decline in the level of incrementalism in the more restrained authorities is due to changes in the cognitive and political conditions within SSDs previously supportive of higher degrees of incrementalism. If this is a reasonable assumption, then it follows that the widespread adoption of the community care strategy is dependent on increased analytical capacity and greater consensus on these policy objectives within SSDs.

An important rival explanation is to be found in the changing weight behind the micro-political interests of politicians, managers, professionals and consumers. These pluralistic interests within SSDs may vary in their ability to define and respond to crises and vary in their capacity to mobilise power to pursue their competing rationalities. Professional 'rationalities' are, for instance, primarily concerned with demand planning: 'what needs should be met and how.' This orientation may not be seen by senior officers and social services committees as central to the problem of 'surviving' with limited resources. Managerial 'rationality,' on the other hand, is in the ascendancy, and provides clearer guidance on the adequate functioning of the agency in response to both resource constraints and changes in level of need/demand for services. The observed non-incremental shifts to community care could result from professional, or indeed consumer, preferences for community care, but, the case for it being a managerial response appears stronger.

Policy shifts, and the forces behind them, are not independent of the institutional environment of local SSDs. There is a recognisable need to relate change in SSDs to central government policies, political balances, and professional developments in addition to demographic change. This would be stating the obvious were it not for incrementalism's 'blinkered' focus on intra-agency forces for stability to the neglect of both change and the wider context of the agency. The dominance of the incrementalist perspective has directed attention away from the problem of analysing both the intra-agency forces challenging incrementalism and their relationship to the organisation's environment.

EXPLORING THE ISSUE

Should Incrementalism Be the Guiding Budgeting Philosophy of Public Agencies?

Critical Thinking and Reflection

1. What is incremental budgeting? What are its strengths and weaknesses as a budgeting philosophy?
2. Is it possible to have incremental policy changes? Why or why not?
3. What aspects of public agencies make incrementalism a useful budgeting strategy?
4. If we do not use incremental budgeting, what other options are possible? How do they compare to incrementalism?
5. In what ways does incrementalism minimize political conflict potentially? Is this healthy for democracy? Why or why not?

Is There Common Ground?

Since the advent of public administration, we have witnessed numerous budgetary paradigms with each new iteration claiming to be the ultimate solution to our nation's needs. Yet, instead of finding the panacea of financial planning, we have faced a revolving door of dominant strategies. More so than others, the concept of incrementalism regularly emerges in budgetary debates and battles. On its face, this continual reemergence makes sense since the idea of slowly increasing or decreasing an agency's funding is easier to envision that zeroing out everyone each year or basing funding completely off of performance.

When it comes to selecting a guiding philosophy, however, it is difficult to determine if there is any single theory that will always work. Policy used to move incrementally from year to year, yet an increasingly polarized electorate seems more willing than ever to change positions as the wind blows. With this fact hanging over public administration, it becomes difficult to assess if incremental budgeting can work in an environment where the system can change quickly. Thus, rather than debating the overall applicability of incrementalism to budgeting today, our time could be better served by figuring out the circumstances under which different budgeting philosophies are most likely to be utilized.

Additional Resources

Hope, J. and R. Fraser, *Beyond Budgeting: How Managers Can Break Free from the Annual Performance Trap* (Boston, MA: Harvard Business Press, 2003)

The annual budgeting process is a trap. Pressured by fixed targets and performance incentives, managers focus on making the numbers instead of making a difference, meeting set goals instead of maximizing potential. With their compensation at stake, managers often resort to deceitful—even unethical—behavior. In the end, everybody loses—the employee, the company, and ultimately the customer. Hope and Fraser argue that companies must abandon traditional budgeting contracts in favor of a radical new model that links performance measurement to evolving competitive benchmarks—and shifts the firm's focus from controlling employee behavior to delivering customer value.

Lee, R.D., R.W. Johnson, and P.G. Joyce, *Public Budgeting Systems,* 8th ed. (Sudbury, MA: Jones and Bartlett, 2007)

Lee, Johnson, and Joyce's book surveys the current state of budgeting throughout all levels of the U.S. government. The text emphasizes methods by which financial decisions are reached within a system as well as ways in which different types of information are used in budgetary decision making.

Meyers, R.T., *Handbook of Government Budgeting* (New York: Jossey-Bass, 1998)

In this comprehensive reference, Roy T. Meyers provides an invaluable tool for anyone who wants to learn how the government budgeting process works, where it does not work, and how it can be improved. Filled with insights and wisdom from 36 contributors, this book presents an encyclopedic account of budgeting innovations today.

Rubin, I.S., *The Politics of Public Budgeting: Getting and Spending, Borrowing and Balancing,* 5th ed. (Washington, DC: CQ Press, 2005)

In this comprehensive reference, Roy T. Meyers provides an invaluable tool for anyone who wants to learn how the government budgeting process works, where it doesn't work, and how it can be improved. Filled with insights and wisdom from thirty-six contributors, this book presents an encyclopedic account of budgeting innovations today.

Shah, A., *Budgeting and Budgetary Institutions* (Washington, DC: World Bank Publications, 2007)

Budgeting and budgetary institutions play a critical role in resource allocation, government accountability, and improved fiscal and social outcomes. This volume distills lessons from practices in designing better fiscal institutions, citizen friendly budgets, and open and transparent processes of budget preparation and execution.

ISSUE 14

Do We Need More Budget Flexibility for Discretionary Spending Compared to Entitlements?

YES: **Ian Hill, Holly Stockdale, and Brigette Courtot,** from "Squeezing SCHIP: States Use Flexibility to Respond to the Ongoing Budget Crisis," *The Urban Institute Series A*, No. A-65 (June 2004)

NO: **Lyndon B. Johnson,** from *Great Society Speech* (May 1964)

Learning Outcomes
After reading this issue, you should be able to: • Define discretionary spending. • Define entitlement programs. • Gain an understanding of why entitlement programs are often considered to be untouchable. • Describe how President Lyndon Johnson was able to convince Americans that his programs were more than simple policies. • Discuss ways that states can use discretionary spending to alleviate potential budget shortfalls. • Understand the importance of this debate for the modern federal budget battle.

ISSUE SUMMARY

YES: Ian Hill, Holly Stockdale, and Brigette Courtot use survey data to demonstrate the manner by which states utilized budgetary flexibility to tailor the SCHIP program to particular state contexts and weather economic conditions.

NO: In a 1964 commencement address, President Lyndon Johnson argued that the Great Society programs achieved a standing higher than mere policy. The combination of public policy and stirring emotional rhetoric demonstrate the attachment many citizens feel to the Great Society programs and perhaps explain why such entitlement programs are deemed untouchable during the budgetary process.

In a 2007 letter to members of Congress, Congressional Budget Office Director Peter Orszag noted that spending by the U.S. government that year would equal roughly $2.7 billion. He goes on to state that 45 percent of that spending comprised three programs: Medicaid, Medicare, and Social Security. Spending for those three programs would be about 9 percent of the Gross Domestic Product of the United States. According to the National Bureau of Economic Research, an economic crisis began in December of 2007. The effects this economic downturn continued to plague the United States well into 2011. A budget deficit occurs when a government budget proposes more spending outlays than it will generate in revenues. The budget deficit in 2007 was $163 billion. In 2010, the budget deficit was nearly $1.2 trillion.

There are generally two approaches to deal with a budget deficit. The first is to increase revenue. The biggest source of revenue for the U.S. government is taxes on the incomes of its citizens. Remaining revenue sources include payroll taxes, corporate income taxes, excise taxes, and miscellaneous duties and fees. States and local governments also generate revenue through an array of methods, primarily tax collection. Essentially, increasing revenue requires raising taxes. However, raising taxes in a time of economic decline or stagnation is often seen as risky political move, leading many political decision makers to focus on the second approach: reducing spending.

Among other functions, a major purpose of a government budget is that it establishes policy priorities of the government by allocating resources and supporting certain activities. The executive budget is a request to the legislature that money be appropriated to the categories listed in the document. The responsibility of the legislature is to determine whether the spending priorities established in the executive budget are congruent with its own preferences. Fundamentally, budgets allocate scarce resources to activities that are considered politically valuable or necessary. However, certain functions of government are deemed to be essential. Spending for these functions is considered mandatory, as program recipients collect benefits as prescribed by law. As a result, essential programs that mandate spending are commonly referred to as entitlements.

Social Security, Medicare, Medicaid are all entitlement welfare programs. Social Security and Medicare are social insurance programs, which are theoretically financed by the recipients of the program. In other words, Social Security benefits are ostensibly funded by the beneficiary through payroll taxes. In contrast, public assistance programs are subsidized by all taxpayers, regardless of whether they receive benefits of the programs. Medicare and Medicaid are both health care programs. However, Medicare is a social insurance program and Medicaid, which is administered and partially funded by states, is a means-tested welfare program, eligibility for which is based primarily on income. However, all three programs share one important condition: If an individual meets eligibility requirements, benefits are required by law to be distributed.

Congressional Budget Office Director Orszag argues that two major factors contribute to the increase in spending on Social Security, Medicare, and Medicaid. The first is the aging population. Orszag notes that for every person aged 65 and older, there are currently five people in the 20–64 age category. By 2030, it is estimated that the ratio will be 1 to 3. Complicating matters is an increasing life expectancy and a relatively low fertility rate. According to Orszag, the second, and more critical factor, is the increasing costs of health care. Orszag warns that the rate of growth in Medicare and Medicaid spending is projected to grow faster than the economy and all other national government programs. Experts predict that spending for the three programs that already comprise 45 percent of the national government budget will continue to grow. Spending for these programs, it is important to remember, is mandatory. Thus, Social Security, Medicare, and Medicaid, classified as entitlement spending, will experience continued growth, together comprising a larger portion of federal spending.

Mandatory spending accounted for just more than 61 percent of the proposed 2010 federal budget. The other 39 percent is known as discretionary spending, which seems to suggest that it is available to be targeted in budget debates. To be sure, mandatory spending is required by law to be spent. However, much of this discretionary spending pays for the day to day operation of the government. This might lead one to wonder how much government spending is truly discretionary. Defense is considered discretionary. However, many political leaders are reluctant to advocate major cuts in defense spending when the U.S. military is currently engaged in active combat. In fact, virtually all discretionary items in the federal budget attract interested parties or clientele groups who will pressure Congress to cut other programs. Thus, some budget items are mandatory by law while others might be considered politically mandatory.

The budget deficit was well over $1 billion in both 2009 and 2010. The consequences of an economic crisis that began toward the end of 2007 continued to plague the United States well into 2011, causing reluctance among national politicians to advocate widespread revenue increases (although targeted increases on high incomes or long-term capital gains have been discussed). The dire situation has led some to question whether political decision makers should have more budgetary flexibility, allowing them to apply cuts to mandatory spending items. In the YES selection, Ian Hill, Holly Stockdale, and Brigette Courtot argue that budgetary flexibility was being utilized by states in times of economic crisis without dramatically affecting citizens. In the NO selection, President Lyndon Johnson, in an address known as The Great Society Speech, establishes the moral foundation of his Great Society programs. Using inspiring rhetoric, Johnson encourages citizens to join together "to give every citizen an escape from the crushing weight of poverty."

YES

Ian Hill, Holly Stockdale, and Brigette Courtot

Squeezing SCHIP: States Use Flexibility to Respond to the Ongoing Budget Crisis

At the beginning of 2003, nearly every state in the nation was facing its third straight fiscal year budget deficit. According to the National Conference of State Legislatures, states confronted a combined budget deficit of $78.4 billion in fiscal year 2004. Early in the economic downturn, states closed gaps using reserves, special "rainy day" funds, budget and accounting maneuvers, and tobacco settlement funds. But increasingly, states have had to make real program cuts to address budget shortfalls. During fiscal year (FY) 2003, 40 states—the most in recorded history—made either across-the-board or selective program cuts totaling $11.8 billion. Few state programs were immune to cuts; even such high-priority programs as Medicaid, K–12 education, higher education, and public safety were reduced in most states.

But how has the State Children's Health Insurance Program (SCHIP) fared during these difficult times? To answer this question two years ago, we interviewed SCHIP administrators and other state officials in 13 states as part of our multiyear SCHIP evaluation conducted under the *Assessing the New Federalism* (ANF) project. We found that SCHIP had largely "dodged the first budget ax" in FY 2002: only one state had reduced eligibility thresholds under the program (for parents, not children); no states had cut benefits (while four states actually expanded coverage of such critical services as dental care); only two states had raised cost sharing; and only one state had cut provider reimbursement. The one program area where a significant number of states had reduced spending— roughly half of the 13 states we studied—was outreach.

State officials explained why SCHIP seemed largely immune to significant cuts, citing its strong popularity among consumers, providers, and politicians; the fact that it was small and inexpensive (relative to Medicaid) and not an entitlement (making it a program that policymakers felt they could "control"); its high federal matching rate (making it a less attractive target for cuts); and its success at its critical objective—insuring low-income children. But these same officials hinted that continued fiscal pressures could result in future cuts to SCHIP.

Given states' ongoing budget difficulties, it was important to repeat our survey last year and update our understanding of how SCHIP programs were

From *The Urban Institute Series A*, A-65, June 2004, pp. 1–10. Copyright © 2004 by The Urban Institute. Reprinted by permission.

affected. Telephone interviews with state SCHIP officials conducted during September and October 2003 found that the program was indeed suffering more severe cutbacks than during 2002. Highlights (or lowlights) include the following:

- While none of our study states actually reduced its upper income eligibility threshold, one state—Texas—did change its methodology for counting family income, effectively reducing its upper limit;
- Three states implemented enrollment freezes, placing thousands of children who would have previously been eligible for coverage onto waiting lists;
- Nearly one-third of states enacted changes in enrollment policies, which will make it more difficult for families to apply for SCHIP;
- Half the states raised cost sharing amounts for enrollees and/or imposed new cost sharing on families that didn't previously have to pay;
- Nearly half the states either froze or reduced reimbursement rates to providers serving SCHIP enrollees; and
- Most states discontinued support for outreach activities.

But not all the news was bad. Only two of the 13 study states reduced benefits for children; two-thirds of the study states reported new efforts to simplify enrollment and renewal procedures; and large states such as California and New York implemented innovative initiatives to enroll more children or dramatically expanded outreach spending. Perhaps most important, every state participating in the survey reported that SCHIP programs retained strong political support and fared quite well, relative to other state programs.

Therefore, depending on one's perspective, SCHIP's glass is either half full or half empty in the aftermath of the FY 2004 budget cycle.

SCHIP Programs in the ANF States

In its brief six-year history, the SCHIP program has dramatically affected uninsurance rates in the United States. Nearly 4 million low-income children were enrolled in the program as of June 2003, and rates of uninsurance among low-income children dropped from 12.6 percent to 10.1 percent between 1999 and 2001. Clearly, however, these important gains reflect the fact that SCHIP was implemented during a dramatic economic expansion; the early years of the program witnessed very rapid implementation by the states, as well as unprecedented investment in both outreach and enrollment simplification. States generally implemented comprehensive benefit packages and imposed relatively low levels of cost sharing.

These trends are certainly well represented by the 13 ANF states, which include the four SCHIP programs with the largest enrollment (California's, Florida's, New York's, and Texas's) and together account for nearly two-thirds of total SCHIP enrollment. However, the study states differ from states generally in a number of important ways. First, more ANF states have "separate" SCHIP programs than is the case nationally (11 out of 13 versus two-thirds), meaning a larger proportion of ANF states are able to impose enrollment caps, benefit reductions, and cost sharing hikes. Second, the ANF states have higher than average eligibility thresholds: in 2003, while the national average upper income threshold for SCHIP was 212 percent of FPL, the ANF state average was 227 percent of FPL. Very few states cover parents of SCHIP enrollees, but three ANF states do (New Jersey, Minnesota, and Wisconsin). Finally, the ANF sample includes two of the three states whose programs were "grandfathered" into SCHIP because of their history as state-funded child health programs (Florida and New York). These last three characteristics may be significant, because they indicate that ANF states have historically had more generous coverage, and may have had a longer history of extending child health coverage to children ineligible for Medicaid, than states generally. As a result, ANF states may have faced even greater pressures on their state budgets in 2003, because of increased enrollment and expenditures. On the other hand, they may also be more resilient in the face of budget pressures, given their long-standing commitment to this vulnerable population.

Table 1 provides additional characteristics of SCHIP programs in the 13 ANF states, including recent enrollment figures and state and federal funding information.

Table 1

Characteristics of SCHIP Programs and Financing in Assessing the New Federalism States

State	Program type	Children enrolled June 2002	Children enrolled June 2003	Change (%)	Financing sources
Alabama	S	53,135	60,383	14	General revenue and tobacco settlement funds
California	C	606,546	720,044	19	General revenue and tobacco settlement funds
Colorado	S	43,679	53,118	22	Designated fund; funded by general revenue and tobacco settlement funds
Florida	C	246,432	330,866	34	General revenue and tobacco settlement funds
Massachusetts	C	50,094	56,261	12	Designated fund; funded by general revenue and cigarette taxes
Michigan	C	44,477	51,424	16	General revenue
Minnesota	M	23	19[a]	−17	Provider taxes

(Continued)

Table 1 (Continued)

State	Program type	Children enrolled June 2002	Children enrolled June 2003	Change (%)	Financing sources
Mississippi	S	52,456	56,690	8	General revenue and tobacco settlement funds
New Jersey	C	95,468	92,170	−3	General revenue and tobacco settlement funds
New York	C	526,204	403,935	−23	Provider taxes
Texas	S	529,980	512,986	−3	General revenue and tobacco settlement funds
Washington	S	6,869	7,305	6	Designated fund; funded by provider, liquor, and tobacco taxes as well as tobacco settlement funds
Wisconsin	M	31,861	35,785	12	General revenue and tobacco settlement funds
	C: 6				General revenue: 10
	M: 2				Tobacco settlement funds: 9
Total	S: 5	2,287,224	2,380,967	4[b]	Other sources: 4

Source: Kaiser Commission on Medicaid and the Uninsured ("Program type"); Smith and Rousseau ("Children enrolled" 2002 and 2003 and "Change"); Campaign for Tobacco-Free Kids ("Financing sources").
C = combination; M = Medicaid; S = separate
[a] Minnesota covered children up to 275 percent of the federal poverty level under its MinnesotaCare program when SCHIP legislation was passed, so few children are covered by SCHIP. Minnesota received an SCHIP waiver in 2001 that allows use of SCHIP funds to cover parents of children in MinnesotaCare.
[b] National change was 7 percent.

How Did SCHIP Programs Change During 2003?

In our interviews with SCHIP officials, we asked directors to describe the budget environments in their states and highlight any policy changes made in the areas of eligibility, enrollment, outreach, benefits, cost sharing, provider reimbursement, and crowd out. We concluded our discussions by focusing on whether SCHIP programs continued to enjoy high levels of political support (as had been the case in 2002) and how much that support may have protected the program from cutbacks.

In 2002, SCHIP administrators in the ANF states reported very few actual cutbacks, especially in eligibility or benefits. In interviews, officials relayed policymakers' reluctance to cut this popular program and emphasized that the need for SCHIP (and Medicaid) was heightened during an economic downturn. But last year a distinctly different picture emerged. During 2003, every state in

Table 2

Changes Enacted or under Consideration in SCHIP

State	Eligibility/ Enrollment cap	Enrollment process	Outreach	Benefits	Cost sharing	Reimburse- ment rates	Crowd out
Alabama	−	+	−	+	−, +		+
California		+	−			−	
Colorado	−		−				
Florida	−	+	−	−	−, +		
Massachusetts	*	−, +			−	−	
Michigan	*	+	−				
Minnesota	*	−		+			
Mississippi		−					
New Jersey		+			−		
New York		+	+				
Texas	−	−, +	−	−	−	−	
Washington	*	−, +				−	
Wisconsin					−	−	−

Source: Urban Institute telephone interviews with state SCHIP administrators.
Key: − = Restrictions enacted
+ = Expansions enacted
* = Expanded eligibility for pregnant women

our sample except New York enacted at least one program cut, indicating that severe budget distress is taking its toll on SCHIP. Cuts were made most often in eligibility, enrollment simplification, cost sharing, and provider reimbursement. Additionally, the majority of officials reported that most, if not all, state money for outreach had been eliminated. On a more positive note, most states continue to work on simplifying their enrollment procedures, and the majority of states have either preserved, or even expanded, their benefit packages.

Table 2 summarizes policy changes in the ANF states in 2003. In the sections that follow, we discuss these changes in more detail.

Eligibility

The most obvious way for states to reduce enrollment or control enrollment growth in a children's health insurance program is to cut eligibility. Even Medicaid programs have this flexibility, although once an upper income threshold for Medicaid is established, all children in families with incomes below that level are *entitled* to coverage. Separate SCHIP programs, however, are explicitly not entitlement programs. Like Medicaid, their eligibility thresholds are flexible, but SCHIP enrollment can also be capped if policymakers decide the budget can no longer sustain the program. While only one study state cut eligibility under SCHIP in 2002 (New Jersey, and for parents, not children), four states took such action in 2003. Texas enacted a de facto reduction in income thresholds. Three other states instituted enrollment caps. Specifically,

- Texas changed its income test from a "net" to a "gross" basis, eliminating all deductions from income and effectively reducing its upper income limit from 240 percent of FPL to 200 percent;
- Texas also imposed a 90-day waiting period before program benefits become effective for new enrollees;
- Alabama capped enrollment in the AllKids program in October 2003 and by March 2004, approximately 11,500 children had been on the waiting list;
- Florida imposed an enrollment cap when Healthy Kids enrollment reached just over 271,000 children and had amassed a waiting list of over 100,000 children by January 2004, roughly 25,000 of whom were noncitizen children eligible for the state-only funded component of the KidCare program;
- Colorado instituted its enrollment cap when enrollment reached approximately 53,000 children; the state does not keep a waiting list.

While these cuts clearly signal a different, and negative, trend, it is worth emphasizing that the vast majority of states chose not to impose such drastic reductions. An equal number of study states (four) actually expanded eligibility under SCHIP during 2003, albeit not to children. Both Michigan and Washington extended eligibility to pregnant women with incomes up to 185 percent of FPL, Massachusetts expanded coverage to this population up to 200 percent, and Minnesota up to 275 percent.

Enrollment Procedures

In 2002, no ANF states were interested in making their enrollment procedures more difficult. Rather, state officials repeatedly told us that they were proud of their progress in simplifying SCHIP (and Medicaid for children) enrollment, and said that reversing this progress would be a real step backward. Fiscal pressures in one-third of our study states were apparently severe enough in 2003 to persuade policymakers to take those backward steps. Specifically,

- Three states—Minnesota, Texas, and Washington—reduced continuous eligibility guarantees from 12 months to six;
- Washington discontinued its policy of allowing families to "self declare" their earnings, and has reverted to requiring parents to submit income verification as part of the application process;
- Texas added an assets test to the eligibility determination process for children in families with incomes over 150 percent of FPL, and Minnesota established a new, uniform assets limit for children stricter than the previous SCHIP limit, but more generous than the Medicaid limit; and
- Massachusetts reduced the amount of time that enrollees have to submit their renewal applications from 60 days to 30.

Despite these setbacks, two-thirds of the study sample actually simplified their enrollment processes. For example,

- Florida, New Jersey, and New York redesigned their SCHIP applications to make them easier, more readable, and more user-friendly;
- Alabama, Michigan, and Washington started preprinting their renewal applications for SCHIP enrollees; and
- Five states continue to develop electronic applications for the coming year (Florida, Massachusetts, Michigan, New Jersey, and Texas).

Of particular note, New York took a number of steps to further simplify the renewal process for children enrolled in Child Health Plus and Medicaid. First, the state simplified its renewal application form. Second, it eliminated the face-to-face interview requirement for renewals under Medicaid. Finally, in an unprecedented move, New York implemented "presumptive eligibility" for SCHIP renewals. Under this policy, if a family submits an incomplete renewal package but appears otherwise eligible, the state will continue to cover the child (presuming he or she is still eligible) until a complete package is submitted for review.

California, despite eliminating all funding for outreach over the past two years, began phasing in two new initiatives that promise to significantly streamline entry into the state's Medi-Cal and Healthy Families programs. The first, "express lane eligibility," will use information gathered on the federal Free and Reduced Lunch Program application to complete children's Medi-Cal applications. The second, "CHDP Gateway," will allow uninsured children who receive check-ups through the state's Child Health and Disability Prevention (CHDP) program to be "pre-enrolled" into two months of temporary Medi-Cal/Healthy Families coverage while CHDP providers complete and submit a formal application on their behalf.

Outreach

By our second survey, most ANF states had virtually eliminated outreach funding. In 2002, a majority of states had begun reducing outreach spending, and Massachusetts, Washington, and Wisconsin had "zeroed out" their outreach budgets. Last year, officials in seven states described additional cuts in outreach during 2003 (Alabama, California, Colorado, Florida, Michigan, Mississippi, and Texas).

While Alabama, Mississippi, and Texas eliminated support for their mass media campaigns, the other states discontinued funding for community-based outreach that often involved assisting families with completing their SCHIP/Medicaid applications. In California, large cuts in 2002 saw the elimination of every outreach effort except its Certified Application Assistor (CAA) program. However, midway through 2003, the CAA program was de-funded as well. Colorado and Michigan eliminated similar application assistance fees. These cuts are likely to reduce enrollment significantly, as application assistance programs have been regarded as one of the more effective strategies for enrolling and retaining children in coverage.

Although outreach funding at the state level has been significantly curtailed, officials described several examples of ongoing outreach at the local level, without formal state funding. In Alabama, regional staff continues to encourage potential recipients to sign up for SCHIP and get on the state's new waiting list. In Colorado, outreach workers are conducting training sessions with hospitals and schools and providing some application assistance, albeit without receiving a fee. Mississippi officials describe working with local grantees of the Robert Wood Johnson Foundation–funded "Covering Kids and Families" program to promote SCHIP and Medicaid enrollment. Michigan is using its limited outreach funds to train local health departments on using the state's new electronic application. And Texas continues to provide grants to community-based organizations to support outreach for Medicaid and SCHIP.

Two states—Minnesota and New Jersey—escaped cuts to their outreach budgets. New York was the only state in our sample to actually increase funding for outreach. New York doubled funding of its "Facilitated Enrollment" program, which puts monies out to a large network of community-based organizations to support staff that help families enroll in Child Health Plus and Medicaid.

Benefits

With two notable exceptions, states largely protected their SCHIP benefit packages in 2003. As in 2002, some states actually expanded their coverage. Alabama increased the maximum number of days it covers for substance abuse services, and liberalized its dental benefit (the state will no longer count the cost of preventive dental care against a child's $1,000 annual cap). Minnesota enhanced mental health benefits for at-risk children.

Two states reduced benefits for children, one more severely than the other. Florida imposed a new annual cap on its dental benefit; children will now be covered only for the first $750 of dental care they receive, an amount that state officials reported would meet the needs of the vast majority of enrollees. Texas cut numerous benefits from its package, including dental, vision, chiropractic, home health, and hospice services, as well as benefits for eyeglasses and hearing aids. The state also tried to scale back its behavioral health coverage, but federal CMS officials judged that such a move would reduce Texas's level of coverage below minimum benchmark standards. A modified behavioral health package was restored in February 2004 and the state is paying claims for services received back to September 2003.

New Jersey is the only other state in our sample that curtailed benefits, but did so for parents (not children) by shifting them into the state's Plan D coverage, which is the most limited package offered under Title XXI and places restrictions on dental, chiropractic, long-term care, and certain behavioral health services.

Cost Sharing

SCHIP rules grant states with separate programs considerable latitude in designing cost sharing policies, and permit states to charge premiums, copayments, and coinsurance totaling no more than 5 percent of a family's income. Until now, while states have made significant use of this cost sharing authority, they have rarely imposed cost sharing at levels anywhere near the federal upper limit. Most charge premiums, annual enrollment fees, and copayments at approximately 1 percent of family income.

Table 3

Modifications of Cost Sharing Requirements during FY 2003

State	Eligibility level affected	Premiums	Copayments
Alabama	133–150% of FPL	New annual fee—$50 per child/$150 family maximum	New copayments imposed on families ($0–$10 for pharmacy and medical services)
	151–200% of FPL	Increased annual fee from $50 per child/$150 family maximum to $100 per child/$300 family maximum	Increased copayments to families ($1–$20 for pharmacy and medical services)
Florida	133–200% of FPL	Increased monthly premiums for all families from $15 to $20 per family	Increased copayments for all families (from $3 to $5 for pharmacy and medical services)
Massachusetts	150–200% of FPL	Increased monthly premiums for all families from $10 per child/$30 family maximum to $12 per child/$36 family maximum	No changes
New Jersey	151–200% of FPL	Increased monthly premiums from $15 to $16.50 per family	No changes
	201–250% of FPL	Increased monthly premiums from $30 to $33 per family	
	251–300% of FPL	Increased monthly premiums from $60 to $66 per family	
	301–350% of FPL	Increased monthly premiums from $100 to $110 per family	
Texas	101–150% of FPL	New monthly premiums of $15 per family (previously annual premium of $15 per family)	Increased copayments for all families with incomes at 100% of FPL or above: office visit copay increases of $2 or $3, as well as increases to emergency room and pharmacy copays (increases vary by eligibility band, 100–150% of FPL band had no copays before this change)
	151–185% of FPL	Increased monthly premiums from $15 to $20 per family	
	186–200% of FPL	Increased monthly premiums from $18 to $25 per family	
Wisconsin	150–185% of FPL	Increased annual premiums from 3% of the family's net income to 5%	Increased pharmacy copayments for fee-for-service population (accounts for about 30% of Badgercare) from $1 ($5 maximum) to $3 ($12 maximum)

Source: Urban Institute telephone interviews with state SCHIP administrators.
Note: Native Americans are exempt from all cost sharing measures.

This pattern is apparently reversing. A majority of states in our sample increased their fees during the past year, and one imposed new cost sharing on the poorest families, which did not have to pay such fees previously. Specific changes are detailed below, and in table 3.

- Representing perhaps the largest increase, Wisconsin raised its monthly premium from 3 percent of family income (already the highest SCHIP premium in the nation) to 5 percent (the maximum allowed by law) for families with incomes between 150 and 185 percent of FPL.

- Alabama imposed a new annual fee of $50 per child ($150 per family maximum) on families with incomes between 133 and 150 percent of FPL. The state also raised its existing annual premium for families with incomes between 151 and 200 percent of FPL from $50 per child ($150 family maximum) to $100 per child ($300 family maximum).
- Florida raised its monthly premium by $5, from $15 to $20 per family, for those earning between 133 and 200 percent of FPL.
- Massachusetts raised its premiums from $10 per child per month/$30 family maximum, to $12 per child per month/$36 family maximum, for families with income between 150 and 200 percent of FPL.
- New Jersey implemented a 10 percent across-the-board premium increase, raising its monthly premiums from $15 to $16.50 per family for those earning between 151 and 200 percent of FPL, from $30 to $33 per family for those earning between 201 and 250 percent of FPL, from $60 to $66 per family for those earning between 251 and 300 percent of FPL, and from $100 to $110 per family for those earning between 301 and 350 percent of FPL.
- Texas also dramatically raised fees for some of its lowest income enrollees. For families with earnings between 101 and 150 percent of FPL, the state switched from a $15 per family *annual* fee, to a new $15 per family *monthly* premium. The state also increased monthly premiums from $15 to $20 per family for those earning between 151 and 185 percent of FPL, and from $18 to $25 per family for those earning between 186 and 200 percent of FPL.

States that raised premiums also tended to ratchet up copayments. Alabama imposed new copayments on the poorest enrollees (children in families earning between 133 and 150 percent of FPL) and raised existing copayments for families earning between 151 and 200 percent of FPL. Florida's copayments for pharmacy and medical office visits increased from $3 to $5 for all Healthy Kids enrollees (earning between 133 and 200 percent of FPL). Texas, like Alabama, imposed new copayments on its poorest enrollees (earning below 150 percent of FPL), and increased copayments for all other families. Wisconsin increased pharmacy copayments from $1 to $3 for children in families with income between 150 and 185 percent of FPL enrolled in fee-for-service arrangements.

To reduce the number of families that disenroll owing to nonpayment of premiums, two states expanded payment options for families. In addition to the customary check or money order, Florida now accepts credit card payments over the Internet and via phone, 24 hours a day. Alabama plans to begin accepting credit card payments over the phone in 2004.

Provider Reimbursement

Typically, provider reimbursement is one of the first places states turn when they need to reduce health program costs. But SCHIP has rarely seen reimbursement rate cuts. Our 2002 survey found that only one of the 13 ANF states reduced provider reimbursement in response to growing fiscal pressures.

Last year, however, nearly half the states in our sample reported either a rate freeze or rate cut to SCHIP providers. California and Wisconsin froze rates to participating health plans, Texas reduced its rates by 2.5 percent, and Massachusetts reduced its rates by 3 percent. Washington brought SCHIP capitation rates down to Medicaid levels by eliminating its $8.00 "CHIP Kicker," a payment adjustment that had been added to Medicaid capitation rates to compensate health plans for the expected higher cost of serving SCHIP enrollees.

Crowd Out

Crowd out (substituting public health insurance coverage for private) was one of the most hotly debated issues during the development of SCHIP legislation. Concerns that SCHIP would crowd out children's existing coverage led many states to include policies that discouraged families from dropping their private insurance. The most common policy was waiting periods, during which children must be uninsured before being allowed to enroll in SCHIP. Worries about substitution have apparently diminished among many state policymakers. An increasing number of states have either reduced or eliminated waiting periods, or added various exemptions to waiting periods for families paying high amounts for existing coverage.

States have rarely turned to their crowd out prevention policies to reduce program costs. This year, however, Wisconsin implemented a new policy requiring parents with employment to provide written documentation that they do not have an offer of health insurance at their place of employment. For those families that do have an offer, state officials will investigate whether it is more cost-effective to subsidize employer-sponsored insurance or enroll the family into direct coverage under BadgerCare. To date, enrollment in Wisconsin's "premium assistance" program has been very low, as few families' employer-sponsored coverage has met the cost-effectiveness test. Therefore, it is hard to predict how much this policy will affect the make-up of the SCHIP program.

Notably, Alabama actually liberalized its crowd out policies in 2003. The state added an exception to its 90-day waiting period for children whose existing insurance is an individual policy or was obtained under COBRA arrangements, because of the typically high costs of such coverage.

Administrative Cuts

We asked SCHIP officials if they have made cuts to their administrative budgets. Most said "yes," but described these cuts as relatively insignificant and as not affecting SCHIP program operations. Only one ANF state (California) reported having to lay off staff, but many officials described how early retirement offers and hiring freezes that have left vacancies unfilled contributed to shrinking staffing levels. Officials from two states reported that attrition among senior staff and the resulting loss of "institutional memory" were significant setbacks.

Is the Glass Half Full, or Half Empty?

On one hand, it would be easy to review the findings from this survey and conclude that SCHIP is in trouble. Without question, cuts to SCHIP programs are more widespread than in 2002. In response to ongoing budget shortfalls, a third of the states in our study either reduced eligibility or capped enrollment, closing thousands of children out of coverage, at least for the time being. Most states have discontinued their outreach efforts, which means fewer families will be made aware of programs that can provide their children with health insurance. One-third of states reinstituted application procedures that will make it harder for parents to enroll their children into SCHIP and Medicaid, likely suppressing enrollment even among eligible children. Two large states ratcheted back on benefits coverage, so some children will have to do without dental care and other services. Out-of-pocket expenses will increase for many families, as half the study states imposed new or increased cost sharing onto parents of enrolled children. Higher premiums may also result in more uninsurance among eligible children. And five states either reduced provider reimbursement or froze it at last year's level (effectively cutting rates that didn't keep up with inflation), which may undermine access to care depending on how providers react to the cuts.

Consistent with these findings, SCHIP programs beyond the ANF sample also scaled back their programs in the past year. Three more states froze enrollment under SCHIP by November 2003 (Maryland, Montana, and Utah) one more reduced its upper income eligibility threshold (Alaska, from 200 percent of FPL to 175 percent); four (Arizona, Connecticut, Indiana, and Nebraska) reduced continuous eligibility for children from 12 months to six and seven instituted or increased premiums for children (Georgia, Kentucky, Maryland, Nevada, New Hampshire, Vermont, and Wyoming). While states were generally more likely to target adults than children, children will still be significantly affected by 2003's cuts to Medicaid, SCHIP, and other state health insurance programs. One group estimated that almost half of all persons losing coverage—490,000 to 650,000—would be children.

On the other hand, some states continued to enhance their SCHIP programs in 2003, even in the face of severe fiscal pressures. Several states added coverage of pregnant women. The two states with the largest programs implemented or expanded innovative initiatives to streamline children's access to coverage. Two-thirds of states in our study took steps to further simplify enrollment. And as many states added benefits to their SCHIP packages as eliminated them.

So many states increasing cost sharing is clearly worrisome, given the potential for premiums and copayments to create barriers to enrollment and service use. Yet almost without exception, state officials said that they were confident that cost sharing increases would not cause serious problems for families. Why? First, the increases were quite small. (Indeed, most premiums increased by $5 or less per month, and most copayments were raised by just a dollar or two. Two exceptions were Texas and Wisconsin.) Second, the increases were, in many cases, the first imposed in the history of the program. This relative stability contrasts sharply with the private insurance sector, where premiums have increased at double-digit rates for several years running. Finally, during the budget development process, proposed increases in cost sharing were described as the *least* controversial of the cuts being considered in children's health programs. Officials took comfort in this, seeing it as a reflection of stakeholders' (including child advocates') view that SCHIP cost sharing was still relatively affordable.

It is also important to consider how SCHIP fared relative to other state programs. Here too one might find at least a modicum of optimism. Recent studies have found that, during 2003, states most often targeted cuts at higher education, state workforce compensation, and aid to localities, among other programs. These studies also documented states' increased willingness to aggressively cut Medicaid by reducing provider reimbursement, eliminating optional benefits, and reducing eligibility standards. But Medicaid coverage for adults was the most common target, as the program was described as "a key component of [states'] efforts to balance their budgets" in fiscal year 2004.

Compared with other state budget cuts, SCHIP cuts were universally described by state officials as among the smallest, and last, cuts to be adopted. Indeed, these officials said that the program retained much of its political support and popularity, and used phrases such as "very painful" and "last resort" to describe how legislators felt about the SCHIP cuts. In 2002, we reported that one reason why SCHIP is so politically popular in states with separate programs is that, since it is not an entitlement, policymakers and state legislators have greater flexibility to control costs through the use of such strategies as enrollment caps, benefit cuts, and cost sharing increases. Clearly, more state officials felt compelled to make use of this flexibility in 2003. By the same token, policymakers may feel free to reverse some of these cuts when fiscal conditions improve.

Conclusions and Outlook

That SCHIP experienced serious cuts in the past year is indisputable. Equally indisputable is that the federal and state capacity to insure poor and near poor children remains strong, and certainly much stronger than it was in 1997 before SCHIP was created. All 50 states (and the District of Columbia) maintain SCHIP programs with upper income eligibility thresholds that average over 200 percent of FPL. Every state's application process can still fairly be characterized as simplified, using shortened forms that can be submitted by mail, requiring minimal verification, and guaranteeing coverage for at least six months. Nearly every state provides coverage of a comprehensive array of benefits, beyond minimum requirements of the Title XXI statute. And while cost sharing in separate programs is widespread, premiums and copayments in all states but one are set at levels well below the maximum permitted by federal law.

SCHIP's early success has been well documented. It has insured nearly 4 million children and, combined with Medicaid, helped reduce the rate of uninsurance among low-income children from roughly 23 percent to just over

17 percent. Yet the program is certainly in transition, and fiscal pressures have led states to implement cuts that threaten to reverse these positive gains.

What the future will hold for SCHIP is uncertain. Bolstered by generous federal matching funds, the program appears to retain much of its political support, which continues to protect it relative to other state programs. State revenue projections are generally improving, creating hope that the worst of SCHIP's cuts are behind it. Yet federal Medicaid fiscal relief, which states acknowledge played a critical role in helping them avert deeper cuts, is due to expire in June 2004, and uncertainty over the adequacy of federal funding for SCHIP remains. More generally, it appears that the residual effects of three years of economic downturn, and state actions to cope with it (including the exhaustion of budget reserves and "rainy day" funds, the redirections of tobacco settlement dollars, and deep cuts to the state workforce and local aid) may last for a considerable time and weaken states' ability to recover quickly.

Six years ago, federal policymakers made a critical commitment to promoting the health of children with the creation of SCHIP, and states followed suit by implementing generous programs quickly and aggressively. Time will tell whether governments will continue to maintain this commitment to our most vulnerable population.

Lyndon B. Johnson  **NO**

Great Society Speech: Remarks at the University of Michigan

President Hatcher, Governor Romney, Senators McNamara and Hart, Congressmen Meader and Staebler, and other members of the fine Michigan delegation, members of the graduating class, my fellow Americans:

It is a great pleasure to be here today. This university has been coeducational since 1870, but I do not believe it was on the basis of your accomplishments that a Detroit high school girl said, "In choosing a college, you first have to decide whether you want a coeducational school or an educational school."

Well, we can find both here at Michigan, although perhaps at different hours.

I came out here today very anxious to meet the Michigan student whose father told a friend of mine that his son's education had been a real value. It stopped his mother from bragging about him.

I have come today from the turmoil of your Capital to the tranquility of your campus to speak about the future of your country.

The purpose of protecting the life of our Nation and preserving the liberty of our citizens is to pursue the happiness of our people. Our success in that pursuit is the test of our success as a Nation.

For a century we labored to settle and to subdue a continent. For half a century we called upon unbounded invention and untiring industry to create an order of plenty for all of our people.

The challenge of the next half century is whether we have the wisdom to use that wealth to enrich and elevate our national life, and to advance the quality of our American civilization.

Your imagination, your initiative, and your indignation will determine whether we build a society where progress is the servant of our needs, or a society where old values and new visions are buried under unbridled growth. For in your time we have the opportunity to move not only toward the rich society and the powerful society, but upward to the Great Society.

The Great Society rests on abundance and liberty for all. It demands an end to poverty and racial injustice, to which we are totally committed in our time. But that is just the beginning.

The Great Society is a place where every child can find knowledge to enrich his mind and to enlarge his talents. It is a place where leisure is a welcome chance to build and reflect, not a feared cause of boredom and

From *Presidential Speech,* May 22, 1964.

restlessness. It is a place where the city of man serves not only the needs of the body and the demands of commerce but the desire for beauty and the hunger for community.

It is a place where man can renew contact with nature. It is a place which honors creation for its own sake and for what it adds to the understanding of the race. It is a place where men are more concerned with the quality of their goals than the quantity of their goods.

But most of all, the Great Society is not a safe harbor, a resting place, a final objective, a finished work. It is a challenge constantly renewed, beckoning us toward a destiny where the meaning of our lives matches the marvelous products of our labor.

So I want to talk to you today about three places where we begin to build the Great Society—in our cities, in our countryside, and in our classrooms.

Many of you will live to see the day, perhaps 50 years from now, when there will be 400 million Americans—four-fifths of them in urban areas. In the remainder of this century urban population will double, city land will double, and we will have to build homes, highways, and facilities equal to all those built since this country was first settled. So in the next 40 years we must rebuild the entire urban United States.

Aristotle said: "Men come together in cities in order to live, but they remain together in order to live the good life." It is harder and harder to live the good life in American cities today.

The catalog of ills is long: there is the decay of the centers and the despoiling of the suburbs. There is not enough housing for our people or transportation for our traffic. Open land is vanishing and old landmarks are violated.

Worst of all expansion is eroding the precious and time honored values of community with neighbors and communion with nature. The loss of these values breeds loneliness and boredom and indifference.

Our society will never be great until our cities are great. Today the frontier of imagination and innovation is inside those cities and not beyond their borders.

New experiments are already going on. It will be the task of your generation to make the American city a place where future generations will come, not only to live but to live the good life.

I understand that if I stayed here tonight I would see that Michigan students are really doing their best to live the good life.

This is the place where the Peace Corps was started. It is inspiring to see how all of you, while you are in this country, are trying so hard to live at the level of the people.

A second place where we begin to build the Great Society is in our countryside. We have always prided ourselves on being not only America the strong and America the free, but America the beautiful. Today that beauty is in danger. The water we drink, the food we eat, the very air that we breathe, are threatened with pollution. Our parks are overcrowded, our seashores overburdened. Green fields and dense forests are disappearing.

A few years ago we were greatly concerned about the "Ugly American." Today we must act to prevent an ugly America.

For once the battle is lost, once our natural splendor is destroyed, it can never be recaptured. And once man can no longer walk with beauty or wonder at nature his spirit will wither and his sustenance be wasted.

A third place to build the Great Society is in the classrooms of America. There your children's lives will be shaped. Our society will not be great until every young mind is set free to scan the farthest reaches of thought and imagination. We are still far from that goal.

Today, 8 million adult Americans, more than the entire population of Michigan, have not finished 5 years of school. Nearly 20 million have not finished 8 years of school. Nearly 54 million—more than one-quarter of all America—have not even finished high school.

Each year more than 100,000 high school graduates, with proved ability, do not enter college because they cannot afford it. And if we cannot educate today's youth, what will we do in 1970 when elementary school enrollment will be 5 million greater than 1960? And high school enrollment will rise by 5 million. College enrollment will increase by more than 3 million.

In many places, classrooms are overcrowded and curricula are outdated. Most of our qualified teachers are underpaid, and many of our paid teachers are unqualified. So we must give every child a place to sit and a teacher to learn from. Poverty must not be a bar to learning, and learning must offer an escape from poverty.

But more classrooms and more teachers are not enough. We must seek an educational system which grows in excellence as it grows in size. This means better training for our teachers. It means preparing youth to enjoy their hours of leisure as well as their hours of labor. It means exploring new techniques of teaching, to find new ways to stimulate the love of learning and the capacity for creation.

These are three of the central issues of the Great Society. While our Government has many programs directed at those issues, I do not pretend that we have the full answer to those problems.

But I do promise this: We are going to assemble the best thought and the broadest knowledge from all over the world to find those answers for America. I intend to establish working groups to prepare a series of White House conferences and meetings—on the cities, on natural beauty, on the quality of education, and on other emerging challenges. And from these meetings and from this inspiration and from these studies we will begin to set our course toward the Great Society.

The solution to these problems does not rest on a massive program in Washington, nor can it rely solely on the strained resources of local authority. They require us to create new concepts of cooperation, a creative federalism, between the National Capital and the leaders of local communities.

Woodrow Wilson once wrote: "Every man sent out from his university should be a man of his Nation as well as a man of his time."

Within your lifetime powerful forces, already loosed, will take us toward a way of life beyond the realm of our experience, almost beyond the bounds of our imagination.

For better or for worse, your generation has been appointed by history to deal with those problems and to lead America toward a new age. You have the chance never before afforded to any people in any age. You can help build a society where the demands of morality, and the needs of the spirit, can be realized in the life of the Nation.

So, will you join in the battle to give every citizen the full equality which God enjoins and the law requires, whatever his belief, or race, or the color of his skin?

Will you join in the battle to give every citizen an escape from the crushing weight of poverty?

Will you join in the battle to make it possible for all nations to live in enduring peace—as neighbors and not as mortal enemies?

Will you join in the battle to build the Great Society, to prove that our material progress is only the foundation on which we will build a richer life of mind and spirit?

There are those timid souls who say this battle cannot be won; that we are condemned to a soulless wealth. I do not agree. We have the power to shape the civilization that we want. But we need your will, your labor, your hearts, if we are to build that kind of society.

Those who came to this land sought to build more than just a new country. They sought a new world. So I have come here today to your campus to say that you can make their vision our reality. So let us from this moment begin our work so that in the future men will look back and say: It was then, after a long and weary way, that man turned the exploits of his genius to the full enrichment of his life.

Thank you. Goodby.

EXPLORING THE ISSUE

Do We Need More Budget Flexibility for Discretionary Spending Compared to Entitlements?

Critical Thinking and Reflection

1. Why are entitlements such a hotly debated political topic? When did they start and why?
2. What effect would more budget flexibility have on policy outcomes in our country?
3. How was Johnson able to convince Americans that they needed to assure money was available for the beneficiaries of his programs? Why have more modern presidents struggled to make the same assertion?
4. How are states able to use discretionary spending to alleviate potential budget shortfalls?
5. What are the political ramifications for getting rid of entitlement programs?

Is There Common Ground?

Entitlement programs, such as Medicare and Social Security, fill the airwaves every night as media outlets discuss the pending budgetary doom our nation faces. The fact is that a high percentage of our annual budget is spent before we begin allocating funds by entitlement programs aimed to protect various groups within society. With a rich history and populist approval, these programs aim to ensure a basic standard of living for all Americans and have grown in demand and scale since the 1960s. With their growth, however, has come a decrease in the discretionary funding available each year. If discretionary spending continues decreasing, politicians will be forced to make a series of difficult choices. First, a smaller number of discretionary programs will be funded. Secondly—and perhaps most importantly for public administration— existing programs and agencies will likely be continually asked to trim fat and do more with less. Between these two factors, government workers will have their day-to-day functioning altered. From a budgetary perspective, what becomes clear is that we must determine a way to balance entitlement programs with the need for an adaptable federal budget that allows for discretionary spending without simply shifting money from other programs or racking up further deficits. Yet, such an outcome relies more on politics than budgetary theory.

Additional Resources

King, R.F., *Budgeting Entitlements: The Politics of Food Stamps* (Washington, DC: Georgetown University Press, 2000)

As budgetary concerns have come to dominate congressional action, the design and implementation of welfare programs have come under greater scrutiny. This book focuses on the food stamp program to examine how the growing integration of welfare and budgeting has affected both politics and people.

National Commission on Fiscal Responsibility and Reform. (2010). *The Moment of Truth: Report of the National Commission on Fiscal Responsibility and Reform.* Retrieved from http://www.fiscalcommission.gov/sites/fiscalcommission.gov/files/documents/TheMomentofTruth12_1_2010.pdf

Cochaired by Erskine Bowles and Alan Simpson, the panel produced an important set of recommendations for reducing the federal deficit. The panel writes: "As members of the National Commission on Fiscal Responsibility and Reform, we spent the past eight months studying the same cold, hard facts. Together, we have reached these unavoidable conclusions: The problem is real. The solution will be painful. There is no easy way out. Everything must be on the table. And Washington must lead."

Santow, L.J. and M.E. Santow, *Social Security and the Middle-Class Squeeze: Fact and Fiction about America's Entitlement Programs* (New York: Praeger, 2005)

Santow and Santow work through data to examine the actual state of entitlement programs in America and the overall impact they have on the national budget each year.

Saturno, J. and B. Heniff, *The Federal Budget Process* (Alexandria, VA: TheCapitol.Net, 2009)

Budgeting for the federal government is an enormously complex process. It entails dozens of subprocesses, countless rules and procedures, the efforts of tens of thousands of staff persons in the executive and legislative branches, and the active participation of the president, congressional leaders, members of Congress, and members of the executive branch. This book discusses the various elements of the federal budget process including the President's budget submission, framework, timetable, the budget resolution, reconciliation, the "Byrd Rule," appropriations, and budget execution.

Schick, A., *The Federal Budget: Politics, Policy, Process,* 3rd ed. (Washington, D.C.: Brookings Institution Press, 2007)

The federal budget impacts American policies both at home and abroad, and recent concern over the exploding budgetary deficit has experts calling our nation's policies "unsustainable" and "system-dooming." As the deficit continues to grow, will America be fully able to fund its priorities, such as an effective military and looking after its aging population?

Internet References . . .

Office of Personnel Management, Performance Management

This performance management guidance relates to the management of employee performance (i.e., planning, developing, monitoring, rating, and rewarding employee contributions), rather than performance-based or performance-oriented approaches to managing, measuring, and accounting for agency program performance.

http://www.opm.gov/perform/overview.asp

US Department of Labor, Affirmative Action

This site explains affirmative action at the federal level and links to all related legislation.

http://www.dol.gov/dol/topic/hiring/affirmativeact.htm

Center on Budget and Policy Priorities

The Center on Budget and Policy Priorities is one of the nation's premier policy organizations working at the federal and state levels on fiscal policy and public programs that affect low- and moderate-income families and individuals.

http://www.cbpp.org/

Peterson-Pew Commission on Budget Reform

To modernize an outdated Congressional budget process in light of the daunting economic challenges facing the nation, the Peter G. Peterson Foundation, The Pew Charitable Trusts and the Committee for a Responsible Federal Budget have launched a landmark partnership to build bipartisan consensus for a core set of reforms.

http://budgetreform.org/

Long-Term Spending on Entitlement Programs

In this letter to Representative Jeb Hensarling, the Congressional Budget Office discusses the implications of long-term entitlement spending on the federal budget.

http://www.cbo.gov/ftpdocs/78xx/doc7851/
03-08-Long-Term%20Spending.pdf

Administrative Ethics

*H*aving spent the first four units of this book demonstrating the significant role played in government and policy by public administrators, now we can turn to examine the ethical behavior of these workers. To begin, we will look at whistleblowing and the protections in place for government employees to bring to light misgivings of our system. From another angle, we will turn to the different types of controls—both intern and external—that have been put in place to try and best control bureaucratic behavior. Lastly, we will closely look at one of the more timely topics—public employee collective bargaining. By going through this unit, students will become more familiar with the ethical dilemmas surrounding public administration and policy.

- Should Whistleblowing Be Encouraged in the Public Service?
- Are External Controls Effective Tools for Ensuring Principled Conduct?
- Should Public Employees Have Collective Bargaining Rights?

ISSUE 15

Should Whistleblowing Be Encouraged in the Public Service?

YES: Tim V. Eaton and Michael D. Akers, from "Whistleblowing and Good Governance: Policies for Universities, Government Entities, and Nonprofit Organizations," *The CPA Journal* (June 2007)

NO: H.L. Laframboise, from "Vile Wretches and Public Heroes: The Ethics of Whistleblowing in Government," *Canadian Public Administration* (March 1991)

Learning Outcomes

After reading this issue, you should be able to:

- Define whistleblowing.
- Gain an understanding of why public administrators need to be concerned with whistleblowing.
- Discuss the conditions under which whistleblowing should be encouraged.
- Understand the potential negative personal impact of whistleblowing.
- Understand the potential negative societal impact of whistleblowing.
- Describe vile wretches and the effects of their actions on public agencies.

ISSUE SUMMARY

YES: Tim V. Eaton and Michael D. Akers argue that, although the Sarbanes-Oxley Act of 2002 applied to corporations, government and nonprofit organizations are not immune from similar problems. Through historical analysis and discussion, the authors contend that whistleblowers should be encouraged and actively protected.

NO: H.L. Laframboise argues that while whistleblowing can be quite useful and necessary, there are some individuals—dubbed vile wretches—whose decisions to blow the whistle actually cause more public problems than the actions they believe they need to expose.

As a result, encouragement can actually harm public perceptions of government.

On November 18, 2004, David Graham testified before the Senate Finance Committee. Graham was the Associate Director of Science and Medicine at the United States Food and Drug Administration. A graduate of Johns Hopkins Medical School, with specializations in internal medicine and neurology, Graham was invited to speak to the committee based on both his field training and his 20-year career at the Food and Drug Administration. The specific purpose of Graham's visit was to provide informed expert opinion on the dangers of Vioxx, a nonsteroidal anti-inflammatory drug (NSAID) that had recently been voluntarily withdrawn by manufacturer Merck in the wake of evidence that it increased the risk of heart attacks. Graham's testimony contained references to nearly a dozen other drugs he had personally researched in his capacity at the FDA that had either been withdrawn or were otherwise investigated for adverse reactions or dangerous side effects.

In this capacity as a trained medical research scientist providing expert testimony, David Graham's behavior is barely notable. Congressional committees regularly rely upon expert opinion when debating and shaping public policy. However, as the object of Graham's testimony turned from Vioxx itself to the process that allowed its approval, his comments became potentially explosive and his role changed from expert witness to whistleblower. Graham completed a 3-year study on the effects of Vioxx to be presented at scholarly conference, the main finding of which was that a high dose of Vioxx significantly contributed to heart attacks. Graham remarked: "I was pressured to change my conclusions and recommendations, and basically threatened that if I did not change them, I would not be permitted to present the paper at the conference." Despite the report's acceptance to a peer-reviewed journal and conference, Graham's managers would not provide clearance for the research to be released. Graham stated that he repeatedly experienced pressure to, at a minimum, diminish his findings.

Perhaps more revelatory was Graham's claim that the undue pressure he experienced during the Vioxx approval process was merely the most recent instance in a pattern of pressure from FDA leadership to alter findings or remain silent. Graham remarked that the process of establishing drug safety often met with two common roadblocks:

> The new drug reviewing division that approved the drug in the first place and that regards it as its own child, typically proves to be the single greatest obstacle to effectively dealing with serious drug safety issues. The second greatest obstacle is often the senior management within the Office of Drug Safety, who either actively or tacitly go along with what the Office of New Drugs wants.

Graham's experience indicates that FDA managers are unwilling to admit to safety problems after a drug has been approved. This suggests the possibility of some degree of agency capture, a situation that occurs when a regulatory agency promotes, rather than independently regulates, the interests of the enterprise it was created to regulate. In other words, Graham claims that the objective advanced by the FDA is not to ensure the health and safety of American citizens but to advance the commercial interests of drug companies. In summary, Graham proclaims, "Vioxx is a terrible tragedy and a profound regulatory failure. I would argue that the FDA, as currently configured, is incapable of protecting America against another Vioxx." A little more than a year after his Senate testimony, Graham told *USA Today,* "The FDA's recent drug safety initiatives serve only as window dressing, diverting attention away from real solutions, such as an independent Office of Drug Safety."

In the aftermath of Graham's testimony, the nonprofit Government Accountability Project claimed to receive anonymous phone calls alleging that Graham was a "demagogue and a bully" and that his research was flawed. Officials from the Government Accountability Project assert that they have evidence, based on phone records and other personal information. Despite his serious accusations of misconduct in the management of the Food and Drug Administration, David Graham continues to work at the FDA in his capacity as Associate Director of the Office of Drug Safety. The public retaliation he received was relatively mild. In 2001, Jesselyn Radack, a Department of Justice attorney, disclosed information to *Newsweek* regarding DOJ handling of the John Walker Lindh interrogation. In the aftermath, Radack received a poor performance evaluation from her supervisor, which led to her seeking another job. It is alleged that DOJ officials provided information to her new employer, a law firm, which led to her being placed on a leave of absence. Eventually, Radack found employment with the Government Accountability Project.

The U.S. Congress has attempted to address the protection of whistleblowers in various statues, notably the Civil Service Reform Act of 1978, the Whistleblower Protection Act of 1989, and the No FEAR Act of 2002. Despite these and other statutory measures, potential whistleblowers face a terrible choice. When public employees witness fraud, waste, abuse, and corruption, should they be encouraged to report that information to authorities? On one hand, if public employees work to serve some component part of the public interest, do they have a responsibility to public trust to blow the whistle? On the other hand, can we expect public employees, who are mere citizens like us, to face the potential ridicule, humiliation, and retaliation that might result from their disclosure? In the YES selection, Tim V. Eaton and Michael D. Akers argue that public employees should be actively encouraged to blow the whistle and that government has a strict responsibility to protect them. Whistleblowers, the authors argue, are essential to good governance. In the NO selection, H.L. Luframboise approaches the issue with a more utilitarian view, suggesting that some attempts to blow the whistle can result in more harm to the public than the benefit that would be provided by the disclosure. The author seems to imply that these "vile wretches" should not be encouraged to engage in whistleblowing.

YES

Tim V. Eaton and Michael D. Akers

Whistleblowing and Good Governance: Policies for Universities, Government Entities, and Nonprofit Organizations

JUNE 2007—The Sarbanes-Oxley Act of 2002 (SOX) has forever changed corporate governance for publicly held corporations. Recent data suggest that the costs of compliance with the provisions of SOX can be very significant. Because these mandated requirements apply almost exclusively to publicly held corporations, some companies have cited the high costs of SOX compliance as a rationale for going private. After all, SOX was developed in response to high-profile corporate scandals that included Enron, WorldCom, and Tyco, and was not designed to address problems in other sectors. Unfortunately, problems in corporate governance are not unique to public corporations.

Problems in the Government and Nonprofit Sectors

Problems exist in the government and nonprofit sectors just as they do in the corporate sector. Recent alleged problems at the World Bank (reported in *U.S. News and World Report*) include kickbacks, payoffs, bribery, embezzlement (a midlevel manager took over $2 million), and collusive bidding.

According to EthicsPoint, a leading provider of technology-based governance, risk, and compliance services, more than 20 separate states' attorneys general have launched 30 investigations into nonprofits all over the United States. In 2002, the United Way scandal (where a director took funds through questionable payments and other executives charged the organization for personal expenses) came to the public's attention. Its aftermath has had a dramatic impact on fundraising. *The Washington Post* reported that the United Way's fall fundraising drive had dropped from a high of $90 million in 2001 to $19 million in 2004. Other notable nonprofit organizations such as the American Red Cross and the Nature Conservancy have also had to deal with scandals and the resulting negative impacts. The Red Cross had funds stolen and additional bonuses taken because of poor internal controls. The Nature

Conservancy encountered problems when the organization engaged in inappropriate business and real estate transactions with its trustees.

Even universities are not immune from scandals. Scandals such as that involving presidential spending at American University often relate to the misuse of athletic, research, or university funds. As part of the termination decision, American University's board of trustees asked its former president to reimburse the institution $125,000 for personal expenses as well as authorize the audit committee to disclose $398,000 in unreported taxable income. Because of the increasing prevalence and publicizing of these incidents, many government and nonprofit entities are not only more aware of SOX, but have already begun the process of implementing certain provisions of SOX within their organizations.

According to a 2004 Grant Thornton study, nearly half of nonprofits have made corporate governance policy changes in the wake of SOX. The study highlights the following statement from Grant Thornton's Larry Ladd: "Many not-for-profits believed that Sarbanes-Oxley was a passing fad or bubble. Today, however, awareness of the act and actions based on the provisions of Sarbanes-Oxley are on the rise. Board members and regulators are now pressing for reform."

While the costs of implementing the provisions of SOX are unquestionably high, certain provisions do have significant benefits. These beneficial components can be selectively applied by noncorporate entities to provide good organizational governance and reduce the potential for fraudulent activity. Additionally, all organizations should consider that failure to respond appropriately today could lead to potential disaster in the future. The consequences may include not only the loss of funds but also the high-profile negative publicity that can severely damage an organization's reputation.

One specific component of SOX that is particularly applicable to noncorporate organizations is whistleblowing, the act of reporting wrongdoing to another party. At the time of the Grant Thornton study, only 29% of nonprofits had a whistleblower policy in place. Organizations of all kinds should better understand what whistleblowing is, what the components of a whistleblowing policy are, and where to turn for more information.

What Is Whistleblowing?

Whistleblowing can be defined in a number of ways. In its simplest form, whistleblowing involves the act of reporting wrongdoing within an organization to internal or external parties. Internal whistleblowing entails reporting the information to a source within the organization. External whistleblowing occurs when the whistleblower takes the information outside the organization, such as to the media or regulators. Establishment of a clear and specific definition of whistleblowing itself should be a fundamental component of every whistleblower policy.

Whistleblowers have garnered attention recently due to the worldwide media exposure of recent accounting scandals. In 2002, *Time* magazine named whistleblowers Cynthia Cooper of WorldCom, Sherron Watkins of Enron, and Coleen Rowley of the FBI as its "Persons of the Year." While the first two individuals are well known and involve financial scandals, Rowley's whistle-blowing was a noncorporate case but with very serious ramifications involving lapses in the intelligence community in the weeks prior to the September 11, 2001, terrorist attacks.

Legislative History

The origins of whistleblowing go back well over a century. In fact, whistle-blowing initially arose not in connection with corporate malfeasance, but in the federal government's False Claims Act.

1863: The False Claims Act's Influence

The False Claims Act was established to offer incentives to individuals who reported companies or individuals defrauding the government. It was intro-duced by Abraham Lincoln in 1863 to target sales of fake gunpowder to the Union during the Civil War. In 1986, the False Claims Act was brought back and Congress added antiretaliation protections. The Act also specifies that the whistleblower can share in up to 30% of the proceeds of the lawsuit. Accord-ing to the Taxpayers Against Fraud (TAF) False Claims Act Legal Center (www .taf.org), this Act has resulted in more than $17 billion dollars of recoveries for the U.S. government since 1986. Major nonprofits that have paid large settle-ments in recent years include major universities and government entities (see www.taf.org/top100fca.htm for a comprehensive list of the largest claims). Finan-cial rewards to whistleblowers can, however, create an incentive to report bogus false claims. The Act imposes monetary penalties on bogus whistleblowers.

1989 and 1994: The Whistleblower Protection Act

Under the Whistleblower Protection Act, passed in 1989 and amended in 1994, federal employees are protected from workplace retaliation when dis-closing waste and fraud. The purpose of the Act and subsequent amendments was to strengthen the protections available to federal employees. Congress has considered reforms that would overhaul the act and enhance protections for federal employees who expose fraudulent activity, waste, and threats to public safety. Such legislation was debated last year, and in 2007, the House of Rep-resentatives approved the Whistleblower Protection Enhancement Act, which overhauls federal whistleblower law.

2002: SOX Requirements

In addition to the changing attitude toward whistleblowing, changes in laws and rights related to whistleblowing have followed. SOX provides an exam-ple of how publicly traded companies have been required to reshape their businesses and their attitudes toward workplace crime. Sections 806, 301, and 1107 of SOX provide additional guidance for whistleblowing.

Section 806 extends protection to employees of publicly traded compa-nies who report fraud to any federal regulatory or law enforcement agency, any member or committee of Congress, or any person with supervisory authority over the employee. This regulation states that whistleblowers who provide information or assist in an investigation of violations of any federal law relating to fraud against shareholders or any SEC rule or regulation are protected from any form of retaliation by any officer, employee, contractor, subcontractor, or agent of the company. Employees who are retaliated against will be "entitled to all relief necessary to make the employee whole" (SOX section 806), including compensatory damages of back pay, reinstatement of proper position, and compensation for litigation costs, expert witness fees, and attorney fees.

SOX also requires audit committees to take a role in whistleblowing and reducing corporate fraud. Section 301, amending the Securities Exchange Act of 1934, compels audit committees to develop reporting mechanisms for the recording, tracking, and acting on information provided by employees anonymously and confidentially. By mandating policies and protection for reporting wrongdoing, the SOX standards go beyond merely encouraging companies to be more responsive to employee whistleblowers.

In SOX section 1107, the reach of whistleblowing policies extends beyond public corporations. This section extends protection to any person who reports to a law enforcement officer information related to a violation of a federal law. These whistleblowers are protected from any retaliation by the offender. A violator may be fined and imprisoned for up to 10 years.

2006: Supreme Court Decision

In May 2006, the Supreme Court ruled in *Garcetti v. Ceballos* that whistleblowers who make statements while performing their jobs may not be constitutionally protected. Richard Ceballos, a supervising deputy attorney, was asked by defense counsel to review a case where defense counsel claimed the affidavit used by the police to obtain a search warrant was inaccurate. Ceballos concluded upon his review that there were significant misrepresentations in the affidavit, and he communicated his findings in a memo to his supervisors, the petitioners, and the trial court. Ceballos later claimed that the petitioners retaliated against him for his memo. Reversing the ruling of the Ninth Circuit Court of Appeals, the Supreme Court found that the memo was not protected because Ceballos wrote it while performing his employment duties. Congress has approved legislation (the Senate approved an amendment to the 2007 National Defense Authorization Act and the House approved the Whistleblower Protection Enhancement Act) that addresses the possible ramifications of this decision. A complete description of this case can be found at www.supremecourtus.gov/opinions/05pdf/04-473.pdf#search='garcetti%20v.%20Ceballos.

Why Implement a Whistleblower Policy?

All organizations, including universities, governmental entities, and non-profits, should consider implementing whistleblowing provisions. Consider these important facts from the Association of Certified Fraud Examiners' 2006 "Report to the Nation on Occupational Fraud and Abus":

- More than $600 billion in annual losses is attributed to fraud.
- Anonymous reporting mechanisms are the antifraud measure with the greatest impact on reducing losses: Companies with anonymous reporting mechanisms reported median losses of $100,000, while those without reported median losses of $200,000.
- Tips from employees, customers, and vendors and anonymous tips account for:
  - 34% of the detection of all fraudulent activity;
  - 34% of the detection of fraudulent activity for not-for-profit organizations;
  - 39.7% of the detection of fraudulent activity for government agencies; and
  - 48% of the detection of owner/executive fraud schemes.

Reporting on internal controls was recommended to the corporate community in the late 1970s, but it took the large scandals (such as Enron) for the SOX legislation to impose such reporting. Recent legislation in California (California's Nonprofit Integrity Act of 2004) and proposed legislation in other states suggest that nonprofit organizations should consider "best practice" governance policies and mechanisms similar to the provisions of SOX, as doing so may prepare them for future legislative requirements.

IRS data indicate that many nonprofit organizations would be categorized as small businesses. Most small businesses struggle with an appropriate level of segregation of duties, making a whistleblower policy a good mitigating control. A whistleblower policy and effective enforcement has the potential not only to significantly reduce fraudulent activity but also to send a signal to both internal and external constituencies that the organization exercises good corporate governance. Just as corporations must answer to shareholders, universities, government entities, and nonprofit organizations must answer to the public regarding the stewardship of resources.

The authors agree with the commentary in *The CPA Journal* (Mary-Jo Kranacher, "Whistleblowing: The Devil in the Details," July 2006) that whistleblowing can significantly affect a whistleblower's life and livelihood. The authors believe that the potentially huge personal impact whistleblowing can have on individual whistleblowers means there is an even greater need for organizations to develop clear whistleblower policies.

Best Practices

Many professional organizations associated with universities, government entities, or nonprofit organizations have recognized certain mechanisms as a best practice and recommend that their constituents implement whistleblower polices. The following are a few examples.

National Association of College and University Business Officers

NACUBO provided whistleblowing guidelines in its Advisory Report 2003-3, "The Sarbanes-Oxley Act of 2002: Recommendations for Higher Education." Although SOX is not required for colleges and universities, NACUBO's recommendations are based on SOX section 301. NACUBO Advisory Report 2003-3 states:

> NACUBO recommends that institutions publicize the complaint mechanism and have it periodically reviewed by the audit committee. Institutions could incorporate the complaint mechanism within existing human resource communication policies. Colleges and universities should also consider establishing hot lines, anonymous voicemail, and anonymous e-mail or secure suggestion drop boxes to facilitate the complaint process. Regardless of the specific mechanisms selected, there should be a process for communicating with employees, receiving information, and addressing identified concerns.

BoardSource and Independent Sector

BoardSource (formerly the National Center for Nonprofit Boards) and Independent Sector (a leadership foundation for charities, foundations, and corporate giving programs) published a joint report, "The Sarbanes-Oxley Act and Implications for Nonprofit Organizations." It overviews the SOX provisions and makes several recommendations to nonprofits, such as the following:

> Nonprofits must develop, adopt, and disclose a formal process to deal with complaints and prevent retaliation. Nonprofit leaders must take any employee and volunteer complaints seriously, investigate the situation, and fix any problems or justify why corrections are not necessary.

National Council of Nonprofit Associations

The NCNA, a network of state and regional nonprofit organizations, developed a sample whistleblower policy for use by small and mid-sized nonprofits. The sample policy covers the following areas: responsibility for reporting violations, preventing retaliation against whistleblowers, methods for reporting violations, the compliance officer's duties, applicable areas of complaints and those responsible for addressing them, the involvement of the audit committee in complaints involving internal controls and auditing, the treatment of malicious or false allegations, confidentiality, and procedures for acknowledging reported violations.

Developing a Whistleblower Policy

A whistleblower policy may be drafted and implemented by management, but it should then be submitted to the audit committee or board of directors. The foundation of any whistleblower policy is a clear and specific definition of whistleblowing. Other key aspects of a whistleblower policy include the following:

- *Clear definition of individuals covered by the policy.* A whistleblower policy should cover individuals within the organization as well as external parties who conduct business with the organization. For example, for a university, those covered could include faculty, staff, student employees, vendors, and customers.

- *Nonretaliation provisions.* Whistleblower policies should prevent discrimination or retaliation against employees who report problems. Policies should also include methods to encourage employees, vendors, customers, and shareholders to report evidence of fraudulent activities. In addition, a whistleblower policy should include a disclaimer that anyone filing a claim must have reasonable belief that an issue exists and act in good faith.
- *Confidentiality.* Protecting whistleblowers' confidentiality is an important part of any whistleblower policy. Confidentiality is of great concern because the goal is to create an atmosphere where employees will feel comfortable submitting their names with claims to allow for further questioning and investigation. Allowing employees to file anonymous claims may increase the possibility of claims actually being reported; however, it may also increase the possibility of false claims being filed. The policy should explain how the claims will be investigated once received and whether the employee should expect to receive any feedback.
- *Process.* A whistleblower policy needs to address the process employees should follow in filing their claims. Organizations may require whistleblowers to direct their claims to a certain person, such as a compliance officer, or, alternatively, to follow a ladder of reporting until they reach the top of management. The latter helps ensure that the employee addresses the claim with a supervisor before heading straight to the CEO or an external party. Specific reporting mechanisms within the process could include telephone or e-mail hotlines, websites, or suggestion boxes.
- *Communication.* A whistleblower policy cannot be effective unless it is communicated to employees, vendors, customers, and shareholders. Employees can be informed through employee handbooks. Training could be provided internally during the human resources orientation process or by an outside party. Information can be posted throughout the company and on intranet sites. Customer service representatives can be trained to answer questions about the whistleblower policy.

Upon completion of the whistleblower policy, the organization should develop implementation and enforcement mechanisms that are consistent with the policy. Although the first step—creating an environment where a whistleblower will report problems that exist—is the crucial one, to be fully effective a whistleblower policy must be consistently implemented, claims investigated and evaluated, and proper enforcement taken when necessary.

H.L. Laframboise  **NO**

Vile Wretches and Public Heroes: The Ethics of Whistleblowing in Government

"**V**ile wretches" are those whose acts of whistleblowing are more offensive to the community or to their peer groups than the acts on which they have blown the whistle. A hill-billy who told the revenuers that his neighbour was making moonshine would be a "vile wretch." "Public heroes," in contrast, are those who blow the whistle on events and conditions deemed by the community or peer group to be so abhorrent as to justify their being reported. Igor Gouzenko was the classical "public hero." Peer group repugnance against "vile wretches" runs very deep, for reasons I will now illustrate.

Growing up in the 1930s as a member of a male neighbourhood gang, I hooked apples, put tin-tacks on windows and played Halloween pranks. In all those years I don't remember anyone in the gang squealing on another member, even to his own parents. This aversion to squealing was reinforced by my experience in the Canadian navy where mass punishments for acts of individuals were a common occurrence. The group would take the punishment rather than point the finger at the culprit. I was further conditioned to keep my mouth shut by my years with the federal public service where secrecy was a fetish. The oath of secrecy was treated as sacred.

Given these values, which I know by observation to be prevalent in communities and among peer groups, whistleblowers are not, *by definition alone,* public heroes.

I will start then by criticizing those who perceive themselves to be standing on such a moral ground that it is their duty to report all infractions. If I were to stand on this high moral ground, I would report friends who had evaded income tax, who had passed through customs with undeclared goods, who had bet with bookies, or who were bookies themselves. In brief, I wouldn't have a friend in the world and, to use that West Midlands expression, would be "put to Coventry." There would be no chair for me at the tavern table.

The illegality or impropriety of a particular act, then, is not in itself justification for blowing the whistle. Only if the act is abhorrent to peer group values is the whistleblowing perceived as justified. Without that distinction a community would disintegrate into a collection of mutually suspicious informers.

From *Canadian Public Administration*, March 1991, pp. 73–77. Copyright © 1991 by Wiley-Blackwell. Reprinted by permission via Rightslink.

Turning now to public administration, it is important first to recognize the supremacy of elected officials over appointed officials. Had I taken to heart the political acts and policies with which I strongly disagree I could not have pursued a public service career. By way of illustration, I once attended a pre-election meeting of senior officials to consider propositions put forward by the government of the day to retain or attract swing voters. My debriefing note to my deputy head was entitled "Rat Holes and Honey Pots," descriptive of pouring more money into popular but unproductive programs, and launching projects in constituencies where a party candidate's chances needed reinforcement. Vote-buying with public funds and patronage appointments are facts of political life. Those officials who are so morally fastidious that they deem it their duty to blow the whistle on vote-buying policies and patronage appointments should leave instead to work under the ethics of the business community. I wish them luck.

Still on the subject of public administration, there were two instances in my career where I had to stand up against what a minister wanted to do, not because he was proposing a corrupt action, but because he was ignorant of the rules laid down by the Treasury Board. In each case, after hearing me out, the minister changed his mind. The education of ministers on administrative and financial rules is a constant element at the seam between elected and appointed officials. Rare indeed are cases where a minister will proceed with an improper act against the firm advice of his or her officials, with emphasis on the word "firm."

On the frequency of improper actions by appointed officials, I have words of praise for the probity of Canadian federal public servants. Given the opportunities they have to extract bribes and to favour their friends, I think their overall record of integrity is little short of marvellous, especially by comparison with that of the business community. Despite the constant scrutiny of an army of institutional fault-finders, few are the instances where they have been found to have betrayed their trust. I have had no experience with governments in the provincial and municipal jurisdictions, but judging by the infrequency of media-reported misdemeanours, what I've said about a commendable level of integrity also applies to them.

I have discussed the subject of whistleblowing with two federal officials among whose main duties are to discover, or to investigate, improper actions by public servants, sometimes alone and sometimes in consort with a law enforcement agency. I wish I had the space to recount their anecdotes. As a rule the investigations were time-consuming, expensive and fruitless. One has to question then if the proposal being mooted about of setting up a central hotline for whistleblowers would be cost-effective. It may be that the whistle will in any case be blown by someone on truly abhorrent acts or conditions, and the expense of following up on other complaints would not be justified by the results.

To further diminish the need for, and the importance of, whistleblowing in Canada I will now make a distinction between American values and behaviour patterns, and those of Canadians.

An article I read in preparation for this paper listed some sixty references to relevant published papers, all by American authors.[1] This evidently is a very hot subject with our neighbours to the south and there are very good reasons.

One is that the drive to excel, to win, to amass wealth or to acquire power is, in my observation, much stronger among Americans than among Canadians. This has its up-side in dedication, hard work and entrepreneurial spirit. But there is a down-side when these goals are pursued over the line into illegal and unethical behaviour.

For the past eight years I've been reading a daily American newspaper during my winters in Florida. At first I perceived reports of corruption as exceptional cases, but as the years went by the anecdotes piled up and I came to realize that college sports are riddled with hypocrisy, that law officers themselves are highly suspect, that corporate policies very often cross over into the unethical, and that the American distrust of its politicians is justifiably very deep. My first point on this Canada–U.S. comparison, then, is that the United States is a much more fertile ground for whistleblowers. We have our scamps, but given our different behaviour patterns they are nowhere in proportion to the United States.

A second reason why the United States needs whistleblowers more than Canada is that their governmental controls are too often non-existent, or weak, or, if strong, rarely enforced. The American adoration of the marketplace as a self-correcting mechanism is much greater than in Canada, where its people insist that governments take a strong role in refereeing the games organizations play.

I hope that Canadian academics looking for subjects to publish on, don't jump on that of whistleblowing. I think that all that merits to be written about it, and maybe more than the subject deserves, has already been put on paper.[2]

I will now turn to the problem of retaliation against whistleblowers. The U.S. federal government has a law and a special counsel dedicated to ensuring that federal employees suffer no retaliation for reporting any act—and here I quote—"reasonably believed to be evidence of a violation of any law, rule or regulation, mismanagement, a gross waste of funds, an abuse of authority or a substantial and specific danger to public health and safety."[3] This legislated protection against reprisal doesn't appear to work worth a darn. Again quoting: "Between 1979 and 1984 only sixteen out of more than 1,500 complaints by federal employees against what they considered unjustifiable reprisals for whistleblowing activities resulted in corrective or disciplinary action, that is, one in a hundred cases."[4]

One reason for these relatively fruitless results is that compulsive moralists tend to be difficult people, and it has been hard for the special counsel to separate reprisals perceived to be due to whistleblowing from those due to personality defects that make these employees such a pain in the neck to work with. They "tend to exhibit a distinctive approach to moral issues and decision making."[5] By "distinctive" it is plain that the authors mean "at odds with peer group values."

During my career I've run across a few of these compulsive moralists. They grieve everything grievable, appeal every competition they lose, incite other employees to complain, and generally make nuisances of themselves. As a class, they are the ones who deliver "brown envelopes" to opposition members and to media people. They have little regard for the oath of secrecy.

Having reduced the subject of whistleblowing from an American mountain to a Canadian molehill, I will now dwell briefly on the rare instances where blowing the whistle is justified. Here I will return to the definition I proposed earlier, that is, that the events or conditions reported upon are more abhorrent to community values than the act of whistleblowing. The standard advice to whistleblowers in such cases is first to pursue the matter within the organization, jumping hierarchial reporting levels if necessary to ensure it gets top-level attention. If that fails to produce results, then it should be brought to the attention of an outside agent or agency. Here is where sound judgment is necessary. Depending on the nature of the misdemeanour, it may be unwise to rely on the organization to take corrective action. Going to an outside agent such as the police, an ombudsman, the media, the central government auditor, or an opposition MP may be the only route likely to be effective.

The courage and conviction of what in these cases would be public heroes are much to be admired. Rarely, however, will they find justifiable whistleblowing to have been a career enhancing act. This is the sacrifice they must be prepared to make if they face up squarely to their responsibilities as citizens or, more narrowly, as public servants.

Notes

1. Philip Jos, Mark E. Thompkins and Steven W. Hays, "In Praise of Difficult People: A Portrait of the Committed Whistleblower," *Public Administration Review* (November/December 1989), pp. 552–61.

2. Kenneth Kernaghan and John Langford, *The Responsible Public Servant* (Halifax: Institute of Public Administration of Canada and Institute for Research on Public Policy, 1990), ch. 4.

3. Gerald E. Caiden and Judith A. Truelson, "Whistle Blower Protection in the USA: Lessons Learned and to be Learned," *Australian Journal of Public Administration* (June 1988), p. 121.

4. Ibid., p. 122.

5. Jos, Tompkins and Hayes, "In Praise of Difficult People," p. 552.

EXPLORING THE ISSUE

Should Whistleblowing Be Encouraged in the Public Service?

Critical Thinking and Reflection

1. Why should public administrators be concerned with whistleblowing?
2. When should whistleblowing be encouraged? Why?
3. When should whistleblowing be discouraged? Why?
4. What impact do "vile wretches" have on public policy? How can these effects be mitigated?
5. In what ways can whistleblowing be negative for both the whistleblower and society at large?

Is There Common Ground?

Whistleblowing—at first glance—appears to be a positive occurrence in the public sector for a variety of reasons. First, whistleblowers alert authorities and the public to individuals (or groups of individuals) that are violating some code or statute within an organization. When it comes to the public sector, such actions typically involve malfeasance of public funding (even if indirectly). Second, it reaffirms the ideals that government workers are more concerned with the public interest than their own personal interests. In this way, whistleblowers almost become selfless martyrs for accountability. There is, however, a second side to the debate. To some, whistleblowers are little more than adult tattle-tales. Their actions may not be well-intentioned and instead motivated out of self-interest. The impact does little to improve government, but still manages to risk public confidence in the functioning of our bureaucrats and public agencies. Thus, it becomes almost a cost-benefit analysis where a potential whistleblower must determine if the malfeasance merits the possible agency-wide consequences. Further, the individual must decide if it merits the risk of retaliation by coworkers and superiors. In terms of the debate, what we can agree on is that illegal or unethical acts by public sector workers should not be tolerated and need to be prevented. However, we are still in the process of determining the best way to handle those situations so that the problem workers are handled without risking the reputation of the agency—or worse—government as a whole.

Additional Resources

Alford, C.F., *Whistleblowers: Broken Lives and Organizational Power* (Ithaca, NY: Cornell University Press, 2002)

Alford conducts research into why whistleblowers choose to go public and challenge their organizations, but he is also interested in what they have learned from their experiences. He is fascinated by the costs incurred by the "autonomous individual" who confronts the organization, an entity that Alford says demands obedience, conformity, and loyalty.

Bowers, J., M. Fodder, J. Lewis, and J. Mitchell, *Whistleblowing: Law and Practice* (New York: Oxford University Press, 2007)

This book provides a detailed and authoritative survey of the law relating to public interest disclosure ("whistleblowing"). Six years on from the coming into force of the Public Disclosure Act 1998 (PIDA), the book looks at how the new system has developed, and provides up-to-date guidance on the key issues that arise in practice. It provides full coverage of protection for whistleblowers under, and outside PIDA; the obligation to blow the whistle; and rules, policies, procedures, and problems in particular sectors.

Hesch, J.D., *Whistleblowing: A Guide to Government Reward Programs* (Goshen Press, 2010)

The most successful whistleblowers receive up to $100 million in government rewards, but 80 percent receive nothing at all. Why is that? Written by a former Department of Justice attorney, *Whistleblowing: A Guide to Government Reward Programs* provides a rare, behind-the-scenes tour of three unique government programs paying significant rewards to citizens for reporting fraud under dozens of federal and state programs, such as Medicare or the military, or for reporting income tax fraud.

Johnson, R.A., *Whistleblowing: When It Works—And Why* (New York: Lynn Rienner, 2002)

With the public's attention drawn to the scandals of Enron, Worldcom, and other corporate giants, there is renewed interest in whistleblowing. The author focuses on the public sector, but her analysis and conclusions are easily transferred to whistleblowing in the private sector.

Miceli, M.P., J.P. Near, and T.M. Dworkin, *Whistle-Blowing in Organizations* (New York: Psychology Press, 2008)

This is a research-based book on whistleblowing in organizations. The three authors describe studies on this important topic and the implications of the research and theory for organizational behavior, managerial practice, and public policy.

ISSUE 16

Are External Controls Effective Tools for Ensuring Principled Conduct?

YES: Victor A. Thompson, from *Without Sympathy or Enthusiasm: The Problem of Administrative Compassion* (University of Alabama Press, 1975)

NO: H. George Frederickson, from "Ethics and Public Administration: Some Assertions," *Ethics and Public Administration* (ME Sharpe, 1993)

Learning Outcomes

After reading this issue, you should be able to:

- Define external controls.
- Describe the relationship between external controls and effectiveness.
- Understand the tension between individual goals and organizational goals.
- Gain an understanding of how external controls are linked to principled conduct in public agencies.
- Describe the differences between internal and external controls.
- Define different kinds of external controls.

ISSUE SUMMARY

YES: Victor A. Thompson argues that since public employees are human, they inevitably pursue individual preferences and goals, sometimes at the expense of organizational goals. Thus, he advocates external controls over public employees.

NO: H. George Frederickson argues that administrative discretion is essential to effective public service. The author acknowledges that while external controls such as codes of ethics and ethics legislation will likely increase democratic accountability, such external controls

346

often amount to "gotcha" mechanisms that punish offenders rather than inculcate ethical mores and encourage proper conduct.

In 1940, when public administration theory was still in its nascent era, two scholars engaged in a debate, the substance of which continues to be relevant today. Although the seeds of the debate were sewn by both scholars in the late 1930s, Herman Finer and Carl Friedrich each published work in 1940 that crystallized their respective points of view. The critical issues of this academic argument were the responsibility of public administrators and the methods by which public employees are held accountable. Finer advocated the use of external control mechanisms to ensure responsible conduct among public administrators. Friedrich maintained that internal controls, in the form of education, training, and professional norms, were the most certain way to encourage public responsibility. Fundamentally, the question Friedrich and Finer attempted to answer was whether ethics laws and codes were more effective at ensuring principled conduct than inculcation of values and norms through training. To properly assess and judge the debate, it is critical to understand what is meant by public responsibility and accountability.

Public administrators' responsibility is complex and multifaceted. Since public agencies tend to be funded by taxpayers, they are expected to carry out their duties in an efficient, cost-effective manner. The agencies and programs for which public administrators work are designed by legislatures and managed by executives. Thus, public administrators are responsible to their political masters, to carry out functions as defined by law or public policy. Finally, public administrators are responsible to perform their duties under whatever constitutional or additional statutory authority exists within the jurisdiction in question. However, there is an interpretative difference between an administrator feeling responsible to someone or something and being held accountable by some entity.

Ultimately, public administrators have accountability relationships between the legislative and executive masters, including whatever oversight or legal mechanisms have been established, and taxpayers. However, since taxpayers have no electoral authority over most public administrators, citizens who are unhappy with appointed administrators must rely upon elected officials to manage the accountability relationship on their behalf. For example, a city manager typically performs the major executive functions of municipal government. Although the fiscal and statutory responsibility to taxpayers is clear, city managers are appointed officials who serve at the leisure of the council. Consequently, citizens, to whom the city manager is most assuredly responsible, maintain no direct accountability mechanism over the city manager. This example underscores the critical issue at stake in the debate between Friedrich and Finer: Are internal or external controls more effective at encouraging responsible conduct among public administrators?

Finer advocated the use of external controls. External controls can be implemented in a variety of forms. Constitutional and statutory controls typically involve the monopoly power of government and the fiscal responsibility of the government to the taxpayer. The U.S. Constitution provides Congress with both legislative power and the power of the purse. Furthermore, Article II presents an executive branch with only two specific actors: the president and vice president. This vagueness allowed Congress to design the executive branch according to demonstrated necessity and policy preferences. Once authorized, government agencies are funded with taxpayer money. In order to fulfill its oversight responsibility, Congress created staff agencies, such as the Government Accountability Office and the Congressional Budget Office. These agencies conduct performance audits of the executive branch to ensure that laws are executed correctly and money is spent properly.

Ethics laws, a second form of external control, tend to follow scandal. In the wake of the Watergate scandal, the U.S. Congress passed the Ethics in Government Act of 1978. The legislation created new public disclosure rules, restricted lobbying by public officials after leaving office, and established the Office of Independent Counsel to oversee government employees. Generally, ethics laws codify rules defining conflict of interest, restrict lobbying by former government employees, and establish public disclosure standards. Fundamentally, ethics laws attempt to encourage responsible conduct by punishing conduct that violates the law. Codes of ethics, a third type of external control, encourage proper conduct by formalizing standards and norms. Public administrators might encounter two types of ethics codes. One brand of ethics codes are established by the government or agency as the proper code of conduct for an employee. A second type, a professional code of ethics, consists of the professional standards and norms of behavior expected by the profession. In either case, the code of ethics is considered an external control since it was composed by an outside entity. However, unlike ethics laws which carry legal penalties, codes of ethics are merely normative standards of conduct, encouraging administrators to behave in ways the profession considers "right."

Internal controls are achieved through education and training. Friedrich argued that public administrators should be adequately trained to appreciate the public responsibility bureaucrats have to the public. Friedrich remarked in *Public Policy and the Nature of Administrative Responsibility* that "the responsible administrator is one who is responsible to these two dominant factors: technical knowledge and popular sentiment." As Cooper notes in *The Responsible Administrator,* both of these factors might be considered to be externally derived. However, Friedrich maintained that any ill effects of administrative discretion might be tempered by training administrators in such a way that they be both technically competent and eager to cherish responsibility inherent in their position. Rather than impose legal penalties or appeal to the possible disapproval of the profession, Friedrich advocated the use of training and education to inculcate critical values and standards.

In the YES selection, Victor Thompson echoes the position of Herman Finer. Thompson argues that human flaws and frailty suggest that administrators might subjugate organizational goals for personal goals and that external controls are necessary to ensure responsible conduct. In contrast, in the NO selection, George Frederickson argues that internal controls produce superior results. Frederickson agrees that while external controls will improve democratic accountability, administrative discretion, which the author believes to be essential to public administrators, is promoted by the use of internal controls.

YES

Victor A. Thompson

Without Sympathy or Enthusiasm: The Problem of Administrative Compassion

. . . Organization-tools are different from others in that the materials of which they are composed are autonomous, goal-forming creatures. They are human beings. As such, they have the need to preserve themselves, their values, and their self-images—they have survival needs. They also have the propensity to interact and thereby to spontaneously generate roles and behavior norms and to enforce them informally upon one another. They have a strong tendency to become interlocked in an unplanned, spontaneous system. Considering that it is spontaneous, unplanned, and without a goal, let us call this system the "natural system" of the organization. Since this system arises without the roles of designer and owner, there is no external criterion to which it is beholden. Its only criterion is internal. As for all other natural systems, this criterion is survival.

The natural system of informal norms and roles grows up spontaneously to protect the survival needs of the incumbents of the functionary roles. Survival-endangering behavior, such as competition, high individual production, and the rate and direction of change, are informally brought under control, to the extent possible. Endangering personal obligations such as responsibility or risk are informally reduced or spread around in some way, if this is possible. To accomplish their "mission," natural systems, if allowed to do so, reach states of equilibrium and develop homeostatic processes to reduce deviating swings from these states and to restore them by counterswings, if possible. The form of the process is much like the negative feedback of a thermostatically controlled heating system. Duplicating methods and capabilities develop informally to reduce the risk of failure with its associated threat to the individual. Strangely enough, many formally important organizational functions, such as innovation, structural flexibility, and much of the motivating, are performed in this unplanned, spontaneous system.

Natural systems do not have decision-making organs and hence cannot be studied by the methods of logical or policy analysis. They are studied by statistically controlled empirical observation. Because a society is a natural system (a prime example of one, in fact), moral evaluations of a society— calling it "irrational," "racist," etc.—are either senseless or a form of poetic license. So, too, is the rather common practice of blaming society for various individual failures. Artificial systems, however, such as governments, do have decision-making organs—legislatures, administrative agencies, constitutional conventions—to which evaluative terms of various kinds, rational or moral, are properly applied. They act; they make choices. They have outputs, whereas natural systems, such as societies, have outcomes. To blame a natural system for anything makes no more sense than to blame nature, also a natural system, or a subsystem of nature such as gravity.

Natural systems are not established. Given the appropriate conditions, they develop. The appropriate conditions seem to be occasions and time for stable interactions. Organizations whose technologies and products are stable undergo such natural systemic development that they become almost impervious to change. Schools are a good example of this process. On the other hand, in organizations that use a dynamic and changing technology, the equilibria and homeostatic processes of natural systems are never fully developed. Such organizations are much easier to change by their designers and owners.

The natural system of an organization, because it develops in response to artificial-system demands and responsibilities, becomes in time a unified system rather than a collection of small natural systems or groups. The artificial system is "monocratic"; it is unified by reference to the owner's goal (which may, of course, be a system or set of consistent goals). What unity the organizational natural system acquires depends upon its derivative nature. It derives from a unified artificial system.

This essay is not the place for further discussion of natural-systems development in organizations or the conditions that facilitate or retard this development. One point, however, must be made. There is a potential conflict between the owner's interest and the natural system—between "cost-benefit analysis" of goal accomplishment and survival needs. This potential conflict raises control to the principal position in all artificial-system processes. Control attempts to assure a reasonable meeting of the external criterion, attainment of the owner's goals. Meeting this test is one, and usually the principal, condition for survival of the natural system.

Whatever else a modern public (or private) organization is, therefore, it is a machinelike instrument or tool of an external power. It is an artificial system of prescribed roles and rules. It is not a person. It is not a parent or friend. It is an abstract system of interrelationships designed to achieve an externally defined goal. Roles are bundles of duties (and powers). They do not care; they have no feelings. Whereas a particular incumbent of a role may "care" for a particular client (or customer, etc.), the caring is not part of the organizational plan. In fact, such a caring relation between the incumbent of a role in a modern organization and a client is regarded as unethical, as giving the client "pull," perhaps in the form of nepotism or favoritism.

We are proud of the fact that modern administration, as compared with administration in the past, is relatively free of such "particularistic" behavior and is "universalistic," instead. We are proud of the fact that modern administration gives jobs to people who merit them rather than to people who need them. Departures from such impersonal (noncompassionate) performance are pounced upon by the media; the departures make good news stories precisely because they violate modern canons of good administration. Why should a modern role incumbent care about a client? Who cares for *him,* other than his family and close friends? He, too, is caught up in an abstract, impersonal network, the artificial system, the organization-tool.

Furthermore, constructing organizations of abstract, impersonal roles eliminates (though not entirely) the relevance of the personal relations between role incumbents, whether they be love, hate, or indifference. The officially prescribed relationships exclude this aspect of interpersonal relations. Otherwise each organization would be unique, like a family, very few organizations would exist, and this country could support no more people than it did in 1492, perhaps about 800,000. The exclusion of personal elements from prescribed role relations has made the modern organization possible and adequate to its logistical task of provisioning hundreds of millions of people.

Most people in economically and politically underdeveloped countries cannot understand an abstract administrative order. Their relationships are personal, their obligations are personal, and they are unable to fashion organization-tools. That is why they are underdeveloped. For lack of organizations, their political actions, obligations, and interests are personal—"compassionate." There is no "public" interest. There is no "owner" of the public organization, the accomplishment of whose goal is the test of said organization. Everyone simply gets all he can get. Compassion monopolizes administration.

Still the problem of administrative compassion remains. Most people are brought up in a small intimate group, the so-called nuclear family. Their earliest and most constant experiences involve emotional dependence and support—involve, that is, compassion. In a thousand ways, we come to need such treatment, to be treated as whole and unique individuals whose feelings are important. We do not experience ourselves as "problem categories." We learn to expect incredible amounts of effort to be expended on our behalf, just because of our feelings. ("We forgot the Teddy Bear. We'll have to drive back [100 miles] and get it.") We do not want to have to justify ourselves, to live with contingency.

We are modern men and women. We believe in the principle of equality before the law, we believe in "universalistic" norms of administration, and yet we are ambivalent. We want administration to be universalistic (noncompassionate) in general, but how could making a little exception in our case hurt anything, an exception that would have no perceptible effect on public administration but would do a tremendous amount of good for us?

Our first experience of the large, abstract, impersonal organization can be devastating. For many young people this first experience is college. Yet how much worse it would be for a person brought up in the extended family or clan of traditional society! It is said that there once existed a tribe (in New Zealand,

I believe) that punished serious infractions of social norms by treating the culprit as a nonperson. Everyone acted as if he were not there—a sort of social banishment. People so treated, it is said, died in about three months, on the average.

Yes, the problem remains. The family has shrunk but it has not disappeared, and it is hard to imagine a viable alternative to it that would eliminate small-group experiences completely. The modern organization, by its nature, can offer only impersonal, categorized, noncompassionate treatment. But many individuals apparently still need personalized, individualized, compassionate treatment by the ever more ubiquitous organization. What are some of the adaptations that occur in attempting to resolve this impasse? . . .

An . . . approach—that is, an approach through personnel administration—is to give special attention to the problem in training those who "meet the public": counter clerks, bus drivers, etc. Although the training of counter clerks and others goes on continuously, it does not seem to solve the problem. One's friendly attitude towards one's fellow man is hardly a result of an administrative training program. Such buffer roles between frustrated and frightened clientele and a basically impersonal (hostile?) and abstract organization—an organization that controls employees' behavior in a roundabout fashion by means of rules and roles performed by functionaries—are not feasible on a large scale. The self-protection of the role incumbents often requires a hostile, or at best disinterested, treatment of the clientele, and the special training is soon forgotten. . . .

Since most of us are members of large bureaucratic organizations, concern for more personalized or compassionate treatment of individuals by organizations naturally extends to employees as well as to clientele (or customers, patients, etc.). Several social psychologists, beginning at least with Elton Mayo, have been working on this problem for years. Many of them consult with organization managements about changing organizations or their supervisory styles. These psychologists have begun to call their field "organization development," and for simplicity's sake I will lump their efforts and theories together under that title.

Organization development seeks to change organizations. It is casual about the purpose and direction of change because it relies upon a natural-system, natural-law concept of the "healthy" organization. Warren Bennis, for example, equates "scientific management" with "organization health." The natural-system (i.e., naturallaw) origin of the concept is clear. "It is now possible to postulate the criteria for organization health. These are based on a definition by Marie Jahoda, according to which a healthy personality '. . . actively masters his environment, shows a certain unit[y] of personality, and is able to perceive the world and himself correctly.' Let us take each of these elements and extrapolate it into organizational criteria." Frequently, it is urged that healthy organizations will be more effective in achieving their goals, but the major emphasis of organization development is that the organization be a more healthful environment in which adults can work. These people gloss over the fact that an organization is a tool of an external power (its "owner"). . . .

When training is conducted by people from outside the organization, as it increasingly is, or by trainers within the organization who have studied with those from without, the subject matter is frequently wholly or in part the natural system (usually natural systems of organizations in general). For the most part, external students of organizations use a natural-system model and study the organization as a complex of statistical distributions. The values they import into their science, and hence into their training programs, are natural-system values—that is, natural laws. Furthermore, they are observers rather than participants and so have interests different from organization members. Understanding is more important than profit (or success defined in some other way). Furthermore, they do not have to take responsibility for the results of their advice. Usually they are academics, and since few people pay any attention to them outside the classroom, they feel free to say whatever they want.

From these outside (and perhaps inside) trainers, therefore, trainees absorb some forbidden fruit. They learn about the natural system, and they may learn natural-law values—such as that of the natural harmony of the organization, or that one should be "people-oriented" rather than "task-oriented," or that their organization is "unhealthy." Natural systems are only dimly understood by participants, though much of their behavior is controlled by them. Armed with this new knowledge, the trainee may attempt to resist organization controls or to manipulate them for personal or group advantage. Or he may wish to realize his new natural law values—e.g., being people-oriented rather than production-oriented. In either case, he cannot be fully trusted by either his peers or his superiors. He may have become more of an observer than a participant and hence not quite trustworthy from the organization standpoint. Tremendous pressure will be put upon him to return to the old, safe, predictable, pretraining role performance. In a few months his training will probably have "washed out." If not, his frustrations may induce him to resign or seek a transfer, or he may be fired. The potential conflict between the external criteria— the owner's goals—and the survival criteria of the natural system is real and inescapable. Tools are not designed to survive or to be happy. Etzioni adds the point that human-relations (naturalsystem) training for foremen assumes that they can be both formal leaders (who are officers of the company) and informal leaders of the men—that they can play influence roles in both the artificial and natural systems. The resulting conflict and stress will render such dual roles intolerable for all but a very small number of very unusual people.

. . . A more irrational reaction to the impersonality of modern organizations is the growth of a spirit of regression to a simpler technology and hence simpler organization forms. Even as the British textile workers of the early nineteenth century followed "General Ludd" in his destruction of new labor-saving technology, many today wish to blame science and technology not only for such problems as pollution but also for the alienation, the frustration and desperation, of the individual. (I should say "some individuals" since most, I suspect, are doing very well.) Commitment to this position seems to be associated with fanaticism, with the charisma of a "movement," and as such it shows a tendency to follow the ancient fallacy that the end justifies the means. There have been suggestions of conscious distortions, even by scientists, by those opposing the Amchitka underground blast, the use of DDT, the SST—and who knows what else? We are told that there are currently (1972) ten times as many college students enrolled in classes teaching astrology as in classes teaching astrophysics. The 1970 and 1971 annual meetings of the American Association for the Advancement of Science were disrupted several times by groups who had defined the enemy as a personified "science" and blamed it for everything from human failure to racial prejudice to war. But if scientists are moving in the wrong direction, it is because they are allowing bureaucrats, politicians, college administrators, and private Luddite groups to define that direction, to push their research in directions contrary to their scientific instincts. . . .

Nearly all administrative organizations have these same problems, though not in such an extreme form, and must resort to some of the "stripping" tactics of the more total institutions. They apply the norm of equality. Even in nondemocratic governments of industrial nations the norm is applied to everyone but the political elite. The "rule of law" in this sense is an administrative necessity in an industrial country. Industrialism is impossible without the lowered unit costs and increased predictability that result. Though it is too late for industrialized and industrializing nations, there are countries that still can choose between personalized, individualized, compassionate administrative treatment of at least some of the population (generally, the aristocracy or others able to buy compassion) and administrative efficiency. For us, it is simply too late.

One set of proposed solutions to the administrative-compassion problem (among other problems) involves combining the roles of owner and functionary, or owner and customer-client, in the same person. Where this solution involves no more than the suggestion for small, independent businesses, it has already been discussed as part of the suggestion that we have smaller organizations. Where this suggestion is made in regard to larger organizations, it requires some special attention.

The suggestion for combining roles is closely related to a confusion between associations and organizations. Much "organization theory" and research is about associations, not organizations. The distinction is very important. Associations require a number of people with a shared interest—not an interest in common. For example, a number of people may share an interest in bird watching, in worshiping God, in farming. Each can pursue this interest alone or in association with others. On the other hand, a group with a common interest would have a common goal. It would be, at least incipiently, an organization. . . .

[H]igh-quality service is functionally organized. The areal generalist is professionally an ignoramus and an incompetent. Areal arrangements arise to meet political problems, not administrative ones. Current suggestions for reviving the areal principle in one form or another reflect a decline in political consensus. Immediately there is a drive to use administrative resources to solve the political or consenual problem. The objective is not better-quality services, better administration, but the acquisition of political power or the trading of administrative resources for consensus. However, it is simply too late to go back to the spoils system or to other preindustrial practices. Quality administration is necessary to support our large population in the style to which it has become accustomed. The consensual problem will be solved, if at all, through our political institutions, not by raids on administration. We cannot afford the "compassionate" administration of the underdeveloped countries. Too many people would starve to death. . . .

Repeatedly in the last few years, journalists, political scientists, and some lawyers have been discussing an old Swedish institution, that of the ombudsman, which was first formally established in Denmark in 1954 and was thus brought to the attention of the world. The ombudsman (or his office) hears complaints of citizens about improper treatment by bureaucrats. He also discovers cases on his own during tours of inspection. The ombudsman has power to secure information from the allegedly offending agency, to make recommendations for change, and to publicize the results. . . .

An institution to correct the acts of organizations needs an independent source of information and a continuing source of power. When it must get its information from the accused organization itself, it is at the organization's mercy. There are dozens of ways of hiding, slanting, or reinterpreting incriminating information. Organization officials who could not protect their organization from an ombudsman's investigation would have to be a bit dull and naïve. As for a continuing source of power, there seems to be none. Good government organizations are both weak and fickle. They go from fad to fad. . . .

A far more drastic attack on the principle of administrative impersonality and objectivity, and on our governmental priorities as well, is beginning to develop within academic ranks, especially among young faculty members. This group denies the possibility of a value-free social science. It declares that quantifiable, observable aspects of human relations and behavior are only partial descriptions and leave out the more important aspects of meaning and feeling. It holds that even our most basic ideas, those that seem natural and undetermined, are the products of presuppositions so fundamental as to be part of consciousness itself. It urges, therefore, that full knowledge requires an expansion of consciousness through development of full communication—communication of both facts and feelings without reservation, without self-serving suppressions and distortions designed as weapons in a battle of each against all. Consequently, it rejects positivism and the philosophy of science and toys with ideas from the philosophy of existentialism and phenomenology. . . .

The role of administration is to be somewhat subversive, promoting these goals regardless of congressional or presidential mandates or the wishes of the "organized interests," and being frankly political on behalf of the poor and downtrodden. Administration should be judged according to how well it serves these values rather than by its responsiveness to an unconcerned majority or its efficiency in achieving its assigned goals. The role of schools of public administration is to recruit and indoctrinate such administrators, aptly termed "short-haired radicals." . . .

H. George Frederickson  **NO**

Ethics and Public Administration

. . . Making Ethical Decisions: Doing Right or Wrong

We shift from the question of whether man is inherently good or bad to the question of the rightness or wrongness of decisions. This suspends the question of contextual variation in definitions of goodness and badness and the nature of man in different contexts and simply asks whether a particular decision, a set of decisions, or a pattern of decisions is right or wrong, and why. The approach used here rests on two broad philosophical traditions; the first is deontological, consisting of decisions based on fundamental principles, the other is teleological, consisting of decisions based on calculations of their likely consequences or results. In the deontological tradition, most particularly associated with Aquinas and Kant, decisions are based on duties or principles that are either right or wrong in themselves, the results being irrelevant to moral judgment.

> Deontological reasoning comes in many shades, depending upon whether the rules of behavior are seen as permanent and universal; knowable or unknowable; derived from revelation, human law, or community norms; and so on. All permutations dictate that there are certain underlying rules according to which behavior is judged, and no matter how desirable the consequences, there are certain things managers (and government) may not do.

The teleological tradition, most particularly associated with Mill and Bentham, is often referred to in the modern context as utilitarianism. In this tradition, decisions are judged by their consequences depending on the results to be maximized—security, happiness, pleasure, dignity. Results can be judged on the basis of the individual, the family, the neighborhood, the group or organization, the political jurisdiction, the nation-state.

Explicit standards of right and wrong are a defining feature of American government. The U.S. Constitution and laws, the state constitutions and laws, and the charters and laws of the lesser jurisdictions of the states when taken together are, by any measure, an impressive collection of definitions of right and wrong. In addition, there are countless administrative regulations adopted pursuant to laws and carrying the force of law. Add to this mix an entire branch of government established in part to interpret and protect the constitutions and the laws. Although it is trite, ours is a nation of laws and not of men. Certainly we have an impressive deontological array of constitutions, laws, and regulations that codify our values and define the principles of right and wrong as we see them. Much of the study of ethics in American government is embedded in the constitutional–legal perspective.

Despite the law, there is some considerable tolerance among the citizens for less egregious forms of corruption such as conflicts of interest, the blatant exercise of political influence, and small monetary exchanges. On the other hand, bribery, extortion, or the exchange of large sums of money are ethically unacceptable. Regardless of the law, there is relatively widespread tolerance of petty corruption in American government. This would seem to indicate that absolute principles of ethics, in the deontological tradition, are usually bent depending on the seriousness of the ethical breach.

If there is among the citizens a considerable tolerance for petty corruption, is there also a problem of "regime legitimacy"? Is government held in low regard and therefore unable to sustain strong public support because of petty corruption? Probably not. But there is strong evidence that people are much more inclined to obey the law if they believe the law to be just and fair and if they are of the opinion that there is procedural justice in the administration of the law. Regime legitimacy is a function of fairness and equity and some level of official benevolence in the administration of the law. To the extent that petty or grand corruption detract from fairness, equity, and benevolence, they reduce regime legitimacy. The larger deontological issue here is the identification of fairness, equity, and official benevolence as high-order ethical principles.

The current disquiet over the electoral advantage of incumbents is a further illustration that issues of fairness and equity seem to be importantly connected to regime legitimacy. Efforts to limit the number of terms served by incumbents presumably would level the electoral playing field. That seems more important to voters than the experience or expertise of legislators.

Procedural controls established during the reform movement to reduce corruption were generally successful. Judged in any comparative way, American government is among the most clean or ethical. But these procedures are the "red tape" that causes government to be slow, non–risk taking, bureaucratic, and nonresponsive. Perhaps the best evidence, however, that these anticorruption procedures work is the research indicating that when such procedures are taken away to make government more businesslike, there is an increase in corruption.

At the time of the reform movement it was thought that elected officials worked in the realm of values in making laws and setting budgets. Administration was neutral, a value-free implementation of law and legislative intent. With the destruction of the policy–administration dichotomy it became clear that values and political power are operative from the agenda-setting stage of the public policy process to the street-level implementation of policy. The values and patterns of moral reasoning of public administrators and civil servants became, then, almost as important as the values of elected officials. Professional associations for public administrators rapidly developed codes of ethics and ethics courses and training programs. Many jurisdictions adopted codes and standards. These documents and programs are primarily deontological—the statement of agreed-upon or settled values. And the assumptions have been Kantian—that there are absolute principles of right and wrong, independent of results or consequences, and that public administrators will adhere to these values. Research on ethics for public administrators indicates that the Kantian assumption is essentially correct, that civil servants are significantly inclined to support values such as civic virtue, honesty, procedural fairness, equity, and human dignity. There is also good evidence that citizens expect their government to be fair and equitable even though those concepts are difficult to define.

On its face this seems an odd finding because public administrators live and work in a world that is unrelentingly teleological, a world in which policy and programs results rule. In this world the public administrator practices, to borrow from Simon, "bounded ethics." In bounded ethics the administrator functions within the limits of enabling legislation, with limited budgets, usually advocating or at least supporting the purposes of the agency. Fundamental questioning of the purposes and practices of the agency, on the basis of issues of morality, is seldom found and rarely encouraged. Whistleblowing is very risky to the whistleblower and seldom results in fundamental organizational change. Following bounded ethics, the public administrator is, within the limits of organizational purpose and funding, almost always honest, virtuous, procedurally fair, and efficient. Indeed, many top public administrators have been and are examples of morality in government. To accept this conclusion, however, one must accept the boundaries within which the public administrator works.

There is another explanation for the apparent relative sense of right and wrong or morality of civil servants. Their work is embedded in rules, guidelines, inspectors, forms, and reports, and the other impedimenta of ethics enforcement. There can be little doubt that these requirements are "ethics enhancing" although it is likely that they slow work, inhibit creativity, and reduce responsiveness. With all of these procedural guides, inspectors, and oversight, why was there a HUD scandal, an Ill Winds scandal, an S&L scandal? The answer is that these are primarily political rather than bureaucratic scandals. As Paul Light puts it when he describes how the impending HUD scandal was regularly reported to Congress by the Inspectors General: "As for the influence-peddling scheme at the top of the agency, the IGs simply were not equipped to pursue such high-level wrongdoing. Their task was primarily to look down for scandal, not *up*."

The antigovernment-probusiness ethos of the last fifteen years has taken its toll on governmental ethics. Concepts of privatization and third-party government are especially in favor. Government, to use the currently trendy word, is being "reinvented" to put together public–private partnerships, to "empower" citizens with choices, and so on. In sum, it is fashionable to degovernmentalize on the promise of saving money and improving services. As previously governmental functions are shifted to the private sector or shared, it is a safe bet that corruption will increase. It is no small irony that government moves in the direction of privatization at the same time that there is a rising concern for governmental ethics.

There is a similar paradox in the universities. In public administration and public policy studies the teleological perspective holds the high ground. The wholesale adoption of policy analysis based on the measurement of results in terms of efficiency is a factor. So too is the popularity of the market model and theories of games, public choice, and cost–benefit analysis. What is right or wrong, what is moral or ethical is to be judged in terms of utility of consequences. That such an approach is without a larger sense of absolute right or wrong is generally understood. Yet in the presence of this utilitarian hegemony the universities are rediscovering ethics. It is especially interesting that many of the leaders of the new ethics groups on campuses are neo-Kantians.

What, then, can be concluded about ethical decision making in government and the doing of right and wrong? First, that the ethics of decisions are often based in the constitution(s), the law, and the regulations. Second, that rules, regulations, reports, oversight, inspectors, and the like do enhance the potential for ethical decisions. Third, that professional standards and codes of ethics also enhance ethical decision making. Fourth, that public administrators practice a form of bounded ethics that generally accepts the purposes and policies of the agency and practices ethics within those bounds. Fifth, that the most notable ethical breaches in recent years have been political rather than administrative. Sixth, that citizens are concerned with issues of fairness, equity, and justice and are likely to view government as less legitimate when these issues are not met and when there are scandals. Seventh, that as government moves in the direction of privatization the potential for ethical breaches increases. Eighth, that the study of public policy and the practice of policy analysis in American universities is teleological and utilitarian while most of the theory coming from those associated with the new centers for the study of ethics is deontological.

Democracy and Ethics: The Issue of Accountability

Central to the practice of government administration is the issue of accountability. Before the policy–administration dichotomy was rendered mythical it was possible to beg the question of accountability, falling back on the rhetoric if not the substance of neutrality. No more. Beginning fifty years ago with Herman Finer and continuing to this day is a stream of scholarship that seeks forms of democratic control over the bureaucracy. In our time Lowi argues for a juridical democracy in which the laws are precise and bureaucratic latitude in carrying out those laws is nil. Gruber seeks bureaucratic control through both legislative and presidential actions. Burke looks for balance between democratic control through legislators and elected executives and informed digression on the part of bureaucrats, but on the assumption that there is a bureaucratic control problem.

Carl Friedrich countered Finer with the argument that the effective conduct of government administration requires bureaucratic expertise and the discretion to apply that expertise. A host of public administration scholars have, over the years, supported this position. In recent years the "taking personal responsibility" for decisions and actions school, especially associated with Dennis Thompson, is put forward as the way to cope with the problems of dirty hands and many hands. A bureaucrat cannot take personal responsibility unless discretion is available, except in the case of refusing to act or to exit. John Rohr argues persuasively that there is a constitutional-legal basis for an extensive bureaucratic discretion. Charles Goodsell claims that without bureaucratic discretion government will be ineffective.

The entire issue turns on the question of whether, or to what extent, bureaucracy acts without controls or accountability. Much of the discussion of bureaucratic controls and accountability simply assumes their absence. In fact, the question of controls and accountability is usually caught up in the political battle between the policy preferences of legislators (Congress, state legislatures, city councils) and elected executives (president, governors, strong mayors). It is standard political rhetoric for presidents or governors to call for greater bureaucratic controls when the administration is carrying out the law and spending authorized appropriations on programs the president or the governor does not like. Legislators do the same. Does this mean that the bureaucracy is out of control or is unaccountable? No. Still, a surprising number of scholars accept the rhetoric as true and proceed to the question of controls and accountability.

Such research as there is on the subject indicates the following: bureaucrats tend to be responsive, within the law and their appropriations, to executive direction; in cases of the absence of accountability or the violation of the law or standards of ethics, such as the FBI under Hoover, both congressional and presidential oversight and controls failed; administrative agencies and their leaders are both experts and advocates for their tasks or missions and will seek support among legislators and elected executives interest groups and clients will support the programs and budgets of agencies supporting their interests.

Simply put, there are very few examples of bureaucratic agencies operating outside the ordinary range of legislative and executive accountability. (The activities of Oliver North in the Reagan administration come to mind, but his was hardly a regularly established administrative agency with enabling legislation, a bureaucracy, or a congressionally approved budget.)

Perception is more important than reality. It is widely believed, particularly among elected officials, that there are serious problems of bureaucratic control and accountability. Consequently, there has been a wide range of legislation establishing prohibitions against conflicts of interest and elaborate reporting procedures designed to prevent such conflicts—"designated ethics officers" in federal agencies, "Inspectors General" in federal departments, agency codes of ethics, ethics hotlines, ethics boards and commissions at the state and local level, and so on. Do they work? Yes, the Inspector General system does serve as an effective check against possible corruption. Yes, codes of ethics "do less than everything and more than nothing." Whistleblowing is a deterrent to possible agency misbehavior. Most important, these controls have very likely increased democratic controls and decreased administrative discretion. We may be close to Lowi's juridical democracy.

The problem, of course, is that the effective administration of governmental affairs is diminished. In addition, unlike earlier managerial ethics controls designed to *prevent* unethical behavior, these procedures are primarily designed to catch those who are unethical. As procedural-managerial controls have been relaxed in many jurisdictions, they have been replaced with "gotcha" ethics controls. That such controls inhibit innovation and creativity is certain.

Consider the opposite argument. Morgan and Kass discovered that local-level public administrators are experiencing a "role reversal" in which elected officials either will not or cannot decide issues and make policy. Is it unethical, under such circumstances, for bureaucrats to do nothing, especially if doing nothing would be fundamentally harmful to the public? Should the civil servant "take responsibility" when elected officials will not or cannot? Is the "policy gridlock" such that there can be no common ground on highly charged emotional issues such as abortion or on especially complicated social issues such as health care policy? Under such circumstances do we have questions of role reversal? Can we turn the policy–administration dichotomy on its head? In the dichotomy, elected officials set policy and appointed officials carry it out—they manage. We appear to be more nearly able to agree on how to do certain things—to manage—than we are able to agree on what should be done. Morgan and Kass call for a revised moral framework that enables administrators to articulate a complex ordering of moral claims that are compatible with our constitutional system of government. This is relatively close to Rohr's description of a constitutional basis for the legitimacy of the administrative role in American government.

There is no evidence, however, that Congress, state legislatures, and city and county councils are inclined to more specificity in the law, to precise policy direction, or to adequate funding to carry out policy or to cease intervening in administrative affairs. The problems for administrators are still there, and now they have less discretion to deal with the problems. As policy gridlock at the national level worsens, will there be a resurrection of the bureaucracy? Or is the administration of the national government so diminished in latitude and so hamstrung with congressional micro-management that we have the worst of both worlds—a Congress that cannot make policy and a bureaucracy that cannot manage?

What can be concluded about ethics and democracy and the issue of accountability? First, there has been the widespread perception that public bureaucracies are beyond control or unaccountable, although there is little evidence to support such perceptions. Second, most evidence indicates that bureaucrats are accountable and controlled. But there is also evidence that certain bureaucracies are powerful participants in the policy-making process and have influential political protectors. Third, there has been a sharp increase in ethics controls on bureaucrats and a decline in latitude or administrative discretion.

Fourth, adding to procedural-managerial approaches to preventing unethical behavior there are now many procedures designed to catch the unethical. Fifth, policy gridlock may result in the possibility of administrative role reversal with an accompanying ethical dilemma for government administrators. . . .

The government reform movement had a lasting effect on American government. Will the current ethics reform movement have the same "staying power" and permanent results? The answer is probably yes, especially if there is a continuing increase in incidence of government corruption. However, in the earlier case corruption was reduced by increasing administrative capacity and decreasing politics. In the present case we are moving in the opposite direction, reducing administrative capacity and increasing political control, with the probability that there will be more rather than less corruption. There are, of course, more controls on political corruption than in the past. Whether they will work remains to be seen.

The end of each section of this chapter sets out a list of assertions. These assertions are preliminary attempts to synthesize and summarize what is known about ethics in government administration. They are meant to stimulate research and analysis and should be thought of as subject to testing and verification.

In addition, I suggest that the future ethics research agenda should include the following six tasks:

1. It is evident that standards of right and wrong vary significantly from context to context. Yet much of the literature on ethics, especially the deontological literature, sets. Out universal standards of behavior. For certain matters of right and wrong this is sensible, such as standards of human dignity, the sanctity of life, adherence to the constitution(s) and the law(s). But for many ethical issues, standards and expectations are situationally determined. Future research should focus on the settings, professions, and cultures in which ethical issues occur and measure behavior against the cultural expectations and professional standards appropriate to the research context.

2. Once this is done, researchers should compare ethical standards and behavior between settings, professions, and cultures. In this way the richness and variety of the common ethical themes and variations on those themes can be described.

3. Researchers should assess the effect or result on the behavior of government officials, both political and administrative, of traditional procedural and managerial controls with modem approaches such as ethics officers, codes of ethics, Inspectors General, and whistleblowers.

4. Education and training are two of the most important modern techniques by which governments, professions, and universities attempt to enhance ethical behavior. Researchers should measure the actual results of education and training on behavior.

5. Researchers should assess the influence of privatization on government corruption and on ethics.

6. Researchers should measure the effects of reduced administrative discretion on both administrative effectiveness and ethics.

Much of the research on ethics in government is based on surveys of opinion. While opinions are important, there needs to be a body of research on government ethics based on field observation. Case studies and post-positivist forms of data gathering are essential to building a reliable body of knowledge. With an improved body of knowledge it will be possible to build a descriptive theory in government ethics to complement and challenge deductive theories.

EXPLORING THE ISSUE

Are External Controls Effective Tools for Ensuring Principled Conduct?

Critical Thinking and Reflection

1. What are external and internal controls? How are they similar and different?
2. In what ways are external controls and effectiveness related?
3. In what ways are external controls linked to principled conduct in public agencies?
4. What are some different kinds of external controls? What are the strengths and weaknesses of each?
5. What is the tension between individual goals and organizational goals? How does this tension relate to external controls?

Is There Common Ground?

When public money is at stake and the ideals of American democracy are on the line, we expect that principled conduct will come from our public administrators. Yet, as the news media and government opponents will regularly remind us, this is not always the case. Government—like any other organization—has moments of unethical conduct. Unfortunately, the misgivings of public agencies are magnified and more regularly brought to the attention of the general public. Within organizations, there are two forms of controls that we have discussed in this debate—internal and external controls. Although both have their merits, they also come with significant questions. With internal controls, our concerns need to be whether agencies can be trusted to police themselves. After all, if there is a systemic cause of the misconduct, we could possibly see a less than genuine response. But with external controls, one can question whether outside influences are familiar enough with the context and culture of the organization to assure principled conduct. Perhaps the best way to frame the discussion is to figure out how both internal and external controls can be utilized together in a way that permits workers to do their jobs while knowing there are both internal and external checks on their actions. By doing this, we can hopefully eliminate the need for either type of control to actually exist.

Additional Resources

Garofalo, C. and D. Geuras, *Common Ground, Common Future: Moral Agency in Public Administration, Professions, and Citizenship* (New York: CRC Press, 2005)

This book examines the public and private roles of the citizen as a moral agent. The authors define this agent as a person who recognizes morality as a motive for action, and not only follows moral principles but also acknowledges morality as his or her principle. The book explains that public administration is a fundamentally moral enterprise that exists to serve the values that society considers significant, and that this moral nature makes public administration a prototype for other professions to emulate, a model of moral governance in American society.

Graham, L., *Internal Controls: Guidance for Private, Government, and Non-Profit Entities* (New York: Wiley, 2007)

Graham provides practical advice about what to do when choosing to make an investment in internal controls for an organization. By doing so, all types of organizations can be prepared as transparent, accountable citizens.

Pfeffer, J. and G. Salancik, *The External Control of Organizations: A Resource Dependence Perspective* (Stanford, CA: Stanford University Press, 2003)

The *External Control of Organizations* explores how external constraints affect organizations and provides insights for designing and managing organizations to mitigate these constraints. All organizations are dependent on the environment for their survival. As the authors contend, "it is the fact of the organization's dependence on the environment that makes the external constraint and control of organizational behavior both possible and almost inevitable." Organizations can either try to change their environments through political means or form interorganizational relationships to control or absorb uncertainty. This seminal book established the resource dependence approach that has informed so many other important organization theories.

Pfister, J.A., *Managing Organizations Culture for Effective Internal Control: From Practice to Theory* (Berlin: Physica-Verlag, 2009)

In times of economic and financial crises, the content of this book rings true. Although we often look at formal compliance procedures, incentive systems and other "technical" ways to ensure effective internal control, this study emphasizes a different perspective: How do the management principles and practices influence organizational culture in order to enhance control effectiveness? New theory is provided on the way that tone at the top—leadership, sustainability, accountability, and other social control aspects—is combined with formal control.

Svaram J.H., *The Ethics Primer for Public Administrators in Government and Non-profit Organizations* (Sudbury, MA: Jones and Bartlett, 2006)

A primer that introduces the reader to the fundamentals of administrative responsibility and ethics, this text seeks to explain why ethics are important to administrators in governmental and non-profit organizations, and how these administrators can relate their own personal values to the norms of the public sector.

ISSUE 17

Should Public Employees Have Collective Bargaining Rights?

YES: Amanda Huffman, from "The Wisconsin Debate—The Basics and Implications of Public Sector Collective Bargaining Legislation," *Georgetown Public Policy Review* (April 2011)

NO: Daniel DiSalvo, from "The Trouble with Public Sector Unions," *National Affairs* (Fall 2010)

Learning Outcomes

After reading this issue, you should be able to:

- Define what is meant by collective bargaining rights.
- Discuss whether public employees should be granted universal collective bargaining rights.
- Gain an understanding of the constitutional and statutory bases for collective bargaining rights.
- Describe how collective bargaining rights relate to pension shortages and budget shortfalls.
- Describe the actions of New Jersey Governor Chris Christie to curb public employee union influences in his state.
- Understand how to maintain a balance in public sector employee union relationships with government employers.

ISSUE SUMMARY

YES: Amanda Huffman argues that the Wisconsin showdown from spring 2011 demonstrates a clear need for public employees to have collective bargaining rights. The challenge, in her eyes, is to discover how to maintain a balance and integrity in public sector employment relationships that provides appropriate checks on both employer and union power.

NO: Daniel DiSalvo argues that public union members will need to willingly make concessions in the future or risk seeing dramatic changes due to the faltering economy. Highlighting the efforts of New Jersey Governor Chris Christie, DiSalvo believes citizens will eventually begin questioning the demands of public employees if they do not begin coming to their senses.

Just weeks prior to the 1980 Presidential Election, Republican challenger Ronald Reagan wrote a letter to the president of the Professional Air Traffic Controllers Organization (PATCO) expressing his direct support for the union, describing the steps he would take within his power as president to remedy the relationship between the national government and air traffic controllers. Reagan boldly observed that "In an area so clearly related to public safety, the Carter administration has failed to act responsibly" (Reagan letter). Despite trade unions' tendency to support sympathetic Democrat candidates, tense negotiation with the Federal Aviation Administration under the Carter administration led PATCO to support Ronald Reagan in the election. In other words, sour relations with old management and Reagan's promise of a "spirit of cooperation" led to an unexpected union.

The warm feelings and high hopes were extinguished on August 3, 1981, when PATCO went on strike, demanding higher pay and improved work conditions, of which a 32-hour workweek was a cornerstone. According to federal law, strikes were not permitted to public sector unions in this circumstance. The Carter administration had recently fired postal workers participating in the 1978 strikes. In Reagan's letter of support to PATCO, he argued that since air traffic controllers are critical to public safety, care should be taken to ensure that working conditions and technology support their work. In turn, he argued that the PATCO strike was a threat to the very public safety protected by air traffic controllers in the first place. As they were in violation of the law, Reagan ordered the employees back to work. About 10 percent of the air traffic controllers did so. In response, Reagan issued a 48-hour ultimatum, demanding that the remaining 11,345 striking air traffic controllers return to work or surrender their jobs. At the conclusion of the 48-hour window, the air traffic controllers were fired. A further penalty, later overturned by President Bill Clinton, was that the fired employees would be barred for life from receiving federal employment. As a result of the showdown between President Reagan and PATCO, PATCO effectively ceased to exist. Beyond merely exhibiting a promanagement position on the part of the Reagan administration, Seth A. Rosen (1988) argues that "the PATCO strike further exacerbated the decline in the (airline) industry's revenue and the downward trend in its collective bargaining settlements" (Rosen *Cleared For Takeoff* 15). Reagan's decision was clearly politically risky, but as Reagan himself succinctly stated in a press conference in the wake of the standoff: "The law is very explicit. They are violating the law."

Collective bargaining is essentially the process of negotiation between an employer and a collective group of employees, the product of which is an agreement delineating the nature of work conditions. As the above example indicates, the debate over the rights and responsibilities of public sector unions in the United States is complicated and controversial, especially when compared to the history and development of collective bargaining in the private sector. Even as ardent an advocate of private sector collective bargaining as Franklin Delano Roosevelt was, he maintained serious reservations about the prospects of collective bargaining among government employees. In a 1937 letter to the president of the National Federation of Federal Employees, Roosevelt remarked the following:

> All Government employees should realize that the process of collective bargaining, as usually understood, cannot be transplanted into the public service. It has its distinct and insurmountable limitations when applied to public personnel management. The very nature and purposes of Government make it impossible for administrative officials to represent fully or to bind the employer in mutual discussions with Government employee organizations. The employer is the whole people, who speak by means of laws enacted by their representatives in Congress.

Roosevelt argued that since the will of the people is at stake, collective bargaining among public sector employees represented too great a threat to both the essential operation of the government machinery and the public interest. Of a potential public employee strike, Roosevelt stated: "Such action, looking toward the paralysis of Government by those who have sworn to support it, is unthinkable and intolerable." The debate brings to mind Wallace Sayre's often quoted statement that "business and public administration are alike only in all unimportant respects." In the case of government, the people are multifaceted: citizens; voters; constituents; and taxpayers. Collective bargaining consists of negotiation between employer and employees, but in the case of the public sector, both the nature of the work and the complex composition of the employer complicate the process.

The United States government and most states place extraordinary limits on public sector unions. In many instances, notably the national government, public employees are permitted to join unions that would be recognized by the government. However, the nature of the interaction is often limited to "discussing" employment issues rather than "negotiating" a work agreement. President John F. Kennedy's Executive Order 10988 permitted public employees to establish and join unions. Additional federal policies merely redefined this condition, never going so far as to permit bargaining over employee wages and benefits. Union rules and collective bargaining limitations for public employees vary by state. Collective bargaining is not permitted in 5 states, is permitted but not required in 11 states, and is required in the rest. Of course, the visibility of the issue of state employee collective bargaining increased dramatically when Wisconsin governor Scott Walker and the Wisconsin state legislature worked to pass a Budget Repair Bill that redefined collective bargaining for state employees. The legislation limited bargaining to wages. The debate sparked massive protests and an invasion of the capitol. Supporters of the bill argued that the change should be permitted in the face of an economic crisis that demanded tough choices. Opponents argued that the bill violated a fundamental right to collective bargaining, leading to calls for impeachment of the governor.

In the YES selection, Amanda Huffman echoes the views of the Budget Repair Bill opponents. She argues that although the concerns for the public interest are well-founded, public employees' right to collectively bargain must be maintained. In the NO selection, Daniel DiSalvo acknowledges the difficulty of completely rescinding collective bargaining rights where they already exist, but argues that the protections granted within civil service statutes and employment law sufficiently defend employee rights.

YES

Amanda Huffman

The Wisconsin Debate—The Basics and Implications of Public Sector Collective Bargaining Legislation

Wisconsin's recently passed legislation to limit public workers' collective bargaining rights has ignited a fiery debate over public sector union power in the United States. Despite the complexity of unions in this country, the discussion is often boiled down to a political faceoff between anti-union conservatives and pro-union liberals. Regrettably, such simplification polarizes the debate and dulls a potentially robust conversation of policy alternatives.

In order to provide a more informed view, this article seeks to examine the dispute over public sector unions by defining the basic debate vocabulary, identifying differences between private and public sector unions, summarizing the arguments for and against limiting collective bargaining rights and previewing the political implications of limiting public sector union strength.

The consequential challenge to policy makers is to create reasonable options more nuanced than either the utter demise or complete domination of unions in America; options in which public sector unions can realistically continue to play their intended role of protecting public sector workers without the incentive or ability to abuse the responsibility.

Basic Terminology and Political Issues

The terms "union", "collective bargaining" and "collective agreement" are frequently used and rarely clarified. Given that misinterpretations can seriously muddle any analysis, basic explanations are provided below:

- A "labor union" is an organization that acts on behalf of workers, generally to collectively bargain with employers to provide a variety of worker protections and benefits;
- "Collective bargaining" refers to a process whereby employees (represented by a union) and employers negotiate to reach a collective agreement; and
- A "collective agreement" is the labor contract between an employer and a union.

From *Georgetown Public Policy Review*, April 2011. Copyright © 2011 by Georgetown Public Policy Review. Reprinted by permission.

A key detail is that the "right to collective bargaining", much like the "right to free speech" or the "right to bear arms" is not black and white. The specific rules that define the process, i.e. the rights afforded to employers and employees in contract negotiations, assume many different shades of grey across various jurisdictions.

Federal collective bargaining rights differ from those provided at the state level, bargaining rights vary across states, private sector bargaining rights diverge from those in the public sector, and distinctions in the negotiation process exist across industries. For instance, some states authorize broader public sector collective bargaining rights than are afforded by federal legislation, which has historically been the case in Wisconsin, while others do not.

Collective bargaining rights can also favor either negotiating party to varying degrees. As a result, much of the political debate over unions is about the particulars and extent of collective bargaining rights. Weak collective bargaining rights diminish union strength, both in contract negotiations and broader union activities, while strong collective bargaining rights increase union strength. Labor unions' overwhelming support for Democratic candidates has led some to view extending or limiting collective bargaining as a political mechanism for strengthening or weakening the Democratic Party.

Consequently, the debate over public sector collective bargaining rights in Wisconsin is not just about public workers sharing the financial burden [of solving the state budget deficit]; it's about weakening union power. Previously, Wisconsin law stated that municipal and state employees had the right to collectively bargain over wages, hours, and conditions of employment. The new law enacted on March 10 removes public sector collective bargaining rights on work rules and non-wage benefits for non-public safety employees. While public sector employees can still collectively bargain for wage increases, these increases are capped in that they can increase no faster than the Consumer Price Index in percentage terms each year.

Noteworthy is that the Wisconsin legislation removes many, but not all, of the rights to collectively bargain for some public workers. And while the rights are not completely stripped, limiting the extent of those rights has the potential to significantly reduce union strength.

Moreover, the legislation limits the power of public, not private, sector unions. Understanding how private and public sector unions differ, and how they are inextricably linked, provides the foundation for arguments to either limit or preserve public sector collective bargaining rights.

Private vs. Public Sector Unions

Legislative Differences

Legislative differences exist between private and public sector unions. The 1935 National Labor Relations Act (NLRA) established union rights to organize by detailing union membership, collective bargaining representation and the right to strike rules in the private sector across the nation.

Union legislation in the public sector is more complex. By Executive Order 10988 (1962), President Kennedy established the legal right to collectively bargain for federal employees; however, the Executive Order does not compare to the NLRA in setting a single standard for the details of union membership, collective bargaining and striking rights. Instead, states have individually established public sector union legislation with varying rules. For example, in one particular state public sector workers may be permitted to strike, while in another state they may be obligated to arbitrate disputes. Further, much of state collective bargaining legislation has been enacted in a piecemeal fashion according to the political influence of specific interest groups looking to gain specific rights. Finally, public employees have gained rights and set precedents in certain states by winning cases of employer abuse in the courts. The result is a particularly convoluted set of public sector employment relations governed by federal, state and local rules.

Incentives to Negotiate

Aside from their legislative differences, private and public sector employers and employees deviate in their incentives to negotiate. In very simple terms, if a private sector union makes demands that are too high for a company to meet and still remain in business, the employer can go bankrupt and its employees will be out of a job. Private sector employers and unions thus have an incentive to negotiate for the benefit of both parties.

In the public sector, most government employers do not have the option of bankruptcy and, as a result, public sector unions do not have the same incentive to mitigate their demands to keep their employer afloat. Additionally, public sector union members are also voters who have a say in who runs their government, i.e. they play a role in choosing the employer with whom they negotiate. The lack of incentive for public sector unions to negotiate and the inherent conflict of interest from employers being elected officials is at the core of the argument to limit public sector collective bargaining.

Arguments For and Against Public Sector Collective Bargaining Power

Public Sector Collective Bargaining Rights Should Be Preserved

The main argument for preserving public sector collective bargaining rights is based on the importance of union strength as a whole to individual worker rights. According to the Bureau of Labor Statistics, 36 percent of public sector workers are unionized compared to less than 7 percent of private sector workers. As union power in the United States is largely concentrated in the public sector, a decline in public sector union strength means a decline in overall union strength. As even non-union workers can gain wages and benefits from collective agreements that meet union demands, deterioration in union influence spells weaker protections for workers across the board.

Public Sector Collective Bargaining Rights Should Be Limited

Often the argument for limiting public sector collective bargaining rights is that public sector worker compensation (including benefits and attempting to account for intangibles, such as job security) is higher than that of private sector workers, and that the disparity is unfair. In fact, according to a study based on the Bureau of Economic Analysis (BEA), public sector workers earn more than private sector workers in 41 states.

However, in a 2010 study comparing public and private sector compensation, authors Bender and Heywood find that public workers at the state and local level receive total compensation including wages and benefits 6.8 and 7.4 percent (respectively) lower than their counterparts with similar levels of education and experience in the private sector.

Regardless of any compensation inequality, a more solid case for limiting public sector collective bargaining rights points to the unique circumstances of public sector unions, where the incentives for public employees and government employers to negotiate toward an economically efficient outcome are weaker than in the private sector. Taxpayers end up footing the bill for aggressive union demands and weak political concessions.

Political Implications of Limiting Public Sector Union Strength

Currently, approximately two-thirds of states grant collective bargaining rights for their public employees. The map below provides a simple illustration of the variation in public sector collective bargaining according to state laws.

However, Wisconsin Governor Scott Walker's success in limiting the public sector worker collective bargaining rights in Wisconsin could create a domino effect wherein other state legislative bodies will follow suit. Weaker unions imply an enormous threat to union campaign contributions, which favor Democratic candidates. The law in Wisconsin prohibits non-union public employees from being required to pay union dues. On the other hand, the controversy in Wisconsin has roused union activists and some speculate that there is potential for a reinvigorated labor movement.

Depending on how the scenarios described above unfold, Democrats may stand to either lose or gain politically. But regardless of the political consequences of Gov. Walker's actions, the role of public sector unions is to protect the rights of public workers, not to fund political campaigns. Further, the incentives that govern public sector employer-employee relationships are misaligned and do not provide an adequate check on union demands. These two facts, however, do not mean that public sector unions do not have a place in America's labor market.

Workers in the United States have organized themselves throughout our nation's history to unite their voices against employer abuses—and public sector employers need to be held accountable just like private sector employers. The fact remains that unions cannot protect workers if their negotiating power with employers is toothless. The policy challenge, then, is not to preclude or mandate membership in and collective bargaining by public sector unions, but rather to discover how to maintain a balance and integrity in public sector employment relationships that provides appropriate checks on both employer and union power.

Daniel DiSalvo

The Trouble with Public Sector Unions

When Chris Christie became New Jersey's governor in January, he wasted no time in identifying the chief perpetrators of his state's fiscal catastrophe. Facing a nearly $11 billion budget gap—as well as voters fed up with the sky-high taxes imposed on them to finance the state government's profligacy—Christie moved swiftly to take on the unions representing New Jersey's roughly 400,000 public employees.

On his first day in office, the governor signed an executive order preventing state-workers' unions from making political contributions—subjecting them to the same limits that had long applied to corporations. More recently, he has waged a protracted battle against state teachers' unions, which are seeking pay increases and free lifetime health care for their members. Recognizing the burden that such benefits would place on New Jersey's long-term finances, Christie has sought instead to impose a one-year wage freeze, to change pension rules to limit future benefits, and to require that teachers contribute a tiny fraction of their salaries to cover the costs of their health insurance—measures that, for private-sector workers, would be mostly uncontroversial.

The firestorm that these proposals have sparked demonstrates the political clout of state-workers' unions. Christie's executive order met with vicious condemnation from union leaders and the politicians aligned with them; his fight with the public-school teachers prompted the New Jersey Education Association to spend $6 million (drawn from members' dues) on anti-Christie attack ads over a two-month period. Clearly, the lesson for reform-minded politicians has been: Confront public-sector unions at your peril.

Yet confront them policymakers must. As Christie said about the duel with the NJEA, "If we don't win this fight, there's no other fight left." Melodramatic as this may sound, for many states, it is simply reality. The cost of public-sector pay and benefits (which in many cases far exceed what comparable workers earn in the private sector), combined with hundreds of billions of dollars in unfunded pension liabilities for retired government workers, are weighing down state and city budgets. And staggering as these burdens seem now, they are actually poised to grow exponentially in the years ahead. If policymakers fail to rein in this growth, a fiscal crack-up will be the inevitable result.

From *National Affairs*, Fall 2010, pp. 3–4, 6–7, 13–19. Copyright © 2010 by National Affairs, Inc. Reprinted by permission.

New Jersey has drawn national attention as a case study, but the same scenario is playing out in state capitals from coast to coast. New York, Michigan, California, Washington, and many other states also find themselves heavily indebted, with public-sector unions at the root of their problems. In exchange, taxpayers in these states are rewarded with larger and more expensive, yet less effective, government, and with elected officials who are afraid to cross the politically powerful unions. As the *Wall Street Journal* put it recently, public-sector unions "may be the single biggest problem . . . for the U.S. economy and small-d democratic governance." They may also be the biggest challenge facing state and local officials—a challenge that, unless economic conditions dramatically improve, will dominate the politics of the decade to come.

. . .

A Unionized Government

The effects of public-sector unionism can be grouped under three broad headings. The first centers on compensation, which includes wages, pensions, health care, and other benefits easily valued in monetary terms—the core issues at stake in collective-bargaining negotiations. The second involves the amount of government employment, or the size of government, as reflected in the number of workers and in public budgets. The third involves the productivity and efficiency of government services. Insofar as unions negotiate detailed work rules, they share the power to shape the day-to-day responsibilities of public servants—which influences what government does, and how well it does it.

These are complex matters that are hard for social scientists to measure, and on which scholars disagree. Nevertheless, the evidence supports a few broad conclusions.

Most economists agree that public-sector unions' political power leads to more government spending. And recently, Chris Edwards of the Cato Institute documented *how* government unionism has abetted growth in public-sector compensation. Generally speaking, the public sector pays more than the private sector for jobs at the low end of the labor market, while the private sector pays more for jobs at the high end. For janitors and secretaries, for instance, the public sector offers an appreciably better deal than the private economy: According to the Bureau of Labor Statistics, the average annual salary for the roughly 330,000 office clerks who work in government was almost $27,000 in 2005, while the 2.7 million in the private sector received an average pay of just under $23,000. Nationwide, among the 108,000 janitors who work in government, the average salary was $23,700; the average salary of the 2 million janitors working in the private sector, meanwhile, was $19,800.

For workers with advanced degrees, however, the public-sector pay scale is likely to be slightly below the private-sector benchmark. Private-sector economists, for instance, earn an average of $99,000 a year, compared to the $69,000 earned by their government colleagues. And accountants in the corporate world earn average annual salaries of $52,000, compared to $48,000 for their public-sector counterparts.

Not as easily captured is the comparable worth of those government workers who lack counterparts in the private sector, such as policemen, firefighters, and corrections officers. But that very monopoly status has given the union representatives of these workers enormous leverage, which they have converted into major gains. For example, in New York state, county police officers were paid an average salary of $121,000 a year in 2006. In that same year, according to the *Boston Globe*, 225 of the 2,338 Massachusetts State Police officers made more than the $140,535 annual salary earned by the state's governor. Four state troopers received more than $200,000, and 123 others were paid more than $150,000. While people whose jobs entail greater risk of life and limb certainly deserve higher pay, union power has clearly added a substantial premium.

When all jobs are considered, state and local public-sector workers today earn, on average, $14 more per hour in total compensation (wages and benefits) than their private-sector counterparts. The *New York Times* has reported that public-sector wages and benefits over the past decade have grown *twice* as fast as those in the private sector. These aggregate pay differentials stem partly from the fact that government work tends to be more white-collar, and that public employees tend to be better educated and more experienced, and to live in urban areas. Another factor is the hollowing out of the middle of the income distribution in the private sector. But union influence still plays a major role.

When unions have not been able to secure increases in wages and salaries, they have turned their attention to benefits. *USA Today* journalist Dennis Cauchon notes that, since 2002, for every $1-an-hour pay increase, public employees have gotten $1.17 in new benefits; private-sector workers, meanwhile, have received just 58 cents in added benefits. Of special interest to the unions has been health care: Across the nation, 86% of state- and local-government workers have access to employer-provided health insurance, while only 45% of private-sector workers do. In many cases, these plans involve meager contributions from employees, or none at all—in New Jersey, for instance, 88% of public-school teachers pay nothing toward their insurance premiums.

The unions' other cherished benefit is public-employee pensions. In California, for example, state workers often retire at 55 years of age with pensions that exceed what they were paid during most of their working years. In New York City, firefighters and police officers may retire after 20 years of service at half pay—which means that, at a time when life expectancy is nearly 80 years, New York City is paying benefits to 10,000 retired cops who are less than 50 years old. Those benefits quickly add up: In 2006, the annual pension benefit for a new retiree averaged just under $73,000 (and the full amount is exempt from state and local taxes).

How, one might ask, were policymakers ever convinced to agree to such generous terms? As it turns out, many lawmakers found that increasing pensions was very good politics. They placated unions with future pension commitments, and then turned around, borrowed the money appropriated for the pensions, and spent it paying for public services in the here and now.

Politicians liked this scheme because they could satisfy the unions, provide generous public services without raising taxes to pay for them, and even sometimes get around balanced-budget requirements.

Unfortunately, the hit pension funds took recently in the stock market has exposed the massive underfunding that results from states' and municipalities' not paying for the public services they consume. In Illinois, for example, public-sector unions have helped create a situation in which the state's pension funds report a liability of more than $100 billion, at least 50% of it unfunded. Yet many analysts believe the figure is much higher; without a steep economic recovery, the Prairie State is looking at insolvency. Indeed, Northwestern University finance professor Joshua Rauh puts the date of collapse at 2018; he also predicts that six other states—Connecticut, Indiana, New Jersey, Hawaii, Louisiana, and Oklahoma—will see their pension funds dry up before the end of fiscal year 2020. What's more, according to the Pew Center on the States, 18 states face long-term pension liabilities in excess of $10 billion. In the case of California, like that of Illinois, the unfunded pension liability exceeds $50 billion. In fact, Pew estimates that, when retiree health-care costs are added to pension obligations, the unfunded liabilities of the states total an astounding $1 trillion.

The skyrocketing costs of public employees' pensions now present a huge challenge to state and local governments. If allowed to persist, such massive obligations will inevitably force a fundamental re-ordering of government priorities. After all, if government must spend more on pensions, it cannot spend more on schools, roads, and relief for the poor—in other words, the basic functions people expect their governments to perform. But because many states' pension commitments are constitutionally guaranteed, there is no easy way out of this financial sink hole. Recent court decisions indicate that pension obligations will have to be fulfilled even if governments declare bankruptcy—because while federal law allows bankruptcy judges to change pension and health-care packages in the private sector, it forbids such changes in public employees' agreements.

Yet as skilled as the unions may be in drawing on taxpayer dollars, many observers argue that their greater influence is felt in the quality of the government services taxpayers receive in return. In his book *The Warping of Government Work*, Harvard public-policy scholar John Donahue explains how public-employee unions have reduced government efficiency and responsiveness. With poor prospects in the ultra-competitive private sector, government work is increasingly desirable for those with limited skills; at the opposite end of the spectrum, the wage compression imposed by unions and civil-service rules makes government employment less attractive to those whose abilities are in high demand. Consequently, there is a "brain drain" at the top end of the government work force, as many of the country's most talented people opt for jobs in the private sector where they can be richly rewarded for their skills (and avoid the intricate work rules, and glacial advancement through big bureaucracies, that are part and parcel of government work).

Thus, as New York University professor Paul Light argues, government employment "caters more to the security-craver than the risk-taker." And because government employs more of the former and fewer of the latter, it is less flexible, less responsive, and less innovative. It is also more expensive: Northeastern University economist Barry Bluestone has shown that, between 2000 and 2008, the price of state and local public services has increased by 41% nationally, compared with 27% for private services.

Finally, insofar as government collective-bargaining agreements touch on a wide range of economic decisions, public-sector unions have extraordinary influence over government policies. In the classic model of democratic accountability, citizens vote in competitive elections for candidates offering distinct policy agendas; once in office, the winners implement their programs through public agencies. But when public-employee unions bargain collectively with the government, elected officials partially cede control of public agencies to unelected labor leaders. Many policy choices are then settled in the course of negotiations between office holders and unions, rather than originating with the people's duly elected representatives. Over the long term, these negotiated work rules can drive public policy in directions that neither elected officials nor voters desire. And once enacted, these policies can prove very hard to reverse, even through elections: A new mayor or governor—no matter how hard-charging a reformer—will often find his hands tied by the iron-clad agreements unions managed to extract from his predecessors.

Stanford University political scientist Terry Moe has made exactly this argument with respect to the education sector. "Teachers unions have more influence on the public schools than any other group in American society," Moe argues. "Their massive memberships and awesome resources give them unrivaled power in the politics of education, allowing them to affect which policies are imposed on the schools by government—and to block reforms they don't like." One need only look at the debates over charter-school caps or merit-pay proposals to see Moe's point.

Public-sector unions thus distort the labor market, weaken public finances, and diminish the responsiveness of government and the quality of public services. Many of the concerns that initially led policymakers to oppose collective bargaining by government employees have, over the years, been vindicated.

As a result, it is difficult for defenders of public-sector unions today to make a convincing case that such unions benefit the public at large. Their argument has basically been reduced to three assertions. One is that most public employees live modest lives, and so criticizing efforts to improve their lot distracts attention from wealthy CEOs and Wall Street bankers who are the real culprits behind today's economic woes. Another is that the unions defend the dignity of public service, thereby preserving a middle class that would otherwise be plunged—through conservatives' efforts to privatize such work—into the vicious race to the bottom that now plagues the private sector. Finally, government-workers' unions help advance leftist politics by keeping the labor movement hobbling along.

To be sure, there is some merit to each of these arguments, though none is especially convincing. But even if these claims were completely true and obvious, they would not offer sufficient reason to put up with the other, manifestly negative consequences of public-sector unionism.

Governing in the Real World

"At some point," New Jersey governor Chris Christie said in a February speech to his state's mayors, "there has to be parity between what is happening in the real world and what is happening in the public-sector world."

Achieving such parity will not be easy, as some early attempts to curtail the power of public-sector unions have shown. Some state and local officials (like California governor Arnold Schwarzenegger) have sought to appeal directly to the people through referenda, only to be thwarted by the unions' electoral clout. Others have pursued stop-gap measures like wage freezes and furloughs of public employees, which inevitably draw some public backlash. There have even been calls for some cities to follow the example of Vallejo, California, and declare bankruptcy so that they can renegotiate employment contracts with the unions.

A few places are attempting more serious long-term solutions. As the *Wall Street Journal* reported in June, public-employee unions in Vermont, Iowa, Minnesota, and Wyoming have recently agreed to modest reductions in pension benefits—though none of the cuts is large enough to bring the finances of that state's pension funds fully into balance. In the Garden State, Governor Christie succeeded in getting the state legislature to approve a 2% annual growth cap on property taxes in order to limit local spending—thereby indirectly curtailing the power of teachers' unions to demand more public dollars. Yet even well-designed tax caps can unleash unpleasant consequences, including more crowded classrooms, layoffs of state workers, and increases in pension debt. Few politicians will want to suffer those consequences, and the unions will fiercely oppose all policies that even hint at reform.

All of these efforts are, of course, attempts to deal only with the symptoms of the looming state fiscal crisis—not with its underlying causes. To address those causes, policymakers may even need to re-open the question of whether government workers should enjoy the privilege of collective bargaining.

After all, even without collective bargaining, government workers would still benefit from far-reaching protections under existing civil-service statutes—more protections than most private-sector workers enjoy. And they would retain their full rights as citizens to petition the government for changes in policy. Public-sector workers' ability to unionize is hardly sacrosanct; it is by no means a fundamental civil or constitutional right. It has been permitted by most states and localities for only about half a century, and, so far, it is not clear that this experiment has served the public interest.

It is true that ending government workers' ability to organize is politically inconceivable today in the states where it exists. But if states' and cities' fiscal ills grow painful enough, the unthinkable could someday become political necessity. For all Americans—including public-sector employees—it would of course be better if the situation did not reach that point of catastrophe. We can all hope that a robust economic revival will take the pressure off of states and cities and give policymakers more room to maneuver. If such a rapid recovery is not forthcoming, though, the most appealing solution will be for everyone to re-enter the real world—if only public officials and public-sector unions can be sensible enough to try.

EXPLORING THE ISSUE

Should Public Employees Have Collective Bargaining Rights?

Critical Thinking and Reflection

1. Should public employees be granted universal collective bargaining rights? Why or why not?
2. In what way can some collective bargaining rights be preserved while not allowing public unions to have full control?
3. How does collective bargaining relate to pension shortages and budget shortfalls?
4. How can we best maintain a balance in public sector employee union relationships with government employers? Why is it important to do so?
5. What are the constitutional and statutory bases for collective bargaining rights?

Is There Common Ground?

With the election of Scott Walker to the position of governor of Wisconsin, the issue of public employee collective bargaining rights has hit a fevered pitch. With protests and ballot measures now appearing throughout the country (particularly in the Midwest), the American public is regularly exposed to the arguments both for and against these rights. Proponents of public employee collective bargaining want to ensure that employees have the ability to negotiate for wages and benefits they desire. Opponents, on the other hand, believe that these employees are either already overcompensated or that they should be subject to the decisions of management as is more prevalent in the private sector.

Given the deeply politicized nature of this debate, it is essential that we attempt to reach some common ground. Although there are few shared values in this debate, what most can agree on is the need for public employees to be satisfied and continue doing their jobs. In that vein, perhaps the more overarching question should look at why public employees feel the need to collectively bargain. If public workers are unsatisfied with benefits and salaries, we—as a society—need to discuss whether their apprehensions are valid and if so how we can better take care of our public employees without having to be concerned with the presence of empowered unions.

Additional Resources

Brock, J. and D. Lipsky, *Going Public: The Role of Labor-Management Relations in Delivering Quality Government Services* (Ithaca, NY: Cornell University Press, 2003)

The public sector currently employs around 40 percent of all union members in the United States. Pressures for cost-effective and quality government services have placed new demands on the labor–management relationship. A fluctuating set of expectations about the appropriate responsibilities of government and a shifting political culture are severely testing the ability of the public sector to meet demands for increased accountability and expanded services. Especially in an age of knowledge workers, the traditional division between labor and management regarding leadership and work may no longer be viable.

Greenhut, S., *Plunder: How Public Employee Unions Are Raiding Treasuries, Controlling Our Lives and Bankrupting the Nation* (Santa Ana, CA: The Forum Press, 2009)

Public employees have become the new American elite. In the past, government workers earned less money but had slightly better job security and benefits than Americans working in the private sector. These days, government workers not only earn more than other Americans, but they also have vastly superior benefits, including pension plans that often allow them to retire as early as age 50 with 100 percent or more of their final year's salary. As government gets bigger and more powerful, government officials have more uncontrolled power over the rest of us to enrich and protect themselves at the expense of the public good. The public's servants have truly become the public's masters.

Kearney, R.C., *Labor Relations in the Public Sector,* 4th ed. (New York: CRC Press, 2008)

This volume recognizes the key role played by unions in the federal government and in a large proportion of state and local jurisdictions, but it also recognizes that much is changing. Fiscal realities and strategic challenges are changing the role of the labor union in the public sector. This is a trend that must be understood if its consequences are to be anticipated and met for the mutual good.

Moe, T., *Special Interest: Teachers Unions and America's Public Schools* (Washington, DC: Brookings Institution Press, 2011)

Moe sets out to examine the relationship between teachers unions and public school performance. By looking at the impact unions have on all aspects of educational policy and practice, he seeks answers as to why they are allowed to continue exerting such dramatic power.

Slater, J.E., *Public Workers: Government Employee Unions, the Law, and the State, 1900–1962* (Ithaca, NY: Cornell University Press, 2004)

From the dawn of the twentieth century to the early 1960s, public sector unions generally had no legal right to strike, bargain, or arbitrate, and government workers could be fired simply for joining a union. This is the first book to analyze why public sector labor law evolved as it did, separate from and much more restrictive than private sector labor law, and what effect this law had on public sector unions, organized labor as a whole, and by extension all of American politics. Slater shows how public sector unions survived, represented their members, and set the stage for the most remarkable growth of worker organization in American history.

Internet References . . .

HowTo.gov

HowTo.gov is a Web site to help government workers deliver a better customer experience to citizens. It is about sharing new ideas, common challenges, lessons learned, and successes across government.

http://www.howto.gov/social-media

CDC—Social Media

This site examines how the Centers for Disease Control and Prevention uses social media to reach out to the American public.

http://www.cdc.gov/socialmedia/

Social Media Presence—Texas

Governments across Texas are using social media such as Twitter, Facebook, YouTube, and Flickr to share information and interact with people like you. Find and connect with them here through one Web site.

http://www.texas.gov/en/Connect/Pages/social-media.aspx

White House Office of e-Government & Information Technology

The Office of e-Government and Information Technology (e-Gov), headed by the Federal Government's Chief Information Officer, develops and provides direction in the use of Internet-based technologies to make it easier for citizens and businesses to interact with the Federal Government, save taxpayer dollars, and streamline citizen participation.

http://www.whitehouse.gov/omb/e-gov/

Kenya e-Government

The site contains information on the e-Government strategy, the monitoring and evaluation of e-Government in Kenya, as well as information on the existing and ongoing e-Government projects. It provides a comparative perspective for students in the United States.

http://www.e-government.go.ke/

Government in the Twenty-First Century: New Avenues of Study

*T*he rampant growth of technology has impacted the way government operates. Although classical and contemporary public administration theories are designed to remain relevant as times change, no one seemed prepared for the technological revolution and the advance of both e-governance tools and society's fascination with social media. Now, different generations of bureaucrats are utilizing different technological tools to reach a diverse citizenry. Proponents claim that these new tools promote efficiency and keep government work at the cutting edge of technologies. Others, however, believe the tools are overglorified and cause more problems than they bring benefits. In this unit, we examine government in the twenty-first century.

- Has e-Governance Had a Dramatic Influence on Public Administration?

- Should Public Agencies Use Social Media to Reach the Citizenry?

ISSUE 18

Has e-Governance Had a Dramatic Influence on Public Administration?

YES: Sang M. Lee, Xin Tan, and Silvana Trimi, from "Current Practices of Leading e-Government Countries," *Communications of the ACM* (January 2004)

NO: Victor Bekkers and Vincent Homburg, "The Myths of e-Government: Looking Beyond the Assumptions of a New and Better Government," *The Information Society* (October 2007)

Learning Outcomes

After reading this issue, you should be able to:

- Define e-governance.
- Describe the relationship between e-governance and public administration.
- Gain an understanding of how technological developments impact government performance.
- Discuss the effects of transitions toward e-governance on American society.
- Describe how e-governance has impacted governments in early adopting countries.
- Gain an understanding of the goals of e-governance.

ISSUE SUMMARY

YES: Sang M. Lee, Xin Tan, and Silvana Trimi examine the impact e-government has had on countries that have been early and leading adopters. Such transitions toward e-governance have created a self-sustaining change in a broad range of closely connected technological, organizational, cultural, and social effects.

NO: Victor Bekkers and Vincent Homburg argue that many of the myths associated with e-government—such as technological inevitability, a new and better government, rational information planning, and empowerment of the intelligent citizen—are not supported by empirical analyses. Instead, they are merely myths that are propagated through American culture.

W hen Barack Obama was elected president, many wondered if his supreme Internet strategies would be carried over from his campaign to his administration. In the wake of his win, reporters labeled him our first Internet president and began wondering who the country's first chief technology officer would be. Obama understood the power of the Internet and how it could be used to reach citizens in ways that encourage involvement. Yet, he also knew that others knew more than him. Hence, when he hired Chris Hughes (a Facebook founder) to handle this element of his campaign, we saw how an Internet star could be turned even brighter with the right support staff. Now three years into his first term, we can examine how much of this campaign magic has been used to further lead the United States toward an era of e-governance.

To begin, we need to be sure we understand what e-government is. According to the United Nations, e-government is the employment of the Internet for delivering government information and services to the citizens. The ultimate goal is to increase both the efficiency and effectiveness of service delivery within the public sector. In an ideal world, e-government would allow anyone visiting a government Web site to communicate and interact with bureaucrats through instant messaging, presentations, and perhaps graphical user interfaces to deliver a higher level of customer service than is available through traditional postal mail or even e-mail. When executed to the fullest extent possible, e-government will allow for (1) the achievement of better government, (2) complete usage in all facets of an organization, and (3) continued optimization of service delivery, constituent involvement, and governance through all available technologies.

Delivery models of e-government include government-to-citizen, government-to-business, government-to-government, and government-to-employees. For our purposes, we will focus on government-to-citizen and government-to-government given the nature and goals of public administration and policy. What we hope to see from e-government when operating optimally is a general pushing of information over the Internet (such as meeting schedules, minutes, and major announcements), two-way communication (whereby users engage directly with government), conducting transactions (like applying for services or grants or transferring service) and governance (through informing, encouraging, and involving the citizen).

The ultimate goal of e-government is to be able to offer a greater number and variety of public services to citizens in a more efficient and cost-effective manner. Further, e-government should lead to enhanced transparency. If citizens are more regularly informed of the happenings of government, they should feel more secure in the actions of government. The mundane activities of bureaucracy—such as name or address changes—can be completed electronically rather than in person. Consider the relationship between Wal-Mart, the Alabama Department of Conservation & Natural Resources, and NIC. Under an agreement, NIC provides an online license service for hunters and fisherman that saves the state agency approximately $200,000. This is the benefit of e-government: no lines, no waits, and taxpayer savings.

Beyond the benefits of speed, ease, and convenience, there are other advantages to e-government. First, the environment benefits as any switch toward technology corresponds with less paperwork being processed and stored. Already the U.S. federal government has turned to www.forms.gov to try and convince federal employees to use .pdf forms rather than printing hard copies. Further, e-government provides more avenues for participation by citizens. Tools from blogs to chat rooms can bring citizens together to discuss and learn about issues facing our nation and the world. If we think back to recent episodes, consider how quickly news spread about the death of Osama bin Laden via social media or the way that the London protesters utilized Facebook and Blackberry Messenger to organize flash mobs. Clearly, technology can help bring news to citizens and citizens together.

Although there are many positive elements of e-government, there are also a series of concerns that deserve mention and discussion. To begin, a full and genuine shift toward e-government will cost a large amount of money in development and implementation. Further, the costs of modification to achieve the system citizens actually want will prove to be even costlier. Not all Americans have Internet access either. Although we have created the National Broadband Plan to try to rectify this, it will take time before individuals who cannot afford access or live in remote rural areas may be connected. If an individual is unable to complete a form in hardcopy due to illiteracy, the odds are likely that they will also struggle with e-government. Simply put, such a movement will still leave citizens behind.

Privacy is another issue of concern when it comes to matters of e-government. The more citizens interact with government via the Internet, the more opportunities government has to track and interact with citizens. Although government proponents will state that they will only use information for legitimate business, volumes of online information could be used in other ways if deemed necessary. According to most polls, however, citizens are willing to promote the prosecution of privacy offenders rather than maintaining strict personal confidentiality if it leads to increased efficiency. Maybe even more importantly, the government ultimately controls these sites and capabilities. How transparent can information be when the inmates run the asylum?

Having a better understanding of e-government in the abstract, we can now turn back to a discussion of the Obama Administration's move toward a more technologically enhanced government. A day after being inaugurated, President Obama signed the Memorandum for the Heads of Executive Departments and Agencies on Transparency and Open Government in which he called for increased transparency and directed the Chief Technology Officer to coordinate with the Director of the Office of Management and Budget and the Administrator of General Services to ensure the memorandum be acted upon. As a result, we see sites like www.recovery.gov and www.data.gov to encourage citizen knowledge and participation. In the YES and NO readings that follow, we will look more closely at whether e-government has had a dramatic influence on public administration at this point in time. In the YES selection, Sang Lee, Xin Tan, and Silvana Trimi argue that e-government has altered the way we conduct government business—especially in nations that were particularly early adopters. And the changes have impacted far more than government, touching on technological, organizational, and social effects as well. Taking the opposite side, Victor Bekkers and Vincent Homburg believe there are a series of myths about e-government that are simply not supported by empirical evidence. As a result, one must assume that the impact of e-government has been largely misconstrued and overstated.

YES

Sang M. Lee, Xin Tan,
and Silvana Trimi

Current Practices of Leading
e-Government Countries

It is transforming the way governments function and valuable lessons
can be learned from the pioneering e-government programs that have
led the charge.

The pervasive adoption of the Internet since the 1990s has stimulated businesses to embrace e-commerce. In the public sector, e-government has emerged and grown enormously as well. Indeed, the development of e-government has clearly mirrored the development of e-commerce.

The core concepts and techniques of putting government online first emerged in the most technologically advanced Western countries, which were pioneers in the adoption of the Internet. In the mid-1990s, the governments of the U.S. and Britain, together with other Western countries such as Canada and Australia, led the way in establishing a basic informational Web presence. Since then, public organizations across the globe and at different governmental levels have been applying Internet technologies in innovative ways to deliver services, engage citizens, and improve performance. Today, the Internet is ubiquitous in the developed world, and developed countries are leading the global phenomenon of e-government.

Most of the existing literature on e-government is based on surveys and case studies, reporting many innovative practices and also some spectacular failures. These studies, especially *Communications'* January 2003 section on digital government, offer valuable findings and insights. Here, we provide a broad overview of the current practices of leading e-government countries and present possible future directions.

e-Government Categorization and Progress

Since the advent of the Internet, government agencies, management consulting firms, and IT companies have led the way in not only exploring e-government initiatives, but also documenting best practices. Academic researchers have conducted case studies and surveys to support the development of e-government. Both streams of literature are useful in understanding

From *Communications of the ACM*, January 2004. Copyright © 2004 by Association for
Computing Machinery. Reprinted by permission via Rightslink.

the development of e-government and supporting government agencies in their strategic planning of e-government initiatives.

E-government is mainly concerned with providing quality public services and value-added information to citizens. It has the potential to build better relationships between government and the public by making interactions between citizens and government agencies smoother, easier, and more efficient. In this respect, e-government serves a similar purpose to customer relationship management (CRM) in the business world.

Existing e-government offerings actually go beyond merely facilitating or transforming the interaction between government and individual citizens. E-government serves a variety of other actors. For instance, some e-government initiatives aim at enabling government agencies to more efficiently work together and provide one-stop service to citizens and businesses. Such practices are somewhat analogous to supply chain management (SCM) in the business world, which stresses coordination and collaboration among supply chain partners. There are also e-government initiatives that focus on the internal efficiency and effectiveness of operations, resembling enterprise resource planning (ERP). Other e-government initiatives are intended to produce an overarching infrastructure to enable interoperability across different e-government practices, akin to the efforts of enterprise application integration practiced by businesses.

By combining the findings from other e-government-related publications and current practices of leading e-government countries, we present the categorization of e-government practices in Table 1. . . . The evolutionary progression of e-government, which consists of four stages: cataloging, transaction, vertical integration, and horizontal integration. E-government progress does not necessarily follow a linear path. Government agencies may skip over certain stages or offer services from different stages simultaneously in a single initiative. For instance, the U.S. Integrated Acquisition Environment (IAE) is an e-government initiative that encompasses transaction, vertical integration, and horizontal integration.

e-Government Practices in Leading Countries

Much of the existing e-government literature focuses on a particular layer of government, for example, the federal government in the U.S. or local government in the European countries. In addition, there are few cross-national comparisons of e-government practices. Here, we provide a concise review of current practices in the leading e-government countries, namely the U.S., the European Union, and some advanced e-government countries in Asia. We chose these three regions because they have been leading the way with e-government initiatives, and developing countries are following their best practices.

The U.S. has been leading the e-government development since the Clinton administration in the 1990s. A 2004 United Nations report rated the U.S. the world leader in e-government. Accenture has ranked the U.S. among the innovative leaders in its comprehensive report on the global e-government leadership for three consecutive years since 2001.

Table 1

e-Government Practice Categories

E-government category	Business metaphor	Description	Sub-category	Example practice
Government to citizens (G2C)	Customer Relationship Management (CRM)	Providing opportunities for greater citizen access to and interaction with the government	Managerial interaction	Government's informational Web sites
			Consultative interaction	E-voting, instant opinion polling
Government to businesses (G2B)		Seeking to more effectively work with businesses	Businesses as suppliers of goods or services	Government's e-procurement
			Businesses as regulated economic sectors	Electronic filing with various government agencies
Government to government (G2G)	Supply Chain Management (SCM)	Enabling government agencies at different levels to work more easily together	Vertical integration	Sharing a database among agencies within the similar functional walls but across different levels of government
			Horizontal integration	Sharing a database among agencies at the similar levels of government but across different functions
Government internal efficiency and effectiveness (IEE)	Enterprise Resource Planning (ERP)	Focusing on internal efficiency and effectiveness	Government to employee	Web-based payroll/ health benefits system
			Integrating internal systems	Implementing ERP-like systems to integrate different functions within a single agency
Overarching infrastructure (Cross-cutting)	Enterprise Application Integration (EAI)	Facilitating the interoperability across different practices	Hardware and software interoperability	Public-key Infrastructure interoperability
			Authentication	e-Authentication across different e-government initiatives

At the federal level, an evolving framework of laws and policies has been influencing the speed, scope, and direction of e-government initiatives in the U.S. Some influential statutes include the Government Performance Results Act of 1993, Clinger-Cohen Act of 1996, Government Paperwork Elimination

Act of 1998, and E-Government Act of 2002. Indeed, the government's effort to protect the public has been a top priority in the wake of the terrorist attacks on Sept. 11, 2001. Title VII of the U.S. Patriot Act of 2001 requires public agencies to share information to protect the nation's critical infrastructure.

The E-Government Act of 2002 includes provisions addressing everything from the funding of e-government initiatives to measures for ensuring security and privacy. The Act established a Federal Chief Information Office within the Office of Management and Budget (OMB) to plan an e-government strategy and oversee the implementation of e-government initiatives. In October 2002, the OMB released the E-Government Strategy, an action plan including 25 initiatives . . . for implementing President Bush's initiative to expand e-government. The government announced newer e-government strategies to implement these initiatives in April 2003.

At the state level, the adoption of e-government is unbalanced. Some states have embraced e-government more extensively than others. The most respected e-government study in the U.S., the Digital States Survey by the Center for Digital Government, examines distinct sectors of e-government in all 50 states. Key sectors include social services, digital democracy, e-commerce, taxation, and revenue. Arizona, Michigan, and Washington are recognized as the leaders in providing e-government services in the latest survey.

While local governments (cities and counties) are increasingly adopting e-government practices, local e-government is still at an early development stage and has yet to achieve many of the promised outcomes. Top online services include paying parking tickets or traffic fines, complaint filing, and service requests. The annual Digital Cities Survey and Digital Counties Survey not only rank e-government applications, but also present the best-of-breed programs to promote e-government adoption by local governments.

The European Union

The nations in the EU have been making e-government a major administrative and political priority since the 1990s. While North America undoubtedly led the way in e-government, European countries were ranked second among all the geographic regions in a UN report. In particular, EU member nations received high rankings in the 2004 e-government readiness index among all the UN member states: Denmark (2), the United Kingdom (3), Sweden (4), Finland (9), the Netherlands (11), Germany (12), Belgium (16), Austria (17), Ireland (19), France (24), Luxemburg (25), Italy (26), Portugal (31), Spain (34), and Greece (36). Some EU member nations, such as Belgium, Denmark, Finland, France, Germany, Ireland, Italy, Netherlands, and U.K., also ranked relatively high in recent Accenture reports. Accenture put EU member nations in either the Visionary Followers or Steady Achievers group, while Canada, Singapore, and the U.S. were in the Innovative Leaders category.

The primary initiators of e-government programs in the EU were the European Commission (EC) and the Information Society Project Office. In December 1999, the EC launched the eEurope initiative to spread the benefits of information society to all Europeans. In the published initiative, supporting e-government (government online) is one of the primary goals. Prodded by the EC, the EU's Council of Ministers approved the eEurope 2002 Action Plan in June 2000. The eEurope 2002 Action Plan provides a detailed description of actions to be undertaken, main players involved, and timing. Table 2 depicts the related actions for supporting e-government. The EC's e-government initiatives are not as ambitious as its U.S. counterpart's. In particular, the Action Plan 2002 does not address consultative interaction between government and citizens, such as e-voting, or the integration of the government's internal systems. In June 2002, eEurope 2005 Action Plan was launched to succeed the eEurope 2002 Action Plan. However, it does not provide specific action plans for e-government initiatives. Therefore, the 2002 Action Plan is still the de facto guideline for e-government development in the EU.

The EC has been using competition to accelerate the adoption of e-government by member nations. The EC's Information Society Office created the e-Europe benchmarking program to assess differences among the member nations in the adoption of new technologies. E-government is among the 23 key indicators. In addition, a competition for the e-Europe Award for Innovation in e-Government was created at the ministerial conference three years ago in Como, Italy.

Various e-government benchmarking reports reveal some features of the current development of e-government among EU member nations:

- E-government has made significant progress in the last few years, especially in the form of portal-based Web sites that provide citizens and firms with access to public administration and services.
- The integration and collaboration of e-government initiatives have not been sufficiently addressed. The e-government indicator of existing eEurope benchmarking programs focuses solely on government Web sites such as government-to-citizen (G2C) and government-to-business (G2B) portals.
- E-government development is heterogeneous among EU member nations, while there is some recent convergence at the EU level in the prioritization of initiatives and development strategies. There is a big gap between the current 15 EU members and the 10 new members.
- There appears to be a lack of coordination in legislation among the EU member states.

Asian e-Government Leaders

In the UN's e-government report, Southern and Eastern Asia was ranked third in the regional comparison, behind North America and Europe. Some individual Asian counties received high rankings in the 2004 E-government Readiness Index, notably the Republic of Korea (5), Singapore (8), and Japan (18). Other e-government surveys and reports, such as Accenture's e-government leadership reports and West's global e-government report, also gave high marks to some developed counties in Asia for their e-government development. These Asian countries do not seek to follow a single path in developing e-government practices.

Table 2

Government Online eEurope Action Plan 2002

Action	Actor (s)	Deadline	E-government category	Sub-category
Essential public data online including legal, administrative, cultural, environmental, and traffic information.	Member States, supported by European Commission	end of 2002	G2C	Managerial interaction
Member States to ensure generalized electronic access to basic public services.	Member States	end of 2002/3	N/A	
Simplified online administrative procedures for business, such as fast-track procedures to set up a company.	Member States, European Commission	end of 2002	G2B	Businesses as regulated economic sectors
Develop a coordinated approach for public sector information, including at the European level.	European Commission	end of 2000	G2G	Horizontal integration
Promote the use of open source software in the public sector and e-government best practices through exchange of experiences across the Union (through the IST and IDA programs).	European Commission, Member States	during 2001	Cross-cutting	Hardware and software standardization
All basic transactions with the European Commission must be available online (funding, research contracts, recruitment, and procurement).	European Commission	end of 2001	IEE	Government to employee
			G2B	Businesses as suppliers
Promote the use of electronic signatures within the public sector.	Member States, European Institutions	end of 2001	Cross-cutting	Authentication across platforms

Singapore

[It] has ranked second in Accenture's surveys for three consecutive years, labeled as an Innovative Leader. It ranked eighth in the UN's benchmarking report. Singapore's e-government initiatives started as early as 1980, with the launch of the Civil Service Computerisation Programme (CSCP). The first e-Government Action

Plan (2000–2003) replaced the CSCP in 2000. The vision of the e-Government Action Plan was "to be a leading e-Government to better serve Singapore and Singaporeans in the new knowledge-based economy"; $1.5 billion (US$900 million) was committed to this plan. The plan prescribes the six programs: Knowledge-based workplaces; e-service delivery; technological experimentation; operational efficiency improvement; an adaptive and robust information and communications infrastructure; and information and communications education.

The first e-Government Action Plan provided a strong foundation for the implementation of the second Plan, "e-Government Action Plan II (2003–2006)," which aims to achieve three distinct outcomes: delighted customers, connected citizens, and networked government.

The e-government action plans are explicitly centered on three critical relationship dynamics—G2C, G2B, and G2G. Internal efficiency and effectiveness (IEE) and cross-cutting are implicitly addressed in the implementation of these programs. The Ministry of Finance oversees the overall e-government initiative, while e-government policy and direction are centrally coordinated by a high-level e-Government Policy Committee. Built on a solid platform, including advanced IT infrastructure and a supportive legal framework, Singapore's e-government practices have steadily grown in number and sophistication.

South Korea

In 1987, the Korean government began initiatives to establish a national computing backbone and to consolidate key databases. As early as the 1990s, Koreans were able to enjoy a number of online services, including registering births and finding new economic statistics. The Korean government invested $5 billion in information and communication technology (ICT) from 1996 to 2001. Today, Korea leads the world in the percentage of households connected to high-speed Internet (over 70%), mobile communication users (over 72%), and the rate of ICT diffusion. Following the development of an IT infrastructure, the Korean government launched an e-Government Special Committee and drafted an e-Government Law in early 2001. The Committee named 11 key tasks in the "Strategy Report Committee for e-Government" in May 2001:

Innovative and Improved Services: Public and Business
- Public-oriented service through a single window
- Linking four major social insurance information systems
- Home Tax Service (HTS) via the Internet
- G2B: An integrated e-procurement system

Productivity and Efficiency: Government
- An integrated national finance management system
- Integrated administration information systems in local governments
- A nationwide education administration information system
- A personnel policy management system
- Government e-document exchange

Building an Infrastructure for e-Government
- A government e-signature and e-seal system
- Consolidation of government computing centers

These key tasks cover most current e-government practices: G2C, G2B, G2G, IEE, and cross-cutting. With a strategy, Korea has made perhaps the most dramatic advances in its e-government program, thus ensuring the second place in West's report.

Taiwan

[It] was rated as the best among the 198 nations and regions in West's report. Even though this report is limited to the analysis of e-government features available online at national government Web sites, Taiwan's top ranking reflects its significant progress in e-government. Taiwan's e-government development was primarily guided by the "Electronic Government Program (2001–2004)," passed by the executive branch of the Taiwan government in April 2001. The objectives of the program include:

- To provide online services to all agencies and civil servants via the government service network.
- To encourage the government work force at all organizational levels to take advantage of the Internet to conduct administrative business and provide public service more efficiently.
- To promote communication and document interchange between organizations at different levels by implementing an electronic document exchange and gateway system.
- To improve the convenience and efficiency of government services and extend the spatial and temporal coverage of government services by providing 1,500 Internet-based application services and one-stop processing services.

Some practices of G2C, G2B, G2G, and IEE are clearly addressed in this program. In addition, electronic certification services for e-government have been implemented through a Public Key Infrastructure and a Privilege Management Infrastructure. The Information Management Department oversees and coordinates all the e-government initiatives. By the end of 2002, 97% of Taiwan government organizations were connected to the Internet, and 4,863 government agency Web sites had been established.

Based on an extensive review, Table 3 presents some specific examples of current e-government practices among the selected leading countries.

Conclusion

Based on the existing research and industry reports on e-government, we discussed categories of e-government practices and conducted a cross-national comparison of current e-government practices among the leading countries, particularly the U.S., the EU, and some advanced ICT countries in Asia. This study is a broad review of current practices and future plans of leading

Table 3

Examples of e-Government Practices Among the Select Leading Countries

Country or region	_____	_____	Examples of e-government practices by category	_____	_____
	G2C	G2B	G2G	IEE	Cross-cutting
The U.S.	GovBenefits .gov: providing a single point of access for citizens to locate and determine potential eligibility for government benefits and services.	Federal Asset Sales: creating a single, one-stop access point for businesses to find and buy government assets.	e-Grants: providing a single, online portal for all federal grant customers to access and apply for grants.	Government Human Resource Integration: streamlining and automating the exchange of federal employee human resources information.	The e-Authentication project: providing a secure infrastructure for online transactions.
The Europe Union	Single Point of Access for Citizens of Europe (an EU-project): supporting citizens' travel within Europe.	The Net-Enterprises Project (France): allowing enterprises, through Internet, to send standardized notifications to government agencies.	Interchange of data between administrations (the IDA program): networking of public administrative units.	Government Secure Intranet (UK): a governmentwide communications infrastructure for joined-up government.	IDA e-Link: a communication middleware solution to enable reliable and secure information exchanges among administrative units across Europe.
Singapore	eCitizen Portal: providing a single access point to government information and services, which are organized and integrated in intuitive categories.	G2B Portal: the entry point for all local and international businesses to access a full suite of aggregated and integrated G2B information and services.	GeBIZ Enterprise: coordinating the purchasing needs of the public sector procurement officers.	InfoComm Education Programme (IEP): facilitating learning and enabling public officers to appreciate and work toward the objective of a "Networked Government."	Singapore Personal Access (SingPass): a nationwide personal authentication framework for e-services.
South Korea	Home Tax Service (HTS) via the Internet: providing 24/7 online service such as tax declaration	Integrated e-Procurement System: a single procurement window, allowing all procurement related	Integrated National Finance Management System: a system for information sharing and linkage for finance related institutions.	Integrated Administration Information System in Local Government: promoting the application of information systems for all	Government e-Signature & e-Seal System: securing reliability for information distribution and e-administration such as private

Table 3 (Continued)

Country or region	G2C	G2B	G2G	IEE	Cross-cutting
	and payment.	processes electronic.		administrative affairs.	information protection and security.
Taiwan	Online motor vehicle services system: providing 21 applications and payment services to individual citizens.	Government Procurement Information Center: enabling government procurement with businesses much more transparent and efficient.	Interdepartmental E-mail Delivery infrastructure: delivering official messages via electronic delivery systems not bound by time and geographical constraints.	Online Central Personnel Administration: improving the administrative efficiency in government human resource management.	Government Root Certification Authority (GRCA): providing the public, businesses, and government agencies with secure and error-free means of making online applications and transmitting data.

Examples of e-government practices by category (spanning header above)

e-government countries. Thus, a detailed comparative analysis of specific categories, examples of success and failure, and associated ICT are not provided.

It appears evident that e-government practices mirror each country's ICT diffusion and government efforts toward political reform. There is incredible diversity in e-government programs and practices among nations, including within a geographic area or even an economic bloc such as the EU. However, it is clear that e-government efforts and best practices are most prevalent in North America, selected EU member nations in Western Europe, and several Asian ICT leading nations. While not discussed here, Australia and New Zealand are also making rapid progress in e-government. In most countries, advanced e-government activities are at the federal or national level, and local governments are generally at the early stage of e-government development.

Public organizations are facing challenges in expanding e-government programs, as the levels of adoption and sophistication of e-government practices vary greatly among governments, even among global e-government leaders. Some governments still lack the fundamental infrastructure, organizational culture, and resources required for the transformation of e-government. An effective e-government program requires successful and seamless integration of appropriate ICT, quality information, engaged public employees, good administrative processes, and government leadership. Otherwise, the existing bureaucracy and ineffective processes may only be exacerbated by leading-edge ICT.

Regardless of the state of each country's e-government efforts, e-government should be implemented, because advanced ICT provides enormous new opportunities to improve public services for citizens and to enhance the efficiency of government operations. The new advances in ICT, such as Very-high-bit-rate Digital Subscriber Line (VDSL) high-speed Internet, Virtual Division Multiple Access (VDMA) mobile communications, WiFi, and Next-Generation Network, will undoubtedly further enhance e-government activities through ubiquitous computing.

**Victor Bekkers and
Vincent Homburg**

The Myths of e-Government: Looking Beyond the Assumptions of a New and Better Government

In general, rhetoric and myth play important roles in policymaking. Myths may inspire collective action but may also mystify and blur views on reality. In this article we identify, analyze, and reflect on the myths underlying the e-government programs of Australia, Canada, the United Kingdom, Denmark, and the Netherlands. We found that in all national policies myths of technological inevitability, a new and better government, rational information planning, and empowerment of the intelligent citizen can be discerned. Although the mobilizing powers of these myths are acknowledged, we conclude that existing empirical studies have generated little support for the inescapable telos of these myths, which makes canvas cleaning effects of e-government initiatives less likely.

E-government—or electronic government—is one of the buzzwords in the discussions on modernizing public administration. Modern information and communication technologies (ICTs), especially Internet and web technologies, are seen as enhancing the access, transparency, efficiency, and quality of public administration. According to Fountain, ICTs could help pave the way to new and better government, since they may be used to restructure existing institutional arrangements and to ensure that these innovations flourish. This new and better government is seen to be (1) more responsive to the needs of citizens and enterprises, (2) more democratic, and (3) more efficient. Notwithstanding the intuitive appeal of these claims, studies have shown that the actual implementation of e-government initiatives has been disappointing.

One could reflect on this cleavage between the rhetoric and the reality of the shop floor in a number of ways. In this article, we do not reflect on the cleavage in a strictly material or instrumental sense (i.e., in terms of managerial issues, or critical economic, technical, or political success factors); instead we reflect on the cleavage in a cultural, narrative sense, by reading against the assumptions embodied in policy documents. We do so by analyzing e-government policies and technologies as myths. Following Mosco, we define myths as hymns to progress, and as utopian visions or promises unfulfilled or unfulfillable. It is important to state at the outset that myths mean more than

From *The Information Society,* October 2007, pp. 373–380. Copyright © 2007 by Taylor & Francis. Reprinted by permission via Rightslink.

falsehoods; rather, myths are used in this article as (1) powerful stories that inspire people to strive for realization of issues that matter, whatever the cost, and (2) discourses in which specific aspects are highlighted and revealed at the expense of other aspects that are (deliberately or unintentionally) concealed. We assume that in order to reflect on the cleavage between the rhetoric and the reality of e-government projects, one should analyze the stories, or paths to transcendence, that inspire redesign of institutional arrangements. In short, the research objective of this article is to describe and critically examine the myths that underlie national e-government initiatives.

We do so by analyzing the first waves (1994–2006) of e-government reforms, in which politicians and administrations embraced the transformative potential of ICT enabled projects. This was the period when Al Gore brought the notion of an information superhighway into the popular imagination. In the analysis, policy documents of the Netherlands, the United Kingdom, Denmark, Australia and Canada are scrutinized. While small selections tend to be dubious, we used a number of criteria to select these countries. First, there is the dispersion of continents. We selected European and North American countries as well as Australia. Second, we looked at a number of countries that deployed a number of e-government initiatives during the period studied. Australia and Canada were among the pioneers, while the Netherlands and the United Kingdom can be characterized as relative laggards. Denmark is interesting because—like the other Scandinavian countries—it has a long-standing practice of using ICT in public administration.

While this research approach seems to indicate a comparative design, this is not entirely true. Our research goal is not to compare the e-government policies of the countries involved, and to link these policies to, for example, the their institutional structures and policies. Moreover, we do not present an assessment of organizational, managerial and technical factors, which could explain the success and failure of the e-government initiatives in the selected countries. Rather, our study aims to develop a preliminary inventory of national e-government policies, their contents, instrumentation, and basic beliefs. This makes it possible to demonstrate that there is a common set of beliefs that inspire e-government initiatives in these countries, and which lift politicians, bureaucrats and policy makers out of the banality of everyday administrative practice and into the possibilities of institutional innovation.

In order to confront the rhetoric with the reality of e-government, we analyze a range of assumptions in the policy documents examined. First, we identify assumptions with respect to the goals and ambitions behind e-government initiatives. What claims are put forth to justify the actions and investments to be made? Second, we examine assumptions with regard to the assessment of the use and effects of ICTs. Such an assessment is of interest because ICTs are often seen as the most important means to modernization and institutional renewal. Third, we look at assumptions with respect to the barriers and problems that should be overcome. Very often these barriers reflect the major problems of government organizations, such as coordination and integration across agencies. We also examine the actions that policy documents stipulate should be undertaken for implementation of e-government initiatives. Given the barriers identified, how do governments act to put e-government into practice? The final set of assumptions examined concern the role of citizens. Most e-government initiatives are directed toward improving service delivery for citizens. How do citizens assess the possibilities of Internet technology in relationship to government? Are citizens portrayed as consumers or are they more than that?

The article is structured as follows. In the first two sections we define the concept of e-government and then look at the role of myth, language, and rhetoric in the policy process. In the subsequent four sections we describe a number of myths. Each section has two components. First, we describe the basic assumptions behind e-government initiatives in the Netherlands, the United Kingdom, Canada, Denmark, and Australia. Second, we interrogate these assumptions and spotlight the chasm between the rhetoric and reality of e-government. In the last section, we will draw some conclusions.

The Concept of e-Government

E-government is a policy and managerial concept for which we have relatively little research, especially theoretical research. There is, however, a vast amount of empirical research available that focuses on the effects of ICT on the functioning of public administration in general.

In many publications e-government is portrayed as a vehicle for fostering customer-orientation in public agencies. The emphasis is primarily on designing and implementing front office electronic communication channels, which enable agencies to communicate electronically and unequivocally with citizens and businesses. In many cases, the focus is on delivery of services.

We extend this view of e-government in a number of ways. First, in order to redesign the front office, it is often necessary to also redesign the back office of agencies—the myriad registration functions in or between agencies that need to be performed in order to actually deliver services. Second, many agencies do not merely interact with citizens as service deliverers; they may also interact with concerned citizens, or with potentially malevolent individuals. We therefore define e-government as public organizations' use of modern ICTs, especially Internet and Web technology, to support or redefine the existing and/or future (information, communication and transaction) relations with stakeholders in their internal and external environment. Relevant stakeholders include citizens, companies, societal organizations, other government organizations and civil servant. Relevant goals in this context include increasing the access of government, facilitating the quality of service delivery, stimulating internal efficiency, supporting public and political accountability, and increasing the political participation of citizens.

E-government is often described in relation to the kind of services to be provided. In general, it is possible to discern information services (focused on the disclosure of government information), contact services (possibilities to ask questions about the applicability of certain rules and programs), transaction services (electronic intakes and handling of requests), participation services (electronic forums and virtual civic communities), and data transfer services (the exchange of information between government agencies and between government and private organizations). In this article the analysis encompasses all kinds of services mentioned above.

The Role of Myths in Policy Processes

In many policy documents and consultants' advice and reports there is a clamor for ICT-enabled reform of government. It is asserted that no government can resist the impact of modern ICTs. In doing so, policymakers, politicians, bureaucrats, and consultants tell stories about the nature of policy problems and how these problems should be tackled. In the language of those who study myths, these storytellers could be characterized as bricoleurs: people who compose heroic narratives to inflict changes in ways of thinking and doing. However enlightening these stories may be, innovations are not necessarily implemented immediately (if at all); nor does the implementation necessarily follow the story lines exemplified in policy documents. But then, the hopes for immediate implementation and fear of lagging behind make for powerful technomania.

We regard the concept of myth as a double-edged sword. On the one hand, myths are seductive tales containing promises unfulfilled or even unfulfillable. They are used by bureaucrats or politicians, for example, to legitimize intervention or application of specific technologies. In Edelman's work, the emphasis is on the symbolic content of policy and politics and how policymakers are involved in exploiting tales, symbols, and language. On the other hand, there is a more positive connotation of myths, which can for instance be found in the work of March and Olsen, Lévi-Strauss, and MacIntyre. March and Olsen promote an institutional approach to public administration that focuses on the rules that guide behavior and interactions of individuals, groups and organizations in public administration. By rules they mean the routines, procedures, conventions, roles, strategies, organizational forms, and technologies around which political activity is constructed. These rules, and their embodiment into myths, function as a shared frame of reference that enables individuals, groups, and organizations to deal with contradictions of politics that can never be fully resolved. They act to integrate behavior in a sensible way: Myths can be seen as a source of inspiration that actors can use to enact social reality.

In understandings of myth, the stories that unfold defy history since they admit no alternative: There is no place for social or natural actions that can stop them. Given the revealing and inspirational character of myths, simply debunking these myths may be of limited value. MacIntyre has pointed out that myths are neither true or false, but living or dead. What is of interest with respect to the actual implementation of e-government is what myths represent and how myths fall short of established bases of meaning and experiences with ICTs in public organizations. Therefore, in the subsequent sections, we analyze what kind of myths can be discerned in national e-government policies, and reflect on the question of whether there is indeed an inescapable telos involved in the e-government myths, or whether otherwise compelling contrary evidence can be envisaged.

Myth I: A New and Better Government

Reconstruction of the Myth of a New and Better Government

The first myth eminent in the analysis of the various national policy documents is the purified image of a new and better government. In such a reformulated government, ICTs are seen as helping the realization, with little effort, of administrative machinery that is responsive, client oriented, and cohesive.

In the UK documents *Modernising Government, e-Government: A Strategic Framework for Public Services in the Information Age*, and *Transformational Government*, e-government is seen as having only one purpose: to make life better for citizens and businesses. The focus upon the improvement of electronic service delivery assumes that it will deliver what people really want, fully exploiting government's information resources:

> New technology offers the possibility of making access to information about government easier . . . The digital age also offers the possibility of a better informed and more participative democracy through electronic consultation and better responses to feedback.

In *Transformational Government*, the promise of a new and better government is stretched further:

> The specific opportunities lie in improving *transactional* services . . . in helping front line *public servants* to be more effective . . . in supporting effective *policy outcomes* . . . in reforming the *corporate services* and *infrastructure* which government uses behind the scenes.

In the UK vision, emphasis is on the notion of intragovernmental cooperation: "To improve the way we provide services, we need all parts of the government to work together."

Australia's *Government Online: The Commonwealth Governments Strategy* articulates the goal as improving the quality of all public services, and increasing responsiveness of public service delivery. *Government Online* is the natural extension of the emphasis on service quality and meeting the needs of clients, which has already been put forward in previous reports, such as *Investing in Growth*. In this specific document, the goal of putting all appropriate government services online by 2001 was established Moreover:

> Government Online will contribute more broadly to service quality beyond just the impact on individual agencies and their service charters. Online technology has the potential to break down traditional barriers faced by clients.

In the 2006 Australian policy document *Responsive Government*, there is also reference to a technologically enabled, seamless governmental apparatus:

> It will be possible to group diverse transactions and complete them at the same time, without navigating the underlying structure and

complexity of government. People will be able to interact with many areas of government without needing to understand exactly which agencies deliver which services.

The mission of the Canadian e-government policies, as formulated in the *Government Online* programs, is to advance the federal government's citizen centred service delivery vision collaboratively across departments and other levels of government.

In the Danish vision on e-government, *From Vision to Action: The Information Society 2000*, e-government is described, conceptualized, and discussed in the context of the network society: a worldwide short circuit of time, space, people, and processes. As such, the Danish case (at least until 2004) is an exceptional case in the sense that ICTs are seen as contributing to free access of information, grass-roots democracy, personal development of individuals in workplace and private life, and transparency of the administrative apparatus:

> The new technologies must give all citizens free access to information and exchange of information, and the possibilities for increasing the citizens' self determination are to be exploited. It must be ensured that the technologies are not used for monitoring citizens or invading their privacy.

In order to accomplish the goals described earlier, policymakers put emphasis on lifelong learning, the stimulation of e-commerce, more effective and cheaper public service delivery, the stimulation of grass-roots digital democratic initiatives, and the establishment of information intensive organizations in specific regions (so-called information technology [IT] lighthouses). The vision just given of e-government contrasts with that of the 2004 policy document *The Danish e-Government Strategy 2004–06*. In this document the vision is articulated in one sentence: "Digitalization must contribute to the creation of an efficient and coherent public service with a high quality of service, with citizens and businesses in the centre."

In the Netherlands, *Action Program for Electronic Government* and *The Digital Delta* present the goals of e-government as increasing the accessibility of government, improving the quality of public services, and enhancing the internal efficiency of government. They portray e-government as a vehicle for getting the Dutch government to actively focus on its role as producer of public services. In a subsequent document, *Contract with the Future*, the scope of e-government is broadened: The political participation by citizens is identified as an area that deserves stimulation.

If one scrutinizes the major barriers that obstruct the realization of e-government objectives, one can observe a wide variety of barriers noted in the texts, including:

- The absence of interoperability and (technical) standards.
- Agencies fostering local interests at the expense of citizens' interests.
- A decentralized approach to ICT development.
- Inability to redefine working routines and develop new ICT-based products.

We see that a new and better government is rhetorically crafted in the wordings of the various policy documents. This new and better government is seen as acting as a whole or *joined up*, as per the British jargon. Technology is seen as playing a decisive role in (1) the actual achievement of a joined-up administrative apparatus (and thus, in the redefinition of information relations with internal stakeholders' see "The Concept of E-Government" section) and (2) realizing online transactions between government, on the one hand, and citizens and businesses (external stakeholders) on the other hand.

Reflections on a New and Better Government

Each of the countries that were studied tries to establish citizen or business centric one-entry points. However, the goal of integrated electronic service delivery—especially in relation to contact and transaction services—leads, in practice, to serious integration and coordination problems. Integrated service delivery implies that several back offices should work together in handling questions, requests, et cetera. They need to share information and knowledge across internal and external organizational boundaries. In essence, the exchange and sharing of information and knowledge between these back offices implies the integration of several information domains, each with its own legal framework, its own information systems, its own data definitions, its own routines and procedures, its expertise and experience, and its own frames of reference. The cooperation of the back offices and integration of different information systems and policies implies that positions and interests will have to change. Thus, ICT is not only a source of innovation but is also a source of resistance or even what is referred to as a "battle of the back offices." This battle is the Achilles heel of e-government. An examination of recent assessments of the e-government initiatives in general and the assessments of e-government practices in Canada, the United Kingdom, Australia, and the Netherlands show that the lack of cooperation between these back offices is still a major problem. In a Dutch study on interorganizational electronic service delivery, Van Venrooij has shown that the most important impediments to integration are coordination problems due to an ambiguous distribution of tasks and legally defined competences among the back offices. While these offices should be working together, the plurality of the actors and interests at stake, together with the lack of a common vision or sense of urgency about the necessity to work together, prevents cooperation. Similarly, a focus on service delivery structures instead of a focus on the processes of service delivery or the incompatibility of data systems and data definitions prevents the desired integration. Remarkably, if the integration problem of the back offices are addressed in various e-government policy documents, it is primarily and predominantly articulated as a technical problem for which a technical solution exists. It is rarely seen as a problem of institutional design, that is, in terms of actors, their interests, their power bases and resources, their relationships and their strategies, and conflict and compromises.

Myth II: The Myth of Technological Progress and Instrumentality

Reconstruction of the Myth of Technological Progress and Instrumentality

In the United Kingdom the various promises of ICT are written in the imperative: "ICT will. . . ," for instance, "make our life easier." Similarly, in the UK "Transformational Government" White Paper, the use of technology is described as "creating and retaining the capacity and capability to innovate and use technology effectively as technology itself develops."

ICT as an exogenous driving force is also evident in Danish documents. Introducing the Internet, the authors of the Danish policy document *From Vision to Action Info Society 2000* speak of a network-like environment that is not amenable to government control. Consequently, the information society is seen as developing into an open and decentralized society: "The numerous global networks with their debates, databases and dissemination of information do not lend themselves to control. They invite both anarchy and refreshing debates." In general the Danish see the information society as a revolution in progress that cannot be missed. The only question is how to respond to it.

Dutch programs like *Digitale Delta* and *Action Program for Electronic Government*, show a strong belief and trust in the potential of modern ICT. Optimism prevails about the progress ICT will bring.

In Australia's *Government Online*, there is hardly any sphere of activity that could not be improved by online government—to achieve more, and to do it more quickly and efficiently. Online access to information is seen as having a significant impact on regional communities, older Australians, and the disabled. Online service delivery is seen as complementing and replacing existing traditional service channels and providing around-the-clock access to government from almost everywhere, breaking down the barriers of distance or mobility that some clients face.

The Canadians also see a changing landscape in which distance perishes and a picture of ubiquitous computing dawns. ICT infiltrates almost every aspects of modern life, resulting in the rise of a new set of expectations and demands. People have nomadic access to their information and computing systems from publicly shared access points. ICTs allow us to imagine new ways of connecting citizens, of eliminating the barriers of distance, and of giving a fuller, richer meaning to democracy and citizenship.

Reflections on Technological Progress and Instrumentality

In the various national policy documents, there is a strong belief and trust in the potential of ICTs. Optimism prevails in the descriptions of the progress the information society and Internet technology will bring. Things that were previously unthinkable will now happen. Public administration has a moral duty to use the most advanced "tools" to reinvent government. The dominant view of technology that is exhibited in several of the policy documents is a selective combination of determinism and voluntarism. Both positions are brought together by the assumption that the emergence of the information society coincides with technologies whose potential cannot be denied.

Using existing reflections on the use of ICTs in organizations, however, it is possible to question the generic effects of ICTs. Often, effects are specific and context dependent, and in the policy documents studied, political, socio-organizational, and institutional settings are hardly mentioned or paid attention to. These effects are limited and context dependent because the introduction of ICT in public administration is a social intervention in a policy and organizational network, which influences the position, interests, values, and (information) domains of the actors involved. Thus, the introduction and use of ICT is not a neutral but a political intervention. ICT in the public sector very often strengthens the existing frames of reference, power relations, and positions within a policy sector. Assuming this is not so can be regarded as another myth: a myth of (unquestioned and ubiquitous) material and technological progress.

Myth III: The Myth of e-Government as Rational Information Planning

Reconstruction of the Myth of Rational Information Planning

In the documents that were studied, a picture emerges in which application of ICT tools (in the right way) is seen as a precondition for institutional renewal. For instance, in the Canadian e-government documents four priorities to stimulate a smooth implementation of e-government are identified: aligning various ICT infrastructures, developing a world-class ICT workforce within government, the improvement of the management and success rate of ICT investments, and the minimizing of risks of ICT projects. In the Danish strategy, collaboration between the private and public sector is seen as a necessary condition for Denmark's transition toward the information society. The focus is on implementing a relatively small number of projects with realistic goals and clear deadlines. In Australia's *Government Online,* a national approach to e-government is promoted based upon a number of priorities: a systematic approach to placing its information and services online, relevant enablers (i.e., authentication, privacy, and security), the development of transaction and payment services, and cross-agency collaboration. In Dutch accounts of electronic government, there is an emphasis upon the establishment of virtual services counters, which are theme oriented, such as "living and building," "care and welfare," "companies," and the reduction of "administrative costs for companies."

When we compare the initiatives across countries we see that the primary focus is on the use of rational planning and management methods to accompany the introduction of ICT. Only the Danes chose an incremental approach; the Dutch paid no attention, in the documents we studied, to an implementation strategy. The secondary focus is on the development of all kinds of technological applications that should be developed and deployed.

Reflections on Rational Information Management

In the UK, Australian, and Canadian documents, corporate information planning and project management techniques are seen as intrinsic to the e-government project. The path forward is presented as a question of setting goals, formulating action plans, allocating budgets, and identifying clear roles and responsibilities. A number of technocratic assessments of the practice of e-government identify pitfalls in the effective implementation of e-government, such as bad planning and bad project management.

In the scholarly literature two serious issues have been raised about such an approach. One, the actual practice of ICT planning and implementation does not always reflect the systematic methods and procedures of information systems management models. ICT-driven innovations in private and public organizations are mostly the result of the bubbling up of new ideas from the bottom. Two, formulating and implementing e-government can be viewed as a governance problem that takes place in the context of a network of organizations. On the one hand, standardization and integration in the back office is needed to allow for interorganizational information exchange, while on the other hand, standardization and integration may intensify existing dependencies and enshrine these dependencies in the technology. Consequently, excessive integration fuels interorganizational tensions and conflicts.

The fact that in various documents the down sides of integration and standardization are ignored and strategic planning practices are heralded gives rise to another myth: the myth of rational information planning.

Myth IV: The Myth of Citizen as Empowered Consumer

Reconstruction of the Myth of Citizen as Empowered Consumer

In many policy documents the citizen is portrayed as an intelligent and "empowered" consumer, while government is presented primarily as a service organization. For instance, a UK report notes, "People are aware of the possibility and benefits of excellent service, and they expect it in all dealings with business. . . . The challenge for the public sector is that the same growing expectations will be applied to government services." Similarly, according to an Australian report, an online environment will allow individuals to to customize their online channel with government, to make it more useful, familiar, convenient, and in many instances transparent. The government should facilitate this by "bringing government closer to people to encourage people to interact with government."

Although all the documents analyzed recognize, at least to some degree, intelligent, technologically empowered citizens-as-clients, two types of refinements can be observed.

One, the notion of citizens as mere customers is modified in the Canadian e-government thinking—they are portrayed as playing the role of good citizens. In this role, citizens are allowed and even encouraged to speak up and participate (electronically) in the democratic process.

Two, the notion of the omnirational consumer (who knows his or her preferences, is able to master both bureaucratic and ICT skills, and actively engages in conversation with government agencies) is refined in the Danish e-government document, in which attention is paid to the increased social polarization into a two tier-society with ICT winners and ICT losers. The Danish report proposes the use of ICT to support the personal development of the citizen and to give individuals the opportunity to exercise their influence to speak up: "Individuals must, themselves, demonstrate their constructive interest in the potential of the info-society and avail themselves of opportunities in the educational system, public libraries, et cetera."

It must be noted, however, that the somewhat enlightened vision of citizens in the Danish documents until about 2000 is abandoned in subsequent documents (see also Myth I). In other words, the multifaceted and somewhat enlightened vision of citizens seems to have become narrowed down to the notion of a consumer of public services.

In the Netherlands, the emphasis is also upon the citizen as a consumer of government services. In *Contract with the Future,* a relationship between the rise of the empowered and intelligent citizens and the process of individualization is identified. These new citizens demand a government that is responsive to their needs and is able to generate an open and horizontal dialogue, and that organizes its internal processes in a transparent way.

We thus see that the dominant image of the citizen is that of someone who acts as and should be approached as a consumer. It is only in the Canadian and Dutch documents that attention is drawn to the democratic and participatory role of citizens, but still the emphasis remains primarily upon the consumer role of citizens.

Reflections on the Citizen as Consumer

The image of an intelligent citizen, who uses the possibilities of the Internet in optima forma to improve his or her position as a consumer of government services, is dominant across the documents. It is assumed that citizens will demand a public administration that also uses the possibilities of the Internet in optima forma: a public administration that enables them to act as empowered and intelligent citizens. These assumptions about the role of the citizen and government are not without risk.

Fountain points to the so-called legitimacy paradox of public service delivery. In her view, the improvement of the quality of public service delivery paradoxically does not increase the legitimacy of government; rather, addressing citizens as consumers and defining government as a production company ignores the public and political character of service delivery. A focus on service delivery (and a focus on the consumer rather than on the citizen) narrows the multidimensionality of citizenship and public administration and may therefore decrease legitimacy. The challenge for e-government is to develop participative forms of electronic service delivery and to address citizens at the same time as their identities as consumer, voter, and a Good Citizen or "citoyen."

Conclusion

In this article we take a cultural perspective on various national e-government policies and interrogate the myths underlying these policies by "reading against policy documents." We analyze and reflect on the inescapable telos that these policies present to us in terms of the words chosen, their visionary sketches, mechanisms, and outlooks. Our basic question was: With what myths did the "bricoleurs" of e-government policies try to supersede the banality of everyday life, and what kind of rhetoric is used to actually celebrate institutional renewal?

Our analysis shows that there is indeed a dominant, powerful mythical component to many e-government policies. Dominant in these policies is an inescapable telos suggesting that technology by itself enables or even causes public sector agencies to transform themselves from self-centered conglomerates to citizen-oriented administrative apparatuses. ICTs are depicted as enabling government and citizens to communicate with each other and to enable the delivery of services in a customer-friendly way. Underlying this core myth of e-government, in which a new and improved government is presented as a seamless web, a number of other myths play an important role: the myth of inevitable technological progress, the myth of rational planning, and the myth of empowered citizens.

From the outset, it has never been our intention to ruthlessly debunk or demystify these rhetorical statements. As has been indicated, myths are created through *bricolage* and have mobilizing capacities that lift politicians, bureaucrats, and citizens out of the banality of everyday administrative practice and into the possibilities of actual (presumably desirable) institutional innovation. As such, they are of value. Nevertheless, the chasm between the ambitious goals and aspirations of e-government policies on the one hand, and the rather disappointing pace of implementation of actual electronic services on the other hand, raises questions about the usefulness of the myths. Are we seeing another case of the incisive observation made by Edelman years before the current e-government craze—"words that succeed and policies that fail?"

We conclude that in evaluating and refining e-government programs, it is important to bear in mind the rhetoric and reflect upon the myths it embodies. It is also vital that the significant chasm between sublime rhetoric of e-government and the muddy practice of actual e-government implementation be the subject of further academic observation and debate. Only then, to paraphrase Karl Popper, will the myth of e-government have a canvas-cleaning effect.

EXPLORING THE ISSUE

Has e-Governance Had a Dramatic Influence on Public Administration?

Critical Thinking and Reflection

1. What is e-governance? What led to its beginning? What are the ultimate goals of e-governance?
2. How is e-governance related to public administration? Do you believe there is a natural connection between technological advancement and government? Why or why not? Is the relationship different in early adopting countries?
3. How do technological developments impact government performance? How do they improve performance? How do they harm performance?
4. How has the transition toward e-governance impacted American society?
5. Is our government too technologically dependent? What would happen if computers disappeared tomorrow for governance?

Is There Common Ground?

Technology seems to be changing at a faster pace than ever before. One could even reasonably argue that we are in a protean environment where daily developments impact the tools we possess. Government has not been immune from these developments and as a result we have clearly witnessed the emergence of e-governance. Unfortunately, governments—given their scope and depth—are not always capable of quickly adopting the newest technological tools available.

For some citizens, any government entanglement with technology is viewed as too much. They view the inability for such a large entity to respond as a positive as it prevents government services from becoming too modernized. Consider such simple transitions as moving toward utilizing EBT cards for food stamp payments in many states and a requirement for direct bank deposits for social security and we can see that individuals can resist programs designed to make life easier.

In this day and age, technology is everywhere. As a result, we must accept that it will impact public administration. E-government is more likely to expand than disappear. If we want to make its impact as positive as possible, we need to make concentrated efforts to help citizens understand the way e-government functions and to ensure them services will continue. Most importantly, public administrators can strive to include citizens in the discussion and help them shape their digital experiences with the state.

Additional Resources

Budd, L. and L. Harris, *e-Governance: Managing or Governing?* (New York: Routledge, 2008)

Taking a multidisciplinary approach, this book explores e-governance in theory and practice with an analytical narrative from heterodox perspectives. Covering such essential issues as global governance of the Internet, the European Knowledge Economy, the transformative promise of mobile telephony, the rise of e-Universities, Internet accessibility for the disabled, and e-governance in transition economies, this book draws on contributions from experienced academics and practitioners with an expertise in an emerging field.

Garson, G.D., *Public Information Technology and E-Governance: Managing the Virtual State* (Boston, MA: Jones & Bartlett Learning, 2006)

Garson looks at the relationship between e-governance and public information technology in order to assess what recent developments mean for new forms of governance.

Manoharan, A. and M. Holzer, *E-Governance and Civic Engagement: Factors and Determinants of E-democracy* (Hershey, PA: Information Science Publishing, 2011)

The book explores the impacts from governments that have engaged their citizens online, discusses issues and challenges in adopting and implementing online civic engagement initiatives globally, and helps guide practitioners in their transition to e-governance.

McNabb, D.E., *The New Face of Government: How Public Managers Are Forging a New Approach to Governance* (Boca Raton, FL: Auerbach, 2009)

This book explores how national leaders are changing the art and practice of government and how public managers are shaping and guiding government's response to the transformation.

Obi, T., *E-Governance: A Global Perspective on a New Paradigm* (Amsterdam, The Netherlands: IOS Press, 2007)

E-governance is regarded as one of the most important subjects in the Information Society. Global e-governance for both public and private sectors is becoming extremely significant in an innovative and seamless world community. In this book, Obi examines the potential impacts for e-governance on the international community.

ISSUE 19

Should Public Agencies Use Social Media to Reach the Citizenry?

YES: Peter R. Orszag, from "Guidance for Agency Use of Third-Party Websites and Applications," *Office of Management and Budget Memo* (June 25, 2010)

NO: Bev Godwin, Sheila Campbell, Jeffrey Levy, and Joyce Bounds, from "Social Media and the Federal Government: Perceived and Real Barriers and Potential Solutions," *Federal Web Managers Council* (December 23, 2008)

Learning Outcomes

After reading this issue, you should be able to:

- Describe various forms of social media that could impact government relationships with citizens.
- Define what is meant by social media.
- Gain an understanding of the federal government's view of social media usage for reaching citizens.
- Describe the arguments for and against using social media to interact with citizens.
- Discuss how social media can potentially complicate the relationship between citizen and government.
- Discuss how social media can increase government transparency and collaboration.

ISSUE SUMMARY

YES: Peter R. Orszag argues that government agencies can benefit by reaching out to common citizens through third-party Web sites and applications. Although cautious about the usage of such applications (especially with regards to privacy), Orszag believes through successful usage, agencies can move toward a system of transparency, public participation, and collaboration.

NO: Bev Godwin, Sheila Campbell, Jeffrey Levy, and Joyce Bounds argue that there are several barriers to the federal government successfully utilizing social media to help reach citizens. Through their argument, we begin to see the ways that social media can actually complicate the relationship between citizen and government.

In spring 2011, U.S. House of Representative member Anthony Weiner taught all of America an invaluable lesson on social media: BE CAREFUL! Weiner forgot the golden rule of all social media outlets, which states that once something has been posted, it will be available for all eternity. It is impossible to delete something quickly enough to prevent someone from seeing it. Although Weiner presents a case of one rogue politician being caught creating problems for himself via social media, it does highlight many of the concerns Americans have about the government moving too close to these new technologies.

In the late 1990s, Robert Putnam alerted Americans to the decline in social capital within our nation. Civic society has witnessed the disappearance of groups like the American Legion and League of Women Voters. The younger generations of America seemingly have instead decided to join Facebook groups and to utilize social networking in place of face-to-face traditional civic life. Perhaps even more tellingly, many groups whose continued existence has long relied on politically active older citizens are seeing their memberships split: younger members prefer tech-savvy means of participating and communicating while older members revert to their traditional means (perhaps mailings or phone calls). The concerns over civic participation are shared in the political realm as well. As a result, it is essential that we attempt to understand how new media may strengthen or further diminish civic and social capital in the United States.

We know that technology has become an ever increasing aspect of the average American life in recent decades. It has affected nearly every facet of our existence, from how we answer questions to how we navigate our way through the world. Political candidates, interest groups, political parties, and civic organizations have started to rely even more on technology—particularly social media—to reach citizens. When designing their message, political and civic campaigns will typically take societal demographics into consideration. They will often investigate the best means through which they can "access" individuals and how they might successfully reach them at their level. As organizations begin relying more frequently on technological advancements, it is possible that some segments of the population might be overlooked.

Current estimates suggest that 75 percent of Americans have Internet access. Research has found that the Internet impacts how we communicate, work, and use leisure time. It has blended into the rhythms of everyday life and presents us with myriad of opportunities—such as playing games, seeking information, and chatting. We can even use it to make important life decisions. In 1996, 3 percent of citizens, for example, stated that they relied on the Internet as their primary source of information on campaigns. By 2008, the number had increased to 28 percent. In 2000, 16 percent of adults claimed they used the Internet to obtain news and information. The percentage increased to 31 percent in 2004 and 40 percent in 2008. Among those who acknowledge Internet usage, 35 percent say they use the Internet to watch videos and 10 percent claim to be part of a social networking site. Of those who are using social networking sites, just under a third admit to using access to discover their friends' political affiliations and around a quarter of respondents state that they have used social networking sites to find campaign information. As the data make clear, the Internet is quickly becoming a place where citizens flock to collect information on politics. And the usage is quickly growing.

When it comes to thinking about information-seeking behaviors, convenience and immediacy tend to be the most attractive aspects of the Internet and social media. There are significantly fewer personal costs associated with becoming involved through the Internet compared with traditional means of participation. However, in order to navigate through technology, there is still the need for some element of efficacy. With efficacy required, there are discrepancies regarding the individuals who choose to actively pursue political and civic information through modern means. Simply being connected does not lead to the successful navigation of the civic Web in the same way that owning a car does not guarantee people will show up at the polls on voting day.

As a result, different scholars have taken different approaches to the relationship between technology and social capital. Some find that technology is diminishing social capital by removing the actual contact between citizens. Others believe technology is merely transforming how we understand social capital. By observing high levels of participation in online communities, we have seen alternative routes presented for group involvement and the pursuit of knowledge. Yet, does government need to be an active participant in the social media scene? The statistics tell us that a majority of citizens are active on various social media sites. They tell us that people pay attention to information observed on these sites. But they also tell us that citizens find social media sites to be their own personal territory. Just as students do not appear to want Facebook or Twitter to be forced upon them as part of their classes, we are not entirely convinced that citizens wish to be inundated on these sites by the government. Since there are low costs involved, some argue that there is really no downside to the government adding social media to its ways of reaching citizens—as long as it does not supplant traditional methods.

In the YES and NO readings, we more closely examine whether public agencies should use social media to reach citizens. In the YES reading, Peter Orszag begins by explaining the benefits of government agencies reaching out to citizens through third-party Web sites and applications. He argues that it is easier to go to the citizens than to expect citizens to come to the government agencies. Most importantly, he sees social media as presenting new opportunities for transparency, public participation, and collaboration. Taking a different view in the NO reading, Bev Godwin, Sheila Campbell, Jeffrey Levy, and Joyce Bounds believe there are many barriers to overcome if the federal government is going to successfully utilize social media to reach citizens. They ultimately believe that social media will do little more than further complicate the relationship between citizen and government.

YES

Peter R. Orszag

Guidance for Agency Use of Third-Party Websites and Applications

This Memorandum requires Federal agencies to take specific steps to protect individual privacy whenever they use third-party websites and applications to engage with the public.

In the *Memorandum on Transparency and Open Government,* issued on January 21, 2009, the President called for the establishment of "a system of transparency, public participation, and collaboration."[1] The President emphasized that "[k]nowledge is widely dispersed in society, and public officials benefit from having access to that dispersed knowledge." Following the President's memorandum, the Office of Management and Budget (OMB) issued the *Open Government Directive,* which required a series of concrete steps to implement the system of transparency, participation, and collaboration.[2]

On April 7, 2010, OMB issued several guidance documents responding to the *Open Government Directive.* One such guidance—the most relevant to this Memorandum—is *Social Media, Web-Based Interactive Technologies, and the Paperwork Reduction Act.*[3] That memorandum focuses on the requirements of the Paperwork Reduction Act (PRA)[4] in connection with social media and web-based interactive technologies; it explains that without triggering the PRA, agencies may use such media and technologies to promote open government in many ways.

Like the April 7, 2010 guidance and OMB's *Guidance for Online Use of Web Measurement and Customization Technologies,*[5] this Memorandum recognizes that open government increasingly relies on Federal agency uses of new technologies, such as social media networks and web 2.0 applications. Such uses offer important opportunities for promoting the goals of transparency, public participation, and collaboration. However, increased use of these technologies also requires greater vigilance by Federal agencies to protect individual privacy.

The purpose of this Memorandum is to help Federal agencies to protect privacy, consistent with law, whenever they use web-based technologies to increase openness in government. As explained below, the Memorandum builds on OMB's existing guidance; it calls for transparent privacy policies, individual notice, and a careful analysis of the privacy implications whenever Federal agencies choose to use third-party technologies to engage with the public.[6]

From *Office of Management and Budget Memo,* June 25, 2010.

Scope

This Memorandum applies to any Federal agency use of third-party websites or applications to engage with the public for the purpose of implementing the principles of the *Open Government Directive*.[7] The guidance also applies when an agency relies on a contractor (or other non-Federal entity) to operate a third-party website or application to engage with the public on the agency's behalf. Whenever an agency uses web measurement and customization technologies, the agency should refer to OMB's memorandum providing *Guidance for Online Use of Web Measurement and Customization Technologies*.

Existing Requirements

Compliance with Existing Requirements

Agencies are reminded of their obligation to comply with applicable privacy laws (including the Privacy Act of 1974[8]) and OMB guidance, as well as to consult established privacy principles.[9] In addition, agencies should coordinate with their Senior Agency Official for Privacy (SAOP).

Modifications to Existing Guidance

This Memorandum modifies the following OMB memoranda:

- OMB Memorandum M-03-22, *OMB Guidance for Implementing the Privacy Provisions of the E-Government Act of 2002*
- OMB Memorandum M-99-18, *Privacy Policies on Federal Web Sites*

General Requirements

Subject to the requirements set forth below, agencies may use third-party websites and applications to engage openly with the public. These websites and applications offer new tools that will help people to connect with their government, promoting the goals of transparency, participation, and collaboration. At the same time, agencies should comply with the requirements in this Memorandum to ensure that privacy is fully protected.

Agencies should also provide individuals with alternatives to third-party websites and applications. People should be able to obtain comparable information and services through an agency's official website or other official means. For example, members of the public should be able to learn about the agency's activities and to communicate with the agency without having to join a third-party social media website. In addition, if an agency uses a third-party service to solicit feedback, the agency should provide an alternative government email address where users can also send feedback.

When using a third-party website or application, agencies should adhere to the following general requirements:

a. **Third-Party Privacy Policies.** Before an agency uses any third-party website or application to engage with the public, the agency should examine the third party's privacy policy to evaluate the risks and determine whether the website or application is appropriate for the agency's use. In addition, the agency should monitor any changes to the third party's privacy policy and periodically reassess the risks.

b. **External Links.** If an agency posts a link that leads to a third-party website or any other location that is not part of an official government domain, the agency should provide an alert to the visitor, such as a statement adjacent to the link or a "pop-up," explaining that visitors are being directed to a nongovernment website that may have different privacy policies from those of the agency's official website.

c. **Embedded Applications.** If an agency incorporates or embeds a third-party application on its website or any other official government domain, the agency should take the necessary steps to disclose the third party's involvement and describe the agency's activities in its Privacy Policy, as specified in this Memorandum.

d. **Agency Branding.** In general, when an agency uses a third-party website or application that is not part of an official government domain, the agency should apply appropriate branding to distinguish the agency's activities from those of nongovernment actors. For example, to the extent practicable, an agency should add its seal or emblem to its profile page on a social media website to indicate that it is an official agency presence.

e. **Information Collection.** If information is collected through an agency's use of a third-party website or application, the agency should collect only the information "necessary for the proper performance of agency functions and which has practical utility."[10] If personally identifiable information (PII) is collected, the agency should collect only the minimum necessary to accomplish a purpose required by statute, regulation, or executive order.

Requirements for Privacy Assessment and Public Notice

a. **Privacy Impact Assessments (PIAs).** While OMB Memorandum M-03-22[11] provides broad guidance on the PIA process, an agency's use of third-party websites and applications raises new questions. For that reason, OMB is modifying its existing guidance to require an adapted PIA, described below, for an agency's use of such websites and applications.

The adapted PIA is required whenever an agency's use of a third-party website or application makes PII available to the agency. Each adapted PIA should be tailored to address the specific functions of the website or application, but adapted PIAs need not be more elaborate than the agency's other PIAs. In general, each PIA should be posted on the agency's official website.

The PIA should describe:

    i. the specific purpose of the agency's use of the third-party website or application;
   ii. any PII that is likely to become available to the agency through public use of the third-party website or application;
  iii. the agency's intended or expected use of PII;

    iv. with whom the agency will share PII;

    v. whether and how the agency will maintain PII, and for how long;

    vi. how the agency will secure PII that it uses or maintains;

    vii. what other privacy risks exist and how the agency will mitigate those risks; and

    viii. whether the agency's activities will create or modify a "system of records" under the Privacy Act.[12]

In general, an agency's use of a third-party website or application should be covered in a single, separate PIA. However, an agency may prepare one PIA to cover multiple websites or applications that are functionally comparable, as long as the agency's practices are substantially similar across each website and application. If an agency's use of a website or application raises distinct privacy risks, the agency should prepare a PIA that is exclusive to that website or application.

An agency should work with its SAOP to determine how many PIAs are needed, to identify when updates to PIAs are necessary, and to ensure full compliance with OMB policies. OMB is available to provide further guidance on the PIA process and to direct agencies to model PIAs and other resources that may be useful.

    b. **Agency Privacy Policies.** OMB Memoranda M-99-18[13] and M-03-22 establish requirements for agency Privacy Policies. Agencies should continue to comply with existing guidance and should also update their Privacy Policy to describe their use of third-party websites and applications, including:

      i. the specific purpose of the agency's use of the third-party websites or applications;

      ii. how the agency will use PII that becomes available through the use of the third-party websites or applications;

      iii. who at the agency will have access to PII;

      iv. with whom PII will be shared outside the agency;

      v. whether and how the agency will maintain PII, and for how long;

      vi. how the agency will secure PII that it uses or maintains; and

      vii. what other privacy risks exist and how the agency will mitigate those risks.

An agency should also, when feasible, provide links to the relevant privacy policies of the third-party websites and applications being used.

    c. **Agency Privacy Notices.** To the extent feasible, an agency should post a Privacy Notice, described below, on the third-party website or application itself. The Privacy Notice should:

      i. explain that the website or application is not a government website or application, that it is controlled or operated by a third party, and that the agency's Privacy Policy does not apply to the third party;

ii. indicate whether and how the agency will maintain, use, or share PII that becomes available through the use of the third-party website or application;
iii. explain that by using the website or application to communicate with the agency, individuals may be providing nongovernment third parties access to PII;
iv. direct individuals to the agency's official website; and
v. direct individuals to the agency's Privacy Policy as described above.

An agency should take all practical steps to ensure that its Privacy Notice is conspicuous, salient, clearly labeled, written in plain language, and prominently displayed at all locations where the public might make PII available to the agency.

Role of the Senior Agency Official for Privacy (SAOP)

When agencies are evaluating whether to use third-party websites or applications, they should consult with their SAOP. OMB Memorandum M-05-08 provides that an agency's SAOP shall have a "central policy-making role" and shall have "overall responsibility and accountability for ensuring the agency's implementation of information privacy protections."[14] Agencies should confer with their SAOP at the earliest possible stage of their planning process, and consult with the SAOP through implementation and postimplementation review.

OMB Assistance

When additional assistance is needed, an agency is encouraged to consult the appropriate Office of Information and Regulatory Affairs (OIRA) desk officer for clarification and guidance. For questions specifically about this Memorandum, agencies may contact OMB at privacy-oira@omb.eop.gov.

Appendix

Definitions

Third-party websites or applications. The term "third-party websites or applications" refers to web-based technologies that are not exclusively operated or controlled by a government entity, or web-based technologies that involve significant participation of a nongovernment entity. Often these technologies are located on a ".com" website or other location that is not part of an official government domain.[15] However, third-party applications can also be embedded or incorporated on an agency's official website.

Personally Identifiable Information (PII). The term "PII," as defined in OMB Memorandum M-07-16[16] refers to information that can be used to distinguish or trace an individual's identity, either alone or when combined with other personal or identifying information that is linked or linkable to a specific individual. The definition of PII is not anchored to any single category of information or technology. Rather, it requires a case-by-case assessment of the specific risk that an individual can be identified. In performing this assessment, it is important for an agency to recognize that non-PII can become PII whenever additional information is made publicly available—in any medium and from any source—that, when combined with other available information, could be used to identify an individual.

Make PII Available. The term "make PII available" includes any agency action that causes PII to become available or accessible to the agency, whether or not the agency solicits or collects it. In general, an individual can make PII available to an agency when he or she provides, submits, communicates, links, posts, or associates PII while using the website or application. "Associate" can include activities commonly referred to as "friend-ing," "following," "liking," joining a "group," becoming a "fan," and comparable functions.

Privacy Impact Assessment (PIA). The term "PIA," which is now subject to the modifications in this Memorandum, was defined in OMB Memorandum M-03-22[17] as:

> [A]n analysis of how information is handled: (i) to ensure handling conforms to applicable legal, regulatory, and policy requirements regarding privacy, (ii) to determine the risks and effects of collecting, maintaining and disseminating information in identifiable form in an electronic information system, and (iii) to examine and evaluate protections and alternative processes for handling information to mitigate potential privacy risks.

Privacy Policy. The term "Privacy Policy" is described in OMB Memorandum M-99-18,[18] and is further explained in OMB Memorandum M-03-22. When the term is used in this Memorandum, it refers to a single, centrally located statement that is accessible from an agency's official homepage. The Privacy Policy should be a consolidated explanation of the agency's general privacy-related practices that pertain to its official website and its other online activities.

Privacy Notice. While a Privacy Policy is a statement about an agency's general practices, the term "Privacy Notice" refers to a brief description of how the agency's Privacy Policy will apply in a specific situation. Because the Privacy Notice should serve to notify individuals before they engage with an agency, a Privacy Notice should be provided on the specific webpage or application where individuals have the opportunity to make PII available to the agency.

Notes

1. President Barack Obama, Memorandum on Transparency and Open Government (Jan. 21, 2009), *available at* http://www.gpoaccess.gov/presdocs/2009/DCPD200900010.pdf

2. OMB Memorandum M-10-06, *Open Government Directive* (Dec. 8, 2009), *available at* http://www.whitehouse.gov/omb/assets/memoranda_2010/m10-06.pdf

3. *Available at* http://www.whitehouse.gov/omb/assets/inforeg/SocialMediaGuidance_04072010.pdf

4. 44 U.S.C. § 3501.

5. OMB Memorandum M-10-22, *Guidance for Online Use of Web Measurement and Customization Technologies* (June 25, 2010), *available at* http://www.whitehouse.gov/omb/assets/memoranda_2010/m10-22.pdf

6. Definitions are provided in the Appendix to this Memorandum.

7. This guidance does not apply to internal agency activities (such as on intranets, applications, or interactions that do not involve the public) or to activities that are part of authorized law enforcement, national security, or intelligence activities.

8. 5 U.S.C. § 552a.

9. Since 1973, a series of government reports—both general and agency-specific—have established Fair Information Practices that set forth many accepted principles of information privacy. *See, e.g.,* U.S. Dep't of Health, Educ., and Welfare, Secretary's Advisory Committee on Automated Personal Data Systems, *Records, Computers, and the Rights of Citizens* (1973), *available at* http://aspe.hhs.gov/DATACNCL/1973privacy/tocprefacemembers.htm

10. OMB Circular A-130, *available at* http://www.whitehouse.gov/omb/Circulars_a130_a130trans4/

11. OMB Memorandum M-03-22, *OMB Guidance for Implementing the Privacy Provisions of the E-Government Act of 2002* (Sept. 26, 2003), *available at* http://www.whitehouse.gov/omb/memoranda_m03-22/

12. *See* 5 U.S.C. § 552a(5).

13. OMB Memorandum M-99-18, *Privacy Policies on Federal Web Sites* (June 2, 1999), *available at* http://www.whitehouse.gov/omb/memoranda_m99-18/

14. OMB Memorandum M-05-08, *Designation of Senior Agency Officials for Privacy* (Feb. 11, 2005), *available at* http://www.whitehouse.gov/omb/assets/omb/memoranda/fy2005/m05-08.pdf

15. *See* OMB Memorandum M-05-04, *Policies for Federal Agency Public Websites* (Dec. 17, 2004) (identifying ".gov," ".mil," and "Fed.us" as appropriate government domains), *available at* http://www.whitehouse.gov/OMB/memoranda/fy2005/m05-04.pdf

16. OMB Memorandum M-07-16, *Safeguarding Against and Responding to the Breach of Personally Identifiable Information* (May 22, 2007), *available at* http://www.whitehouse.gov/OMB/memoranda/fy2007/m07-16.pdf

17. OMB Memorandum M-03-22, *OMB Guidance for Implementing the Privacy Provisions of the E-Government Act of 2002* (Sept. 26, 2003), *available at* http://www.whitehouse.gov/omb/memoranda_m03-22/

18. OMB Memorandum M-99-18, *Privacy Policies on Federal Web Sites* (June 2, 1999), *available at* http://www.whitehouse.gov/omb/memoranda_m99-18/

Bev Godwin, Sheila Campbell, Jeffrey Levy, and Joyce Bounds

 **NO**

Social Media and the Federal Government: Perceived and Real Barriers and Potential Solutions

The Context for Using Social Media Within the Federal Government

As leaders of the Federal Web Managers Council, we've seen that social media in government has become the number one topic of discussion within our government web manager community over the past year. The prospect of agencies using social media sites such as YouTube, Facebook, Wikipedia, Twitter, and SecondLife has raised a myriad of legal, contractual, and policy questions. As the new Administration looks to leverage these new tools to create a more effective and transparent government, it's an opportune time for us to share what we've learned and propose solutions for how to best use these new tools across government. These recommendations are based on our first-hand experience using social media within our own agencies and from hundreds of conversations with web managers across the country.

Some agencies are already using social media tools with great success. They've shown how these tools can transform how we engage the public, include people in the governing process, and accomplish our agency missions. (See WebContent.gov for examples of agencies successfully using social media: http://www.usa.gov/webcontent/technology/other_tech.shtml). But many agencies are not using these tools, either because of perceived or real lack of resources, cultural resistance, or legal or other barriers. There are varying interpretations around what is allowed across the federal government, and some agencies do not yet understand how these tools will help them achieve their missions.

The purpose of these recommendations is to address the perceived and real barriers to using social media, and to propose solutions that will result in greater consistency and a clearer understanding of what is expected and permitted across federal agencies.

We hope this paper will facilitate dialogue on these important issues, both within and outside the government. As this topic evolves, we'll use Webcontent .gov and various social media tools to continue the conversation. We also invite you to read the Federal Web Managers Council white paper, "Putting Citizens First: Transforming Online Government," which offers recommendations for

From *Federal Web Managers Council*, December 23, 2008.

transforming online government beyond social media (http://www.usa.gov/web-content/documents/Federal_Web_Managers_WhitePaper.pdf).

Barriers and Potential Solutions

Cultural Issues and Lack of a Strategy for Using These New Tools

Issue: Many agencies view the use of social media as a technology issue, instead of a communications tool, and management decisions are often based solely on technology considerations. In many cases, the focus is more on what can't be done rather than what can be done. The default approach should be openness and transparency. For this reason, agencies need to be prepared that the decision to use social media will have cultural implications throughout government. Some agencies have leadership and legal support and have shown that the benefits of using social media outweigh the risks; but many have not. The result: social media is not consistently applied across government.

Proposed solution: The new Administration should communicate a government-wide strategy for using social media tools to create a more effective and transparent government. The new Administration's Chief Technology Officer (CTO) should require each agency to, within three months, develop their own social media/Web 2.0 communications strategy that describes how it will use their agency website and the larger Web to accomplish its mission, reach new audiences, and engage the public. The strategy should include resources needed to accomplish these goals.

Employee Access to Online Tools

Issue: Many agencies block their employees from using sites like YouTube, Facebook, and Wikipedia. They make one of three arguments, all of which can be addressed through effective policies and management controls:

1. Security: IT security specialists raise concerns that these high traffic sites pose a greater risk for malware and spyware. However, agencies can implement security measures to mitigate these risks, just as they do for other high traffic sites such as Google and Yahoo. Certain agencies may still need to restrict access for specific groups, but this should be the exception, not the rule.
2. Employees will waste time: this is the same argument that has been used to say employees shouldn't have access to phones, email, etc. It's not unique to Web 2.0. It should be addressed by agency managers as a management issue, not a technology problem.
3. Bandwidth: this is a legitimate concern for sites such as YouTube that consume considerable bandwidth. However, agencies need to budget for this, as they do for other infrastructure needs. If opening all computers to all sites is an issue, agencies should at least provide access to agency staff that need to understand and use these tools to communicate with the public.

Proposed solution: The new Administration should require agencies to provide access to social media sites unless the agency head justifies blocking certain employees or certain sites.

Terms of Service

Issue: Most online sites require account owners to agree to terms of service that federal agencies can't agree to, in particular:

1. Indemnification and defense: if a federal employee, on behalf of their agency, creates an account on a social media site, they must agree not to sue the site, nor allow the site to be included in suits against the agency. Many sites also require the account owner to pay the site's legal costs arising from such suits. Under the Anti-deficiency Act, federal agencies can't commit to either provision.
2. Applicable law and court jurisdiction: most terms of service also assert that a certain state's laws (usually California) apply to the terms of use and that the state's courts will adjudicate disputes. This is problematic since federal agencies follow federal law and go to trial in federal court.

Many companies have been willing to negotiate on these issues, but they don't want to negotiate separate agreements with dozens of different agencies. Similarly, it's not efficient for agencies to work out agreements with an unending list of potential companies.

Proposed solution: The new Administration (through the National CTO, GSA, OMB, or some other central organization) should:

a) Establish a single terms of service that covers all social media sites, which excludes the federal government from the provisions described above. (If this isn't possible, at a minimum, create a standard federal terms of service with each site and establish a process for adding new agreements as new sites are identified.)
b) Alert federal agencies that the benefits of using these sites outweigh the risks and that they should use social media sites pending agreements on terms of service.

Advertising

Issue: Many vendor sites place ads on all their pages; this is how they earn money from free accounts. For some agencies, this raises ethical concerns when government content appears near inappropriate advertisements (pornography, hate, political, etc), because it can give the appearance that the government is endorsing the content. What constitutes "advertising" is interpreted differently across government.

Proposed solution: The new Administration should:

1. Issue a memo stating that government agencies should accept this kind of contextual advertising as a byproduct of using social media

sites, that advertising online is no different than advertising in a magazine, newspaper, radio, or TV, where you can't control exactly how your content will appear in context. However, if this is not possible:
2. Set criteria for all agencies for when such ads are acceptable. For example, ads could be acceptable when:
   - They are ubiquitous, appearing on all similar pages on a site, regardless of the account owner
   - They do not include pornography or violence
   - There isn't confusing language that implies endorsement by the account owner (e.g., "promoted" or "sponsored" material)

Procurement

Issue: Government procurement rules didn't anticipate the flood of companies offering free tools to anyone who wants to use them. Attorneys at different agencies interpret the rules differently, leading to confusion and hesitation. Agencies that want to use these tools face three issues:

1. Gratuitous services and gift authority: there are rules governing when agencies are allowed to accept free services or gifts. Some agencies have gift authority and others don't. Potential concerns include giving the offering company inappropriate inside information that lets it tailor a later commercial product or possibly coming back later and billing the government.
2. Choosing winners without competition: the government shouldn't arbitrarily decide which companies will be given the cachet of providing our content, which can provide value to their sites. For example, federal agencies should have criteria to determine which video sharing sites they will publish their videos to (YouTube, Yahoo Video, AOL Video, etc).
3. Contract authority: Ordinarily, only specific employees are given authority to bind an agency contractually. This is very cumbersome when trying to establish accounts on social media sites.

Proposed solution: The new Administration should work with procurement and ethics attorneys to ensure that:

1. Agencies can use free Web products and services.
2. Agencies do not need to use all products and services offered, as long as they have criteria for deciding which ones they use.
3. Employees with a clear business need can create accounts to use free services, as long as they have managerial approval.

Privacy

Issue: There is no guarantee that social media sites will protect people's privacy to the same degree as federal agencies.
Proposed solution: The new Administration should direct agencies to use a standard disclaimer to display on social media sites where they publish

content (i.e. EPA's Facebook page or Twitter page). The disclaimer would alert the public that they are no longer on a federal site and that the private sector site's own privacy policy applies, with a link to that policy.

Persistent Cookies

Issue: Agencies are banned from using persistent cookies without approval from their agency head, which effectively means the federal government isn't using them. This greatly limits our ability to serve customers' needs because our sites can't remember preferences or settings. It also means we can't take advantage of sophisticated web services and analytic tools that rely on persistent cookies.

Proposed solution: The National CTO or OMB should immediately rescind the previous guidance prohibiting persistent cookies and replace it with guidance that allows agencies to use persistent cookies to better serve customers' needs. The new guidance should state that it's acceptable for agencies to use social media sites that rely on persistent cookies. However, the government should retain the ban on tracking cookies, since they specifically track where visitors go between sites.

Surveys

Issue: The Paperwork Reduction Act, subsequent OMB regulations, and OMB draft guidance require that agencies complete a lengthy process to obtain an OMB control number to survey and request information from the public. This requirement is interpreted by most agencies to include voluntary online surveys, polls, and other applications that are intended to improve customer service. The Act predated the Internet and doesn't anticipate the use of social media and other customer service tools.

Proposed solution: The National CTO or OMB should issue immediate guidance that outlines exceptions to the PRA, such as using online surveys to solicit public opinion about federal websites, using social media to have online discussion forums with the public, etc.

Access for People with Disabilities

Issue: Under section 508 of the Rehabilitation Act of 1973, all information provided to the public via agency websites must be equally accessible to people with and without disabilities. Many social media tools are automatically accessible because they are primarily text (e.g., blogs). However, some multimedia sites do not currently provide the opportunity to include transcripts or captioning, and many agencies lack sufficient resources to provide these services on their own.

Proposed solutions:

1. The National CTO should issue guidance requiring agencies to post their materials in accessible formats on their own websites, and that non-governmental sites may not be the sole location where content is posted. This will ensure that people with disabilities always have

an accessible version of the content, and that the official version of content is located on a government website.

2. The National CTO and GSA should collaborate on developing a government-wide procurement vehicle to purchase tools that assist with 508 compliance, such as captioning software to make videos and webcasts available to people with disabilities.

3. The National CTO should work with major companies to make Web software, including social media software, fully accessible to people with disabilities.

Administrative Requirements During Rulemaking

Issue: The Administrative Procedure Act (APA) of 1946 sets rules for how agencies can communicate with the public during rulemaking, accept public comment on proposed regulations, etc. The Act didn't anticipate the collaborative tools now available, leading to hesitation and confusion as to how to incorporate them during the rulemaking process.

Proposed solution: The National CTO or OMB should issue guidance to help agencies use collaborative social media tools to enhance the rulemaking process, while still complying with the APA.

EXPLORING THE ISSUE

Should Public Agencies Use Social Media to Reach the Citizenry?

Critical Thinking and Reflection

1. What is social media? How is it similar to and different from traditional media?
2. What are the various forms of social media? How can each potentially impact government relationships with citizens?
3. How can social media potentially complicate the relationship between citizen and government? Likewise, how can it increase government transparency and collaboration?
4. Should government use social media to interact with citizens? Are there privacy concerns to be considered? What could go wrong if government relies too much on social media?
5. What policies has the federal government already put in place regarding social media? Do you believe the policies are written to fulfill their objectives? Are they too restrictive or not restrictive enough?

Is There Common Ground?

Although all forms of technology continue to develop, social media has truly become a facet of everyday American life in the past five years. Platforms such as Facebook, Twitter, and YouTube have radiated throughout society as more and more users join on every day. For as long as we have had government, Americans have been concerned with assuring political participation. Although in the early years of the new republic, our politicians seemed to want to limit uninformed citizens from having too much say, politicians and bureaucrats today seem to want to reach citizens where it is most convenient: online.

If all citizens utilized social media, such an approach would likely be far more acceptable. However, turning toward social media makes a few troubled assumptions. First, such a transition implies that all Americans have Internet access and the ability to access government information provided through social media. Second, and perhaps even more troubling, the use of social media suggests citizens want government to communicate with them through this medium. If neither of these presumptions proves true, the use of social media does little more than create confusion. The key for public administrators then is to determine ways social media can be utilized to reach interested citizens seeking a more direct connection with government. And if they choose to push forth with social media regardless, they must figure out how to create a genuine relationship via these services.

432

Additional Resources

Brander, M.N., *Social Media Use in the Federal Government* (New York: Routledge, 2010)

Brander discusses federal government usage of social media as a tool for reaching citizens and for working within the bureaucracy. As one of the first texts to examine these new technological advancements, Brander's efforts deserve consideration by public administration scholars and practitioners.

Chester, J., *Digital Destiny: New Media and the Future of Democracy* (New York: The New Press, 2008)

Chester assesses the development of new media and examines ways that these new forms can negatively impact democracy as we know it.

Eggers, W.D., *Government 2.0: Using Technology to Improve Education, Cut Red Tape, Reduce Gridlock, and Enhance Democracy* (Lanham, MD: Rowman & Littlefield, 2007)

Government 2.0 journeys across America and overseas to demonstrate the promise and perils of the emerging technological world and offer a likely road map to its implementation.

Fox, R.L. and J.M. Ramos, *iPolitics: Citizens, Elections, and Governing in the New Media Era* (Boston: Cambridge University Press, 2011)

Among other things, contributors to this volume analyze whether the public's political knowledge has increased or decreased in the new media era, the role television still plays in the information universe, the effect bloggers have had on the debate and outcome of health care reform, and the manner in which political leaders should navigate the new media environment.

Lanthrop, D. and L. Ruma, *Open Government: Collaboration, Transparency, and Participation in Practice* (Sebastopol, CA: O'Reilly Media, 2010)

Through a collection of essays and case studies, leading visionaries and practitioners both inside and outside of government share their ideas on how to achieve and direct this emerging world of online collaboration, transparency, and participation.

Contributors to This Volume

EDITORS

WILLIAM J. MILLER is assistant professor of political science at Southeast Missouri State University. He received his doctorate in 2010 in public administration and urban studies from the University of Akron along with a master's degree in applied politics (campaign management and polling). He focuses his studies on campaigns and elections, public opinion toward public policy (domestic and international), and the pedagogy of political science. He recently edited *Tea Party Effects on 2010 U.S. Senate Elections: Stuck in the Middle to Lose* (Lexington Books). His research appears in *Journal of Political Science Education, Journal of Political Marketing, Studies in Conflict and Terrorism,* and *Journal of Common Market Studies.* Book chapters have been included in Stephen Craig and David Hill's *The Electoral Challenge* (CQ Press) and John Ishiyama and Marijke Breuning's *Twenty-First-Century Political Science* (Sage). He is currently working on three other book projects: *State and Local Government and Politics: Where Government Takes Action* (National Social Science Press), *The Election's Mine—I Draw the Lines: Redistricting in the American States* (Lexington Books), and *Scope and Methods of Political Science* (Cognella). He has also served as a political consultant for eleven campaigns in the past five years. In this role, Miller has assisted in fundraising, Web site development, voter targeting, polling (design and implementation), and overall management of the campaigns. He has worked across both sides of the aisle and for varying levels of candidates.

JEREMY D. WALLING is associate professor of political science at Southeast Missouri State University. He received his Ph.D. in 2005 from the University of Kansas and his MPA from Missouri State University in 1998. He studies state politics and intergovernmental relations, American national institutions, and public administration ethics and accountability. He recently edited *Tea Party Effects on 2010 U.S. Senate Elections: Stuck in the Middle to Lose* (Lexington Books). His work has appeared in *The Constitutionalism of American States, The Handbook of Administrative Ethics,* and *Public Personnel Management,* the last two with H. George Frederickson. He is currently working on *The Election's Mine—I Draw the Lines: Redistricting in the American States* with William J. Miller.

AUTHORS

MICHAEL D. AKERS is Charles T. Horngren Professor of Accounting and Chair, Department of Accounting at Marquette University. In addition to serving on the editorial advisory board of two journals, he has authored more than 50 articles in academic and professional journals.

DOUGLAS J. AMY is professor of politics at Mount Holyoke College and specializes in voting systems, proportional representation, and American politics.

JULIA BECKETT is associate professor of public administration and urban studies at the University of Akron. She has published in the areas of public budgeting and finance, government accountability, democratic governance, and public law.

JENNA BEDNAR is associate professor of political science at the University of Michigan. Her research is on the analysis of institutions, focusing on the theoretical underpinnings of the stability of federal states.

ROBERT D. BEHN is lecturer in public policy at Harvard Kennedy School and faculty chair of the school's executive program, Driving Government Performance: Leadership Strategies that Produce Results. He specializes in governance, leadership, and the management of large public agencies and conducts custom-designed executive education programs for public agencies.

VICTOR BEKKERS is professor of public administration at Erasmus University Rotterdam. He holds the chair on the empirical study of public policy and public policy processes. He is also academic director of the Center of Public Innovation.

THOMAS BIRKLAND is associate dean for research, extension, engagement, and economic development in the College of Humanities and Social Sciences at North Carolina State University. His research interests have centered on the politics of natural hazards and industrial accidents. He approaches his work from two angles—as a subject matter expert in this field and as a contributor to public policy theory.

JOYCE BOUNDS is ambassador of Canada to the Organization for Economic Cooperation and Development and President Emeritus of the Canadian Public Service.

NAOMI CAIDEN is Emeritus Professor of political science at California State University, Los Angeles. Her research focuses on public administration, public policy, budgeting, and comparative administration.

SHEILA CAMPBELL is director of the Government Web Best Practices Team for the General Services Administration of the U.S. government.

BRIGETT COURTOT is a research associate in the Urban Institute's Health Policy Center. Her current work focuses on Medicaid and Children's Health Insurance Program (CHIP) policies relating to eligibility and enrollment, managed care delivery systems, and health care quality measurement.

DANIEL DISALVO is assistant professor of political science at the City College of New York. He received his doctorate in Politics from the University of Virginia and was previously Andrew W. Mellon Visiting Professor at Amherst College. His scholarly work focuses on political parties, elections, public policy, and American political thought.

TIM V. EATON is associate professor of accountancy at Miami University. His research focuses on financial accounting, pensions, and whistleblowing.

H. GEORGE FREDERICKSON is Edwin O. Stene Distinguished Professor of Public Administration at the University of Kansas. Prior to that, he served for more than 10 years as the president of Eastern Washington University at Cheney and Spokane, Washington.

LEONARD C. GILROY is the director of Government Reform at Reason Foundation, a nonprofit think tank advancing free minds and free markets. Gilroy, a certified urban planner (AICP), researches privatization, government reform, transportation, infrastructure, and urban policy issues.

BEV GODWIN is director of the Center for New Media and Citizen Engagement for the General Services Administration of the U.S. government.

CHARLES T. GOODSELL is Professor Emeritus at the Center for Public Administration and Policy at Virginia Tech University. His research most notably focused on public bureaucracy and the future of public administration.

IAN HILL is senior fellow of health policy at the Urban Institute. He possesses more than 25 years of experience directing evaluation and technical assistance projects focused on public health insurance programs for disadvantaged children and families. He is a nationally recognized qualitative researcher with extensive experience developing in-depth case studies focused on the implementation of health policies and programs.

VINCENT HOMBURG is associate professor at the Faculty of Social Sciences, Erasmus University Rotterdam. He specializes in public management and e-government.

AMANDA HUFFMAN is Editor-in-Chief of the *Georgetown Public Policy Review*.

RALPH P. HUMMEL is Emeritus Professor Public Administration and Urban Studies at the University of Akron and a director of the Institute of Applied Phenomenology in Science and Technology, Spruce Head Island, Maine. He has published numerous articles on American bureaucracy, phenomenology, and the theoretical foundations of public administration.

LYNDON B. JOHNSON was the 36th president of the United States of America.

HERBERT KAUFMAN is Visiting Fellow in Political Science at Yale University since 1987, was professor of political science at Yale from 1953 to 1969, senior fellow in governmental studies at the Brookings Institution from 1969 to 1985, and Thomas P. O'Neill Visiting Professor of American Politics at Boston College from 1986 to 1987. His main areas of study are public administration and organization theory and behavior.

AIDAN KELLY is senior lecturer at Goldsmiths, University of London, in Sociology. He provides postgraduate training in quantitative methods for the Doctoral Training Centre in the social sciences at Goldsmiths and Queen Mary, University of London.

ANTHONY KENNEDY is Associate Justice of the United States Supreme Court after being appointed by President Ronald Reagan.

JOHN F. KENNEDY was the 35th president of the United States of America.

SANG M. LEE is currently the University Eminent Scholar, Regents Distinguished Professor, and executive director of the Nebraska Productivity and Entrepreneurship Center. His research interests include global business strategies, strategic innovation, technology convergence, ICT for business solutions, and value networking.

JULIAN LE GRAND has been the Richard Titmuss Professor of Social Policy at the London School of Economics since 1993. From 2003 to 2005, he was seconded to No. 10 Downing Street as Senior Policy Adviser to the Prime Minister.

JEFFREY LEVY is director of Web Communications for the Environmental Protection Agency.

DAVID E. LEWIS is professor of political science and law (by courtesy) at Vanderbilt University and co-director of the Center for the Study of Democratic Institutions. His research interests include the presidency, executive branch politics, and public administration.

GREGORY B. LEWIS is professor of public management and policy in the Andrew Young School of Policy Studies at Georgia State University. He is known primarily for his research on race and sex differences in career patterns in the federal civil service and on attitudes of federal employees. More recently, his research focuses on the status of lesbians and gay men in American society and on public opinion on gay rights.

H.L. LAFRAMBOISE is a former assistant deputy minister for Government of Canada.

KRISTEN NORMAN-MAJOR is associate professor and chair of public administration at Hamline University. She combines her extensive public sector and academic experience to examine public policy and administration issues from a practical standpoint. Her current areas of interest include social policy related to children and families, social equity and diversity, and cultural competency in public policy and administration.

SEONG SOO OH received his Ph.D. from a joint program Georgia State University and Georgia Institute of Technology. He has since been an instructor and researcher at Georgia State and California State University—Stanislaus.

PETER R. ORSZAG is the seventh Director of the Congressional Budget Office. His four-year term began on January 18, 2007. Before joining CBO, Dr. Orszag was the Joseph A. Pechman Senior Fellow and deputy director of economic studies at the Brookings Institution.

JAMES L. PERRY is Chancellors' Professor in the School of Public and Environmental Affairs (SPEA) and Adjunct Professor of Philanthropic Studies and Political Science at Indiana University. He has also held faculty appointments at the University of California, Irvine, the Chinese University of Hong Kong, and the University of Wisconsin, Madison. His recent research focuses on public service motivation, community and national service, collaboration, and government reform.

B. GUY PETERS earned his Ph.D. from Michigan State University and is currently the Maurice Falk Professor of American Government at the University of Pittsburgh. Dr. Peters has also served as a research professor at the University Center for International Studies (UCIS), a senior fellow at the Canadian Centre for Management Development, and honorary professor at City University of Hong Kong. His research focuses on public policy and administration and American administration policy.

LYMAN W. PORTER is Professor Emeritus of Organization & Strategy at the Paul Merage School of Business at the University of California, Irvine. His research focuses on the fundamental aspects of employee–organizational relationships.

JIM POWELL is policy adviser to the Future of Freedom Foundation and a senior fellow at the Cato Institute.

HOLLY STOCKDALE is analyst in health care financing for the Congressional Research Service.

XIN TAN is assistant professor of Management Information System at Fairleigh Dickinson University after he received his Ph.D. in business (information systems) from University of Nebraska—Lincoln. Dr. Tan's research interests include systems development method, conceptual modeling, and management of emerging information technologies.

VICTOR A. THOMPSON was professor of political science at the University of Florida.

SILVANA TRIMI is associate professor of management at the University of Nebraska—Lincoln. Her research interests include e-government, m-government, technology convergence, web 2.0, electronic business, and privacy and security issues in e-business.

PAUL R. VERKUIL is an attorney, former dean of the Tulane University Law School, former president of the College of William and Mary, and former dean of Cardozo School of Law at Yeshiva University. He has also served as the CEO of the American Automobile Association from 1992 to 1995. He is currently on the faculty of the Cardozo School of Law.

SARAH WATERMAN is founder of vtresponse.com—a Web site devoted to helping victims of Hurricane Irene. Prior to this, she was a research assistant at the University of Vermont College of Medicine. She received a Master of Public Administration at University of North Carolina, Chapel Hill.

WILLIAM F. WEST holds the Sara Lindsey Chair at the Bush School and has previously served as the Master of Public Service and administration program's director. Dr. West specializes in the study of administrative institutions, regulatory policy, the oversight of bureaucracy, bureaucratic politics, administrative law, and the Congress. A graduate of the United States Military Academy, Dr. West earned his Ph.D. in political science at Rice University.

AARON WILDAVSKY was an American political scientist known for his pioneering work in public policy, government budgeting, and risk management. He spent the majority of his career at the University of California at Berkeley.

WOODROW WILSON was the 28th president of the United States of America.